THE JEWISH IMPERIAL IMAGINATION

Leo Baeck (1873–1956) was a rabbi, public intellectual, and the official leader of German Jewry during the Holocaust. *The Jewish Imperial Imagination* shows the myriad ways in which the German imperial enterprise left its imprint on his religious and political thought, and on modern Judaism more generally. This book is the first to explore Baeck's religious thought as political, and situate it within the imperial context of the period, which is often ignored in discussions of modern Jewish thought. Baeck's work during the Holocaust is analyzed in depth, drawing on unpublished manuscripts written in Nazi Germany and in the Theresienstadt Ghetto. In the process, Yaniv Feller raises new questions about the nature of Jewish missionizing and the German-Jewish imagination of the East as a space for colonization. He thus develops the concept of the "Jewish imperial imagination," moving beyond a simple dichotomy of ascribing to or resisting hegemonic narratives.

YANIV FELLER is Assistant Professor of Religion and Jewish Studies at the University of Florida, Gainesville. His articles, on topics ranging from Christmas trees to modern gnosis, have appeared in journals such as *New German Critique, Comparative Studies in Society and History*, and *Jewish Studies Quarterly*.

IDEAS IN CONTEXT

Edited by DAVID ARMITAGE, RICHARD BOURKE and JENNIFER PITTS

The books in this series will discuss the emergence of intellectual traditions and of related new disciplines. The procedures, aims, and vocabularies that were generated will be set in the context of the alternatives available within the contemporary frameworks of ideas and institutions. Through detailed studies of the evolution of such traditions, and their modification by different audiences, it is hoped that a new picture will form of the development of ideas in their concrete contexts. By this means, artificial distinctions between the history of philosophy, of the various sciences, of society and politics, and of literature may be seen to dissolve.

A full list of titles in the series can be found at: www.cambridge.org/IdeasContext

THE JEWISH IMPERIAL IMAGINATION

Leo Baeck and German-Jewish Thought

YANIV FELLER
University of Florida

Shaftesbury Road, Cambridge CB2 8EA, United Kingdom

One Liberty Plaza, 20th Floor, New York, NY 10006, USA

477 Williamstown Road, Port Melbourne, VIC 3207, Australia

314–321, 3rd Floor, Plot 3, Splendor Forum, Jasola District Centre, New Delhi – 110025, India

103 Penang Road, #05-06/07, Visioncrest Commercial, Singapore 238467

Cambridge University Press is part of Cambridge University Press & Assessment, a department of the University of Cambridge.

We share the University's mission to contribute to society through the pursuit of education, learning and research at the highest international levels of excellence.

www.cambridge.org
Information on this title: www.cambridge.org/9781009321891

DOI: 10.1017/9781009321877

© Yaniv Feller 2024

This publication is in copyright. Subject to statutory exception and to the provisions of relevant collective licensing agreements, no reproduction of any part may take place without the written permission of Cambridge University Press & Assessment.

First published 2024

A catalogue record for this publication is available from the British Library.

Library of Congress Cataloging-in-Publication Data
NAMES: Feller, Yaniv, author.
TITLE: The Jewish imperial imagination : Leo Baeck and German-Jewish thought / Yaniv Feller, Wesleyan University, Connecticut.
DESCRIPTION: First edition. | New York, NY : Cambridge University Press, 2024. | Includes bibliographical references and index.
IDENTIFIERS: LCCN 2023006711 (print) | LCCN 2023006712 (ebook) | ISBN 9781009321891 (hardback) | ISBN 9781009321884 (paperback) | ISBN 9781009321877 (epub)
SUBJECTS: LCSH: Baeck, Leo, 1873-1956–Philosophy. | Baeck, Leo, 1873-1956–Political and social views. | Rabbis–Germany–Biography.
CLASSIFICATION: LCC BM755.B32 F45 2023 (print) | LCC BM755.B32 (ebook) | DDC 296.092 [B]–dc23/eng/20230228
LC record available at https://lccn.loc.gov/2023006711
LC ebook record available at https://lccn.loc.gov/2023006712

ISBN 978-1-009-32189-1 Hardback

Cambridge University Press & Assessment has no responsibility for the persistence or accuracy of URLs for external or third-party internet websites referred to in this publication and does not guarantee that any content on such websites is, or will remain, accurate or appropriate.

Contents

Acknowledgments		*page* vi
Introduction: Jewish and Colonial Questions		1
1	Under the Aegis of Empire	20
2	Saving Christianity from Itself	48
3	Vulnerable Existence	73
4	Forced Labor	101
5	Seeking Hope	130
6	Cold War Judaism	154
Epilogue: Remembering German Jewry, Forgetting Empire		179
Bibliography		193
Index		228

Acknowledgments

In the process of writing this book, I encountered many people who shared my interests, tolerated what at times were no more than semi-coherent ideas, and offered advice and encouragement. It gives me great pleasure to thank them.

I started thinking about Leo Baeck when writing a dissertation at the University of Toronto. My *Doktorvater* David Novak embodies, in life and scholarship, the commitment to Judaism and philosophical thinking alike. Bob Gibbs, Willi Goetschel, and Joseph Mangina planted, in various ways, the seeds for the argument of this book, and I am grateful for their support of the project from its inception. Pamela Klassen encouraged me to move from ideas to material culture, and from the past to the present.

At the University of Florida, I am fortunate to have Norman Goda, Roy Holler, Rebecca Jefferson, Dragan Kujundžić, Terje Østebø, Anna Peterson, and Gayle Zachmann as colleagues. Much of this manuscript has been completed at Wesleyan University. For their support and friendship, I thank Ron Cameron, Peter Gottschalk, Yu-ting Huang, Dalit Katz, Liza McAlister, Ulrich Plass, Justine Quijada, Andy Quintman, Mary-Jane Rubenstein, Daniel Smyth, and Daniel Steinmetz-Jenkins.

I am grateful to friends and colleagues who shared with me their insights on various aspects of the book, including Dustin Atlas, Dan Avnon, Brigidda Bell, Itamar Ben-Ami, Ian Brown, Yemima Hadad, Emily Filler, Michal Friedlander, Anna Hájková, Martin Kavka, George Kohler, Alan Mittleman, Michael Morgan, Matthias Morgenstern, David Myers, Paul Nahme, Ryan Olfert, Randi Rashkover, Larisa Reznik, Martin Ritter, Benjamin Schvarcz, Adam Stern, and Eli Stern.

Doris Bergen, Christina von Braun, and Michael Meyer, who kindly shared his own work on Baeck before it was published, read an earlier version of the entire manuscript, and made invaluable suggestions. I am grateful for their time and support. Susannah Heschel was always available

Acknowledgments

vii

for consultation and spent hours discussing the manuscript with me in ways that honed the argument and helped me find my voice.

Invitations to present aspects of this work made me refine my argument. Many thanks to Asher Biemann (University of Virginia), Irene Aue-Ben-David (Leo Baeck Institute Jerusalem), Cedric Cohen-Skalli (Haifa University), Elad Lapidot (University of Lille), and Ufuk Topkara (Humboldt University), as well as to all participants in the discussions.

The Leo Baeck Fellowship of the Studienstiftung des deutschen Volkes, Ontario Trillium Scholarship and Naim S. Mahlab Ontario Government Scholarship in Jewish Studies, and scholarships from the Anne Tanenbaum Centre for Jewish Studies at the University of Toronto helped fund the research. A semester fellowship at the Center for the Humanities at Wesleyan University provided much needed time for revisions. I thank its director Natasha Korda and all the fellows for invigorating conversations. I was also fortunate to spend half a year at the Ludwig-Uhland-Institut für empirische Kulturwissenschaft at the University of Tübingen. It was a surreal time, completing the work amidst a pandemic while sitting in a tower in Schloss Hohentübingen. I am grateful to Monique Scheer for making it possible, and for her generous hospitality and friendship.

This research benefited from various archives. I thank the staff of the Leo Baeck Institute New York, LBI Jerusalem, Jewish Museum Berlin, Centrum Judaicum, Terezin House, Erich Fromm Institute, Prague Military Archive, Wiener Library, and the Israeli National Library. Many thanks also to the interlibrary loan staff at Wesleyan University and the University of Florida.

At Cambridge University Press, I am very grateful to Liz Friend-Smith for her encouragement and faith in the manuscript, as well as to Elliot Beck and Mark Fox. Lena Emilia-Schenker provided research assistance, J. Naomi Linzer prepared the index, and Hilary Levinson helped with the proofs. The Jordan Schnitzer First Book Publication Award of the Association of Jewish Studies supported the publication of this book.

For many years now, I have been fortunate to share the joys and sorrows of research and writing with Netanel Anor, Omri Grinberg, Adi Livny, Ron Makleff, Marc Volovici, and Alexandra Zirkle. Thank you for your kindness and constant willingness to be there with sage advice. Haggay and Leah Ben Ami, Tor Tsuk, and Guy Kobani and Bianca Limbächer have provided home away from home and much needed distractions from writing.

My deepest gratitude goes to my parents, Maya and Zvi Feller, for their unwavering support. For always providing a good laugh, and just the right amount of interest in the work, I thank my siblings Guy and Anat, and their families: Carmit, Noga, Nadav, Noam, Yarden, Shay, and Gili.

Finally, to my wife Rachel, with love. Thank you for everything, and for everything to come.

Introduction
Jewish and Colonial Questions

In August 1938, Leo Baeck, the official leader of German Jewry under Nazism, published a short text titled "The Distance." Within the span of a few lines the revered rabbi took his readers on a transnational journey, moving from medieval letter exchanges to Jews joining Christopher Columbus and Vasco da Gama, paving new sea-paths, discovering the New World, and heading to the "legendary lands of the East." The present moment, he suggested to the readers of the German-Jewish magazine *Der Morgen*, was no different. German Jews were "colonists" and "colonizers" who were journeying into the world, like the great discoverers of old.[1]

Why should Jews in Germany, in 1938, care about Columbus? What did this have to do with their fate under Nazism? By that point, persecution had become a daily reality. Jews in Germany experienced physical and verbal violence, lost their livelihood, and watched non-Jewish friends desert them. Those who stayed behind would not or could not leave. More than a quarter of the Jews living in Germany were deported or fled the country since the Nazis took power in 1933.[2]

The Evian Conference, convened in July 1938, was meant to find an international solution to the plight of the refugees. Yet it ended with a whimper and did not offer much hope. Out of the thirty-two countries present, only the Dominican Republic was willing to admit additional refugees in an attempt to rehabilitate the country's international image

---

[1] Leo Baeck, "Die Ferne (1938)," *Werke* 6, 281; on *Der Morgen* see Sarah Fraiman, "The Transformation of Jewish Consciousness in Nazi Germany as Reflected in the German Jewish Journal *Der Morgen*, 1925–1938," *Modern Judaism* 20, no. 1 (2000): 41–59.

[2] Before 1938, about 130,000 out of 520,000 Jews left. Their numbers would significantly increase after the November state-sponsored pogrom known as Kristallnacht. See Marion Kaplan, *Between Dignity and Despair: Jewish Life in Nazi Germany* (New York: Oxford University Press, 1999), 73; Abraham Margaliot, "Emigration: Planung und Wirklichkeit," in *Die Juden im nationalsozialistischen Deutschland: The Jews in Nazi Germany, 1933–1943*, eds. Arnold Paucker et al. (Tübingen: Mohr, 1986), 303; Herbert Strauss, "Jewish Emigration from Germany: Nazi Policies and Jewish Responses (I)," *Leo Baeck Institute Year Book* 25, no. 1 (1980): 326.

2   The Jewish Imperial Imagination

after the brutal massacre of around 15,000 Haitians in 1937. Accepting
German Jews was in this sense a public relations maneuver. It was also,
however, motivated by the idea that European immigration could be a
positive economic and civil catalyst for the country.[3]

In "The Distance," Baeck attempted to help Jews in Germany imagine a
world in which they might leave the only home most of them ever knew.
"Colonies are being founded," he told his readers, "and they will remain
after the motherland disappears."[4] As Nazi domination was growing in
influence, at that point through the annexation of Austria in March 1938,
it became clear that the motherland rejected its Jews. It was time to go
forth, implied Baeck, for they had no future in Germany. In making his
case, Baeck offered a striking image: Jews as part of the colonial enterprise
and colonizers of their own volition for the sake of a Jewish future. The
year 1492, which is associated with Columbus's arrival to Hispaniola, was
momentous also in Jewish history. It marked the expulsion of the Jews
from Spain, one of the most traumatic experiences in Jewish history.[5] In
contrast with the negative feeling of forced emigration under duress
associated with expulsion, Columbus stood as a symbol of proud participation in exploration and colonization.

The choice of colonial imagery in "The Distance" is far from coinci-
dental. Baeck had a lifelong engagement with imperial constellations. Born
in Lissa in East Prussia (today's Leszno in Poland) in 1873 to a family with
a long rabbinic lineage, Baeck studied at the Jewish Theological Seminary
in Breslau (today Wrocław in Poland), which was associated with positive-
historical Judaism. Before completing his studies, he transferred to the
Liberal *Lehranstalt für die Wissenschaft des Judentums* in Berlin, where he
completed his rabbinical training alongside a doctorate at the Friedrich
Wilhelm University under the supervision of Wilhelm Dilthey. In 1897,
Baeck was appointed as a rabbi in Oppeln (today Opole in Poland), where
he would serve for the next decade. In this period, the young Baeck
married Natalie Hamburger, and their only daughter, Ruth, was born.
Subsequent career moves took the family to Düsseldorf, before Baeck

---

[3] Lauren Derby, *The Dictator's Seduction: Politics and the Popular Imagination in the Era of Trujillo* (Durham, NC: Duke University Press, 2009); Richard Turits, *Foundations of Despotism: Peasants, the Trujillo Regime, and Modernity in Dominican History* (Stanford: Stanford University Press, 2003); Marion Kaplan, *Dominican Haven: The Jewish Refugee Settlement in Sosua, 1940–1945* (New York: Museum of Jewish Heritage, 2008); Allen Wells, *Tropical Zion: General Trujillo, FDR, and the Jews of Sosúa* (Durham, NC: Duke University Press, 2009).

[4] Baeck, "Die Ferne (1938)," 282.

[5] On the connection between 1492 and the Holocaust, see Sarah Phillips Casteel, *Calypso Jews: Jewishness in the Caribbean Literary Imagination* (New York: Columbia University Press, 2016).

Introduction

accepted a position in Berlin in 1912, where he was also appointed as a faculty member at the *Lehranstalt*.

During the First World War, Baeck was one of the first rabbis to volunteer as an army chaplain (*Feldrabbiner*) on behalf of the Jewish community. He served for almost the entire duration of the war, first on the Western and then on the Eastern front. During the Weimar Republic, Baeck's stature as a scholar grew, and he became a public intellectual who not only held positions within the Jewish community but was also frequently invited to speak to non-Jewish audiences about Judaism.

When the Nazis came to power in 1933, Baeck was appointed as the head of the *Reichsvertretung der deutschen Juden* (Reich Representation of German Jews), a Jewish umbrella organization uniting most Jews in Germany. He remained in this role even after the 1938 November Pogrom, when the Reichsvertretung changed its name and character and became the *Reichsvereinigung der Juden in Deutschland* (Reich Association of Jews in Germany), a Gestapo-controlled organization. In 1943, Baeck arrived at Theresienstadt Ghetto, where he survived the war. After liberation he moved to London to be with Ruth, and quickly resumed his scholarly and public activities. He died in 1956.

As this biographical sketch shows, Baeck, one of the most prominent German-Jewish intellectuals of the twentieth century, experienced several imperial constellations throughout his long life. He grew up at a time when the Wilhelmine Empire was at its peak, and saw its dissolution and loss of colonies in the Great War. During the Nazi empire under Hitler, Baeck navigated difficult and uncertain conditions. After the Holocaust, he witnessed and conceptualized the rise of a new world order during the Cold War, and the place of Jews therein.

The myriad ways in which the context of German imperialism left its mark on Baeck have gone unacknowledged because the nation-state, this perceived unity of a group of people (nation) and political rule (state), still occupies much of European history in general, and German-Jewish philosophy in particular.[6] This book shows what happens when we move

---

[6] Ann Laura Stoler and Frederick Cooper, "Between Metropole and Colony: Rethinking a Research Agenda," in *Tensions of Empire: Colonial Cultures in a Bourgeois World*, eds. Frederick Cooper and Ann Laura Stoler (Berkeley: University of California Press, 1997), 22; Antoinette Burton, "On the Inadequacy and the Indispensability of the Nation," in *After the Imperial Turn: Thinking with and through the Nation*, ed. Antoinette Burton (Durham, NC: Duke University Press, 2003), 1–23. For the "imperial turn" in Jewish Studies, see the contributions by Ra'anan Boustan, Jonathan Boyarin, Sarah Stein, and Ivan Kalmar and Derek Penslar in Riv-Ellen Prell, ed., "Empire in Jewish Studies," *AJS Perspectives*, Fall 2005, 7–19; and the discussion below.

4 The Jewish Imperial Imagination

beyond the nation-state and turn our attention to the role German imperialism played in the formation of twentieth-century Jewish philosophy. The result is not only a better understanding of Baeck, but of the German-Jewish philosophical tradition. The analysis offered here, and the imperial context it provides, reveals how German-Jewish thought was shaped by, and responded to, empire.

New questions emerge when the imperial context is taken seriously. Baeck argued, for example, that Judaism is a missionary religion that has pursued, and should pursue, proselytizing among non-Jews. Such an idea is lost or left undertheorized if one does not account for the idea of an imperial civilizing mission and the role missionaries played in the colonial enterprise. The imperial context thereby challenges the idea that Jewish mission, a favorite topic of German-Jewish thought, was merely ethical monotheism, that is to say a belief in Jewish monotheism as a vehicle for the promotion of a more just vision of the world.[7] Focusing on empire shows that even at times when ethical monotheism served as an alternative to imperial violence, the idea of a Jewish mission borrowed on imperial language and was shaped by it.

In other cases, the imperial context brings forth a new understanding of well-known themes. An example is the war enthusiasm expressed by many German-Jewish thinkers during the First World War, including Hermann Cohen and Martin Buber. The war was an outburst of fervent nationalism and many Jews felt an opportunity to prove themselves as Germans. Yet the Jewish support for the war cannot be fully explained on those terms. Baeck's reflections from the front, in sermons and texts sent home, provide a new interpretive layer. They show how support for the war was part of a comprehensive Jewish imperial imagination of colonization and the spreading of German, and German-Jewish, culture to the Polish territories.

Baeck offers a unique opportunity for studying the impact of the German imperial context on the shaping of modern Jewish thought. First, in his long and productive life, Baeck experienced multiple imperial constellations. One goal of *The Jewish Imperial Imagination* is to move beyond a focus on Baeck's personality and place him in the context of the imperial imaginations that contributed to his thought. My interest is

---

[7] Adam Sutcliffe, *What Are Jews For? History, Peoplehood, and Purpose* (Princeton: Princeton University Press, 2020); Robert Erlewine, *Monotheism and Tolerance: Recovering a Religion of Reason* (Bloomington: Indiana University Press, 2010); Robert Erlewine, "Samuel Hirsch, Hegel, and the Legacy of Ethical Monotheism," *Harvard Theological Review* 113, no. 1 (2020): 89–110; Wendell Dietrich, *Cohen and Troeltsch: Ethical Monotheistic Religion and Theory of Culture* (Atlanta: Scholars Press, 1986); Ehud Benor, *Ethical Monotheism: A Philosophy of Judaism* (New York: Routledge, 2017).

Introduction

therefore not that of a biographer, although the argument unfolds historically and thereby follows the contours of Baeck's biography and the various empires he encountered.[8]

Second, Baeck was a public intellectual and community leader. Unlike other contemporary Jewish intellectuals, Baeck did not have the privilege of staying in the ivory tower. He wrote technical essays about topics such as Jewish mysticism or the canon of the New Testament, as well as political pamphlets, articles for the popular press, and sermons. His writing was pitched at audiences spanning middlebrow and highbrow readers alike. Because of this fact, Baeck's oeuvre offers insights into the various registers in which German-Jewish thought engaged empire.

Finally, there is Baeck's fame. In her eulogy to Baeck, Eva Reichmann, who fled Germany after the November Pogrom and became one of the first historians of the Holocaust and the director of the Wiener Holocaust Library in London, called Baeck "a symbol of German Jewry."[9] This widespread admiration for Baeck began during his lifetime. He had been called the "Pope of German Jews," and "a saint for our time," because he could have fled Nazi Germany but chose to stay with his community. Baeck also had his detractors, who accepted his centrality as a leader in order to criticize him. Hannah Arendt, reporting for the *New Yorker* on the Eichmann trial in Jerusalem, called Baeck "the 'Jewish Führer'," a statement she later deleted.[10]

"Laurels have no nutritional value," Baeck once quipped, but if named institutions are indicators of recognition and admiration, then Baeck is still held in the highest regard.[11] The Leo Baeck Institute, with branches in New York, London, Jerusalem, and Berlin, serves as the main archive and research institute for German-Jewish history. The Leo Baeck summer school and fellowship support young scholars. The Central Council of Jews in Germany is based at the Leo Baeck House in Berlin. In Haifa and Toronto, Jewish day schools are named after him; in Los Angeles and Buenos Aires, synagogues bear his name. The legacy of Leo Baeck's thought thus sheds light on the German-Jewish tradition that he embodied.

---

[8] For a biographical focus, see Michael Meyer, *Rabbi Leo Baeck: Living a Religious Imperative in Troubled Times* (Philadelphia: University of Pennsylvania Press, 2020); Leonard Baker, *Days of Sorrow and Pain: Leo Baeck and the Berlin Jews* (New York: Macmillan, 1978).

[9] Eva Reichmann, "A Symbol of German Jewry," *Leo Baeck Institute Year Book* 2, no. 1 (1957): 21–26.

[10] Leonard Baker, *Days of Sorrow and Pain*, 1; Joshua Liebman, "A Saint for Our Times: The Most Unforgettable Character I've Met," *Reader's Digest*, July 1948; Hannah Arendt, "A Reporter at Large: Eichmann in Jerusalem – III," *New Yorker*, March 2, 1963, 42.

[11] Leo Baeck, "Aphorismen (n.d.)," *Werke* 6, 56.

6 The Jewish Imperial Imagination

Emancipation and Empire

Born shortly after German unification, Baeck lived with the promise of emancipation and equal rights. He also experienced its deterioration and ultimate reversal under Nazism.[12] In the German-speaking lands, Jewish emancipation was understood by Jews and non-Jews alike throughout the late eighteenth and nineteenth centuries as a gradual and conditional process. Rights were deemed dependent upon the "civic improvement" of the Jews, that is to say the giving away of the communal structures of the *kehila*, and discarding particular Jewish elements in favor of what was seen as a way of becoming productive members of the new polity.[13] Even though equal rights had been theoretically won by the time Baeck was born, this notion of conditional emancipation was still very much present in unified Germany. It is a legacy Baeck would constantly engage.

Emancipation in Germany was tied to nascent German national feelings and the emergence of the nation-state as a polity that promised equal citizenship to all its members. The distinction between "civic" and "ethnic" is sometimes used to categorize different nation-states, with France serving as a model of "civic" nationalism whereas Germany typifies "ethnic" nationalism. The former is characterized as "liberal, voluntarist, universalist, and inclusive" while the latter as "illiberal, ascriptive, particularist, and exclusive." As Rogers Brubaker observes, the categories' apparent neatness does not hold upon closer scrutiny. Depending on whether they are defined narrowly or broadly, they either leave too much of a middle grey zone or over-determine the case in question to an extent that no longer corresponds to reality.[14] Instead, the value of these analytical categories is in exposing the Janus-face of the

---

[12] On emancipation as a nonlinear process, see David Sorkin, *Jewish Emancipation: A History across Five Centuries* (Princeton: Princeton University Press, 2019).

[13] Jacob Katz, *Out of the Ghetto: The Social Background of Jewish Emancipation, 1770–1870*, trans. Henry L. Feingold (Syracuse: Syracuse University Press, 1998); Reinhard Rürup, "Jewish Emancipation and Bourgeois Society," *The Leo Baeck Institute Year Book* 14, no. 1 (1969): 67–91; Werner Mosse, "From 'Schutzjuden' to 'Deutsche Staatsbürger Jüdischen Glaubens': The Long and Bumpy Road of Jewish Emancipation in Germany," in *Paths of Emancipation*, eds. Pierre Birnbaum and Ira Katznelson (Princeton: Princeton University Press, 1995), 59–93. For a critique of Katz's approach of treating Germany as the paradigmatic case, see Pierre Birnbaum and Ira Katznelson, "Emancipation and the Liberal Offer," in *Paths of Emancipation*, 15–18.

[14] Rogers Brubaker, "The Manichean Myth: Rethinking the Distinction between 'Civic' and 'Ethnic' Nationalism," in *Nation and National Identity: The European Experience in Perspective*, eds. Hanspeter Kriesi et al. (West Lafayette: Purdue University Press, 2004), 56, 62; Rogers Brubaker, *Citizenship and Nationhood in France and Germany* (Cambridge, MA: Harvard University Press, 2009).

Introduction 7

project of the nation-state as extending rights to all citizens but also a harbinger of illiberal sentiments.

German Jews were often proponents of the German national movement in the nineteenth century, not the least because they firmly believed in its liberal promise and hoped for inclusion and equal rights. They were confronted, however, with the other side of the coin: the idea of the nation as an ethnic, primal unit. This idea was used in antisemitic discourse, with growing vehemence since the 1880s, to deny those very rights.[15]

This debate about the place of the Jew in modern society has been called the Jewish Question, a term emerging in the late eighteenth century, although its appearance by this name is quite sparse until the 1830s. The Jewish Question received numerous manifestations and was also appropriated by Jews as part of a self-legitimation discourse. At its core, the Jewish Question was about the possibility of the majority to tolerate difference and grant legal and political rights to Jews.[16] The persistence and expansion of the Jewish Question during the 1880s, after the de jure granting of full rights, shows that the Jewish Question was never solely a matter of civil or political rights.[17]

Karl Marx observed that the Jewish Question was not about the Jews, but about society. In "Bruno Bauer: The Jewish Question" (1844) – before the granting of full rights to Jews – he rejected Bauer's claim that Jews needed to give away all their particularity in order to be integrated into the emerging nation, claiming instead that the Jew is emblematic of modern capitalist society, which in Marx's description was laden with anti-Jewish stereotypes such as huckstering and greed.[18] The Jewish Question in Germany was thus a German Question, serving to clarify, in Peter Pulzer's words, "German concepts of the nation and political rule."[19]

---

[15] George Mosse, *The Crisis of German Ideology: Intellectual Origins of the Third Reich* (New York: Schocken Books, 1981).

[16] Jacob Toury, "'The Jewish Question': A Semantic Approach," *The Leo Baeck Institute Year Book* 11, no. 1 (1966): 85–106; Alex Bein, *The Jewish Question: Biography of a World Problem*, trans. Harry Zohn (London and Toronto: Associated University Presses, 1990), 18–25.

[17] Hans-Ulrich Wehler noted at least 500 publications on the Jewish Question between 1873 and 1890. See Hans-Ulrich Wehler, *The German Empire, 1871–1918*, trans. Kim Traynor (New York: Berg Publishers, 1985), 106.

[18] Karl Marx, "On the Jewish Question," in *The Marx-Engels Reader*, ed. Robert Tucker (Princeton: Princeton University Press, 1978), 26–52; Elad Lapidot, *Jews Out of the Question: A Critique of Anti-Anti-Semitism* (Albany: SUNY Press, 2020), 223–54.

[19] Peter Pulzer, *Jews and the German State: The Political History of a Minority, 1848–1933* (Cambridge, MA: Blackwell, 2003), 30; Peter Gay, *Freud, Jews, and Other Germans: Master and Victims in Modernist Culture* (New York: Oxford University Press, 1978), 19; Paul Rose, *German Question/Jewish Question: Revolutionary Antisemitism in Germany from Kant to Wagner* (Princeton: Princeton University Press, 1990).

8   The Jewish Imperial Imagination

As a question about society, the Jewish Question was hardly the only one being asked. Nor was it confined to the nation-state. Holly Case called the period starting in the nineteenth century and lasting until after the Holocaust the "Age of Questions." It was an era in which the model of a question that required an answer was a prominent feature of public discourse. Alongside and at times intersecting with the Jewish Question were, to name a few, the Eastern Question, Social Question, Transylvania Question, and Woman Question.[20]

Thinkers in the Age of Questions understood this entanglement of issues. Paul de Lagarde, a nineteenth-century antisemitic German bible scholar and orientalist, made connections between the Jewish and Catholic Questions. Writing in the context of the *Kulturkampf*, Bismarck's attempt to secure state authority and national identity after German unification by diminishing the power of the Catholic church, de Lagarde commented a person "deludes himself" if he thinks "that the Jewish Question is a religious or tolerance question. It is just as much a question of power [*Machtfrage*], just like the Catholic question is a question of power."[21]

Jewish intellectuals also saw connections between the Jewish Question and other questions. Theodor Herzl, the founder of political Zionism, initially thought the Jewish Question was a subset of the Social Question. In 1890, he wrote that "the Jewish Question is neither national nor religious but is rather social. It is a formerly navigable arm of the great stream, which is called the Social Question."[22] In various texts throughout his career, Baeck also brought together various questions, including the emancipation of Jews alongside that of women, describing the Jewish Question alongside the Peasants' Question, and even drawing parallels between the legal status of Jews in Nazi Germany and Blacks in the United States.[23]

---

[20] Holly Case, *The Age of Questions, or, A First Attempt at an Aggregate History of the Eastern, Social, Woman, American, Jewish, Polish, Bullion, Tuberculosis, and Many Other Questions over the Nineteenth Century, and Beyond* (Princeton: Princeton University Press, 2018); Wendy Brown, *Regulating Aversion: Tolerance in the Age of Identity and Empire* (Princeton: Princeton University Press, 2006), 48–77; Michael Galchinsky, "Africans, Indians, Arabs, and Scots: Jewish and Other Questions in the Age of Empire," *Jewish Culture and History* 6, no. 1 (2003): 46–60; Anne McClintock, *Imperial Leather: Race, Gender, and Sexuality in the Colonial Contest* (New York: Routledge, 1995); John Kucich, *Imperial Masochism: British Fiction, Fantasy, and Social Class* (Princeton: Princeton University Press, 2009).

[21] Paul de Lagarde, *Deutsche Schriften* (Göttingen: Dieterich, 1878), II.107; on Jewish-Catholic relations, see Ari Joskowicz, *The Modernity of Others: Jewish Anti-Catholicism in Germany and France* (Stanford: Stanford University Press, 2013).

[22] Quoted in Derek Penslar, *Theodor Herzl: The Charismatic Leader* (New Haven: Yale University Press, 2020), 60.

[23] Leo Baeck, "Frauenbund (1929)," *Werke* 3, 226–231; Leo Baeck, "Von Moses Mendelssohn zu Franz Rosenzweig (1956)," *Werke* 5, 180; "Lehrhaus eröffnet. Ansprache der Leiter – Leo Baeck erhält der Eröffnungsvorlesung," *Jüdische Allgemeine Zeitung* 14, no. 88 (November 7, 1934): 1–2.

Introduction

In the 1880s, at the same time the Jewish Question was racialized and hotly debated in Germany, another question emerged. The Colonial Question (*Colonial-Frage*) was about Germany's desire, often described as need, to establish colonies as part of its claim to the status of world-power.[24] The Jewish and the Colonial Questions share important similarities in this regard, as noted already by Hannah Arendt in *The Origins of Totalitarianism* (1951). Arendt argued that both political antisemitism and imperialism challenged the nation-state by attempting to transcend it. The peak of German imperialist expansion during the Wilhelmine Empire coincided with the rise of antisemitism, as the logic of othering and attempts to achieve a sense of German homogeneity were turned both outward and inward.[25] Aamir Mufti explains that the logic of the Jewish Question, as a question about citizenship and belonging, was not limited to the Jewish Question in Germany. In his account, it was transposed to the issue of partition between India and Pakistan.[26] Arendt and Mufti help elaborate this overlooked connection between the Jewish Question and the Colonial Question. Like the Jewish Question, the Colonial Question was about the shape of German society and power relations within it.

The contemporaneous prominence of both questions calls for an intellectual history that sheds light on how German imperial aspirations shaped modern Jewish thought. Reading the history of Germany as an empire has consequences for theorizing the Jewish imperial experience more broadly.[27] Recent scholarship explored the ways in which thinking about Jews as part of empires enables the inclusion of marginalized voices, including those of Jews in Arab lands and Sephardic Jews under the Ottoman Empire. This approach has expanded the canon of Jewish thought, for example, by bringing it into discussions about the Global South.[28] One of the appealing features of empire for this scholarship is that it allows for the coexistence of minorities. What Jews found appealing in

---

[24] The popularization of the Colonial Question is often attributed to Friedrich Fabri's enthusiasm for German colonization. See Friedrich Fabri, *Bedarf Deutschland der Colonien? Eine politisch-ökonomische Betrachtung*, 3rd ed. (Gotha: Friedrich Andreas Perthes, 1879).

[25] Hannah Arendt, *The Origins of Totalitarianism* (New York: Harcourt, 1973); Stefan Vogt, "Contextualizing German-Jewish History," in *Colonialism and the Jews in German History: From the Middle Ages to the Twentieth Century*, ed. Stefan Vogt (London: Bloomsbury, 2022), 5.

[26] Aamir Mufti, *Enlightenment in the Colony: The Jewish Question and the Crisis of Postcolonial Culture* (Princeton: Princeton University Press, 2007).

[27] Doron Avraham, "Between Concern and Difference: German Jews and the Colonial 'Other' in South West Africa," *German History* 40, no. 1 (2022): 38–60.

[28] Willi Goetschel and Ato Quayson, "Jewish Studies and Postcolonialism," *The Cambridge Journal of Postcolonial Literary Inquiry* 3, no. 1 (2016): 1–9; Ethan Katz et al., eds., *Colonialism and the Jews* (Bloomington: Indiana University Press, 2017); Bryan Cheyette, *Diasporas of the Mind: Jewish and*

10 The Jewish Imperial Imagination

many empires, according to this reading, was the idea of imperial citizenship. This understanding of empire makes a clear demand of the present. It serves as an antidote to contemporary Jewish nationalism in the State of Israel by pointing to alternative paths.[29]

Germany is often excluded from these discussions because it is perceived as a paradigmatic example of a relatively homogenous nation-state, which is posited in opposition to the idea of empire.[30] Yet the Wilhelmine Empire or *Kaiserreich*, as it was known, had a Kaiser (emperor) and it was a Reich (empire). From German unification in 1871 until its dissolution in the aftermath of the First World War in 1918, Germany was not as multiethnic as other empires where the majority of Jews lived – above all the Habsburg, Ottoman, and Russian empires – but it nonetheless occupied Polish territories and Alsace-Lorraine, had a Danish population in Schleswig-Holstein, and by the turn of the century also established colonies in Africa, China, and Polynesia. At its height, it was the third largest

---

Postcolonial Writing and the Nightmare of History (New Haven: Yale University Press, 2013); Santiago Slabodsky, *Decolonial Judaism: Triumphal Failures of Barbaric Thinking* (New York: Palgrave Macmillan, 2015). Many of the works on Jews and empire are historical. On the Ottoman Empire: Sarah Abrevaya Stein, *Extraterritorial Dreams: European Citizenship, Sephardi Jews, and the Ottoman Twentieth Century* (Chicago: University of Chicago Press, 2016); Julia Phillips Cohen, *Becoming Ottomans: Sephardi Jews and Imperial Citizenship in the Modern Era* (Oxford: Oxford University Press, 2014); Michelle Campos, *Ottoman Brothers: Muslims, Christians, and Jews in Early Twentieth-Century Palestine* (Stanford: Stanford University Press, 2011). On France: Joshua Schreier, *Arabs of the Jewish Faith: The Civilizing Mission in Colonial Algeria* (New Brunswick: Rutgers University Press, 2010); Lisa Leff, *Sacred Bonds of Solidarity: The Rise of Jewish Internationalism in Nineteenth-Century France* (Stanford: Stanford University Press, 2006); on the British Empire: David Feldman, "Jews and the British Empire c.1900," *History Workshop Journal* 63, no. 1 (2007): 70–89; Elizabeth Imber, "Jewish Political Lives in the British Empire: Zionism, Nationalism, and Imperialism in Palestine, India, and South Africa, 1917–1939," Thesis, Johns Hopkins University, 2018. On Russia and parts of the Habsburg Empire: Israel Bartal, *The Jews of Eastern Europe, 1772–1881*, trans. Chaya Naor (Philadelphia: University of Pennsylvania Press, 2006).

[29] Dmitry Shumsky, *Beyond the Nation-State: The Zionist Political Imagination from Pinsker to Ben-Gurion* (New Haven: Yale University Press, 2018); Julie Cooper, "In Pursuit of Political Imagination: Reflections on Diasporic Jewish History," *Theoretical Inquiries in Law* 21, no. 2 (2020): 255–84.

[30] An example of such a distinction is Malachi Hacohen, *Jacob & Esau: Jewish European History between Nation and Empire* (Cambridge: Cambridge University Press, 2019). The focus on multiethnic empires is also present in other comparative studies of empire, for example, Jörn Leonhard and Ulrike von Hirschhausen, eds., *Comparing Empires: Encounters and Transfers in the Long Nineteenth Century* (Göttingen: Vandenhoeck & Ruprecht, 2011). The theoretical point on nation-states expanding outward is made by Étienne Balibar and Partha Chatterjee, who argue from different perspectives: Étienne Balibar, "The Nation Form: History and Ideology," in Étienne Balibar and Immanuel Wallerstein, *Race, Nation, Class: Ambiguous Identities* (London: Verso, 1991), 86–106; Partha Chatterjee, *Nationalist Thought and the Colonial World: A Derivative Discourse* (Minneapolis: University of Minnesota Press, 1993).

Introduction

European power in territory and the fifth in terms of population.[31] In addition, unified Germany, that is to say the Wilhelmine Empire, was the result of the unification of different states or *Länder*, each with its own rich history and tradition that it would not easily give away. Finally, it had a rich mix of religious traditions, including Protestants, Catholics – primarily in the south and in the Polish territories of East Prussia – and various Jewish denominations. Imperial Germany was therefore not homogenous, but contained multiple tensions.

The Kaiserreich perceived itself and was perceived by other empires as an empire. A brief comparison with France and the British Empire supports the idea of treating Germany as an empire and exposes several shared features that would prefigure in Baeck's thinking. First, empires used a rhetoric of civilizing mission to expand their control over vast territories. Second, despite the rhetoric of a civilizing mission, distinctions were clearly drawn along racial lines. The third feature of empire in the late nineteenth and early twentieth century was expansion outward, toward acquiring territory by conquest or economical control. Finally, this expansion served to amplify the power of the nation and its standing vis-à-vis other world-powers.[32]

Leo Baeck's thought is complex and cannot be read as a consistent resistance to empire, nor merely as following imperial ideas. On the one hand, Baeck did not see imperial power as a guarantor of Jewish existence and thriving, but often standing in opposition to Judaism. On the other hand, he ascribed to ideas about colonization and the ways in which Jewish settlers improve upon the land in comparison with the natives. A similar tension is evident in his contributions to the academic study of religion. While he opposed theological colonization, namely, the idea of Christianity superseding Judaism, Baeck had no qualms about using Buddhism and the colonial idea of the savage as negative foils in making

---

[31] Wolfgang Mommsen, *Imperialismus: Seine geistigen, politischen und wirtschaftlichen Grundlagen* (Hamburg: Hoffmann und Campe, 1977), 37–38; Helmut Walser Smith, *Germany: A Nation in Its Time* (New York: W.W. Norton & Company, 2020), 272–83.

[32] Edward Ross Dickinson, "The German Empire: An Empire?," *History Workshop Journal* 66, no. 1 (2008): 129–62; Sebastian Conrad, *German Colonialism: A Short History* (Cambridge: Cambridge University Press, 2012), 3; and Andrew Porter, *European Imperialism, 1860–1914* (New York: Palgrave Macmillan, 1994), 5. Lora Wildenthal argues that this neglect is part of a dominant historiographical trend in West Germany from the 1960s to diminish Germany's colonial legacy, for example, by describing it as a short-lived, failed experiment or focusing on its role for domestic politics. See Lora Wildenthal, "Notes on a History of 'Imperial Turns' in Modern Germany," in *After the Imperial Turn: Thinking with and through the Nation*, ed. Antoinette Burton (Durham, NC: Duke University Press, 2003), 144–56.

The Jewish Imperial Imagination

his arguments in favor of Judaism.[33] By examining Baeck's thought in the context of empire, tensions and contradictions emerge, exposing a more nuanced perspective of Baeck, and the German-Jewish culture in which he was embedded.

Political Imagination

The experience of living as a Jewish minority in German empires lurked behind the questions Baeck asked, yet the exact meaning of empire was left understated in his writing.[34] It constitutes what David Scott called a problem-space "in which the objects have all but become self-evident so that the questions through which they were called into being in the first place have faded from view."[35] *Jewish imperial imagination* is a mediating concept between the shadow of empire in Baeck's thought and its real-life, political manifestations, thereby making imperial ideas visible.

The definitions of empire and imperialism, like that of colonialism, are often contentious and far from fixed. Baeck used several, at time overlapping, notions of colonies in his writings, from a distinct minority group with defined legal rights to an outgrowth of an imagined Jewish spiritual empire aimed at converting people to its faith. Often, he drew upon an understanding of colonies as agricultural settlements that did not have the pejorative connotations of violence, exploitation, occupation, and dispossession. At other times, however, he stressed the violence of empire.

Instead of ascribing to a narrow definition of empire, I opt for a broad one. Empires are large political units that conquer, annex, and exercise control over populations that are deemed different than that of the metropole, often through the use of violence but also through economical exploitation. This is true of land-based conquest and colonization (such as the German annexation of Polish territories) as well as of territories considered far away (such as German colonies in Africa). In this sense, as well as in everyday usage, the distinction between colonialism and

---

[33] On thinking about supersessionism in light of postcolonial theory, see Susannah Heschel, *Abraham Geiger and the Jewish Jesus* (Chicago: University of Chicago Press, 1998).

[34] In focusing on the imperial context and political implications of Baeck's thought, I diverge from earlier research such as Albert Friedlander, *Leo Baeck: Teacher of Theresienstadt* (London: Routledge and Kegan Paul, 1973).

[35] David Scott, *Refashioning Futures: Criticism after Postcoloniality* (Princeton: Princeton University Press, 1999), 8; see also Edward Said, *Culture and Imperialism* (New York: Vintage, 1994), 6; Suzanne Marchand criticizes Said's reasoning from absence, see Suzanne Marchand, *German Orientalism in the Age of Empire: Religion, Race, and Scholarship* (New York: Cambridge University Press, 2009), xxv.

Introduction 13

imperialism is fluid. At different historical moments, Baeck's Jewish imperial imagination engaged a number of these aspects of empire, depending on the exact context.[36]

Imperial imagination thus means working, whether consciously or unconsciously, with ideas about empire. In its broadest sense, imagination is a faculty of the human mind, one often associated with creative activity and aesthetics. There is also a sense, however, in which it is not limited to an individual. One can speak of imagination as a social and political category.[37] Charles Taylor and Cornelius Castoriadis, among others, speak of the social imagination – or the imaginary – as standing at the heart of the symbolic order that shapes social and political life. In Taylor's definition, social imagination represents "the ways people imagine their social existence, how they fit together with others, how things go on between them and their fellows, the expectations that are normally met, and the deeper normative notions and images that underlie these expectations."[38] Such an idea of the social or political imaginary as constituting political reality is also evident in Benedict Anderson's *Imagined Communities*, which argued that the idea of the nation as a shared community required an act of imagination because it went beyond the scope of immediate acquaintance. The constructed nature of a nation does not make it any less real or present in the world.[39]

Political imagination is constitutive of society and shapes the individuals living in it. At the same time, by being a creative act, imagination can

[36] Jennifer Pitts, "Political Theory of Empire and Imperialism: An Appendix," in *Empire and Modern Political Thought*, ed. Sankar Muthu (Cambridge: Cambridge University Press, 2012), 354–55; Richard Koebner and Helmut Dan Schmidt, *Imperialism: The Story and Significance of a Political Word, 1840–1960* (Cambridge: Cambridge University Press, 1964), 1–26; Krishan Kumar, "Colony and Empire, Colonialism and Imperialism: A Meaningful Distinction?," *Comparative Studies in Society and History* 63, no. 2 (2021); George Steinmetz, "Empires and Colonialism," in *Oxford Bibliographies in Sociology* (Oxford: Oxford University Press, 2017), www.oxfordbibliographies .com/view/document/obo-9780199756384/obo-9780199756384-0090.xml?q=Empires+an%E2% 80%A6.

[37] Christina von Braun, *Versuch über den Schwindel: Religion, Schrift, Bild, Geschlecht* (Zurich and Munich: Pendo, 2001), 551–5; Amy Kind, "Exploring Imagination," in *The Routledge Handbook of Philosophy of Imagination*, ed. Amy Kind (Abingdon: Routledge, 2016), 1; Avshalom Schwartz, "Political Imagination and Its Limits," *Synthese* 199, no. 1 (2021): 3326.

[38] Charles Taylor, *Modern Social Imaginaries* (Durham, NC: Duke University Press, 2004), 23; Cornelius Castoriadis, *The Imaginary Institution of Society*, trans. Kathleen Blamey (Cambridge: Polity, 1987), 145.

[39] Benedict Anderson, *Imagined Communities: Reflections on the Origin and Spread of Nationalism* (London: Verso, 2006); cf. Partha Chatterjee, "Whose Imagined Community?," in *The Nation and Its Fragments: Colonial and Postcolonial Histories* (Princeton: Princeton University Press, 1993), 3–13.

14   The Jewish Imperial Imagination

move beyond the influence of external structures.[40] Yaron Ezrahi divides what he calls "performative political imagination" into three, at times overlapping, modes: the reflective, the fantastic, and the instrumental. The reflective is the common-sense realism of a given society. It is grounded in what is perceived to be connected to and grounded in reality. The fantastic, by contrast, is not something one expects to find embodied in life. It remains fiction, but this does not take away from its political efficacy. Finally, the instrumental mode is that of science and scientific metaphors such as "the body as a machine." The fantastic mode "could produce performative scripts that either idealize the regime or subvert it by radically transcending existing political practices," whereas the reflective mode is often conservative.[41]

Today we identify fantasy with the unreal, or unfounded in reality, but Ezrahi's division serves as an important reminder of the connection between fantasy and the imagination, the latter being a Latin translation of the former.[42] Susanne Zantop analyzed what she called "colonial fantasies" in German travel accounts, translation projects, and world histories in the eighteenth and nineteenth centuries. At a time in which there was no unified Germany, German writers imagined themselves as noble, better colonizers than the British or Spanish.[43] These colonial fantasies did not reflect a German colonial reality but nonetheless served as an underlying stratum in the emerging German imperial imagination.

With the lack of German colonial subjects, Jews were imagined as the ersatz colonized. They were the ultimate candidates for this transference because they have been, as Susannah Heschel argued, the long-time Other

---

[40] Chiara Bottici, *Imaginal Politics: Images beyond Imagination and the Imaginary* (New York: Columbia University Press, 2014), 3–5.

[41] Yaron Ezrahi, *Imagined Democracies: Necessary Political Fictions* (Cambridge: Cambridge University Press, 2012), 51.

[42] Bottici, *Imaginal Politics*, 15–31; a preference for fantasy is found in works such as Jacqueline Rose, *States of Fantasy* (Oxford: Clarendon Press, 1996); Joan Scott, "Fantasy Echo: History and the Construction of Identity," *Critical Inquiry* 27, no. 2 (2001): 284–304; Pamela Klassen, "Fantasies of Sovereignty: Civic Secularism in Canada," *Critical Research on Religion* 3, no. 1 (2015): 41–56.

[43] Susanne Zantop, *Colonial Fantasies: Conquest, Family, and Nation in Precolonial Germany, 1770–1870* (Durham, NC: Duke University Press, 1997); Birthe Kundrus, "Die Kolonien - 'Kinder des Gefühls und der Phantasie,'" in *Phantasiereiche: Zur Kulturgeschichte des deutschen Kolonialismus*, ed. Birthe Kundrus (Frankfurt am Main: Campus Verlag, 2003), 7–18; Russell Berman has shown the construction of a colonial space in travelogues and popular literature in the eighteenth and nineteenth centuries, but these do not always foster hierarchical structures or calls for active settler-colonialism in the areas identified. See Russell Berman, *Enlightenment or Empire: Colonial Discourse in German Culture* (Lincoln: University of Nebraska Press, 1998).

Introduction

of Christianity.[44] Yet Jews were not passive subjects in this regard. In the eighteenth century, Moses Mendelssohn utilized colonial language in his plea for toleration. He defined Jews in Prussia as "indigenous colonists" (*eingebohrnen Colonisten*), a seemingly paradoxical expression, in which Jews were both colonists in the sense of a distinct group, like the Huguenots in Berlin, as well as natives. Precisely because they are both indigenous and colonists, Mendelssohn argued, Jews could maintain particularity yet had inalienable rights deriving from their belonging to the "mother-nation."[45]

In the nineteenth century, Jews turned to historical research to oppose theological and scholarly othering. Abraham Geiger, the leading thinker of Reform Judaism in the nineteenth century, for example, turned to textual criticism in order to argue that Jesus was a Jew, thereby challenging Christian supersessionist claims.[46] Baeck is part of the intellectual lineage that starts with Mendelssohn and moves through Geiger, yet his concerns were different. Mendelssohn and Geiger, while imagining themselves and being imagined as colonial subjects, lived prior to German colonial expansionism. Baeck, by contrast, was living through the actualization of German imperial aspirations worldwide, first in the Wilhelmine period and later under Nazism.

The term counterhistory has been used by scholars to denote the intellectual move of Geiger and other Jewish scholars who presented a historical narrative that rejected or subverted the hegemonic discourse produced by the majority. In formal terms, counterhistory is an inversion of negative stereotypes into positive ones and vice versa.[47] Although useful

---

[44] Heschel, *Abraham Geiger and the Jewish Jesus*; Jonathan Hess, *Germans, Jews and the Claims of Modernity* (New Haven: Yale University Press, 2002); Jonathan Boyarin, *The Unconverted Self: Jews, Indians, and the Identity of Christian Europe* (Chicago: Chicago University Press, 2009).

[45] Willi Goetschel, *The Discipline of Philosophy and the Invention of Modern Jewish Thought* (New York: Fordham University Press, 2013), 178–88; on the use of the word colony in this sense, see Eduard Muret, *Geschichte der französischen Kolonie in Brandenburg-Preußen, unter besonderer Berücksichtigung der Berliner Gemeinde* (Berlin: Büxenstein, 1885); Jacob Toury, "Emanzipation und Judenkolonien in der öffentlichen Meinung Deutschlands (1775–1819)," *Jahrbuch des Instituts für deutsche Geschichte* 11 (1982): 17–53.

[46] Heschel, *Abraham Geiger and the Jewish Jesus*.

[47] David Biale, *Gershom Scholem: Kabbalah and Counter-History* (Cambridge: Harvard University Press, 1979); Amos Funkenstein, "History, Counterhistory, and Narrative," in *Perceptions of Jewish History* (Los Angeles: University of California Press, 1993), 22–49; Susannah Heschel, "Jewish Studies as Counterhistory," in *Insider/Outsider: American Jews and Multiculturalism*, eds. David Biale et al. (Berkeley: University of California Press, 1998), 101–35; Susannah Heschel, "Revolt of the Colonized: Abraham Geiger's Wissenschaft des Judentums as a Challenge to Christian Hegemony in the Academy," *New German Critique* 77 (1999): 61–85; Christian Wiese, *Challenging Colonial Discourse: Jewish Studies and Protestant Theology in Wilhelmine Germany*, trans. Barbara Harshav (Boston: Brill, 2005).

16 The Jewish Imperial Imagination

as a way of stressing Jewish agency, the conceptual framework of counter-history fails at times in accounting for the complex German-Jewish engagement with empire. Baeck's thought is a case in point. There are times in which Baeck was clearly offering a counterhistory to the prevailing Christian narrative. One example is his claim that Christianity without Judaism became a Marcionite-romantic religion that has no ethical foundation. At other times, however, the picture is opaque. Baeck viewed, for example, Jewish occupational patterns of concentration in commerce and living in the metropole as "unhealthy" and detached from the soil. Was Baeck ascribing to stereotypes here or was he attempting to refute them? Is this counterhistory? Working with the framework of counterhistory risks assuming agency and creating a heroic narrative that might obscure, rather than highlight, the extent to which imperial imaginaries shaped German-Jewish thought.[48]

The Jewish imperial imagination is at times a contestation of imperial imaginaries, but it also draws on those very same imaginaries in its understanding of Judaism. The two adjectives, the Jewish and the imperial, modify one another.[49] Conceptions of Judaism were sometimes used to critique imperial perceptions of the Jew as an Other. At the same time, Jewish thought was profoundly shaped by imperial ideas. The tensions in the Jewish subject therefore do not ascribe to simple binaries of resistance or collaboration. They were an integral part of existence as a minority in an imperial order.

Imperial Constellations

It would be helpful to outline how *The Jewish Imperial Imagination* develops the argument about Baeck's thought and its engagement with empire. The argument unfolds chronologically and thematically, with certain imaginaries recurring as leitmotifs in more than one chapter. While Baeck remained steadfast in certain aspects of his thought, such as his belief in the value of Judaism as an ethical force in the world, other

[48] Sven-Erik Rose, *Jewish Philosophical Politics in Germany, 1789–1848* (Waltham, MA: Brandeis University Press, 2014), 11–13.

[49] On this idea of co-constitution, despite the discrepancy in power relations, see Aimé Césaire, *Discourse on Colonialism*, trans. Joan Pinkham (New York: Monthly Review Press, 2000); Albert Memmi, *The Colonizer and the Colonized*, trans. Howard Greenfeld (Boston: Beacon Press, 1991); Frantz Fanon, *Black Skin, White Masks*, trans. Richard Philcox (New York: Grove Press, 2008); Homi Bhabha, *The Location of Culture* (London: Routledge, 2004); Catherine Hall, *Civilising Subjects: Metropole and Colony in the English Imagination 1830–1867* (Chicago: University of Chicago Press, 2002).

Introduction 17

aspects changed or were expanded in important ways depending on the imperial context.

Baeck's formative ideas emerged as he was coming of age as a scholar in the Wilhelmine Empire. The first chapter is dedicated to this era, which was ripe with numerous intersecting visions of supersessionism, expansion, and domination. A major challenge for Baeck was Adolf Harnack's turn-of-the-century popular lectures and subsequent book titled *The Essence of Christianity*. Harnack presented a pure and positive essence of Christianity against a legalistic and negative Jewish tradition. Baeck's first major work, *The Essence of Judaism* (1905), responds to Harnack and subsequent challenges from the History of Religions School. Yet this type of response was shaped by the heydays of German imperialism, both abroad and in the attempts to colonize the former Polish territories.

Imperial imagination shaped Baeck's perception of the Great War. Chapter 2 analyzes Baeck's sermons and writing from the front as well as his subsequent reflections during the Weimar Republic. Baeck's emphasis on the idea of culture and description from the Eastern front exemplify the way his imperial imagination was grounded in the idea of Poland as a colonial space, along with a belief that Jewish colonization was nonviolent. After the establishment of the Weimar Republic, Baeck confronted once more the question of theological colonization, which took a radical form during the 1920s. Baeck recognized the figure of second-century heretic Marcion, who called for a de-canonization of the Hebrew Bible, as vital for the German theological and political imagination. Against neo-Marcionite attempts to detach Christianity and Germany from Judaism and the Jews, Baeck offered a presentation of Judaism that stressed its place as the ethical foundation of Christianity.

Baeck's fears of the political implications of neo-Marcionism were realized with the rise of Nazism. The next three chapters offer a detailed account of Baeck's thought from the rise of Nazism to the end of the Second World War. "Vulnerable Existence" details Baeck's role as the head of German Jewry between the years 1933 and 1935. Baeck was a leader of a persecuted minority trying to navigate uncertain terrain. In search of explanations of antisemitism, Baeck turned to surprising sources such as Heidegger and Matthias Grünewald's magnificent Isenheim altar, while stressing the Jewish ability to stand before God as the foundation for steadfastness against Nazi adversity.

The fourth chapter covers the relation between imperial violence and the need of a minority to narrate its history for the oppressor. It does so by turning to Baeck's most contested text, a 1200-page unpublished manuscript of which only three copies survived. Although Baeck claimed he produced it for the conservative resistance, archival documents suggest that it was written at the command of Nazi officers. Baeck's discussions of race and Jewish colonization throughout history as they appear in this text reveal that he is treading very cautiously, citing Nazi scholarship on the one hand, while insisting on the rights of Jews on the other. This ambiguity is best explained by treating this manuscript as intellectual forced labor, an understanding that sheds light on Baeck's imperial imagination at a time when the organization he headed needed to make difficult choices, including regarding deportations.

Baeck arrived at Theresienstadt Ghetto in January 1943. Chapter 5, "Seeking Hope," builds on the available evidence to reconstruct Baeck's imperial imagination while in the ghetto. Despite the harsh conditions, Baeck insisted that hope was possible and in fact necessary. He made this point by contrasting the biblical prophets with the Western historiographical tradition, which he identified as espousing historical pessimism. Evil empires that thrived only on power and violent means, he comforted his audience in the ghetto would eventually collapse and be left in ruins. This for him was the message of the prophets in Theresienstadt. Baeck returned to earlier ideas after liberation, identifying Marcionism as well as the historical pessimism as giving rise to Nazism.

In the postwar era, Baeck imagined Jewish history as bifocal, like an ellipse. The contemporary centers of Jewish existence were the young State of Israel and the United States. In this new constellation, both needed each other. American Jews needed the State of Israel in order to be reminded of their particularity; the State of Israel needed American Jews to serve as a guard against nationalism and deification of the state. The Cold War brought with it new geopolitical constellations. Baeck imagined the United States as Atlas carrying the world. It played an important role not only in fostering Jewish life, but in serving as a bulwark against communism, and leading the United Nations in a more religious direction.

The epilogue turns to the presence of empire and the memory of genocide today by looking at institutions that bear Baeck's name, including the Leo Baeck House in Berlin, the Leo Baeck Institute in New York, and the Leo Baeck Temple in Los Angeles. I contend that the fact that Baeck, and other German-Jewish thinkers, are often treated without regard to the imperial context has a corollary in contemporary debates in Germany about the relation between the colonial past and the memory

Introduction 19

of the Holocaust. Such heated debates, for example, the Mbembe Affair, show that the intertwining of the Jewish and Colonial Question is still very much a German Question.

As these chapters demonstrate, the imperial context is essential to a full historical understanding of German-Jewish thought since the late nineteenth century. By treating Baeck's oeuvre as expressing a Jewish imperial imagination, it is possible to see the political undertones of religious thought. Many of these ideas, including Baeck's view of Poland, missionizing, Jesus's Jewishness, and the distinction between state power (*Macht*) and spiritual energy (*Kraft*) emerged in the context of the Wilhelmine Empire. To understand Baeck's response to it requires turning to Berlin at the turn of the twentieth century.

CHAPTER I

Under the Aegis of Empire

The auditorium of the Friedrich Wilhelm University in Berlin was packed with around 500 students. They all gathered to listen to Adolf Harnack's lectures on the essence of Christianity. In a vivid style and with scholarly authority, Harnack, a Protestant theologian and the leading church historian of the era, offered a historical view of the essence of Christianity and its contemporary relevance. The eponymous book, published shortly thereafter in 1900, became an immediate bestseller. In the five years following its publication, almost 500 reviews, articles, and books related to *The Essence of Christianity* appeared. It ran through multiple editions and was translated into several languages.[1] What made Harnack's lectures so popular, noted Ernst Troeltsch, was his ability to capture the spirit of the time and the anxieties of the age. At a period when historicizing tendencies and the popularity of scientific materialism were threatening to overwhelm Christian faith, Harnack turned to history in order to present a clear essence of Christianity.[2]

In his lectures, Harnack claimed the superiority of Christianity over Judaism, which was facing its own legitimacy crisis in Germany at the time.[3] Jewish scholars felt obliged to reply to Harnack's challenge. In

---

[1] Nittert Janssen, *Theologie fürs Volk: Der Einfluß der religionsgeschichtlichen Schule auf die Popularisierung der theologischen Forschung vor dem Ersten Weltkrieg* (Frankfurt am Main: Peter Lang, 1999), 150; Thomas Hübner, *Adolf von Harnacks Vorlesungen über das Wesen des Christentums unter besonderer Berücksichtigung der Methodenfragen als sachgemässer Zugang zu ihrer Christologie und Wirkungsgeschichte* (Frankfurt am Main: Peter Lang, 1994), 250–92, 312–57.

[2] Ernst Troeltsch, "What Does 'The Essence of Christianity' Mean?," in *Writings on Theology and Religion*, eds. Robert Morgan and Michael Pye (Louisville: Westminster John Knox Press, 1977), 164.

[3] Uriel Tal, *Yahadut Ve-Natsrut Ba-'Raikh Ha-Sheni'* (Jerusalem: Magnes University Press, 1969); Uriel Tal, "Theologische Debatte um das 'Wesen' des Judentums," in *Juden im wilhelminischen Deutschland, 1890–1914*, ed. Werner Mosse (Tübingen: Mohr, 1976), 599–632; Uriel Tal, "Al Bakashat 'Mahut Ha-Yahadut' Ba-Dorot Ha-Achronim U've-Yamenu," in *Mitos U-Tevunah Be-Yahadut Yamenu*, eds. Amos Funkenstein and Asa Kasher (Tel-Aviv: Tel-Aviv University, 2011), 181–215; Hermann Levin Goldschmidt, *The Legacy of German Jewry*, ed. Willi Goetschel and trans.

Under the Aegis of Empire   21

1901, a young, unknown rabbi from Oppeln in East Prussia, Leo Bäck – he would modernize it to Baeck around 1912 – was one of the first scholars to publish a critical review of Harnack. *The Essence of Judaism* (hereafter *Essence*) followed in 1905, marking Baeck as an important voice of German Jewry.

Baeck's *Essence* was much more than a reply. It was a self-standing presentation of his philosophy, popular long after the essence debate subsided. It ran through four editions by 1926 and was translated into several languages.[4] Harnack appeared only three times in the text, and only in the footnotes. This was not just a polemic by way of ignoring the adversary.[5] Baeck engaged not only Harnack, but also other debates about the originality of the Hebrew Bible and Judaism. In the *Essence*, Baeck imagined Jews and Judaism, from within the imperial context in which he lived, as a minority with expansionist aspirations. Jewish uniqueness, he argued, lay in the fact that unlike other colonizers, Jews did not resort to power and violence. Instead, their colonization was spiritual in nature.

Theological Colonization

Harnack was appealing, and provocative, because he insisted on the simplicity of the essence of Christianity, which was centered in his view on the person of Jesus as a moral exemplar. From this, Harnack derived a threefold definition of that essence: "First, the kingdom of God and its coming. Secondly, God the Father and the infinite value of the human soul. Thirdly, the higher righteousness and the commandment of love."[6]

The task of the historian, for Harnack thought the determination of the essence was a task that belonged to historians, was to separate the "kernel" from the "husk," the essential from the contingent.[7] An element is essential, according to Harnack, if it has a lasting presence throughout the

---

David Suchoff (New York: Fordham University Press, 2007), 124–32; Wiese, *Challenging Colonial Discourse*, 159–69.

[4] Theodore Wiener, "The Writings of Leo Baeck: A Bibliography," *Studies in Bibliography and Booklore* 1, no. 3 (1954): 109; since the publication of Wiener's bibliography, the *Essence* has also appeared in Hebrew and French: Leo Baeck, *Ma'hut Ha'yaha'dut*, trans. Lea Zgagi (Jerusalem: Bialik, 1967); Leo Baeck, *L'essence du judaïsme*, trans. Maurice-Ruben Hayoun (Paris: Presses Universitaires de France, 1993).

[5] Friedlander, *Leo Baeck*, 61.

[6] Adolf von Harnack, *Das Wesen des Christentums: Sechzehn Vorlesungen vor Studierenden aller Facultäten im Wintersemester 1899/1900 an der Universität Berlin gehalten* (Leipzig: J. C. Hinrichs, 1900), 6; Adolf von Harnack, *What Is Christianity?*, trans. Thomas Baily Saunders (London: Williams & Norgate, 1901), 9.

[7] Harnack, *What Is Christianity?*, 10, 12–13, 39, 85–86, 118.

22   The Jewish Imperial Imagination

development of Christianity in a way that relates to the original essence found in the words and acts of Jesus. Christianity as a whole should be looked at in light of historical developments, but the emphasis on the principles laid down by Jesus implied that there were inessential aspects to Christianity in its various later manifestations.

Harnack claimed Jesus's singularity, grounding his claim in a two-pronged approach. First, Harnack separated Jesus from subsequent dogmatic formulations that were part of the kernel. This was also the motivation beyond his *magnum opus,* the seven-volume *History of Dogma.*[8] In taking this approach, Harnack offered a theology based on history rather than dogma. Critics accused him both of taking the role of history too far and for not taking it far enough. The historically inclined Catholic thinker Alfred Loisy, for example, insisted on the interplay between kernel and husk that could only be understood when taken together. Later church writings and dogmas would thereby have a role to play in determining the essence. Ernst Troeltsch, on the other hand, criticized Harnack for focusing too much on Jesus's words and not taking the social conditions of Jesus's message and its historical developments fully into account.[9]

Second, Harnack recognized that Jesus was a Jew, but contrasted him with his contemporaries, the Pharisees. Harnack used harsh language to bring Jesus's singularity across. Whereas "they thought of God as of a despot guarding the ceremonial observances" and "saw Him only in His law, which they had converted into a labyrinth of dark defiles, blind alleys and secret passages," Jesus "breathed with God" and "saw and felt Him everywhere" proclaiming the one truth of God as opposed to the Pharisees' "thousand commandments."[10]

The stakes of such a debate were not merely academic. Harnack popularized an image of Judaism that Jews could not accept. In a 1901 review of Harnack published in the leading scholarly organ of the Science of Judaism, Baeck insinuated that the church historian lacked the relevant knowledge of Semitic languages. Harnack, he argued, also failed to distinguish between different layers of Jewish texts, namely, between

---

[8] Harnack, *What Is Christianity?,* 94–95; Adolf von Harnack, *History of Dogma,* trans. Neil Buchanan (New York: Dover, 1961), 1:73.

[9] Alfred Loisy, *The Gospel and the Church,* trans. Christopher Home (New York: Scribner's Sons, 1912); Troeltsch, "What Does 'The Essence of Christianity' Mean?," 138, 152; Lori Pearson, *Beyond Essence: Ernst Troeltsch as Historian and Theorist of Christianity* (Cambridge, MA: Harvard University Press, 2008); Stephen Sykes, *The Identity of Christianity: Theologians and the Essence of Christianity from Schleiermacher to Barth* (Philadelphia: Fortress Press, 1984), 127–30.

[10] Harnack, *What Is Christianity?,* 36.

halakha (law) and *aggadah* (non-legal lore). Finally, aspects Harnack identified as the essence of Christianity, such as the emphasis on the commandment of love, were in fact Jewish, which was not surprising because Jesus was a Jew.[11] In the *Essence*, Baeck made a similar point about the importance of Jewish sources for a proper understanding of Christianity. He constantly referenced the Talmud, he wrote, because of "the history of its misjudgment."[12] Baeck also wryly noted that luckily the Sermon on the Mount was part of the New Testament and not the Hebrew Bible or Talmud, "otherwise it would not have gained the grace of the Old and New Testament scholars, who would use it as a sign of the narrow-mindedness of the Israelite religion."[13]

By claiming Jesus as a Jew, Baeck challenged Harnack's opposition between Pharisees and Jesus.[14] He followed on this point the pioneering work of the nineteenth-century Jewish scholar Abraham Geiger, who showed that Jesus was a Pharisee. In her analysis of Geiger, Susannah Heschel, inspired by postcolonial theory, showed how supersessionist claims can be thought of as theological colonization that attempted to displace Judaism in favor of Christianity. She called Jewish scholarly responses that reject these claims a "revolt of the colonized."[15] This term highlights the minority position of German Jews in academic discourse, but also the political stakes. If Jesus was a Pharisee, then the Pharisees, and by implication Judaism, were of great and essential value to Christianity, a position that Baeck would insist upon even under Nazi persecution.

For all his critique of Harnack, Baeck shared with the church historian an understanding of religion as based on ethical content and a focus on the individual.[16] In the *Essence*, Baeck summarized that "it is not only that Judaism is ethical, *but ethics forms its principle, its essence.*"[17] These ethics

---

[11] Leo Bäck, "Harnack's Vorlesungen uber das Wesen des Christentums," *Monatsschrift fur Geschichte und Wissenschaft des Judentums* 45 (1901): 100n1, 106–10.

[12] Leo Baeck, *Das Wesen des Judentums* (1905), in *Werke* 1, eds. Albert Friedlander et al. (Gütersloh: Gütersloher Verlagshaus, 2006), 418.

[13] Baeck, *Das Wesen des Judentums* (1905), 351.

[14] Bäck, "Harnack's Vorlesungen," 118; Baeck, *Das Wesen des Judentums* (1905), 338; Reinhold Mayer, *Christentum und Judentum in der Schau Leo Baecks* (Stuttgart: W. Kohlhammer, 1961), 50–58.

[15] Heschel, "Revolt of the Colonized"; Heschel, *Abraham Geiger and the Jewish Jesus*; on Jewish scholarship on the historical Jesus, see Gösta Lindeskog, *Die Jesusfrage im neuzeitlichen Judentum: Ein Beitrag zur Geschichte der Leben-Jesu-Forschung* (Darmstadt: Wissenschaftliche Buchgesellschaft, 1973).

[16] Michael Zank, "Vom Innersten, Äußersten und Anderen: Annäherungen an Baeck, Harnack und die Frage nach dem Wesen," in *Religious Apologetics: Philosophical Argumentation*, eds. Yossef Schwartz and Volkhard Krech (Tübingen: Mohr Siebeck, 2004), 42.

[17] Baeck, *Das Wesen des Judentums* (1905), 343 – emphasis in original.

24   The Jewish Imperial Imagination

are grounded in a sense of duty (*Pflicht*) and acting (*Tun*) in this world.[18] This definition of Judaism is tied to Baeck's general definition of religion. In a 1909 essay in *Liberales Judentum* titled "Christian Culture," Baeck wrote religion "has to do with the personality, with the individual world of the soul, which should be made moral [*versittlicht*] and refined through the constant content of the religion."[19]

Methodologically, Baeck, like Harnack, focused on the exemplars of religion, locating the essence of religion "in the religious genius," just as "the essence of art is grasped in the great artists and their works."[20] Harnack found the essence of Christianity in the words of its founder, Jesus of Nazareth. Baeck found the essence of Judaism in the prophets. This turn to the prophets was part of a counterhistory aimed at Protestant scholarship, and especially Julius Wellhausen's distinction between the earlier prophetic layer and the later "legalistic" layer of the Hebrew Bible, which he claimed was already a distortion.[21] The shift from the singular genius to the plural of the prophets has a further important implication. There is a difference of kind between claiming that a group determines the essence or an individual. A religion, Baeck suggested, that was centered on one personality – Christianity with its focus on Jesus as the founder, Buddhism and the Buddha, and Islam and Muhammad – would quickly exhaust itself when this person departed. A religion based on a group's relation to God could last past its founders.[22] Baeck could therefore claim that Judaism was, and remained, an ethical religion of the prophets.

Harnack was not the only target of Baeck's *Essence*. Between Harnack's lectures and the *Essence* only five years had passed, but in that time, other debates were raging about the originality of Judaism and its contribution to civilization. Two such debates of the year 1903 are especially noteworthy: the Babel-Bible controversy provoked by the Assyriologist Friedrich Delitzsch, and the work of the comparativist Wilhelm Bousset.

---

[18] This understanding of ethics can be traced back to Immanuel Kant via the Jewish neo-Kantian philosopher Hermann Cohen, to whom Baeck recognized his debt in the endnotes. See Baeck, *Das Wesen des Judentums* (1905), 418; on Cohen's influence on Baeck, see Alexander Altmann, "Theology in Twentieth-Century German Jewry," *Leo Baeck Institute Year Book* 1 (1956): 198.

[19] Leo Baeck, "Christliche Kultur (1909)," *Werke* 6, 61; Leo Baeck, "Religion (n.d.)," 19.

[20] Baeck, *Das Wesen des Judentums* (1905), 331.

[21] Christian Wiese, "Counterhistory, the 'Religion of the Future' and the Emancipation of Jewish Studies: The Conflict between the *Wissenschaft des Judentums* and Liberal Protestantism 1900 to 1933," *Jewish Studies Quarterly* 7, no. 4 (2000): 367–98.

[22] Baeck, *Das Wesen des Judentums* (1905), 328; Leo Baeck, "Zur Frage der Christusmythe (1910)," *Werke* 6, 78.

Under the Aegis of Empire

The methodological focus of this strand of scholarship, known as the History of Religions School, was a comparative and developmental perspective on religion that drew on philological work to make claims about the origins of religion and its development. If earlier Jewish responses to Christian scholarship focused on showing Christian dependence upon Judaism, now the originality and primacy of Judaism was challenged by putting it in a broader perspective. Delitzsch and Bousset looked to Near Eastern empires and cultures for precedence and influence on the Hebrew Bible and Judaism more broadly.[23] As with Harnack, the language might be that of the academic study of religion, but Bousset and Delitzsch turned to ancient empires in order to think not only about the past but also about contemporary identity.

Bousset used a comparative perspective to argue for Persian influences on Christianity, mediated through Hellenistic Judaism. He thereby displaced Judaism as central for Christianity by making it, at best, a conduit. Such an approach had the potential to decentralize Christianity itself and give space for other religions, yet for Boussest, and indeed in most cases, Protestant Christianity de facto was defined as the highest level of religious development.[24] Delitzsch was even more radical in his discussion of the Assyrian and Babylonian empires. In lectures in front of the German Oriental Society, with the Kaiser in attendance, Delitzsch described recent deciphering of cuneiform tablets that forced in his view a reckoning with the status of the Hebrew Bible as an original, let alone revealed, text. In his second and most provocative lecture, Delitzsch claimed that everything valuable in the Hebrew Bible could be traced back, in a much purer form, to Babylonian culture, which was ethically superior. The prophet Isaiah, long a source of inspiration for Jewish and Christian claims about prophetic morality, turned in Delitzsch's hands to a violent, warmongering "Bedouin."[25] Given the aforementioned centrality of the prophets in Protestant theology as the ethical, pre-legalistic layer in the Hebrew

---

[23] Marchand, *German Orientalism in the Age of Empire*; Wiese, *Challenging Colonial Discourse*, 177–215.

[24] Wilhelm Bousset, *Das Wesen der Religion dargestellt an ihrer Geschichte* (Halle: Gebauer-Schwetschke, 1906), 176; see also Ernst Troeltsch, *The Absoluteness of Christianity and the History of Religions*, trans. David Reid (Louisville: Westminster John Knox Press, 1971); Tomoko Masuzawa, *The Invention of World Religions, or, How European Universalism Was Preserved in the Language of Pluralism* (Chicago: University of Chicago Press, 2005), 309–24.

[25] Friedrich Delitzsch, *Babel and Bible: Two Lectures*, trans. Thomas McCormack and W. H. Carruth (Chicago: Open Court, 1903), 70.

26 The Jewish Imperial Imagination

Bible, such a claim was highly provocative not only to Jews but also to many Christians, including Harnack.[26]

The *Essence* tackled this new type of methodological challenge in a twofold way. First, Baeck sought to participate in this discourse by developing a typology that would present Judaism in a positive light. There were, in his scheme, religions grounded in optimism and those grounded in pessimism. The former is exemplified by Judaism with the firm prophetic messianic belief at its center. The latter was identified with Buddhism, which in Baeck's description was godless and goal-less with regard to ethical life.[27] In his struggle against the Protestant supersessionist imagination of Judaism, Baeck created his own hierarchy, diminishing another religious tradition in an attempt to elevate Judaism. It was not merely a counterhistory but a shifting of the terms of debate drawing on the orientalist imagination of religions similar to the one his thought was meant to combat when it came to Judaism.

Second, Baeck claimed Jewish monotheism was a radical paradigm shift in which "the 'One God' of Israel is not the *last* word of an old, developed until that point, way of thinking but the *first* word of a new thinking."[28] The criterion for religious novelty, according to Baeck, was not in newness per se or in the question who was there first. Those who search for "embryology" in philosophy of religion were missing the point. Against the progressive development argument of the History of Religions, Baeck contended monotheism was a new religious phenomenon, a revolution in world-history. Judaism might have used images of earlier traditions but was a radical break from them.[29] Whereas Baeck would not grant Harnack that Jesus radically brought something new into the world, he made the same type of argument in the name of Jewish monotheism.

Converting the World

In contrast to the prevailing academic study of religion, which placed Judaism as a national religion, Baeck strove to present Judaism as a

---

[26] Yaacov Shavit and Mordechai Eran, *The Hebrew Bible Reborn: From Holy Scripture to the Book of Books*, trans. Chaya Naor (Berlin: De Gruyter, 2007), esp. 305–54.

[27] Baeck, *Das Wesen des Judentums* (1905), 357; Sebastian Musch, *Jewish Encounters with Buddhism in German Culture: Between Moses and Buddha, 1890–1940* (New York: Palgrave Macmillan, 2019), 82–85.

[28] Baeck, *Das Wesen des Judentums* (1905), 343 – emphasis in the original.

[29] Baeck, *Das Wesen des Judentums* (1905), 324–25. See also Yeḥezkel Kaufmann, *The Religion of Israel*, trans. Moshe Greenberg (New York: Schocken Books, 1972).

Under the Aegis of Empire

universal world religion. This was aimed at refuting longstanding accusations of Jewish particularism. Judaism was a "world religion" (*Weltreligion*) and not a national one because it proclaimed the progress of humanity toward the messianic age.[30] Judaism, he wrote, had a steadfast faith that "Humanity is destined to realize the good in it more and more ... the concept of the moral development from generation to generation, *the ethical concept of world-history* is thereby connected with the idea of the good."[31] Since this prophetic ideal transcended national boundaries, it meant Judaism was a world religion.[32]

The argument was manifested implicitly in the structure of the *Essence*. The first part, "The Character of Judaism," progresses from a methodological consideration in the first section to "The Prophetic Religion and the Community of Faith," and from there to "Revelation and World-Religion." Similarly, the section titled "Faith in the Human" in the second part, progresses from "Faith in Ourselves," through "Faith in Our Neighbor (*Nebenmensch*)," and all the way to "Faith in Humanity." The last section, "The Preservation of Judaism" shows the need to maintain particularity, but even this was done in the name of universality, with the one subsection, "History and Task," emphasizing Judaism's role in the world.

This was a non-preordained teleology of history. Progress – Baeck followed Hermann Cohen on this point – was based on the never-ending ethical task of human ethical action in the world. Jews had a "*world-historical vocation*, the *mission of Israel* ... All of Israel is the messenger [*Bote*] of the Lord, the messiah, the Servant of God, who carries the religion to all the lands, who brings the light and salvation to all people."[33] The Servant of God, often referred to as the Suffering Servant, is a biblical reference to the book of Isaiah. It is widely understood by Christians to refer to Jesus. Baeck, in the tradition of Jewish commentators, argued by contrast that the entire people of Israel was the Servant of God. This interpretation was consistent with Baeck's shift from the singular genius to the group, even extending beyond the

---

[30] On the classification, see Masuzawa, *The Invention of World Religions*, 108–20.

[31] Baeck, *Das Wesen des Judentums* (1905), 400 – emphasis in original.

[32] Baeck, *Das Wesen des Judentums* (1905), 405; see also Leo Baeck, "World Religion and National Religion (1953)," *Werke* 5, 551–58.

[33] Baeck, *Das Wesen des Judentums* (1905), 347; Yaniv Feller, "What Hope Remains? Leo Baeck as a Reader of Job," in *Hope*, eds. Ingolf Dalferth and Marlene Block (Tübingen: Mohr Siebeck, 2016), 357–60.

28 The Jewish Imperial Imagination

prophets to describe all of Israel as endowed with a world-historical mission.[34]

The idea of a Jewish mission was central to the German-Jewish imagination. In the Enlightenment, non-Jewish prominent figures – including Herder, Schiller, and Lessing – argued Jews were participating in a universal mission of educating humanity. This claim, which assigned Jews a higher role than witnesses to the triumph of the Church, nonetheless still treated Judaism as a stepping stone toward the higher morality of Christianity, followed by reason.[35] In the nineteenth century, however, a variety of Jewish thinkers from Abraham Geiger to Samson Raphael Hirsch adopted the idea of a Jewish mission as part of an agenda of showing Judaism's value in the modern era.[36]

Baeck worked within this tradition of a Jewish mission, but the "*world-historical vocation, the mission of Israel*" contains two distinguishable aspects. First, it has the meaning of a collective world-historical role that the people of Israel play in the advancement of justice in the world. This can be seen as an intrinsic attitude Jews should adopt. They should behave morally. Second, this mission also imbues a certain relation to the world and other nations, that of being a "light unto the nations" (*or lagoyim*) and promoting ethical monotheism in them. Israel should be ethical not just for its own sake, but for that of others. The mission was for Baeck a promotion of universality, a turning toward the world, while also maintaining particularity and not losing one's uniqueness.[37]

---

[34] Adele Berlin and Marc Zvi Brettler, eds., *The Jewish Study Bible* (New York: Oxford University Press, 2014), Is. 42:1–9; Is. 52:13–53:12; Martin Buber, *The Prophetic Faith*, trans. Carlyle Witton-Davies (New York: Harper, 1960), 217–18.

[35] Sutcliffe, *What Are Jews For?*; Richard Cohen, "'Jewish Contribution to Civilization' and Its Implications for Notions of Jewish Superiority in the Modern Period," in *The Jewish Contribution to Civilization: Reassessing an Idea*, eds. Jeremy Cohen and Richard Cohen (Oxford: Littman Library of Jewish Civilization, 2008), 11–23; Nils Roemer, *Jewish Scholarship and Culture in Nineteenth-Century Germany between History and Faith* (Madison: University of Wisconsin Press, 2005), 18–22; Ofri Ilany, "The Jews as Educators of Humanity: A Christian-Philosemitic Grand Narrative of Jewish Modernity?," in *The German-Jewish Experience: Contested Interpretations and Conflicting Perceptions*, eds. Steven Aschheim and Vivian Liska (Berlin/Boston: de Gruyter, 2015), 1–14.

[36] Michael Meyer, "Concerning D. R. Schwartz: 'History and Historiography – "A Kingdom of Priests" as Pharisaic Slogan,'" *Zion* 46, no. 1 (1981): 57–58.

[37] Jacques Derrida called this paradoxical claim for universality and particularism at the same time "philosophical nationality." Jacques Derrida, "Onto-Theology of National-Humanism (Prolegomena to a Hypothesis)," *Oxford Literary Review* 14, no. 1/2 (1992): 4, 10; Dana Hollander, *Exemplarity and Chosenness: Rosenzweig and Derrida on the Nation of Philosophy* (Stanford: Stanford University Press, 2008), esp. 101–17. On this tension as central to the idea of election, see David Novak, *The Election of Israel: The Idea of the Chosen People* (Cambridge: Cambridge University Press, 1995).

The last section of the *Essence*, "History and Task," opened with the following description, which expands the idea of the Jewish mission in an important way:

> All presuppositions of Judaism lead in principle to this, that it seeks to *convert [bekehren]* the world to its ideas. Its faith in God as well as its faith in man demands it. When the fight for religious existence left it [Judaism] for the first time in repose and no longer demanded all its strength, the propaganda began immediately. With the progress of the diaspora, which expanded the domain of Judaism over the borders of the old homeland, the mission kept the same pace, and expanded the realm of the faithful beyond the people of Israel.[38]

When Baeck talked about Jewish mission, he meant very concretely conversion of non-Jews. This was part of the mission of Judaism, an idea that Baeck found in the past in ways that served as a model for the present.[39] There are two key components here: the Jewish task to proselytize, and the role of the diaspora in this mission.

In order to understand Baeck's call for missionizing, often absent from other Jewish thinkers, the imperial context needs to be addressed. Baeck worked with prevailing imperial imaginaries at the turn of the century, in which ideas of spreading one's religion and culture played an important role. Despite Bismarck's early reluctance, by the time the *Essence* was written the Kaiserreich had colonies and outposts in Togo, Cameroon, German Southwest Africa, and German East Africa (1884); Kiaochow (Qingdao) in China (1897); and Samoa (1899). In 1897, Bernhard von Bülow, then the secretary for foreign affairs, summed up the German imperial aspirations known as world-politic (*Weltpolitik*), claiming that Germany did not seek to shadow anyone but demanded its rightful place "in the sun."[40] To have a place in the sun meant Germany needed to militarize and expand outward.

---

[38] Baeck, *Das Wesen des Judentums* (1905), 409 – emphasis in the original. In the second edition of the *Essence*, Baeck added a qualifier: "even more precisely: not so much to convert it [the world] as to try and teach it." The fact that Baeck tempered the statement of the first edition could be read as clarifying its intended meaning, but it could also signify the changing context after the loss of German colonies in the Great War. See Baeck, *Das Wesen des Judentums* (1926), 279. Baeck would return to the idea of Jewish missionizing in the postwar era.

[39] For contemporary discussions of Jewish missionizing, see Oswald John Simon, "Missionary Judaism," *Jewish Quarterly Review* 5 (1893): 664–79; Oswald John Simon and Israel Zangwill, "The Mission of Judaism," *Jewish Quarterly Review* 9 (1897): 177–223.

[40] Bernhard von Bülow, "Bernhard von Bülow über Deutschlands 'Platz an der Sonne' (1897)," in *Deutsche Geschichte in Bilder und Dokumente*, eds. Roger Chickering et al., vol. 5 (Washington, DC: German Historical Institute), http://germanhistorydocs.ghi-dc.org/sub_document.cfm?document_id=783, accessed June 29, 2020.

30 The Jewish Imperial Imagination

The renegotiation of where Germany was to be found, and who was German, was tied to the Jewish Question. Different views of German expansionism led to different attitudes toward Jews and their place in the body politic. The growing colonial experience led to an increase in racializing discourse, which made the theorizing of Jews as racially others more prevalent.[41] German antisemitic nationalists, such as the Pan-German League, saw Jewish presence in Germany as a problem in ways that were similar to their rejection of the presence of colonized people on German soil. Jews in fact posed a greater problem in the antisemitic imagination precisely because they had equal rights and lived amidst Germans.[42]

On the other hand, there were Jews, and people of Jewish descent, who were active in the colonial enterprise. Just like their German compatriots, they did not necessarily settle in the colonies but expressed support in other ways. Colonial acquisition and claiming Germany's "place in the sun" allowed these Jews to express their loyalty as citizens of a German empire. To be a good German in this understanding was to be pro-colonization. Such a view was shared across the spectrum of Jewish positions in the Wilhelmine Empire, evident in the widely read *Allgemeine Zeitung des Judentums*, representing the integrationist position, as well as the Zionist newspaper *Die Welt*.[43] Imperialism was therefore a space in which Jews could be included or excluded, be a vanguard of the empire, or be seen as an irreconcilable other.

The imperial imagination was reflected in, and shaped by, popular works. The entry "Colonies" in the sixth edition of the popular encyclopedia *Meyers Großes Konversationslexikon* (1902–1908) reflects a common sentiment. It called some of the German colonies "protectorates" (*Schutzgebiete*), recognized that they were not as economically productive as those of other world powers, but insisted that they were still works in

---

[41] Claudia Bruns, "Antisemitism and Colonial Racisms: Genealogical Perspectives," in *Colonialism and the Jews in German History: From the Middle Ages to the Twentieth Century*, ed. Stefan Vogt and trans. Alissa Jones Nelson (London: Bloomsbury, 2022), 25–55.

[42] Christian Davis, "Colonialism and the Anti-Semitic Movement in Imperial Germany," in *German Colonialism in a Global Age*, eds. Bradley Naranch and Geoff Eley (Durham, NC: Duke University Press, 2015), 228–45; Dennis Sweeny, "Pan-German Conceptions of Colonial Empire," in *German Colonialism in a Global Age*, eds. Bradley Naranch and Geoff Eley (Durham, NC: Duke University Press, 2015), 265–82; Geoff Eley, *Reshaping the German Right: Radical Nationalism and Political Change after Bismarck* (Ann Arbor: University of Michigan Press, 1991).

[43] Christian Davis, *Colonialism, Antisemitism, and Germans of Jewish Descent in Imperial Germany* (Ann Arbor: University of Michigan Press, 2012); Philipp Nielsen, *Between Heimat and Hatred: Jews and the Right in Germany, 1871–1935* (New York: Oxford University Press, 2019), 24–25; Avraham, "Between Concern and Difference."

Under the Aegis of Empire 31

progress. Part of the reason for their lack of development, it was suggested, was that most German colonies, except for Southwest Africa, were unsuitable for large European migration, that is to say, to settler colonialism. The German colonies were not described as colonies by conquest (*Eroberungskolonien*) but rather as commerce or plantation colonies. The Herero Revolt of 1904 was mentioned in one line as an explanation for the current strong military presence in the area.[44]

Empire had also been part of commercial and entertainment culture, including advertisement, toys, novels, magazines, and imported products. The 1896 Colonial Exhibition in Berlin brought objects and products from the colonies to the heart of the empire. Among the presentations were also non-white people who were transported from their homes in order to amuse and edify the public in the metropole.[45] This was not unique but part of a larger phenomenon of "peoples exhibitions" (*Völkerschauen*) in zoos and travelling exhibitions throughout Europe. Little is known of the people who were presented, but some of them never saw their home or family again. Victor (age 7) and Alberta (age 5), for example, were transported to Copenhagen from the Danish colony of St. Croix in 1905 for the Danish Colonial Exhibition. After the exhibition ended, they were placed in a boarding school and never saw their parents again. Alberta died of tuberculosis in her teens, while Victor grew up in Denmark, where he became a musician, teacher, and vice headmaster of a local school.[46]

The Colonial Exhibition in Berlin was a huge success, attracting more than a million visitors.[47] Baeck, still a student in the city at the time, could have visited or read about it. A text about a similar exhibition by Theodor Herzl, a journalist and the leader of the Zionist movement, presents one way in which a leading German-speaking Jewish intellectual imagined people of color in the wake of such exhibitions. The 1899 exhibition in the Prater in Vienna included members of the Beja people (Bisharin), from Sudan and Southern Egypt. Herzl reflected in a text in the popular

---

[44] "Kolonien," in *Meyers großes Konversationslexikon*, 6th edition, https://woerterbuchnetz.de/?sigle=DWB#9.

[45] Jeff Bowersox, *Raising Germans in the Age of Empire: Youth and Colonial Culture, 1871–1914* (Oxford: Oxford University Press, 2013); David Ciarlo, *Advertising Empire: Race and Visual Culture in Imperial Germany* (Cambridge, MA: Harvard University Press, 2011).

[46] See Rikke Andreassen, *Human Exhibitions: Race, Gender and Sexuality in Ethnic Displays* (New York: Routledge, 2015), 29–31, 96–100. I thank Rashida Shaw McMahon, who currently traces their lives, for pointing out this story.

[47] For that number, see Ciarlo, *Advertising Empire*, 58.

32 The Jewish Imperial Imagination

newspaper *Neue freie Presse* that "whoever conquers them can only improve them, for they stand on one of the lowest levels of human consciousness, and bear barely a trace of concepts of bodily and moral purity." They were "doomed to extinction," not the least because their contact with Europeans already forced them to put on a show and play a role. They know they "must not behave tamely, like government officials, but must balefully roll their eyes, threateningly brandish their crude weapons, and fill the petty bourgeois with fear."[48]

Conceptualizing non-whites, the way Herzl did, allowed Europeans in the metropoles to construct an idea of whiteness and European progress, in contrast to those people deemed savages untainted by modernity. Given that skin color and a notion of civility were the determining factors, Jews could claim whiteness and belonging to the majority culture. Although Baeck did not reflect on these issues at the time, the notion of savages as those who are lacking historical consciousness, and Blacks as losing their historical consciousness due to the Middle Passage and slavery, would come to preoccupy him explicitly in his later writings.[49]

Baeck developed his argument about the place of Jews in the world and the Jewish mission in the context of this tension between two political imaginaries that were present in the German imperial pursuits: racial ideas and civilizing mission.[50] At times, the two collided, with racial theories suggesting that there can be no significant improvement in the state of lesser races. Furthermore, the fact that Germany was a latecomer to the imperial stage meant that the policies it adopted were different, and often civilizing mission did not play an important role on the ground, although this varied by colony.[51]

This does not mean, however, that an imperial imagination of Germans as civilizers was not present. The two imaginaries also worked in tandem, as in the claim that because Germans are the more advanced race it is their

---

[48] Theodor Herzl, "Das Bischari-Lager," *Neue freie Presse*, April 30, 1899; Penslar, *Theodor Herzl*, 140.

[49] *Jüdische Allgemeine Zeitung* 14 (November 7, 1934): 1–2; Leo Baeck, "Geschichtsschreibung (1944)," *Werke* 6, 345; Baeck, "Epochen der jüdischen Geschichte (1956)," *Werke* 5, 227–28.

[50] The idea of a civilizing mission was common to many empires. See Jennifer Pitts, *A Turn to Empire: The Rise of Imperial Liberalism in Britain and France* (Princeton: Princeton University Press, 2009); Alice Conklin, *A Mission to Civilize: The Republican Idea of Empire in France and West Africa, 1895–1930* (Stanford: Stanford University Press, 1997); Mary Louise Pratt, *Imperial Eyes: Travel Writing and Transculturation* (New York: Routledge, 2008), 7; Leff, *Sacred Bonds of Solidarity*.

[51] Davis, *Colonialism, Antisemitism, and Germans of Jewish Descent in Imperial Germany*, 7–8; George Steinmetz, *The Devil's Handwriting: Precoloniality and the German Colonial State in Qingdao, Samoa, and Southwest Africa* (Chicago: Chicago University Press, 2007).

moral responsibility to help those "less fortunate."[52] Friedrich Fabri (1824–1891) – a prominent advocate of German colonization and the leader of a missionary society – provides an example of this tension. In his manifesto *Does Germany Need Colonies?*, he claimed that a people that had reached the peak of its power could only remain there if it "recognizes and shows itself to be a carrier of a cultural-mission [*Cultur-Mission*]," without which political power would lead to barbarism.[53] Understood this way, there is no necessary contradiction between espousing liberal causes in the name of a civilizing mission, the promotion of values such as an open civil society, the rule of law, and scientific and educational development and support for colonialism because the two can be seen as complementary.[54]

Missionaries played an important role in civilizing claims, and the language of proselytizing that Baeck used had been a staple of empire. Although there were important distinctions between missionary groups – for example, between German Catholic and Protestant missionaries as well as regional differences among the colonies – several common features can be identified: First, missionaries were an integral part of the German imperial vanguard even before formal colonization took place. In order to preach, missionaries studied the local language through mediators, at times producing the first dictionaries. Second, a corollary to learning the native language was that missionaries also taught German, often establishing schools in the process that also corresponded with the more broadly understood cultural mission of education to work and punctuality. Finally, the missionary work, like the colonial exhibitions, brought the colonies home. Baeck might have been exposed to some of the activity of missionizing and colonial enterprises through their fundraising

---

[52] Conrad, *German Colonialism*, 77; Ulrike Linder, "Trans-Imperial Orientation and Knowledge Transfers," in *German Colonialism: Fragments Past and Present*, eds. Sebastian Gottschalk et al. (Berlin: Deutsches Historisches Museum, 2016), 25–26.

[53] Fabri, *Bedarf Deutschland der Colonien?*, 111.

[54] Birthe Kundrus, *Moderne Imperialisten: Das Kaiserreich im Spiegel seiner Kolonien* (Cologne and Weimar: Böhlau Verlag, 2003); Matthew Fitzpatrick, *Liberal Imperialism in Germany: Expansionism and Nationalism, 1848–1884* (New York: Berghahn Books, 2008); Jens-Uwe Guettel, *German Expansionism, Imperial Liberalism and the United States, 1776–1945* (Cambridge: Cambridge University Press, 2012); Erik Grimmer-Solem, *Learning Empire: Globalization and the German Quest for World Status, 1875–1919* (Cambridge: Cambridge University Press, 2019); on the connection between liberalism and empire beyond the German context, see Jeanne Morefield, *Covenants without Swords: Idealist Liberalism and the Spirit of Empire* (Princeton: Princeton University Press, 2009); Uday Singh Mehta, *Liberalism and Empire: A Study in Nineteenth-Century British Liberal Thought* (Chicago: University of Chicago Press, 1999); Pitts, *A Turn to Empire*.

34   The Jewish Imperial Imagination

campaigns, which included distribution of newspapers, lectures, and festivals.[55]

This imperial imagination about the role of missionaries and civilizing mission informed Baeck's understanding of Jewish missionary drive. In his historical account in the *Essence*, the Roman Empire meant the end of Jewish proselytizing, as imperial edicts made conversion to Judaism punishable by death. From that point on, Judaism focused all its energy (*Kraft*) on self-preservation; its mere existence now became the most urgent task.[56] The desire to missionize, however, still lived in Judaism according to Baeck. In historical junctures in which Jews "had a moment to breathe, almost always the old propaganda was stirred anew," such as in the case of Jews in Arabia or the conversion of the Khazar Kingdom. This reference is to a story, told most famously in Judah Halevi's *Book of Refutation and Proof on Behalf of the Despised Religion* better known as the *Kuzari*, in which the king, and later the people, of this kingdom near the Black Sea converted to Judaism in the early medieval period.

Jewish missionizing was not just a historical relic for Baeck. He made clear in a 1912 private letter that Jewish missionizing would not only win converts but would also serve to awaken religious sensibilities among Jews, and contribute to the strength of the Jewish community. Missionizing, Baeck insisted, was part of a Jewish "commandment of self-preservation."[57] The fact that others would recognize the value of Judaism would also awaken pride among Jews in their own religion. Baeck believed that if one was earnest about their religion, they would try to convince others of this value, thereby missionizing. He claimed that this was true of Christians, as it was of Jews, but the former turned in the past to the sword and forced conversions, rather than making a compelling case for their religion.[58]

---

[55] Rebekka Habermas, "'Do You Want to Help the Heathen Children?': Missionary Work in the German Colonies," in *German Colonialism: Fragments Past and Present*, eds. Sebastian Gottschalk et al. (Berlin: Deutsches Historisches Museum, 2016), 50–57; Ulrich van der Heyden, "Christian Missionary Societies in the German Colonies, 1884/1885–1914/1915," in *German Colonialism: Race, the Holocaust, and Postwar Germany*, eds. Volker Langbehn and Mohammad Salama (New York: Columbia University Press, 2011), 215–52; Glen Ryland, "Translating Africa for Germans: The Rhenish Mission in Southwest Africa, 1829–1936," Thesis (University of Notre Dame, 2013); Richard Hölzl, "'Mitleid' über große Distanz: Zur Fabrikation globaler Gefühle in Medien der katholischen Mission (1890–1940)," in *Mission Global: Eine Verflechtungsgeschichte seit dem 19. Jahrhundert*, eds. Rebekka Habermas and Richard Hölzl (Cologne: Böhlau, 2014), 265–94.

[56] Baeck, *Das Wesen des Judentums* (1905), 410.

[57] Leo Baeck to an unnamed recipient, February 11, 1912, in Leo Baeck Collection AR 66, Subgroup 3, Leo Baeck Institute; Meyer, *Rabbi Leo Baeck*, 244n125.

[58] Baeck, *Das Wesen des Judentums* (1905), 416. On Christian missionizing during this period, see Christopher Clark, *The Politics of Conversion: Missionary Protestantism and the Jews in Prussia, 1728–1941* (Oxford: Clarendon Press, 1995), 242–81.

Tilling the Heathen Fields

Judaism, according to Baeck, never abandoned the desire to convert the world. For most of its history, however, Judaism was severely limited in its ability to missionize. Its ethical message, however, was spread by proxy. Christianity and Islam qua world religions were based on Judaism and in this, Baeck said, they also had a similar mission (*Sendung*). Yet what guaranteed those religions would not go astray? Baeck's answer was clear: Jews must remain Jews and promulgate Judaism. Jewish mission was not only the promotion of ethics and the messianic vision, but also serving as a reminder to other monotheistic religions of the ethical mission.[59]

Christianity expanded throughout the Roman Empire, eventually becoming the official imperial religion. For Baeck, the success of Christian missionizing in antiquity was grounded in two factors: the propagation of the Jewish message and the use of the Jewish networks of communities across the Roman Empire and Egypt. On the latter point, Baeck relied on none other than Harnack, who in *The Mission and Expansion of Christianity* calculated around a million converts to Judaism based on the available demographic numbers. Jewish missionary zeal genuinely surprised Harnack. He explained it by claiming the ceremonial system, or Jewish law, was not central for Jews outside Palestine. Drawing on a racialized language, he added that those who converted were mostly "kindred Semites of the lower class."[60]

Baeck said the expansion of Christianity was "unthinkable" without the Jewish diaspora, without "Judaism's tilling of the heathen fields and without the base [*Stützpunkt*] of Jewish provincial communities."[61] He thereby did not treat the Jewish diaspora as exile as a result of divine punishment, but instead understood it in light of what Amos Funkenstein called "missionary theodicy," a way of making sense of the exile through the idea that "because of their dispersion, the Jews can and did disperse the knowledge of God among the nations."[62] Being spread across the world allowed Jews to spread their message more effectively.

---

[59] Baeck, *Das Wesen des Judentums* (1905), 404–5.

[60] Adolf von Harnack, *The Mission and Expansion of Christianity in the First Three Centuries*, trans. James Moffatt (London: Williams and Norgate, 1908), 8; for an overview of current scholarship on Jewish missionizing and demographics in antiquity, see Brian McGing, "Population and Proselytism: How Many Jews Were There in the Ancient World?," in *Jews in the Hellenistic and Roman Cities*, eds. John Bartlett and Sean Freyne (Abingdon: Taylor & Francis, 2002), 88–106.

[61] Baeck, *Das Wesen des Judentums* (1905), 409.

[62] Funkenstein, "Polemics, Responses, and Self Reflection," in *Perceptions of Jewish History*, 205.

36 The Jewish Imperial Imagination

The terms "tilling of the fields" and "provincial communities" were potent political imaginaries for thinking about expansion and diaspora. The etymology of "colonizer," from the Latin *colonus* or farmer, tiller, and planter, already suggests agrarian activity.[63] There was, in other words, a relation between relation to the land, agriculture, and the mission of the Jews. Like the language of missionizing and the discussion of overseas colonies in the last section, these terms show engagement with the German imperial imaginary, in this case the colonization of Poland.

The inner, or adjacent, colonization of Poland was Germany's most prominent colonial enterprise. More than 120,000 Germans settled in East Prussia, fivefold the number of Germans in all the overseas colonies.[64] Baeck's biography suggests he was likely exposed to discourse about Poles and Polish territories. Lissa, where Baeck was born and raised, was part of the province of Posen which was at the heart of the inner colonization efforts. Jews in Lissa in general, and Baeck's family specifically, often sided with the German policies, evident, for example, in his father Samul Bäck's decision to preach in German and Leo's education in a German gymnasium. Furthermore, Baeck wrote the *Essence* while living in Oppeln, a city in a former Polish territory.[65]

Following the Partitions of Poland that erased its status as an independent state in the late eighteenth century, discussions in Prussia and German-speaking lands conceptualized it as a colonial space. In the National Assembly of 1848, Prussia's right to the Polish territories was justified as "conquest of the plowshare."[66] The logic is seemingly straightforward and common in colonial discourse. If vast swaths of lands are not being used, the argument goes, then there is a duty to improve them, thereby also staking a claim to those lands.[67]

At first, the German approach was meant to "Germanize" the Polish population, not the least by weakening the power of the Catholic church.

---

[63] Kumar, "Colony and Empire, Colonialism and Imperialism," 286.

[64] Philipp Ther, "Beyond the Nation: The Relational Basis of a Comparative History of Germany and Europe," *Central European History* 36, no. 1 (2003): 45–73; Sebastian Conrad, "Internal Colonialism in Germany: Culture Wars, Germanification of the Soil, and the Global Market Imaginary," in *German Colonialism in a Global Age*, eds. Geoff Eley and Bradley Naranch (Durham, NC: Duke University Press, 2015), 247–54.

[65] Baker, *Days of Sorrow and Pain*, 16–17.

[66] Franz Wigard, *Stenographischer Bericht über die Verhandlungen der deutschen constituirenden Nationalversammlung zu Frankfurt am Main* (Frankfurt am Main: J.D. Sauerländer, 1848), 1146.

[67] Such an idea was present, for example, in John Locke, *Two Treatises of Government and a Letter Concerning Toleration*, ed. Ian Shapiro (New Haven: Yale University Press, 2003), II. chap. 5, esp. par. 41; see also David Armitage, "John Locke: Theorist of Empire?," in *Empire and Modern Political Thought*, ed. Sankar Muthu (New York: Cambridge University Press, 2012), 84–111.

Under the Aegis of Empire 37

James Bjork has shown that there were instances where preference during elections was given to confessional over national questions in the Polish territories, proving that the issue was not merely national but also religious.[68] Put differently, this is another example of intertwining questions, in this case what to do with the Polish territory and the *Kulturkampf* about the place of Catholicism in unified Germany.

Especially since the 1880s, the German policy toward the Polish territories increasingly shifted toward settler colonialism in the hope of creating a German majority. This approach, however, strengthened rather than weakened Polish nationalism. In 1902, the acclaimed Polish author Henryk Sienkiewicz advised "Prussian Poles" not to hate the Germans despite the "glowing hatred of the Poles, their traditions, and ideas" that "is spreading in Germany." Anti-Polish sentiments, he added, had "one good effect, namely, it renders our Germanization impossible. The Germanism that is thrust upon us through force and hatred will nevermore pass into Polish blood. It is at best but varnish, which can be immediately removed."[69]

Poland was imagined differently than the colonies abroad during the Kaiserreich. The Germans, according to the *Meyers großes Konversationslexikon* (6th edition), had colonized this area since the eighth century CE and completed colonization by the fourteenth century. The implication was that the land had been substantially and permanently altered.[70] Alongside its conceptualization as an old German territory, Germany's Wild East – to use Kristin Kopp's turn of phrase – was thought of as the equivalent of the American Wild West, a landscape imagined to contain wild or uncivilized natives, a space that held potential for expansion through the taming of both nature and the local population.[71] Since the late nineteenth century, North America served as an important site for German thinking about its imperial place in the world, not the least because so many Germans emigrated there. The United States inspired

[68] James Bjork, *Neither German nor Pole: Catholicism and National Indifference in a Central European Borderland* (Ann Arbor: University of Michigan Press, 2009), 21–36.

[69] "Warns Prussian Poles," *The New York Times*, September 28, 1902; Sienkiewicz's thought is another example of colonial entanglements. Protesting the Prussian occupation of Poland, he had few qualms about German colonization in Africa. See Lenny Valerio, *Colonial Fantasies, Imperial Realities: Race Science and the Making of Polishness on the Fringes of the German Empire, 1840–1920* (Athens: Ohio University Press, 2019), 187–95.

[70] "Kolonien;" Wolfgang Wippermann, *Die Deutschen und der Osten: Feindbild und Traumland* (Darmstadt: Primus, 2007), 65.

[71] Kristin Kopp, *Germany's Wild East: Constructing Poland as Colonial Space* (Ann Arbor: University of Michigan Press, 2017); Vejas Liulevicius, *The German Myth of the East: 1800 to the Present* (Oxford: Oxford University Press, 2009), esp. 71–130.

38   The Jewish Imperial Imagination

policies of land management, ideas of a national frontier, and agricultural and international commerce. Leading economists such as Max Sering, who helped theorize the benefits of imperial expansion, worked in North America and held close ties to it.[72]

The imperial imagination of the Wild East was also manifested in popular literature. Gustav Freytag's 1855 novel *Soll und Haben* (Debit and Credit) sold 100,000 copies by 1900. It is a *Bildungsroman* that tells the story of Anton Wohlfart, a young man who settles on Polish territories as a self-declared German colonist. The contrast between Wohlfart, representing the diligent, industrious bourgeoisie, and the Polish people as uncivilized and violent is a central motif in the novel, as it was of later novels in the popular turn of the century genre known as *Ostmarkroman*. *Soll und Haben* shows not only the protagonist's personal growth, as is typical of a *Bildungsroman*, but also his ability to spatially expand what is considered in the novel to be the productive and moral virtues of Germanness.

Wohlfart thereby epitomizes both the civilizing mission and the tilling of the fields, and *Soll und Haben* is another example of the entanglement of questions. Wohlfart is employed in the import of colonial wares. Furthermore, his image is contrasted not only with Poles, but also with German aristocrats, and with Jewish characters that stand, following antisemitic stereotypes, for urbanity and constant desire for profit. The Jewish, Polish, and Colonial Questions all merge in this novel that conceptualizes Polish space as unruly and in need of German civilizing mission through settlement.[73]

Baeck's idea of Jewish missionizing as "tilling the heathen fields" drew on these imperial imaginaries of the East. The concern was about Jewish colonization both in spiritual terms of conversion and missionizing, and of physical settlement and agriculture. The Jewish "tilling of the heathen fields"

---

[72] Robert Nelson, "The Archive for Inner Colonization, the German East, and World War I," in *Germans, Poland, and Colonial Expansion to the East: 1850 through the Present*, ed. Robert Nelson (New York: Palgrave Macmillan, 2009), 65–93; Robert Nelson, "A German on the Prairies: Max Sering and Settler Colonialism in Canada," *Settler Colonial Studies* 5, no. 1 (2015): 1–19; Dörte Lerp, "Beyond the Prairie: Adopting, Adapting and Transforming Settlement Policies within the German Empire," *Journal of Modern European History* 14, no. 2 (2016): 225–44; Guettel, *German Expansionism, Imperial Liberalism and the United States, 1776–1945*; Grimmer-Solem, *Learning Empire*.

[73] Gustav Freytag, *Soll und Haben* (Leipzig: S. Hirzel, 1866); Kopp, *Germany's Wild East*, 29–56; similar attitudes toward Poles and the Polish territory were evident in *Die Gartenlaube*, one of the most popular illustrated weeklies in the German-speaking world. See Angela Koch, *DruckBilder: Stereotype und Geschlechtercodes in den antipolnischen Diskursen der "Gartenlaube"* (Colonge: Böhlau Verlag, 2002), esp. 49–136.

Under the Aegis of Empire

was to be done in the realm of spirit, but its connection to the settlements of the Jewish diaspora alluded to the fact that Jews needed to establish outposts. It was a religious imaginary about conversion that participated in a discourse about the economically and politically desired Jewish professions.

The question of whether Jews can be farmers and till the land had been a trope in discussions of the Jewish Question since the late eighteenth century. Was the absence of Jewish farmers the result of their exclusion from certain professions, a situation that could be remedied with their emancipation, or was it a testimony that they were incapable of working the land? Jewish vocational patterns and the possibility of changing them were thus tied to the ideas of the improvement of the Jew and emancipation, with the antisemitic picture of the Jew as an unproductive member of the polity with inauthentic relation to the land hanging above Jews even after they received equal rights.[74]

The Jewish Colonization Association (est. 1891) tried to alleviate the plight of Russian and Romanian Jews by the establishment of agricultural colonies. Colonies in this sense were agrarian enterprises, in line with the etymology of the word.[75] Although German Jews on the whole did not share the same pressing economical need, some of them sought to refute anti-Jewish stereotypes by partaking in the enterprise of inner colonization, among others via the *Bodenkulturverein* (Association for the Advancement of Agriculture among the Jews of Germany) (founded 1898).[76] Like support for the colonies in Africa, the image of the Wild East proved a fertile ground for German Jews of diverse denominations and political opinions who sought a relation to the soil and a reform of their vocations. They could all gather behind the basic aim of fostering Jewish agricultural enterprises in a way that would prove Jews could have an authentic and productive relation to the soil. Although Baeck was not a member of the *Bodenkulturverein*, he expressed similar concerns about Jewish urbanization. In a 1931 article in *Der Morgen*, for example, he called for a move away from the artificial lights of the city and a return to nature and rural areas.[77]

---

[74] Sucher Weinryb, *Der Kampf um die Berufsumschichtung: Ein Ausschnitt aus der Geschichte der Juden in Deutschland* (Berlin: Schocken, 1936), 14–17; Alexandra Zirkle, "Re-forming Professions: Salomon Herxheimer and Ludwig Philippson on the Past and Future of Jewish Farmers," in *Deutsch-jüdische Bibelwissenschaft: Historische, exegetische und theologische Perspektiven*, eds. Daniel Vorpahl et al. (Berlin and Boston: De Gruyter, 2019), 41–56.

[75] Derek Penslar, *Shylock's Children: Economics and Jewish Identity in Modern Europe* (Berkeley: University of California Press, 2001), 223–54.

[76] Nielsen, *Between Heimat and Hatred*, 23–37.

[77] Leo Baeck, "Mensch und Boden: Gedanken zur Soziologie des Großstadtjuden (1931)," *Werke* 6, 201–3.

40 The Jewish Imperial Imagination

The *Bodenkulturverein* and its focus on agriculture and connection to the land attracted Jews interested in another idea of Jewish agricultural settlement, namely on the soil of Palestine. Being Zionist was not an exclusive identity in this regard. Otto Warburg, a leading Zionist, for example, was also a member of the *Bodenkulturverein*, and a supporter of German colonialism.[78] Baeck showed an early positive attitude toward the idea of Jewish settlement in Palestine. After the first Zionist congress in Basel in 1897, the executive board of the Association of German Rabbis condemned the Zionist movement. Among more than ninety rabbis, only three refused to vote yes to this decision, one of whom was the recently ordained Leo Baeck.[79]

Why would Baeck, a young unknown rabbi from the province, risk going against the vast majority of his peers, likely including his father? While Baeck was not a Zionist in the strict sense, he could see value in the movement. First, Baeck took seriously the idea that Zionism could reach Jews that are disenchanted from the present Jewish communal institutions. Second, Baeck believed that the noun Judaism is more important than the adjectives that precede it such as Liberal, Orthodox, or Zionist. Years later, in a presidential address to the Union of Progressive Judaism in 1947, he said that there are many legitimate expressions of Judaism, one should not condemn other Jews.[80] Finally, the imperial context provides another explanation for Baeck's support of Zionism. The Jewish world-historical vocation, its civilizing mission, required both the securing of Jewish identity and the spreading of ethical monotheism. Zionism had the potential to contribute to both. It revived interest in Jews who were detached from Judaism or the Jewish community while also helping to spread the mission.

Baeck saw in Zionism one option among others to spread the mission in a new land. This view is elaborated in his essay "The Foundation and Content of Life," published in Martin Buber's Zionist journal *Der Jude* during the First World War. Baeck wrote that although "the thought of Jewish mission has been mocked from within and without . . . it would be a great day, in which the first emissaries will go out once again to proclaim the truth of our God."[81] Settlement in the land would provide an outlet for those among the Jews, presumably those disaffected from the official

---

[78] Stefan Vogt, *Subalterne Positionierungen: Der deutsche Zionismus im Feld des Nationalismus in Deutschland, 1890–1933* (Göttingen: Wallstein, 2016), 172–95.

[79] Hermann Levin Goldschmidt, "Der junge Leo Baeck," *AJR Information* 28, no. 5 (May 1963): 2.

[80] Leo Baeck, "Die Prinzipien der Progressiven Bewegung des Judentums (1947)," *Werke* 6, 522.

[81] Leo Baeck, "Lebensgrund und Lebensgehalt (1917/1918)," *Werke* 3, 121.

A Struggle for Existence

In refusing to condemn Zionism, Baeck was in the minority. Most German Jews initially opposed Zionism because claims for German nationhood and demands for a Jewish state could be interpreted as mutually exclusive. Nowhere was this attitude more evident than in what quickly became one of the biggest Jewish organizations in Germany, the *Centralverein* or C.V. (Central Association of German Citizens of Jewish Faith). Founded in 1893, the C.V.'s goal was to fight the rise of political and racial antisemitism that argued Jews as irrevocably distinct from, and inferior to, Germans. Although fighting discrimination against Jews was a goal shared by the C.V. and Zionists, the C.V.'s position was that Zionists came too close to adopting the presuppositions of antisemites. As Eugen Fuchs, one of its cofounders, put it: Zionists, "just like the antisemites, wish to detach the German Jews from the fatherland."[82]

Baeck was aware of these fears and the potential accusation of dual loyalty. In the *Essence*, he wrote that although state and society were blind to Jewish suffering, Jews remained loyal citizens and faithful to their country. That their patriotism and love for the fatherland often went unrequited proved, in his mind, it was pure.[83] Patriotism and being proud Germans, while still insisting on Jewish difference, was for Baeck part of the Jewish predicament as a minority. Jews, he wrote at the beginning of the *Essence*, "have always been a minority," but they did not live in a "spiritual ghetto." As a minority, they strove for intellectual and spiritual independence out of necessity: "a minority is compelled to think ... In the mental quarrel, it must win for itself, time and again, the consciousness of truth, which for the ruler appears guaranteed through the possession of power [*Macht*]."[84] Jews did not have the privilege of complacency and always had to struggle to maintain their mission and particularity.

[82] Quoted in Avraham Barkai, *"Wehr Dich!": Der Centralverein deutscher Staatsbürger jüdischen Glaubens (C.V.) 1893–1938* (Munich: C.H. Beck, 2002), 51; Ismar Schorsch, *Jewish Reactions to German Anti-Semitism, 1870–1914* (New York: Columbia University Press, 1972), 117–48; Hagit Lavsky, *Before Catastrophe: The Distinctive Path of German Zionism* (Detroit: Wayne State University Press, 1996).

[83] Baeck, *Das Wesen des Judentums* (1905), 415–6.

[84] Baeck, *Das Wesen des Judentums* (1905), 321–2.

42   The Jewish Imperial Imagination

The minority's creativity was hard won and necessary for its survival. Baeck turned to a language of struggle and fighting in describing the experience of the Jewish minority. One of the sources for such militarized language was religious polemics, a word whose etymology relates to waging a war. A common metaphor in this regard is that of polemics as the sword and apologetics as the shield.[85] Baeck followed this line of thought in the *Essence*, saying that as a minority, Jews had to be "armed" for the fight. Drawing on the statement in *Pirkei Avot* (1:1) that the Sages made a "hedge around the Torah," Baeck claimed rabbinic law "is not the teaching itself, but a defensive bulwark [*Schutzwehr*] for it."[86] "It is easy to ask," Baeck added, "whether this fence which surrounded and still surrounds Judaism has in fact been necessary," a common question in the Jewish Liberal tradition to which Baeck belonged. Unlike those who would too easily do away with the fence, however, Baeck recognized its value. Thanks to its defenses, the community survived "in the middle of a hostile world. Yet no one knows what would have been without its existence."[87]

The need for a defensive bulwark is articulated in the title of the last section of the *Essence*: "The Preservation of Judaism." Baeck developed in it a distinction between worldly success and the ethical task, between forced conversions with the sword and the Jewish spiritual work. The constant persecution of Jews, first by the Roman Empire, and then by Christendom as the new world power, led in Baeck's description to hundreds of thousands of victims. But these were nothing more than a "victory of power [*Macht*], harmless and without glory."[88] Whereas Jewish missionizing attempted to colonize in the spirit, using energy (*Kraft*), empires used violence and terror in the spreading of its message. In "Life's Foundation and Content," Baeck made this distinction clear: "the concept of power [*Macht*] has completely transformed itself into energy [*Kraft*] in Jewish existence."[89] The distinction between *Kraft* and *Macht*,

---

[85] Bäck, "Harnack's Vorlesungen," 120; Moritz Friedländer, *Geschichte der jüdischen Apologetik als Vorgeschichte des Christentums: Eine historisch-kritische Darstellung der Propaganda und Apologie im Alten Testament und in der hellenistischen Diaspora* (Amsterdam: Philo Press, 1973), 1; Hanne Trautner-Kromann, *Shield and Sword: Jewish Polemics against Christianity and the Christians in France and Spain from 1100–1500* (Tübingen: Mohr Siebeck, 1993).

[86] Baeck, *Das Wesen des Judentums* (1905), 411.

[87] Baeck, *Das Wesen des Judentums* (1905), 413–4.

[88] Baeck, *Das Wesen des Judentums* (1905), 416.

[89] Baeck, "Lebensgrund und Lebensgehalt (1917/1918)," 119; Franz Rosenzweig similarly spoke in *The Star of Redemption* about the Church's imperial power, but he did not condemn it. See Franz Rosenzweig, *Der Stern der Erlösung* (Frankfurt am Main: Suhrkamp, 1988), 391; Benjamin Pollock, "From Nation State to World Empire: Franz Rosenzweig's Redemptive Imperialism," *Jewish Studies Quarterly* 11, no. 4 (2004): 332–53.

Under the Aegis of Empire   43

spiritual energy and physical power, was a constant throughout Baeck's career, and he returned to it often in order to critique coercion and violence.

The rejection of coercion and violence also allowed Baeck to wage a hidden polemic with Harnack on the question of dogma. Harnack claimed that dogmas were part of a later historical development in Christianity, the husk and not the kernel of Christianity. Baeck, by contrast, connected dogmas to the history of Christian violence, because dogmas required a totalizing religious authority that had the means to enforce decisions against dissent. The "cohesive power of obligatory dogmas" led to the view that "he who has the power, possesses the truth."[90] The word *Macht* is used consistently to refer to state-power, but also to that of the church, which stood under the influence of this idea of power.[91]

Baeck described the fight for the validity of dogmas in the early days of Christianity as an armed conflict. Christianity, in other words, was violent from its early days. In the second edition of the *Essence*, Baeck added that decisions were made using weapons "or an imperial edict," thereby highlighting the role of Christianity as an imperial religion.[92] In Judaism, by contrast, such a body that demanded obedience and fought dissent did not exist since at least the days of the Sanhedrin. True to his notion of prophetic world-history, Baeck argued that worldly power is not a measurement of true success, "world-*church* and world-*religion* are not identical, and even less so world-religion [*Weltreligion*] and religion all over the world [*Allerweltsreligion*]."[93]

The term chosen by Baeck to describe the Jewish struggle was *Kampf ums Dasein*, a "struggle for existence," which he called a "compulsory spiritual fight" against the demands of conquering powers.[94] This term evokes Heinrich Georg Bronn's translation of Darwin's "struggle for existence" in *On the Origin of Species*. Although the term predates Darwin, in the late nineteenth century the idea became associated with

---

[90] Baeck, *Das Wesen des Judentums* (1905), 321–22. In the nineteenth century, debate around dogma was part of the formative phase of Jewish denominations. By Baeck's time, however, it was once more primarily an inter-religious debate. See Michah Gottlieb, "Does Judaism Have Dogma? Moses Mendelssohn and a Pivotal Nineteenth-Century Debate," *Yearbook of the Maimonides Centre for Advanced Studies* 2 (2019): 240; Kerstin von der Krone, "Jüdische Wissenschaft und modernes Judentum: Eine Dogmendebatte," in *Die "Wissenschaft des Judentums": Eine Bestandsaufnahme*, eds. Andreas Kilcher and Thomas Meyer (Paderborn: Wilhelm Fink Verlag, 2015), 115–38.

[91] Baeck, "Lebensgrund und Lebensgehalt (1917/1918)," 119.

[92] Baeck, *Das Wesen des Judentums* (1926), 46; cf. Baeck, *Das Wesen des Judentums* (1905), 322.

[93] Baeck, *Das Wesen des Judentums* (1905), 352.

[94] Baeck, *Das Wesen des Judentums* (1905), 323, 345.

44 The Jewish Imperial Imagination

his understanding of the term. Bronn's translation, in fact, offered a stronger notion of a zero-sum game in the fight between species.[95]

This naturalist concept was tied to racial classifications and justification of empire. Bernhard von Bülow used the term to explain Germany's need for a strong fleet.[96] Ernst Haeckel, one of the influential popularizers of Darwin in Germany and an advocate for German imperialism, used *Kampf ums Dasein* in his *Natural History of Creation* (1868) to describe the history of humanity. The "Indo-German race," he argued, had "surpassed all other races and species by virtue of its higher development of the brain." Although some lesser races were protected to an extent by dint of their better acclimatization to tropical conditions, Haeckel believed others would sooner or later "completely succumb" in the *Kampf ums Dasein*.[97]

At the time Baeck composed the *Essence*, he could have read in the newspapers about such struggles in which the German Empire was involved: The Boer War in southern Africa against the British Empire (1899–1902); the Boxer Rebellion (1899–1901) in China; and the Herero Uprising (1904) in German Southwest Africa.[98] The latter was part of the German settler colonialism program in Africa that resulted in genocide. In response to the German confiscation of land, oppression by the settlers, and the loss of their livelihood, the Herero rebelled. This should have come as no surprise. Justus, a Herero man from Okahanja, warned the missionary August Kuhlmann that the oppression was unbearable.[99]

The response to the Herero Uprising was brutal. After several months of fighting, General Lothar von Trotha was appointed by the Kaiser to quench the revolt. In an infamous order from October 2, 1904, known

[95] U. Kutschera, "Struggle to Translate Darwin's View of Concurrency," *Nature* 458, no. 7241 (2009): 967; Ernst Mayr, *The Growth of Biological Thought: Diversity, Evolution, and Inheritance* (Cambridge, MA: Belknap, 1982), 482–85.

[96] Bernhard von Bülow, "Bernhard von Bülows 'dynamische' Außenpolitik (1899)," in *Deutsche Geschichte in Bilder und Dokumente*, eds. Roger Chickering et al., vol. 5 (Washington, DC: German Histroical Institute), http://germanhistorydocs.ghi-dc.org/docpage.cfm?docpage_id=2845, accessed June 29, 2020.

[97] Ernst Haeckel, *Natürliche Schöpfungsgeschichte* (Leipzig: A. Kröner, 1924), II.395–6; Daniel Gasman, *The Scientific Origins of National Socialism* (New York: Routledge, 2017). The philosophical challenge of Haeckel's materialist monism influenced Jewish thought; see Paul Nahme, *Hermann Cohen and the Crisis of Liberalism: The Enchantment of the Public Sphere* (Bloomington: Indiana University Press, 2019), 115–19; Eliyahu Stern, *Jewish Materialism: The Intellectual Revolution of the 1870s* (New Haven: Yale University Press, 2018), 102–11.

[98] I focus here solely on the Herero Uprising, rather than the Herero and Nama, because this is the one Baeck most likely would have heard about as he was completing the *Essence*. In a later campaign against the Nama people, about half of them fell victim to the German brutality.

[99] Matthew Fitzpatrick, *The Kaiser and the Colonies: Monarchy in the Age of Empire* (Oxford: Oxford University Press, 2022), 142.

Under the Aegis of Empire

as the *Vernichtungsbefehl* (extermination order), he ordered not to accept surrender and execute anyone, including women and children, who would not leave. The German army pushed the Herero population to the scorching desert, which was supposed "to complete," in the words of an official report, "the job that the German weapons had started: the annihilation of the Herero people."[100] The war, wrote the Rhenish missionary Johann Irle, "turned Hereroland into a desert, full of human corpses and the cadavers of livestock. Everywhere we encounter the bleaching bones of the Herero and the graves of brave German soldiers. The country has become a giant cemetery in which whites and blacks rest facing one another."[101] When the Kaiser ordered a stop to this policy in December, forced labor camps with cruel working conditions were established for the surviving Herero. This genocidal policy decimated the Herero population by about eighty percent.[102]

Already at the start of the campaign – under the colonial administrator Theodor Leutwein – Social Democrats such as August Bebel protested attacks of women and children. The newspaper *Tägliche Rundschau*, by contrast, rejected any negotiations with the Herero because "the national honor and the future of the colony require punishment and suppression of the rebels via force of weapons and the superiority of the white man."[103] After von Trotha's campaign, and another conflict in German East Africa known as the Maji-Maji Uprising (1905–1907), the colonies and how to rule them became a matter of public debate. Soldiers from the colonial campaigns began publishing pamphlets and reports justifying their actions, while politicians such as Matthias Erzberger from the Center Party criticized the government for the high costs of maintaining control of the colonies. The argument was primarily, but not solely, economic. The shock at the colonial violence in Germany was a result of breaking the imaginary of the German as a civilizing force and a noble colonizer. If beforehand Germans could imagine themselves to be morally better than

---

[100] Quoted in Steinmetz, *The Devil's Handwriting*, 195.

[101] Steinmetz, *The Devil's Handwriting*, 195.

[102] Jan-Bart Gewald, *Herero Heroes: A Socio-Political History of the Herero of Namibia, 1890–1923* (Athens: Ohio State University Press, 1999). Isabel Hull argues that the German military ethos propagated extreme brutality, thereby supporting genocidal acts. See Isabel Hull, *Absolute Destruction: Military Culture and the Practices of War in Imperial Germany* (Ithaca: Cornell University Press, 2013). Susanne Kuss rejects such a claim, among others by pointing to the perception, shared by many nations, that the colonies were a theater of war with its own rules. See Susanne Kuss, *German Colonial Wars and the Context of Military Violence*, trans. Andrew Smith (Cambridge, MA: Harvard University Press, 2017), 138, 2–3.

[103] Quoted in Hull, *Absolute Destruction*, 13. For early critiques and responses, see 13–21.

46 The Jewish Imperial Imagination

the violence of Spanish or British colonizers, after the genocides and prevalent violence, such a position was hard to maintain.[104]

The mixed attitudes toward the colonies was also reflected in Jewish newspapers. In 1908, the Berlin Orthodox journal *Die jüdische Presse* praised the courage of Jewish soldiers in the colonial campaigns. Similarly, the *Allgemeine Zeitung des Judentums* celebrated in July 1914 the fact that Jewish participation in the colonial campaigns in China and in Africa was recognized in the *Frankfurter Zeitung*. Participation in what were seen as military campaigns was an opportunity to prove Jewish masculinity through combat and assert Jewish patriotism. On the other hand, many Jews also shared the critique of the German violent colonial policies that became evident in the genocide of the Herero.[105]

Baeck's thought offered an alternative to violent imperialism, without addressing the colonial atrocities. His use of *Kampf ums Dasein* for the Jewish spiritual struggle implied a critique of imperial violence. Those that struggle for existence were the minorities, those refusing to succumb to the stronger powers. Baeck generalized from the Jewish predicament to the idea of the treatment of minorities in general:

> Already through its mere existence, it [Judaism] expresses the *ethical principle of minority*. Judaism witnesses the power of the idea as against the power of mere numbers and external success ... If Judaism did not exist, one would have had to invent it. Without minorities there is no world-historical goal. And because of that, Judaism has become a *standard of measurement of the level of morality*.[106]

Baeck connected the idea of a world-history with the Jewish task in the world, but this time the task was described as being-there. The role of the Jew as a minority witnessing the morality of the world was a consequence of persecutions that prevented proselytizing. The fate of Israel was exemplary in showing the long distance from the messianic era.[107]

This was an inversion of one of the most influential views determining the status of Jews and Judaism under Christian rule. Augustine wrote in

---

[104] Kuss, *German Colonial Wars and the Context of Military Violence*, 238–41; Medardus Brehl, "'Das Drama spielte sich auf der dunklen Bühne des Sandfeldes ab': Die Vernichtung der Herero und Nama in der deutschen (populär-)Literatur," in *Völkermord in Deutsch-Südwestafrika: Der Kolonialkrieg (1904–1908) in Namibia und seine Folgen*, eds. Jürgen Zimmerer and Joachim Zeller (Berlin: Ch. Links Verlag, 2016), 86–87; Grimmer-Solem, *Learning Empire*, 340–44.

[105] Avraham, "Between Concern and Difference," 58, 49–51.

[106] Baeck, *Das Wesen des Judentums* (1905), 415 – emphasis in original; see also Leo Baeck, "Unsere Stellung zu den Religionsgesprächen (1910)," *Werke* 6, 83.

[107] Baeck, *Das Wesen des Judentums* (1905), 415.

Under the Aegis of Empire

the fourth century CE – and his thought shaped a lot of the Church's relation to the Jews in the Middle Ages – that Jews were living witnesses to Christ until the Second Coming. The preservation of the Jews, whom Augustine compared to Cain, was therefore required. They were not to be slain but rather forced to subjugation.[108] Jews were indeed witnesses, Baeck implied, but it was not to the triumphal church but to the current state of the world. In this sense, too, Jews were the Suffering Servant of whom Isaiah spoke. They embodied the messianic promise and the need to realize it in the world, but also the suffering involved in such a task.

Baeck envisioned Jews and Judaism as a minority with a world-historical mission, which included spreading ethical monotheism and expanding through converting the world. He did not reject the idea of empire per se, but he opposed the use of power in the imperial context, the attempt to coerce people using violence. The alternative to violence and power was the Jewish model, spiritual in nature and without the state-apparatus. This meant being a minority with a task in the world. Such a position often led to a struggle for existence, but this struggle was part of what it meant to be a minority in the world of empires.

---

[108] Paula Fredriksen argues that such a position defends the Jews, emphasizing their indispensability until the end of times, see Paula Fredriksen, *Augustine and the Jews: A Christian Defense of Jews and Judaism* (Toronto: Doubleday, 2008).

CHAPTER 2

Saving Christianity from Itself

On August 1, 1914, Germany declared war on Russia and mobilized to conquer Belgium on its way to France. The Great War had started. Kaiser Wilhelm II called for a German *Burgfrieden*, a civic truce from all political disputes and disagreements. "Today," he declared, "we are all German brothers and only German brothers."[1] The First World War was first and foremost a war between empires, a global affair unlike the world had ever seen. The war was waged on land and in sea, where naval supremacy was paramount because of the reliance on colonies for the transportation of materials, goods, and soldiers. At least four million non-whites partook in the war in combat and non-combat roles, primarily in the armies of the two largest colonial powers, France and Britain.[2]

Jews in many countries saw in the war an opportunity to refute the common antisemitic accusations of lack of patriotism, courage, or willingness to sacrifice.[3] In Germany, despite some critique and opposition, the war was generally greeted by German Jews and non-Jews alike.[4] From C.V. to

[1] Wolfdieter Bihl, ed., *Deutsche Quellen zur Geschichte des Ersten Weltkrieges* (Darmstadt: Wissenschaftliche Buchgesellschaft, 1991), 49; cf. Ralph Haswell Lutz, ed., "The Kaiser's Speech from the Balcony of the Royal Palace, Berlin, August 1, 1914," in *Fall of the German Empire, 1914–1918*, trans. David G. Rempel and Gertrude Rendtorff (Stanford: Stanford University Press, 1932), 4.

[2] John Morrow, *The Great War: An Imperial History* (New York: Routledge, 2016); John Darwin, *The Empire Project: The Rise and Fall of the British World-System, 1830–1970* (Cambridge: Cambridge University Press, 2011), 305–58; Roger Chickering, *Imperial Germany and the Great War, 1914–1918* (Cambridge: Cambridge University Press, 2014), 94–110.

[3] On the history of Jews in the military, see Derek Penslar, *Jews and the Military: A History* (Princeton: Princeton University Press, 2013). On the Jewish experience of the war from a transnational perspective, see Marsha Rozenblit and Jonathan Karp, eds., *World War I and the Jews: Conflict and Transformation in Europe, the Middle East, and America* (New York: Berghahn Books, 2017); Sarah Panter, *Jüdische Erfahrungen und Loyalitätskonflikte im Ersten Weltkrieg* (Göttingen: Vandenhoeck & Ruprecht, 2014).

[4] Pulzer, *Jews and the German State*, 195; Ulrich Sieg, *Jüdische Intellektuelle im Ersten Weltkrieg: Kriegserfahrungen, weltanschauliche Debatten und kulturelle Neuentwürfe* (Berlin and Boston: De Gruyter, 2001); Mordechai Breuer, *Modernity within Tradition: The Social History of Orthodox*

Saving Christianity from Itself

Zionists, from Liberals to Orthodox, more than 100,000 Jews of various backgrounds served in the German army throughout the war, among other reasons because it was fought against Tsarist Russia, who mistreated Jews. Martin Steinhardt from Mannheim was only fourteen when he volunteered for service and won the Iron Cross for his bravery. He fell on October 18, 1914, one of 12,000 German Jews who died in the war.[5]

Baeck was part of the initial patriotic wave engulfing Germany and volunteered to serve as a Jewish chaplain for almost the entire four years of the war. His texts from this period, while never endorsing war and violence as such, infused it with greater world-historical meaning in ways that imagined parallels between the Jewish position as a minority and a support for the German army. By the end of the Great War, with the surrender of Germany, the abdication of the Kaiser, and the loss of colonies and territories, a new Germany emerged, the Weimar Republic. In developing his Jewish postimperial imagination, Baeck once more turned to theology and the history of religion. He came to recognize certain contemporary trends in Protestant Christianity as a gnostic-Marcionite vision of redemption from the world. This theological position, he argued, was unethical and politically dangerous. Against complete inwardness to the extent of world-negation, Baeck offered a Jewish theopolitical imagination that insisted on the Jewish foundation of Christianity. The antidote to anti-Judaism and antisemitism, he claimed, was to strengthen the Jewish element within Christianity.

Cultural Conquest

A few days after the war began, German Jews joined their Christian countrymen in a day of prayer for the success of the military campaign. Such an event was not without precedent. At least since the late sixteenth century, Jews, like their Christian counterparts, participated in special national days of fasting and prayer, for example, after natural disasters or the coronations of monarchs.[6] On August 5, Baeck delivered a sermon at the Fasanenstrasse Synagogue in Berlin. Already half an hour before the

---

Jewry in Imperial Germany, trans. Elizabeth Petuchowski (New York: Columbia University Press, 1992), 385–87; Nielsen, *Between Heimat and Hatred*, 73–78. The support for the war was by no means unanimous; see Gideon Reuveni and Edward Madigan, "The First World War and the Jews," in *The Jewish Experience of the First World War*, eds. Edward Madigan and Gideon Reuveni (London: Palgrave Macmillan, 2019), 1–5.

[5] Peter Appelbaum, *Loyal Sons: Jews in the German Army in the Great War* (Portland, OR: Vallentine Mitchell, 2014), 54.

[6] Marc Saperstein, *Jewish Preaching in Times of War, 1800–2001* (Oxford: The Littman Library of Jewish Civilization, 2008), 5–12.

50   The Jewish Imperial Imagination

start of the special service, thousands of people gathered. All 1720 seats were taken and the public also filled the hallways, with more gathered outside. The demand was so high the service was repeated that day for those who could not enter the building.

The service began with a singing of Psalm 130 – "Out of the depth I called thee, O Lord" – to a Yom Kippur melody, before moving to a sermon on Psalm 94:15, "Judgement shall again accord with justice and all upright shall rally to it." Recent days, Baeck said, had made all feel how "the life of the fatherland is our life; the conscience of the people echoes in ours. The consciousness of justice [*Recht*], the clear conscience, unites all. We all understand each other, because we understand our duty." The war, Baeck promised his audience, was not a territorial war. Rather, it was a "war, which will decide on the culture and ethos of Europe, whose fate lies in the hands of Germany and its allies."[7] The German triumph would be a triumph of justice, concluded Baeck, before moving to a moment of contemplative silence and a final prayer.

In his sermon, Baeck alluded to the idea of German culture as necessitating going to war. He was hardly the only one to offer such an interpretation. Culture (*Kultur*) was a central category at that time, signifying both a particular national culture and a shared idea of European culture.[8] The war, and claims of moral superiority, were done not only in the name of defending the nation but also in the name of promoting culture. At the start of the war, descriptions, not least by British propaganda, began to emerge of violence and horrific scenes during Germany's conquest of the neutral Belgium.[9] In response, German intellectuals published an appeal to the *Kulturwelt*, which in English was translated as "To the Civilized World!" because of the different connotations of the words culture and civilization in German and English.[10]

Ninety-three of Germany's leading intellectuals signed the text, which was published in October 1914. The list reads as a Who's Who of Science and Culture: renowned scientists Max Planck, Fritz Haber, Wilhelm Röntgen, and Ernst Haeckel; artists such as Max Liebermann and Fritz August von Kaulbach; the poets and novelists Gerhardt and Carl Hauptmann, Ludwig Fulda, and Richard Dehmel; the philosophers

---

[7] "Der Bettag am 5.August," *Allgemeine Zeitung des Judentums* 78, no. 33 (August 14, 1914): 385.

[8] Jörg Fischer, "Zivilisation, Kultur," in *Grundgeschichtliche Begriffe*, eds. Reinhart Koselleck et al., vol. 7 (Stuttgart: Klett-Cotta, 1992), 669–774.

[9] John Horne and Alan Kramer, *German Atrocities 1914: A History of Denial* (New Haven: Yale University Press, 2009).

[10] Fischer, "Zivilisation, Kultur," 760–61.

Saving Christianity from Itself

Wilhelm Windelband and Max Wundt; Adolf von Harnack and Reinhold Seeberg among the theologians; Gustav von Schmoller among the economists, and the list goes on. Thirty-three of the signees were or would later be elected to the Prussian Academy of Sciences, including several past and future Nobel Prize laureates. With the exception of Social Democrats and parties to its left, all of German society was represented: liberals and conservatives, Protestants, Catholics, and Jews stood together to defend what they saw as defamation of German culture and morality.[11]

In a series of statements that began with "It is not true that . . ." the signees insisted that Germany was not responsible for the outbreak of the war, did not use excessive violence against Belgians, nor did it violate international law. They protested the "lies of our enemies" and argued against attempts to distinguish between German culture, as emerging in the Enlightenment, and German-Prussian militarism that was associated with the Wilhelmine Empire. Without German militarism, they wrote, German culture would have been long gone: "German army and the German people are one and the same." They appealed to their international reputation: "Believe us! Believe that we will fight this battle until the end as a people of culture [*Kulturvolk*], for whom the legacy of a Goethe, a Beethoven, a Kant was as holy as its hearths and homes."[12] Culture became a justification for the war, and a counterargument against those accusing the Germans of being militaristic, brutal, and barbaric.

Baeck left for the front in September 1914. Unlike Christian army chaplains, the rabbis' serving were not paid by the army but directly by the Jewish community, who even had to pay for Baeck's uniform. The army did recognize, however, the role of the rabbis as chaplains and provided assistance such as transportation.[13] "The Drama of History," a short text Baeck composed for the newsletter of the Jewish community of Berlin after arriving at the Western front, called for a return to the Bible, which he describes as a "book of struggle," but not in the sense of "conflict

---

[11] Bernhard von Brocke, "Wissenschaft und Militarismus: Der Aufruf der 93 'An die Kulturwelt!' und der Zusammenbruch der internationalen Gelehrtenrepublik im Ersten Weltkrieg," in *Wilamowitz nach 50 Jahren*, eds. William Calder et al. (Darmstadt: Wissenschaftliche Buchgesellschaft, 1985), 657–58.

[12] Brocke, "Wissenschaft und Militarismus," 718; Lutz, ed., "The Manifesto of the German University Professors and Men of Science," 74–78. It achieved the exact opposite purpose, becoming a sign for neutral observers, for example, in the USA, for the extent to which chauvinism infested the German academy. See Brocke, "Wissenschaft und Militarismus," 665, 676–81.

[13] Editors' introduction in Sabine Hank et al., eds., *Feldrabbiner in den deutschen Streitkräften des Ersten Weltkrieges* (Berlin: Hentrich & Hentrich, 2013), 30.

52   The Jewish Imperial Imagination

and quarrel." [14] It was a spiritual struggle, "the struggle is for the ideal [*Idee*], the great tasks of history. Our prophets have created this concept of struggle, because they created the concept of world-history." [15] Consistent with his position in the *Essence* about Jewish struggle as spiritual, and without necessarily intending to do so, Baeck, like his Christian counterparts, weaponized the prophets. [16] This was not a counterhistory resisting a Christian interpretation, but rather a reading that was in line with a prevalent imperial imagination during a world conflict. The struggle might be for an ideal, but it was fought in real trenches.

In another text, circulated as a publication for Jewish soldiers for the holiday of Shavuot in 1915, Baeck once again turned to the Bible as a source of inspiration for those heading to battle. "An urge forward came into the duty and gave it a great push," he said. "All the hundreds of thousands rushed into the struggle ... The biblical spirit blew through the land, our holy text was once more seized." In a holiday marking the giving of the Torah, Baeck celebrated the value of the sacred text, while also alluding to the beginning of the book of Genesis, thereby giving the impression that going to war was an act of new creation. [17]

In adopting biblical language, Baeck achieved a twofold purpose. First, he conveyed to Jewish soldiers, and the wider Jewish public, that Jewish sources had value for the present moment. In this, he called them to strengthen their relation to Judaism. Second, the current situation offered a new interpretation of the text, and Baeck's ideas about Judaism. This two-way street led to a position that never explicitly endorsed the war, but implied de facto spiritual underpinning and support.

War, however, could not be for war's sake alone. According to Baeck it needed to serve the purpose of a lasting peace and not merely cessation of hostilities. The exact meaning of peace was left understated. At Baeck's most patriotic moments, peace involved a new world order in which German culture would take a leading role. The war was a "war for peace," in that it led toward "a new Germany ... it is what we dream of." [18] This imagined imperial *pax Germania* was tempered by Baeck's repeated emphasis that one also needed to maintain, as much as possible, positive relations to the conquered people. In a small booklet of reflections on the Sabbath for Jewish

[14] Leo Baeck, "Das Drama der Geschichte (1914)," *Werke* 6, 120–21.
[15] Leo Baeck, "Das Drama der Geschichte (1914)," 121.
[16] Susannah Heschel, "Ecstasy versus Ethics: The Impact of the First World War on German Biblical Scholarship on the Hebrew Prophets," in *The First World War and the Mobilization of Biblical Scholarship*, eds. Andrew Mein et al. (London: T&T Clark, 2019), 187–206.
[17] Leo Baeck, "Du Sollst! (1915)," *Werke* 6, 126.   [18] Leo Baeck, "Du Sollst! (1915)," 127.

Saving Christianity from Itself

soldiers, Baeck argued that honor and dignity, both of the fatherland and of one's faith community, were dependent upon the soldiers' behavior. Those whose land the Germans occupied had suffered greatly, he wrote, and one should treat them with kindliness in a fair and decent manner. The ethical reasoning for the war should be attested in how one behaved in victory.[19]

Baeck's focus was on ethical resolve rather than just military might. The struggle could not be only for earthly power, he argued, in which case it was meaningless in the long term.[20] Every people "must create a place for itself, in which it can work for humanity, through which it carries what it has to offer for the sake of world-history, for the culture of all."[21] Baeck makes a claim for moral ideals, arguing that only a people that possesses those would have a future and a right to exist before God. Not coincidentally, however, this rhetoric recalls the German colonial discourse of "a place in the sun." The Germans' attempt to secure this place was not only justified, Baeck suggested, it was necessary for moral progression and the triumph of culture.

The language of spiritual struggle in describing the German forces was similar to the ways in which he described Judaism's struggle in the *Essence*. In making the connection between being German and being Jewish, Baeck was participating in discussions about the meaning of Germanism and Judaism, and the relation between the two. The most famous contemporary example was Hermann Cohen's "Deutschtum und Judentum" or "Germanism and Judaism" (1915/1916), two essays under the same name in which Cohen stressed Jewish and German spiritual affinity. The motivation for such essays, Cohen wrote, emerged from an understanding that just as the German spirit was misunderstood and maligned in the time of the war – we have seen a similar claim in the Manifest of the Ninety-Three – so was the Jewish spirit.[22] The affinity between Germans and Jews, Cohen suggested, was not only historical, but also philosophical, with German idealism finding its counterpart in Judaism's monotheistic faith.[23] Baeck's texts from the early years of the war made similar connections between the German and the Jewish condition.

---

[19] Leo Baeck, "Draussen und Drinnen (n.d., likely 1915)," *Werke* 6, 129; Baeck, "Das Drama der Geschichte (1914)," 123.

[20] Baeck, "Das Drama der Geschichte (1914)," 123; cf. Baeck, "Du Sollst! (1915)," 127.

[21] Baeck, "Das Drama der Geschichte (1914)," 123.

[22] Hermann Cohen, "Deutschtum und Judentum," in *Jüdische Schriften*, eds. Bruno Strauss and Franz Rosenzweig, vol. 2 (Berlin: C.A. Schwetschke, 1924), 292; Frederick Beiser, *Hermann Cohen: An Intellectual Biography* (Oxford: Oxford University Press, 2018), 307–11, 326–29; Sieg, *Jüdische Intellektuelle im Ersten Weltkrieg*, 231–56.

[23] Nahme, *Hermann Cohen and the Crisis of Liberalism*, 69–82; Miguel Vatter, *Living Law: Jewish Political Theology from Hermann Cohen to Hannah Arendt* (New York: Oxford University Press,

54   The Jewish Imperial Imagination

After serving until October 1915 on the Western front, Baeck moved to the Eastern front. The need to fight on two fronts and the fear of encirclement between the Russian and French empires were guiding the logic behind the German military strategy known as the Schlieffen Plan, which aimed at a quick defeat of France on the Western front before turning all the forces toward Russia on the Eastern front.[24] In a pamphlet sent to Jewish soldiers for the holiday of Hanukkah – a celebration of the victory of the Maccabees over their Hellenistic opponents in the second century BCE – Baeck connected the German fear of encirclement and the Jewish sense of being a minority.

Baeck defined two types of people: those who only wanted to be part of the masses; and those who found a sense of firmness within their own soul and could therefore have their place among the few. The struggle between the two "is the actual content of the history of the peoples." Jews firmly belonged in the latter and the message of Hanukkah was that "spirit is more meaningful than the number. It celebrates the energy [*Kraft*] that resides in the few." It had always been the Jewish task "to stand over against the many" and now Baeck added that it was also a German task. Knowledge about the victory of the spirit carried with it "the strong confidence that Germany will remain successful in its struggle against the enemies surrounding it, and we Israelites in the land, we feel this trust especially intimately and deeply." Baeck repeated this point at the end of his sermon: "Encircled by enemies, the German people have now experienced and demonstrated it. We, children of our community of faith in the fatherland, we also know it from long ago. We have to tend in war as in peace to the heritage of the Maccabees."[25]

During the war, Baeck imagined the German condition as if it were the Jewish minority in danger in the world, struggling for its rightful place. Baeck's reflections on Hannukah during the Great War had a lasting impression on certain German Jews. The text was reprinted and excerpted by *Der Schild*, the organ of the Jewish veterans' association (*Reichsbund jüdischer Frontsoldaten* –RjF), on Hannukah 1935, just a few months after the passing of the racist Nuremberg Laws. The memory of the war, and the sense of Jewish struggle as German struggle had an appeal for Jewish

---

2021), 59–76; Dana Hollander, *Ethics Out of Law: Hermann Cohen and the "Neighbor"* (Toronto: University of Toronto Press, 2021), 17–19.

[24] John Keegan, *The First World War* (New York: Knopf, 1999), 28–34.

[25] Leo Baeck, "Die Kraft der Wenigen (1915)," *Werke* 6, 130–33. On the theme of Hanukkah during the war, see Tim Grady, *A Deadly Legacy: German Jews and the Great War* (New Haven: Yale University Press, 2017), 41.

veterans as they were trying to maintain their German patriotism and make sense of their existence under Nazism.[26]

A report by Baeck after moving to the Eastern front underscores the German imperial imagination of the East as a space to be colonized. Baeck described it as a wide "borderless land ... street, meadow, and forest appear to be one, everything is undefined and unlimited."[27] It was, in other words, an empty space waiting to be civilized by the Germans. This description stood in stark contrast to a report Baeck sent from the western front, in which he celebrated the beauty of the countryside as well as commented on the advanced railroad system.[28]

German military successes furthered support for colonization of the East as a buffer zone against the Russians, either through Germanization or by "civilizing" the local population. In Ober Ost, Erich Ludendorff led a brutal occupation regime that included expropriations and forced labor, while still attempting to promote a sense of German *Kultur*. By contrast, Hans Hartwig von Beseler, the Governor-General of Warsaw, tried to implement reforms whose aim was a modernized Polish state that would be autonomous but fully subordinate to Germany in foreign matters. Both approaches failed in subduing the local population. A popular adage in Poland at the time was that asking whether the Germans were preferable to the Russians was like asking which was better, plague or cholera.[29]

The expansion eastward brought numerous East European Jews under German control. On the ground Baeck tried, like other rabbis, to alleviate their suffering, for example, by helping them acquire wheat for the production of matzos for Passover. Steven Aschheim described the German-Jewish perception of Eastern European Jews as that of "brothers and strangers."[30]

---

[26] Leo Baeck, "Die Kraft der Wenigen," *Der Schild* 14, no. 51 (December 20, 1935): 1.

[27] Report to the Jewish community of Berlin from November 1915, quoted in Ulrich Sieg, "Empathie und Pflichterfüllung: Leo Baeck als Feldrabbiner im Ersten Weltkrieg," in *Leo Baeck, 1873–1956: Aus dem Stamme von Rabbinern*, eds. Fritz Backhaus and Georg Heuberger (Frankfurt am Main: Jüdischer Verlag im Suhrkamp Verlag, 2001), 49–50.

[28] Report from October 2, 1915, in Peter Appelbaum, "Leo Baeck: Chaplain and Neo-Kantian Philosopher," in *Loyalty Betrayed: Jewish Chaplains in the German Army during the First World War* (Portland, OR: Vallentine Mitchell, 2014), 150–51.

[29] Vejas Liulevicius, *War Land on the Eastern Front: Culture, National Identity, and German Occupation in World War I* (Cambridge: Cambridge University Press, 2000), 114; Jesse Kauffman, *Elusive Alliance: The German Occupation of Poland in World War I* (Cambridge, MA: Harvard University Press, 2015), 52–53.

[30] Steven Aschheim, *Brothers and Strangers: The East European Jew in German and German Jewish Consciousness, 1800–1923* (Madison: University of Wisconsin Press, 1982).

56   The Jewish Imperial Imagination

The *Ostjuden*, as they were often called, were seen as brethren in need that should be helped. At the same time, their otherness was stressed, and they were clearly demarcated in the German-Jewish imagination from the latter's middle-class, educated status. East European Jews were in this sense a canvass – the Freudian *Projektionsfläche* – for German-Jewish desires and anxieties. They were presented at times, such as in Martin Buber's example of Hasidim, as a model of simpler authenticity that was lost to Western Jews.

This Jewish primitivism, as Samuel Spinner calls it, was not unlike the turn to the native as a noble savage in artworks such as Paul Gaugin's depiction of Tahiti. But in the case of Jewish primitivism, these were Jews imagining Jews. In fact, this treatment of primitivism was not limited to German Jews' reflection on the more observant East European Jews and their communities. A similar move was done by modernized East European Jews. The Yiddish literary critic Bal Makhshoves, for example, described how he studied the Jews of Warsaw "like Aztecs," while at the same time recognizing that they were in fact his siblings, "like children from one father."[31]

The perception of foreignness and nearness shaped not only artistic sensibilities but also the German-Jewish imperial imagination. The Zionist Franz Oppenheimer, for example, argued that German Jews had tribal consciousness (*Stammesbewußtsein*), an affiliation based on shared past historical experience. *Ostjuden*, on the other hand, had in his description national consciousness (*Volksbewußtsein*), which was a matter of the present. This distinction, popular among German Zionists, informed contemporary Jewish discussions in Germany about Eastern European Jews. Acting on this political imagination, among others by attempting, during and after the war, to secure a Jewish national or cultural autonomy for Eastern European Jews, was often done without consulting Eastern European Jews, who did not necessarily agree to such visions.[32] During the war, for example, a small group of German Jews, the Committee for the East, suggested to anyone who would listen, among others to General Hindenburg, that because of the linguistic similarity of Yiddish to German, and because they required "civilizing," East European Jews could

---

[31] Quoted in Samuel Spinner, *Jewish Primitivism* (Stanford: Stanford University Press, 2021), 3.
[32] Yfaat Weiss, "'Wir Westjuden haben jüdisches Stammesbewußtsein, die Ostjuden jüdisches Volkesbewußtsein': Der deutsch-jüdische Blick auf das polnische Judentum in den beiden ersten Jahrzehnten des 20. Jahrhunderts," *Archiv für Sozialgeschichte* 37 (1997): 157–78; Till van Rahden, "Germans of the Jewish *Stamm*: Visions of Community between Nationalism and Particularism, 1850–1933," in *German History from the Margins*, eds. Neil Gregor et al. (Bloomington: Indiana University Press, 2006), 27–48.

Saving Christianity from Itself 57

be utilized as a vanguard for German colonization. In this Jewish imperial imagination, the Ostjuden would be the first locals to be Germanized.[33]

The Committee for the East was a relatively marginal organization, but similar views were found among other parts of German Jewry. Hermann Cohen, for example, believed the war would bring about German spiritual rejuvenation and would help promote the German world-mission (*Weltmission*) of serving as the "schoolmaster of the world."[34] Even before the war broke out, Cohen imagined a specific German-Jewish task. He thought that a civilizing mission toward the Ostjuden was needed. Bringing liberation, that is to say Germanizing them, would be, Cohen said, "the greatest triumph of the German Jew."[35]

Like Cohen and the Committee for the East, Baeck implied that the East was inherently German. In a series of lectures given in Germany shortly before his death, Baeck claimed that Yiddish "as it is known in modern times" was in fact medieval German, spoken for a while by Jews in Germany, "as well as in their colonies in the East."[36] While this is a legitimate linguistic argument, the language Baeck used in order to describe it was once more that of colonies. He argued for the Germanness of Yiddish because in his view Jews from Germany moved to the East as colonizers in order to improve it.

As the Great War dragged into its third year, hopes for a quick German victory vanished. Baeck called for perseverance, writing in a report to the Jewish community in November 1916 that while a short war can be carried on the storm of emotions, a longer war "with its ups and downs of events and suffering, demands moral energies [*Kräfte*]."[37] The prolonged war challenged the moral standing not only of the soldiers of the front, but also of the decision makers and the broader population. The search for a culprit turned inward toward those perceived as a foreign element: Alsatians, Danes, Poles, and Jews. Following accusations that Jews were not doing their part in the war effort on the front, the army ordered in October 1916 a census or "Jew-count" (*Judenzählung*). The

---

[33] Grady, *A Deadly Legacy*, 79–85, 130–31.   [34] Cohen, "Deutschtum und Judentum," 263.

[35] Hermann Cohen, "The Polish Jew," in *The Jew: Essays from Martin Buber's Journal Der Jude, 1916–1928*, ed. Arthur Cohen (Alabama: University of Alabama Press, 1980), 59; Cedric Cohen-Skalli, "Cohen's Jewish and Imperial Politics during World War I," in *Cohen im Netz*, eds. Hartwig Wiedebach and Heinrich Assel (Tübingen: Mohr Siebeck, 2021), 177–97.

[36] Leo Baeck, "Von Moses Mendelssohn zu Franz Rosenzweig (1956)," 166; on the politics of the relation between Yiddish and German, see Marc Volovici, *German as a Jewish Problem: The Language Politics of Jewish Nationalism* (Stanford: Stanford University Press, 2020).

[37] Baeck, "Berichte des Feldgeistlichen Rabbiner Dr. Leo Baeck an den Vorstand der jüdischen Gemeinde – Bericht 51 (1916)," *Werke* 6, 139.

58 The Jewish Imperial Imagination

result was never officially published, apparently because it would have refuted the claim that Jews were underrepresented in the front.[38]

Gathering statistical data in and of itself was not unique. German Jews, like Jews in other countries, attempted to collect data on their own during the war in order to locate where spiritual help such as that offered by Baeck and the other chaplains was needed, and after the war ended, in order to prove Jewish valor. Only in Germany, however, was statistical data gathered by the state to vilify part of its own army.[39] For those who hoped participation in the war would prove Jewish loyalty, the census was seen as a breach of trust and a violation of what they saw as an implicit agreement: Jews would prove their loyalty in combat and would not be discriminated against. The *Judenzählung* led to protests in many of the Jewish newspapers and among Jewish intellectuals. Hermann Cohen, for example, called it an "insult to our sons who serve on the front."[40] Baeck did not write about it explicitly. In fact, many Jewish soldiers did not comment about the *Judenzählung* in their letters home, perhaps due to shame, perhaps because the ongoing experience of war and survival quickly relegated it to secondary importance.[41]

By the end of the war, little was left of the initial enthusiasm, in Baeck as in many other Germans. Baeck, recipient of the Iron Cross Second Class for his work as a chaplain, returned to Berlin in June 1918. The war would end several months later, in November, with German surrender and Berlin in turmoil. Germany lost more than 1,750,000 people in the war, and many more were wounded. It also perceived itself, and was perceived later, as financially burdened by the reparations set in the Treaty of Versailles.[42]

Peace and the Prussian State

Germany lost its colonies in the war. The pacific colonies fell in 1914. German Southwest Africa was lost in May 1915, and Cameroon by

[38] Werner Angress, "The German Army's 'Judenzählung' of 1916: Genesis – Consequences – Significance," *The Leo Baeck Institute Year Book* 23, no. 1 (1978): 117–38; Gavin Wiens, "A Mixed Bag of Loyalties: Jewish Soldiers, Ethnic Minorities, and State-Based Contingents in the German Army, 1914–1918," in *The Jewish Experience of the First World War*, eds. Edward Madigan and Gideon Reuveni (London: Palgrave Macmillan, 2019), 137–58.

[39] Jacob Segall, *Die deutschen Juden als Soldaten im Kriege 1914–1918* (Berlin: Philo Verlag, 1921); Panter, "Beyond Marginalization," 29–31.

[40] Quoted in Sieg, *Jüdische Intellektuelle im Ersten Weltkrieg*, 93; on the discussions in Jewish press, see Appelbaum, *Loyal Sons*, 253–61.

[41] Derek Penslar, "The German-Jewish Soldier: From Participant to Victim," *German History* 29, no. 3 (2011): 428; Grady, *A Deadly Legacy*, 138–50; cf. Appelbaum, *Loyal Sons*, 253–66.

[42] Sally Marks, "The Myths of Reparations," *Central European History* 11, no. 3 (1978): 231–55.

February 1916. German East Africa was also largely done with by 1916. The treaties that finalized Germany's borders after the war, most notably the Versailles Treaty of June 1919, also meant that Alsace-Lorraine became part of France and vast territories in the east were given to the newly established Poland, which – adding salt to injury from a German perspective – demanded, but did not receive, Cameroon as a colony. All in all, the former empire lost about 13% of its territory.[43]

With the abdication of the Kaiser and the territorial losses, the Wilhelmine Empire was no longer. It was not the only empire to have collapsed. The Habsburg and Ottoman Empires ceased to exist, and Russia experienced the October Revolution and was now a communist state. Yet Great Britain, France, and the United States – the countries Germans often viewed as peers – all increased their power. In a world still governed by empires, in which it strove for its place in the sun, Germany had lost its status as a world-power.

The Weimar National Assembly, which drew up the constitution of the new republic, declared with 144 in favor and 7 opposed that it desired the "restoration of Germany's colonial rights." This was a legal claim that expressed the ongoing desire for colonialism, which now had to remain latent and unfulfilled. A revisionist view portrayed the East and the German colonies as part of Germany. This was evident, for example, in popular atlases and maps that depicted Poland as a German "cultural-soil" (*Kulturboden*), thereby de-legitimizing the new state by suggesting that its current productive abilities were only due to earlier German tilling of the land dating all the way back to the medieval period.[44]

School textbooks similarly spoke of the ways in which Germans civilized Africa, calling these territories by their colonial names. The genre of *Afrikabuch*, looking nostalgically at the colonial experience, grew in popularity. Former colonial officers such as Heinrich Schnee continued to lecture and propagate German expansionism. The most prominent version of this revisionist tendency during the Weimar Republic was Hans Grimm's popular 1926 novel *People without Space* (*Volk ohne Raum*), in which he suggested that all of Weimar's current troubles were related to the unfulfilled German yearning for expansion.[45]

---

[43] Valerio, *Colonial Fantasies, Imperial Realities*, 168.   [44] Kopp, *Germany's Wild East*, 124–59.

[45] Wolfe Schmokel, *Dream of Empire: German Colonialism, 1919–1945* (New Haven: Yale University Press, 1980), 1–8; Britta Schilling, *Postcolonial Germany: Memories of Empire in a Decolonized Nation* (Oxford: Oxford University Press, 2014), 13–40; Susann Lewerenz, "Colonial Revisionism," in *Historical Companion to Postcolonial Literatures: Continental Europe and Its*

60 The Jewish Imperial Imagination

Among the stories celebrated in this nostalgia for the colonies was that of General Paul von Lettow-Vorbeck, who recruited African troops known as *askari* and waged guerrilla war against the British army until the end of the war in November 1918. Although fewer than twenty German Jews participated in the war over the colonies, their stories were highlighted in Jewish newspapers such as *C.V.-Zeitung* and *Der Schild*. Showcasing examples of bravery and patriotism of Jewish service in the military was an essential component of the agenda of the RjF, and the organization can be seen as the leading Jewish organization participating in the revisionist efforts of glorifying the lost empire.[46]

Baeck did not offer a revisionist history, but he contributed to *Der Schild* an essay that drew on the conservative theme of anti-urbanism, calling for a *"way out of the metropolis and back to nature."*[47] Since the late nineteenth century the city and the Jews became equated as two facets of modernity as represented in commerce, the mixture of people, and the rapid social changes. *Völkisch* movements, especially in their explicitly antisemitic formulations, professed a return to rural settling and the soil as a way to regain authenticity supposedly not available in the city, and not accessible to the Jews, who were not as rooted in the soil.[48] Baeck's call for a return to nature worked against these claims, while adopting the basic imaginary about the artificiality of the city, whose constant lights he lamented. The rural settlement was part of a constellation of ideas of Jewish task and rejuvenation to which Baeck ascribed, even if he did not speak of a resettlement in the colonies.

During the interwar period Baeck developed friendships with prominent figures from the old imperial strata such as Count Paul Thun-Hohenstein, Count Hermann von Keyserling, and Baron Hans-Osso

---

Empires, eds. Prem Poddar et al. (Edinburgh: Edinburgh University Press, 2008), 224–25; Christian Rogowski, "'Heraus mit unseren Kolonien!': Der Kolonialrevisionismus der Weimarer Republik und der 'Hamburger Kolonialwoche' von 1926," in *Phantasiereiche: Zur Kulturgeschichte des deutschen Kolonialismus*, ed. Birthe Kundrus (Frankfurt am Main: Campus Verlag, 2003), 243–62.

[46] Avraham, "Between Concern and Difference," 58–59; Penslar, "The German-Jewish Soldier," 439–40.

[47] Leo Baeck, "Mensch und Boden (1931)," 203 – emphasis in the original; see also Leo Baeck, "Gemeinde in der Großstadt (1930)," *Werke* 3, 218–25; Leo Baeck, "Geist und Blut (1931)," *Werke* 3, 72–73.

[48] George Mosse, "The Influence of the Volkish Idea on German Jewry," in *Germans and Jews: The Right, the Left, and the Search for a "Third Force" in Pre-Nazi Germany* (London: Orbach & Chambers, 1971), 105; Hillel Kieval, "Antisemitism and the City: A Beginner's Guide," *Studies in Contemporary Jewry* 15 (1999): 3–18; Joachim Schlör, *Das Ich der Stadt: Debatten über Judentum und Urbanität, 1822–1938* (Göttingen: Vandenhoeck & Ruprecht, 2005).

Saving Christianity from Itself

von Veltheim-Ostrau. These personal connections were meaningful for Baeck. Keyserling contributed to Baeck's rising stature by inviting Baeck to lecture in the School of Wisdom he founded in Darmstadt in 1920, alongside figures such as Ernst Troeltsch, Max Scheler, and Carl Jung.[49] Baeck and Veltheim-Ostrau maintained connection even during the Nazi period and in 1943, he entrusted Veltheim-Ostrau with a draft of *This People* for safekeeping.

These nobles belonged to what Dina Gusejnova called an "imperial intelligentsia," a loose group of nobility who "lived in an age in which empires declined, yet imperialism persisted."[50] Often working transnationally, members of the imperial intelligentsia engaged in imaging Europe in the aftermath of the Great War. Like members of the imperial intelligentsia, Baeck, while still living in a world dominated by empires, did not imagine a return to an old imperial order. Instead, he turned toward working for peace, joining, for example, the short-lived Jewish League for Peace and the Inter-Denominational Working Group for Peace. In a text written for a publication of the latter, Baeck wrote that people who did not desire power, and in whom the religious element was present in both motivation and act, saw "in the moment of decision, the way to peace only through war," they "were drawn to the war with certainty that they responded to a duty that was more than a human duty."[51] This was perhaps a way of self-reflecting on the patriotism and religious duty that had guided his own thought during the Great War. Whereas in 1914 Baeck participated in a day of prayer for the success of the troops, in September 1930 the Jewish League for Peace organized Synagogal Peace Celebration that involved more than thirty rabbis and community leaders.[52]

The trauma of the Great War led to an extensive culture of memory in which sacrifice of life for the fatherland was glorified.[53] In a memorial service at the *Lehranstalt* shortly after the war's end, Baeck celebrated the teachers who passed away, and the students who sacrificed their lives. He

---

[49] Keyserling used his connection to Baeck as an argument for his quick rehabilitation after the end of the Second World War. See Ludwig Marcuse, "Graf Klingeling und Leo Baeck," *Aufbau* 11, no. 50 (December 14, 1945): 3.

[50] Dina Gusejnova, *European Elites and Ideas of Empire, 1917–1957* (Cambridge: Cambridge University Press, 2016), xxvi–xxvii; letters testifying to Baeck's connection to these figures are in *Werke* 6, 586–621.

[51] Leo Baeck, "Friedensbahn und Friedensziel (1930)," *Werke* 3, 176.

[52] Virginia Holmes, "Integrating Diversity, Reconciling Contradiction: The Jüdischer Friedensbund in Late Weimar Germany," *Leo Baeck Institute Year Book* 47 (2002): 178.

[53] George Mosse, *Fallen Soldiers: Reshaping the Memory of the World Wars* (Oxford: Oxford University Press, 1990); Jay Winter, *Remembering War: The Great War between Memory and History in the Twentieth Century* (New Haven: Yale University Press, 2006).

62 The Jewish Imperial Imagination

used the occasion to offer an analysis of the troubles at the core of Prussian, and by extension German, identity. Baeck argued that the two intellectual pillars of Prussia – the two foundations of its political imagination – were Luther and Kant, or more broadly Lutheranism and Enlightenment. In making this separation, Baeck was rejecting the position in the Manifest of Ninety-Three about the unity of Prussian culture.

Enlightenment had a positive influence on the status of the Jews. It was thanks to it, Baeck argued, that the idea of emancipation emerged and became significant. Lutheranism, in his description, started positively with the Jewish idea of equality expressed in the notion that the community should become a nation of priests, but ended horrendously. Luther was a contested figure in German-Jewish thought, and emotions regarding him ran the gamut from admiration to contempt. For some leaders of the Reform movement in Judaism, Luther was a model to be imitated – just as he broke the shackles of the Catholic Church and reformed Christianity, modern Jews should reform Judaism. In criticizing Luther, Baeck was adopting a different stance, which criticized Luther's concessions to earthly power.[54] In his dissertation on the early reception of Spinoza in Germany, completed in 1895 under the supervision of Wilhelm Dilthey, Baeck explained that Luther's idea of being "subservient to authority" was a result of the gratitude the reformer felt for the protection provided to him by some of the princes against the Catholic Church. After the Great War, however, Baeck thought this reliance on earthly power was integral to Protestant doctrine. Luther's moral failure was due to a lack of "inner relation to the Old Testament," which took away from Lutheranism its ability to act in the world.[55]

Alluding to Jesus's statement "render unto Caesar the things that are Caesar's, and unto God the things that are God's" (Mt. 22:21), Baeck suggested that Catholicism tried to give everything to the Church. Luther, on the other hand, decided to rely on state-power and protection to enforce his Reform, thereby conceding everything worldly to the state. Luther's insistence on *sola fide*, redemption by faith alone, meant that the

---

[54] Susannah Heschel, "Theological Ghosts and Goblins: Martin Luther's Haunting of Liberal Judaism," in *Polyphonie der Theologie: Verantwortung und Widerstand in Kirche und Politik*, ed. Matthias Grebe (Stuttgart: Kohlhammer Verlag, 2019), 325–44; Christian Wiese, "'Let His Memory Be Holy to Us!': Jewish Interpretations of Martin Luther from the Enlightenment to the Holocaust," *The Leo Baeck Institute Year Book* 54 (2009): 93–126.

[55] Leo Bäck, *Spinozas erste Einwirkung auf Deutschland* (Berlin: Mayer & Müller, 1895), 8; on Dilthey's influence on Baeck, see Friedlander, *Leo Baeck*, 19–22, 62–63; Alexander Altmann, "Theology in Twentieth-Century German Jewry," *Leo Baeck Institute Year Book* 1 (1956): 199.

Saving Christianity from Itself

ethical duty and deed in this world were meaningless, which led to a position by which the princes and rulers were the ones responsible for the ethical sphere, or rather, "the moral is, what the authority demands."[56]

Baeck turned to Luther to explain not just the foundations of the German political imagination, but also the Great War. It was really a war between two branches of Christianity: Calvinism, represented by the Anglo-Saxon states of Great Britain and the United States, and Lutheranism, represented by Germany. This dichotomy, admittedly a very partial description, helped Baeck carve an image in which the Entente won because they were spiritually stronger. "Calvin here has carried away the victory over Luther – this as well is like a piece of the history of Judaism," because Calvinism maintained, in his view, the Jewish messianic teaching.[57] The radicalness of this statement should not be overlooked. Less than a year after the end of the war, in which Baeck himself participated on the German side, he claimed that Germany's loss was to an extent a victory of Judaism over Lutheranism. The substrata of the imperial Great War that had just ended was in fact religious. On this level, Judaism was regarded as part of the victorious powers through its commitment to a better future for humanity.

The New without the Old

The ethical passivity of Lutheranism and its political implications became a recurrent theme in Baeck's thought. Just as in the *Essence*, Baeck turned to religious and theological discourse in his understanding of the contemporary political sphere. Earlier theological colonization, that is to say supersessionism, was aimed at replacing Judaism with Christianity. Because of that, it was concerned with minimizing the originality or importance of Judaism for Christianity, for example, by stressing Jesus' singularity. In the radicalized environment of the Weimar Republic and the theological crisis provoked by the Great War, new trends took place, with some thinkers trying to sever Christianity from Judaism completely.

The figure of Marcion, and Adolf Harnack's interpretation of it, was an important example as well as a catalyst to this imagination. Little certain is known about Marcion of Sinope (ca. 85–160 CE), since the information

---

[56] Leo Baeck, "Heimgegangene des Krieges (1919)," *Werke* 3, 386.
[57] Baeck, "Heimgegangene des Krieges (1919)," 388. Baeck ignored the fact that Catholic states such as France and Austro-Hungary fought each other, or the influence of Russian Orthodoxy on Slavic identity.

64   The Jewish Imperial Imagination

available comes from his opponents.[58] It was generally agreed at the time, however, that Marcion posed a serious challenge to what became the established Church. Marcionite theology separated the Creator, the God of the Jews who created this world, and the true good God, the Redeemer, who must therefore be – this is the fundamental logic of Marcion – separate from this world and can have nothing to do with it. This God is the Alien God.

Already as a student, Harnack wrote an award-winning essay on Marcion (1870), in which he identified the heretic as a "modern believer" and "the first reformer." He would later call Marcion his "first love in theology."[59] The rise of the figure of Marcion was connected to earlier discussions in the late nineteenth century and the first half of the twentieth century, when historians of early Christianity lumped Marcion with another category of heresy, namely, Gnosticism. This umbrella term was used, and is still in use, to describe deviant groups for whom gnosis (lit. knowledge) was central.[60] In a generalized description, the gnostic worldview maintained that that the creator God, described as malicious Demiurge, was separate from the good, redeeming God. Humans were torn from within and were alien to this world. On the one hand, they were bound to this physical existence, to the world of the evil Demiurge. On the other, however, they contained within themselves a spark of the divine, of the good God. It was through mystical, not normally accessible knowledge (gnosis) that some humans were redeemed and freed from the created world.[61]

Marcion shared with the Gnostics a dualistic worldview and the question about the place of the Old Testament in Christianity. Harnack wrote, however, that "Marcion cannot be numbered among the Gnostics in the strict sense of the word," because unlike them he managed to avoid

---

[58] Judith Lieu, Marcion and the Making of a Heretic: God and Scripture in the Second Century (New York: Cambridge University Press, 2015), 56.

[59] Adolf von Harnack, Marcion: The Gospel of the Alien God, trans. John Steely and Lyle Bierma (Durham, NC: Labyrinth Press, 1990), ix; Adolf von Harnack, Marcion, der moderne Gläubige des 2. Jahrhunderts, der erste Reformator: Die dorpater Preisschrift (1870), ed. Friedemann Steck (Berlin: de Gruyter, 2003).

[60] On the problem with bringing together the categories of Gnosticism and heresy, see Michael Williams, Rethinking "Gnosticism": An Argument for Dismantling a Dubious Category (Princeton: Princeton University Press, 1996), esp. 33–51; Karen King, What Is Gnosticism? (Cambridge, MA: Harvard University Press, 2003).

[61] Harnack's summary of gnostic teaching is in Harnack, History of Dogma, I.233–34 and cf. Hans Jonas, The Gnostic Religion: The Message of the Alien God and the Beginnings of Christianity (Boston: Beacon Press, 1963), 42–47; see also Benjamin Lazier, God Interrupted: Heresy and the European Imagination between the World Wars (Princeton: Princeton University Press, 2008), 28–29; Manfred Bauschulte, Religionsbahnhöfe der Weimarer Republik: Studien zur Religionsforschung 1918–1933 (Marburg: diagonal-Verlag, 2007), 241–72.

Saving Christianity from Itself 65

syncretism. The Gnostics attempted to discard the Old Testament and its god only by introducing myths borrowed from the mystery cults, thereby creating "syncretism from another side." Marcion, by contrast, "is the consistent one; *true religion must be plain and transparent, just as it must also be alien and absolute-paradoxical.*"[62] This distinction was often lost on German-Jewish thinkers such as Baeck or Buber, who conflated Marcionism with Gnosticism, but their interpretation of this tendency in contemporary Protestantism did not change because of that.

Harnack showed sympathy for Marcion's attempt to purify Christianity and believed that in offering a third-way between gnostic syncretism and the emerging Church's reliance on the Old Testament, Marcion adhered to Pauline theology. Paul's distinctions between works and faith, law and gospel, flesh and spirit were taken by Marcion *in extremis* to their logical conclusion. Marcion's metaphysical dualism allowed him to hold these antitheses by ascribing one side of the equation (law, flesh, works) to the Creator God, and another (gospel, spirit, faith) to the Alien God. In *History of Dogma*, Harnack wrote that "Marcion was the only Gentile Christian who understood Paul, and even he misunderstood him."[63] In *Marcion*, he followed this line, suggesting that Marcion was a true disciple of Paul, but Luther was an even better interpreter of the apostle.[64]

Marcion's significance for Harnack lay in his consistent method of purging the Christian canon. Nothing was allowed to stand next to the gospel. It was with this strict and consistent theological dualism that Marcion read the Christian texts available to him. Based on this principle, Marcion was the first Christian to form a Christian canon, which for him consisted of one gospel, probably showing similarities to Luke but edited in order to wipe out any elements of the "Jewish God," as well as ten Pauline epistles.[65]

In a chapter about Marcion's contemporary relevance, Harnack made the contemporary stakes of the canon debate clear:

> *the rejection of the Old Testament in the second century was a mistake which the Great Church has rightly avoided; to retain it in the sixteenth century was a*

---

[62] Harnack, *Marcion*, 12 – emphasis in the original, 65; Harnack, *History of Dogma*, I.267.

[63] Harnack, *History of Dogma*, I.89; see also John W. Marshall, "Misunderstanding the New Paul: Marcion's Transformation of the *Sonderzeit* Paul," *Journal of Early Christian Studies* 20, no. 1 (2012): 1–29.

[64] Harnack, *Marcion*, 131.

[65] For a summary of the scholarly debate about the relationship between Marcion's gospel and the canonic gospels, see Matthias Klinghardt, Jason BeDuhn, and Judith Lieu, "Marcion's Gospel and the New Testament: Catalyst or Consequence?," *New Testament Studies* 63, no. 2 (2017): 318–34.

66   The Jewish Imperial Imagination

fate from which the Reformation was not yet able to withdraw, to still conserve it as a canonical document in Protestantism since the nineteenth century is the result of a religious and ecclesiastical paralysis.[66]

In a later lecture, Harnack clarified that, unlike Marcion, he had no intention of doing away with the Old Testament completely.[67] He did insist, however, that the Old Testament should be relegated to a secondary level and be treated as a collection of texts that, in the words of Luther, were "good and useful" to read as part of the prehistory of the Church but not to its essence. That he needed to clarify his position shows how easily his argument about the canon could be misunderstood.

Harnack created an image of historical continuum beginning with Paul, going through Marcion, and ending with Luther, or perhaps even with Harnack's own reading of Marcion. Comments about Luther were inserted in several strategic places in *Marcion*. When explaining how Marcion expounded the difference between gospel and law and how Marcion saw in his opponents Judaizers of the gospel, for example, Harnack rhetorically exclaimed: "Who does not think here of Luther?!"[68] The bringing together of Marcion and Luther did not mean that Harnack offered a complete endorsement of Marcion, despite his rhapsodic tone. After discussing the clarity and simplicity of Marcion's message – that gospel and law, Old and New Testament, did not belong together – Harnack added that it is "only Luther with his justification-faith manages to rival Marcion here."[69] Luther was a better interpreter of Paul than Marcion according to Harnack because of his ability to offer salvation in this world and ethics, something Marcion's strict dualism must cede.

In a moment of theological crisis, Harnack called for the de-canonization of the Hebrew Bible combining the trailblazing insight of Marcion with Luther's theology.[70] The responses to Harnack's *Marcion* fell into several categories. On the Protestant side, scholars specializing in the Old Testament rejected Harnack's position and tried to show the value of the Old Testament. Catholic theologians similarly held to the canon and rejected Harnack's position. Among liberal Protestants not working on the Old Testament, opinions varied. It is hardly surprising that despite being far from them politically himself, Harnack's work found a warm reception among supporters of racial and *völkisch* understandings of

---

[66] Harnack, *Marcion*, 134 – emphasis in original.
[67] Harnack, "Marcion: Der radikale Modernist des 2. Jahrhunderets. Vortragskonzept (Uppsala, 13. März 1923)," in *Marcion, der moderne Gläubige*, 398.
[68] Harnack, *Marcion*, 18.   [69] Harnack, *Marcion*, 62.   [70] Harnack, *Marcion*, 135.

Saving Christianity from Itself

Christianity such as Friedrich Andersen.[71] For Jewish thinkers, the claim that the Old Testament was not canonical was especially troublesome. It demeaned the sacred text of Judaism, severed the relation between Christianity and Judaism, and, by way of implication, could imply the casting out of Jews from Christian majority society. Once again, Baeck was quick to reply to Harnack.[72]

Romantic Experience

Baeck's "Romantic Religion" (1922) was intended as part of a larger project, never completed, on "Classical and Romantic Religion."[73] The text is presented as a critique of romanticism and romantic religion as unethical attitudes in the world.[74] The underlying current, however, was an attack on Harnack's call to de-canonize the Old Testament as a growing tendency in the Protestant imagination in Germany. Attempts to de-Judaize Christianity, Baeck warned, were leading to passivity and obedience to authority that could be dangerous.

Several pieces of evidence suggest Marcionism and Gnosticism were the main target of Baeck's argument. First, in the second, expanded edition of *The Essence of Judaism* (1922), Baeck used the term "gnosis" – absent from the first edition – in several places. The main thrust of these additions was to contrast between the Torah and the prophetic teachings and gnosis, a point Baeck raised during the Wilhelmine Empire, but he developed it into a full critique only in the Weimar Republic by drawing on the vocabulary of gnosis.[75]

---

[71] Wolfram Kinzig, *Harnack, Marcion und das Judentum nebst einer kommentierten Edition des Briefwechsels Adolf von Harnacks mit Houston Stewart Chamberlain* (Leipzig: Evangelische Verlagsanstalt, 2004), 116–45.

[72] On some other Jewish responses, see Paul Mendes-Flohr, "Martin Buber and the Metaphysicans of Contempt," in *Divided Passions: Jewish Intellectuals and the Experience of Modernity* (Detroit: Wayne State University Press, 1991), 207–36; Lazier, *God Interrupted*; Yaniv Feller, "From Aher to Marcion: Martin Buber's Understanding of Gnosis," *Jewish Studies Quarterly* 20, no. 4 (2013): 374–97; Benjamin Pollock, *Franz Rosenzweig's Conversions: World Denial and World Redemption* (Indianapolis: Indiana University Press, 2014); Robert Erlewine, "Redeeming This World: Buber's Judaism and the Sanctity of Immanence," in *Judaism and the West: From Hermann Cohen to Joseph Soloveitchik* (Bloomington: Indiana University Press, 2016), 78–104.

[73] Leo Baeck, "Romantische Religion," in *Festschrift zum 50jährigen Bestehen der Hochschule für die Wiessenschaft des Judentums in Berlin* (Berlin: Philo Verlag, 1922), 3.

[74] Ernest Rubinstein, *An Episode of Jewish Romanticism: Franz Rosenzweig's The Star of Redemption* (Albany: SUNY Press, 1999); Yaniv Feller, "Romantic Politics in the Thought of Gustav Landauer and Leo Baeck," in *Skepsis and Antipolitics: The Alternative of Gustav Landauer*, eds. Cedric Cohen-Skalli and Libera Pisano (Leiden: Brill, 2022), 276–85.

[75] Leo Baeck, *Das Wesen Des Judentums*, 79–80, 68–69; Leo Baeck, "Griechische und jüdische Predigt (1914)," *Werke* 4, 155.

68 The Jewish Imperial Imagination

Second, in a letter to Franz Rosenzweig, who critiqued Baeck's presentation of Christianity in an essay titled "Apologetic Thinking" (1923), Baeck admitted an intentional simplification of Christianity. He explained to Rosenzweig that he thought

> it could be valuable to present Christianity for once as 'pure' Paulinism, in order to depict the way it is, and in theory also has been, when it should or would want to be freed from its Jewish, when it should or would want to be gnostic, Marcionite – cf. Harnack: *Marcion*. That the pure romantic remains then residual, that this thus is the 'pure' Christianity."[76]

Such Christianity, Baeck conceded, was a construct. It never existed practically in history but was an ideal type. This letter points to the true adversary Baeck wished to confront in his essay, namely, the Marcionite position that severed Judaism from Christianity.

Finally, "Judaism in the Church" (1925), an essay published in English at the *Hebrew Union College Annual*, could be seen as a companion piece to "Romantic Religion." In it, Baeck mentioned Marcion as a successor to the tradition of Paul. In a manner akin to Harnack, Baeck singled out Marcion as the one who strove most ardently to achieve "pure Paulinism."[77] "Judaism in the Church" was even more explicit than "Romantic Religion" about the political implications of the Marcionite position and its contemporary relevance. Baeck ended the essay by claiming that most forms of Protestantism relied on Judaism, yet "[t]o be sure, there are ideas in German Protestantism, most of them of an antisemitic inspiration, which, like the ideas of Marcion, would blot everything Jewish out of Christianity."[78] Put differently, antisemitism, Marcionism, and the erasure of the Jewish elements in Christianity were all connected.

Read in this light, "Romantic Religion" is a critique of certain strands in contemporary Protestantism, and by extension of the imaginaries present in Protestant society. As in the *Essence*, the critique was couched in typology of religions. Baeck began by asserting there are two ideal types of religion: the classical and the romantic, with the former manifested historically in Judaism and the latter in Christianity. The "romantic" – following Friedrich Schlegel's definition of the romantic book – was "one which treats sentimental material in a phantastic form" and Baeck added

---

[76] Leo Baeck to Franz Rosenzweig, March 8, 1923, *Werke* 6, 578. For Rosenzweig's critique, see Franz Rosenzweig, "Apologetic Thinking," in *Philosophical and Theological Writings*, ed. and trans. Paul Franks and Michael Morgan (Indianapolis: Hackett, 2000), 95–108.

[77] Leo Baeck, "Judaism in the Church (1925)," in *The Pharisees and Other Essays*, 75–6, 79. Baeck cites Harnack's *History of Dogma* when discussing Marcion.

[78] Baeck, "Judaism in the Church (1925)," 90.

Saving Christianity from Itself

that "tense feelings supply its content, and it seeks its goals in the now mythical, now mystical vision of the imagination. Its world is the realm in which all rules are suspended ... that which lies beyond all reality, the remote hereafter of all things."[79] The vocabulary Baeck used to describe the aspiration of the romantic to a world "which lies beyond all reality" and to the "remote hereafter" suggests that romantic religion was not concerned with this world but, like gnosis, with what was beyond it.

The true founder of Christianity in Baeck's text was Paul, because Jesus was and remained a Jew according to Baeck. It was Paul's genius, Baeck wrote, that created a powerful syncretistic new religion that combined the Jewish messianic idea and mystery cults. Christianity's roots in mystery cults are shared by the Gnostics, so that "Gnosticism is Christianity without Judaism and, in that sense, pure Christianity. Whenever Christianity wanted to become pure in this way, it became gnostic."[80]

Baeck argued the romantic tendencies in Paul were not manifested equally among various Christian denominations. Calvinism, as in Baeck's speech in the aftermath of the Great War, received positive treatment because it stressed earthly works. Catholicism was criticized for its mystification of the sacrament. Protestantism was the most romantic according to Baeck.[81] Luther was indeed a close reader of Paul, Baeck implicitly agreed with Harnack, but in "Romantic Religion" this was hardly meant as praise.[82] Protestantism is the closest to a gnostic fantasy because it is the most consistent in its attempts to sever Judaism from Christianity. This was Marcion's attempt, it was Luther's, and "Romantic Religion" alluded to the fact that such an attempt was also contemporary.

At one point in the text, Baeck summarized his argument by juxtaposing Paul's romantic religion with classical religion. Romantic religion was "absolute dependence as opposed to the commandment, the task, of achieving freedom ... There the human being is the subject; here, in romantic religion, the object." Romantic religion "does not go beyond itself ... In classical religion, man is to become free through the commandment, in romantic religion he has become free through grace."[83]

---

[79] Leo Baeck, "Romantic Religion," in *Judaism and Christianity*, trans. Walter Kaufmann (Philadelphia: Jewish Publication Society of America, 1960), 189–90.

[80] Leo Baeck, "Romantic Religion," 250.

[81] Baeck, "Volksreligion und Weltreligion (1931)," *Werke* 3, 160; Baeck, "Romantic Religion," 213.

[82] For "Romantic Religion" as a critique of Luther, without taking into account the context of Marcionism, see Walter Homolka, *Jewish Identity in Modern Times: Leo Baeck and German Protestantism* (Providence: Berghahn Books, 1995), 76–97.

[83] Baeck, "Romantic Religion," 211.

70   The Jewish Imperial Imagination

Judaism *qua* classical religion was active in the world and ethical, oriented toward redemption of the world; Christianity *qua* romantic religion was passive and tried to escape this world. The Jewish element in Christianity was in this reading the only thing preventing it from becoming immoral. The claim that Protestantism needed to return to its Jewish roots is consistent with Baeck's position during the Wilhelmine Empire, but in the Weimar Republic he came to fully realize the political and ethical stakes.[84]

The experience of faith (*Glaubenserlebnis*) stood according to Baeck at the heart of Pauline Christianity, which took from the mystery cults "the exuberance of emotion, the enthusiastic flight from reality, the longing for an experience [*Erlebnis*]."[85] The term *Erlebnis* captures much of Baeck's critique of romantic-Marcionite religion. *Erlebnis* – from the same root as life (*Leben*) – conveys a type of experience that is lived, intense, and often centered around one's own feeling. It is distinguished from *Erfahrung*, the experience of the external world.[86] In Baeck's critique, the term was understood along these lines as a subjective, inner, and intense kind of experience that led to a detachment from the world. One who sought *Erlebnis* was focused on one's own feelings and not the external world, where ethics took place through a relation to others.

Baeck made clear in a lecture at Keyserling's School of Wisdom that *Erlebnis* was self-centered, exclusivist, and passive.[87] The person receiving grace in romantic religion was already at the goal, no further action, moral or otherwise, was required on her part. Instead of treating life as a question and an ethical task, subjective feeling was presupposed to be the whole truth. The romantic believer "wants to be [*dasein*], without being there independently [*durch sich sein*], he wants less to live [*leben*] and much more to experience [*erleben*]."[88]

---

[84] Leo Baeck, "Die Umkehr zum Judentum (1909)," *Werke* 6, 63–69; Wiese, *Challenging Colonial Discourse*, 307–14.

[85] Baeck, "Romantic Religion," 196. See also 204, 208, 230, 236, 243.

[86] *Erlebnis* was popularized in the late nineteenth century among others by Baeck's teacher Wilhelm Dilthey. See Wilhelm Dilthey, *Das Wesen der Philosophie* (Hamburg: F. Meiner, 1984), xvii–xix; Charles Bambach, *Heidegger, Dilthey, and the Crisis of Historicism* (Ithaca: Cornell University Press, 1995), 152–60; on *Erlebnis* and *Erfahrung*, see Martin Jay, *Songs of Experience: Modern American and European Variations on a Universal Theme* (Berkeley: University of California Press, 2005), 11; Nitzan Lebovic, *The Philosophy of Life and Death: Ludwig Klages and the Rise of a Nazi Biopolitics* (New York: Palgrave Macmillan, 2013), 16–19; Yotam Hotam, *Gnosis Moderni Ye-Tsiyonut: Mashber Ha-Tarbut, Filosofyat Ha-Ḥayim Ve-Hagut Le'umit Yehudit* (Jerusalem: Magnes University Press, 2007).

[87] Leo Baeck, "Vollendung und Spannung (1923)," *Werke* 3, 34.

[88] Baeck, "Romantische Religion," 44; Baeck, "Romantic Religion," 193.

Saving Christianity from Itself

Romantic redemption was not a redemption *of* the world, but a redemption *from* the world. This longing for experience of grace was based according to Baeck on a "feeling of absolute dependence," a definition he took from the influential romantic theologian Friedrich Schleiermacher.[89] This feeling of passivity led according to Baeck to political indifference, or worse, to the adoption of a redeeming figure outside oneself on whom one is totally dependent.[90] These positions left no room for improvement of the current conditions, and as such stood in opposition to Judaism's task in this world. If the Redeemer had truly come and salvation was *sola fide*, then human works are meaningless. This world, in other words, was at best negligible and at worst evil. This was the reason, according to Baeck, that Luther and Paul rejected the Law. "Pauline lawlessness" was, at its core, gnostic:

> the anarchical principle of Gnosticism, 'everything is permitted,' is therefore only the new justice carried to its logical conclusion. In principle and theoretically, it is a matter of indifference for the Pauline doctrine how man behaves in action, whether he does good or evil. For deeds are deeds and have nothing to do with religion; they always involve a valuation of the human subject and a denial that only faith in grace remains.[91]

Presented this way, *Erlebnis* based on a feeling of absolute dependence offered no foundation for ethics. The Pauline-Marcionite-Lutheran denial of the Law extended in this interpretation not only to the so-called ceremonial law but encompassed every ethical law in the Bible.

Baeck's critique of *Erlebnis* was not a wholesale objection to the importance of religious experience. Early in his career, he adopted a position common in Liberal Judaism that rejected mysticism as irrational and therefore opposite to Judaism. From the 1910s, however, and much more consistently throughout the Weimar Republic, Baeck reevaluated Jewish mysticism positively as expressing a profound dimension of Jewish life. This change of position, evident also in the works of several other rabbis of the era, was expressed in a twofold way in Baeck's work. First, Jewish mysticism became a field of scholarly investigation for Baeck. He started publishing, primarily in Jewish venues such as the *Monatsschrift für Geschichte und Wissenschaft des Judentums*, on Jewish mysticism, its origins,

---

[89] Baeck, "Romantic Religion," 192; Friedrich Schleiermacher, *Der christliche Glaube nach den Grundsätzen der evangelischen Kirche* (Halle: O. Hendel, 1897), 13 (par. 4).

[90] This approach is similar to the idea of fatalism, see Franziska Rehlinghaus, *Die Semantik des Schicksals: Zur Relevanz des Unverfügbaren zwischen Aufklärung und Erstem Weltkrieg* (Göttingen: Vandenhoeck & Ruprecht, 2015).

[91] Baeck, "Romantic Religion," 250.

72   The Jewish Imperial Imagination

and its canonical works.[92] Second, during the Weimar Republic, Baeck gave a central place in his thinking to the idea of the mystery (*Geheimnis*) as a counterpart to the commandment (*Gebot*). This is evident in the eponymous essay "Mystery and Commandment," which emerged from a lecture at Keyserling's School of Wisdom, as well as in the revised edition of the *Essence*. The mystery provided depth to Jewish religious life, giving deeper meaning to one's relation to the commandment. The choice of term is telling. *Geheimnis* was distinguished from *Erlebnis*, which disregards the commandment, and from what he saw as the *Mysterium* of the sacrament and the passive acceptance of grace. In short, the mystery in Judaism was posited against self-centeredness, the accompanying feeling of passivity, and the detachment from the world. Instead, it led to acting ethically in the world.[93]

These were no mere theoretical discussions. The *Erlebnis* of grace determined the relation to state power. Protestantism had no qualms about letting earthly rulers control this world, because the believer was concerned with a flight from this-worldly reality. The Marcionite and Protestant believer was egocentric and concerned only with himself and his own redemption. This view, which Baeck traced to Paul, led "to the point of first tolerating every despotism and of then soon consecrating it."[94] Protestantism, like Marcionism, had no interest in offering a moral alternative to the earthly ruler because its entire enterprise was to flee this world. This type of political imagination can lead to disregard for the rights of others, especially the Jews whose foundational text would no longer be considered part Christianity. Eleven years after the publication of "Romantic Religion," Baeck would see his fears about romantic Christianity's relation to Judaism materialize.

---

[92] He republished some of them in *Aus drei Jahrtausenden* (1938). See Leo Baeck, *Werke* 4, 251–91; Kurt Wilhelm, "Leo Baeck and Jewish Mysticism," *Judaism* 11, no. 2 (1962): 123–30; Alexander Altmann, *Leo Baeck and the Jewish Mystical Tradition* (New York: Leo Baeck Institute, 1973); Christian Wiese, "Geheimnis und Gebot: Leo Baecks liberales Judentum zwischen Vernunftreligion und Mystik," in *Glaube und Vernunft in den Weltreligionen*, ed. Werner Zager (Leipzig: Evangelische Verlagsanstalt, 2017), 99–132; on Baeck as part of a broader reevaluation of Jewish mysticism, see Michael Brenner, *The Renaissance of Jewish Culture in Weimar Germany* (New Haven: Yale University Press, 1996), 43–46.

[93] Leo Baeck, "Geheimnis und Gebot (1921–1922)," *Werke* 3, 45–55.

[94] Baeck, "Romantic Religion," 214.

CHAPTER 3

Vulnerable Existence

In a presaging passage in "Romantic Religion" (1922), Baeck wrote of the resurgence of gnostic thought in modern times. He called it a form of "racial scholasticism" whose faith was that "grace works through the dark abysses of the blood." Race was a "modernized *pneuma*," a term that Baeck used to connect it to gnosis. The pneuma was a component of the spirit that gnostic knowledge promises to release from this world.[1] Like Gnosticism, Baeck said, this racial scholasticism promised salvation through a supposed return to pure origins.

With the appointment of Hitler to chancellor on January 30, 1933, the realization of what Baeck called a gnostic myth and the delusional focus on blood quickly took a distinctively political form, that of Nazi dictatorship. "Our time," Baeck warned in an article in *Der Morgen* that October, "experiences a resurgence of a religious 'gnostic' dualism."[2] Not much had changed between contemporary Germany and late antiquity. Now as then, Baeck implied, people saw in Judaism the great realm of darkness diametrically opposed to the light of salvation.

The rise of Nazism and the changing political circumstance led to new questions and pressing concerns. Baeck's essays from this period reveal a new iteration of his Jewish imperial imagination, one that centered less on Jewish missionizing and expansion. Instead, there was an attempt to understand the Jewish minority position in the world in light of antisemitism. In an uncertain time, Baeck stressed Jewish precarity, turning in the process to unexpected sources of inspiration such as Martin Heidegger. But Baeck's engagement with the Nazi empire was not limited to intellectual activity. As the leader of German Jews, he had to form policy and coordinate actions in a constantly shrinking sphere of action.

---

[1] Leo Baeck, "Romantic Religion," in *Judaism and Christianity*, 207. See also Leo Baeck, "Geist und Blut (1931)," 70–81.

[2] Leo Baeck, "Das Judentum in der Gegenwart (1933)," *Werke* 6, 217.

74   The Jewish Imperial Imagination

Race and Space

To understand Baeck's thought and actions in this period, it is necessary to understand the new intellectual and political context in which he had to operate. Doris Bergen sums the Nazi worldview as grounded in two pillars: race and space. The two were interconnected. Accentuating a discourse already present during the Wilhelmine Empire, Hitler believed in the need for German expansion for the survival and thriving of the Aryan race. The East in particular was conceptualized as a space for expansion. The assumed superiority of this race was also the justification for such a conquest.[3]

Race and space were tied to a changing understanding of what it means to be a *Volk*, a word commonly translated to English as people, but at times as nation. The adjective *völkisch* rose in popularity after 1917 as a signifier of hardline right-wing nationalistic politics. It was a favorite of Hitler in *Mein Kampf* and his early speeches. *Volksgemeinschaft* or national community, by contrast, had different connotations. In the first decade of the Weimar Republic, the term was invoked in an appeal for national unity in the aftermath of the First World War. Unlike the adjective *völkisch*, *Volksgemeinschaft* symbolized a more inclusive approach.[4]

The Nazi ideology included a transformation of the idea of the *Volksgemeinschaft*, imbuing it with the same exclusionary, racist, and ultra-nationalistic ideas of the adjective *völkisch*. Claudia Koonz identifies four elements of this understanding. First, a biological concept of the life of the *Volk* as that of an organism; second, a belief in the development of this life according to the nature of the *Volk* and its environment; third, a justification of violence against elements that are not part of the *Volk*; finally, an acceptance that the government had the right to annul legal protections of persons and groups deemed as outside the *Volk*, even if they were citizens of the state.[5] At the heart of the *Volksgemeinschaft*, in other words, stood a society purged from all unwanted elements.

The Nazi imperial imagination was grounded in ideas of imperial expansion and inward expulsion of elements seen as not part of the nation. The place of Jews as part of the latter was unlike that of any other group. Race thinking alone does not explain German hatred not only toward the

---

[3] Doris Bergen, *War and Genocide: A Concise History of the Holocaust* (Lanham: Rowman & Littlefield, 2016), 36–40; Gerhard Weinberg, "The World through Hitler's Eyes," in *Germany, Hitler, and World War II: Essays in Modern German and World History* (Cambridge: Cambridge University Press, 1995), 32–8, 41–4.

[4] Smith, *Germany*, 299–300.

[5] Claudia Koonz, *The Nazi Conscience* (Cambridge, MA: Belknap, 2003), 6–8.

Vulnerable Existence

Jews as racially different but also toward Judaism. Explaining the Nazi perception of the Jew, Saul Friedländer coined the term "redemptive anti-Semitism" to describe the Nazi apocalyptic vision that promised redemption for themselves and the world by excising the Jews from within them.[6]

The anti-Jewish policy, indeed the definition of a Jew, was not predetermined form the outset.[7] Between 1933 and the mid-1930s, Nazi policies were aimed at the social and economic status of the Jews as harbingers of everything bad in modernity, including capitalist greed and bolshevism. With the Nuremberg Laws of 1935, the Nazis consolidated their power and began to imagine in earnest a world without Jews. The exclusion of Jews, and of Judaism, from the public sphere on both a national and a local level took, among others, the form of symbolic acts of violence such as the desecration of cemeteries, the destruction of synagogues, and the burning of Torah scrolls.[8]

The German religious landscape was also shaped by the Nazi imperial imagination, as is evident in the 450th anniversary of Luther's birth that took place in November 1933. The day was christened as "German Luther Day" and the reformer was described as a "national Hercules" who rose "from German blood and soil." Alfred Bierschwale, one of the leading organizers of the festivities, made this point clearly: "Today, 450 years after Luther's birth, Adolf Hitler completed Luther's work. German unification has become an immutable fact." Hermann Göring, one of the strongest people in the Nazi state, similarly used the occasion to say that just as the "divinely gifted" Luther fought for the soul of the Germans in the past, "the German people under the leadership of Hitler is today fighting for the resurgence of our fatherland."[9] A leading religious player in this celebration was the antisemitic movement of German Christians (*Deutsche Christen*), founded in 1932, which quickly became one of the most prominent Protestant groups in Germany after 1933. Seeing themselves as followers of Luther's teachings, they attempted to minimize the role of the Old Testament in Christian life.[10]

---

[6] Saul Friedländer, *Nazi Germany and the Jews: The Years of Persecution* (New York: Harper Collins, 1997), 73–112.

[7] Dan Stone, *Histories of the Holocaust* (Oxford: Oxford University Press, 2010), 64–112.

[8] Alon Confino, *A World without Jews: The Nazi Imagination from Persecution to Genocide* (New Haven: Yale University Press, 2014), 85, 99.

[9] Quotes from Ulrich Prehn, ed., *"Überall Luthers Worte...": Martin Luther im Nationalsozialismus* (Berlin: Stiftung Topographie des Terrors, 2017), 42, 47, 49; the image of Luther as Hercules was based on the eponymous 1520 woodcut by Hans Holbein the Younger (66).

[10] Doris Bergen, *Twisted Cross: The German Christian Movement in the Third Reich* (Chapel Hill: University of North Carolina Press, 1996); Richard Steigmann-Gall, *The Holy Reich: Nazi Conceptions of Christianity, 1919–1945* (Cambridge: Cambridge University Press, 2003).

76   The Jewish Imperial Imagination

This is not to say that all Protestants supported Nazism or that only Protestants supported Nazism. Yet the vision of excising Judaism from amidst the German *Volk* and Christianity was in line with what Baeck identified during the Weimar Republic as the Marcionite inclinations of Protestantism. Such a theological approach received institutional support with the establishment of the Institute for the Study and Eradication of Jewish Influence on German Church Life in 1939, which promoted scholarship that presented Jesus, as Susannah Heschel writes, as "an antisemite and proto-Nazi."[11] To an extent, this position was not unprecedented but rather an extreme version of earlier tendencies.[12] Yet the fact that such ideas were now deployed and supported by a totalitarian regime meant that scholarship now lent credibility, and financial resources, to such endeavors.

Against this theological attitude, Baeck published *The Gospel as a Document of the History of the Jewish Faith* (1938) as part of the Schocken Jewish Library, a series of slim volumes with a distinct design between 1933 and 1939. Written and edited by Jewish scholars, these works served as sources of Jewish knowledge and comfort for some Jewish readers.[13] Baeck took up the question of Jesus's Jewishness once more in this text, claiming the synoptic gospels as Jewish texts and part of the Jewish tradition. It was "a piece, not inconsiderable, of Jewish history – a testimony of Jewish faith."[14] Baeck's book served as a counterhistory and a methodological guise for an attack on the entire enterprise of de-Judaizing the New Testament under Nazism. The radical implication of his argument was that there was no access to Jesus except through Judaism.[15] For most Jews living in Germany, however, this might have been of little comfort. They had more immediate and everyday concerns about their lives and livelihood.

---

[11] Susannah Heschel, *The Aryan Jesus: Christian Theologians and the Bible in Nazi Germany* (Princeton: Princeton University Press, 2008), 27.

[12] Anders Gerdmar, *Roots of Theological Anti-Semitism: German Biblical Interpretation and the Jews, from Herder and Semler to Kittel and Bultmann* (Leiden: Brill, 2009).

[13] Renate Evers, "Die 'Schocken-Bücherei' in den Nachlasssammlungen des Leo Baeck Institutes New York," *Medaon* 14 (2014), www.medaon.de/de/artikel/die-schocken-buecherei-in-den-nachlasssammlungen-des-leo-baeck-institutes-new-york/.

[14] Leo Baeck, "The Gospel as a Document of the History of the Jewish Faith," in *Judaism and Christianity*, trans. Walter Kaufmann (Philadelphia: Jewish Publication Society of America, 1960), 42.

[15] Christian Wiese, "Das Evangelium als 'Urkunde der jüdischen Glaubensgeschichte': Spuren der zeitgenössischen jüdischen geistigen Widerstand gegen die theologisch-völkische Religionswissenschaft des eisenacher 'Entjudungsinstitut,'" in *Das eisenacher ‚Entjudungsinstitut': Kirche und Antisemitismus in der NS-Zeit*, eds. Christopher Spehr and Harry Oelke (Göttingen: Vandenhoeck & Ruprecht, 2021), 132–38.

Vulnerable Existence 77

A Jewish Civic Truce

The exclusion of Jews from economic and public life started shortly after the Nazis rose to power. The first major public action was calling a boycott of Jewish businesses on April 1, 1933. It was a haphazardly organized affair with varying degrees of local success. In the short term, it did not significantly curtail Jewish economic life and resulted in criticism abroad.[16] In hindsight, Baeck saw in it the day of "great cowardice" that signified the start of the great decline. The boycott, he told members of the Association of Jewish Refugees in Great Britain twenty years later, was not only against Jewish business, "in truth justice was boycotted. The Jewish businesses survived for a while; justice did not survive that day."[17]

The boycott can be seen as a first attempt at what Christoph Kreutzmüller called "the destruction of economic existence of Jews," a long, twisted process that included implicit and explicit threats, comprehensive legislation limiting the scope of permissible Jewish economic activity, and the use of violence.[18] Among the anti-Jewish legislation in April 1933, for example, were laws dismissing Jews from the civil service and limiting their ability to practice law and medicine. The flurry of legislation was not limited to economic activity. In 1933 alone more than two hundred anti-Jewish laws were enacted, including the prohibition of kosher slaughtering in Germany and a *numerus clausus* limiting the number of Jewish children who could attend public school.[19] Lore Gang-Salheimer from Nuremberg, whose father was a war veteran, was eleven in 1933. She was allowed to remain in her public school but felt such alienation from her classmates that she left in 1935.[20]

Feelings of German patriotism, hope that the Nazis would not stay in power for long, or belief in the ability to adjust to the new conditions also meant that many Jews decided to stay in Germany. The prohibitive costs of emigration, and the fear of starting anew, often at an old age, meant that

---

[16] Karl Schleunes, *The Twisted Road to Auschwitz: Nazi Policy toward German Jews, 1933–39* (Urbana: University of Illinois Press, 1990), 76–91; Avraham Barkai, *From Boycott to Annihilation: The Economic Struggle of German Jews, 1933–1943*, trans. William Templer (Waltham, MA: University Press of New England, 1989).

[17] Leo Baeck, "Zum Boykott Tag (1953)," *AJR Information*, April 1973, 3.

[18] Christoph Kreutzmüller, *Final Sale in Berlin: The Destruction of Jewish Commercial Activity, 1930–1945*, trans. Jane Paulick and Jefferson Chase (New York: Berghahn Books, 2015), 7–8.

[19] Joseph Walk, ed., *Das Sonderrecht für die Juden im NS-Staat: Eine Sammlung der gesetzlichen Maßnahmen und Richtlinien* (Heidelberg: C. F. Müller Juristischer Verlag, 1981).

[20] Deborah Dwork, *Children with a Star: Jewish Youth in Nazi Europe* (New Haven: Yale University Press, 1991), 22–23.

78   The Jewish Imperial Imagination

leaving was not always a viable option. There was hope for the best, because at times exceptions were made, among others to Jewish spouses in interfaith marriages and to veterans of the First World War. This was further complicated by the lack of clear definition of Jewishness, which was not legally codified and clarified until the Nuremberg Laws. All these factors led to the result that while 37,000 Jews emigrated from Germany in 1933, that number declined to 21,000–25,000 yearly until the November Pogrom of 1938.[21]

In navigating the political and legal quicksand, German Jews organized collectively. The result was the formation of the *Reichsvertretung der deutschen Juden* (Reich Representation of German Jews, hereafter Reichsvertretung) in September 1933. This umbrella organization provided assistance and support for Jews in the fields of education, vocational training, economic and social support, and immigration.[22] Baeck was chosen as the president of the newly established organization, thereby taking further responsibilities alongside his other positions as rabbi and teacher. Despite multiple opportunities to flee Germany during these years, he decided to stay, saying that as long as there was a *minyan*, a quorum of ten Jews required for prayer, he would stay in Germany.[23]

Baeck's leadership, and the work of the Reichsvertretung, was met with some resistance within the Jewish community. The Reichsvertretung brought together opposing factions of Jewish society, including the two largest organizations: the C.V. (Central Association of German Citizens of Jewish Faith) and the Zionist Federation for Germany. Notably absent, and at times openly critical of the Reichsvertretung, was the Representation of Independent Orthodoxy (*Vertretung der unabhängigen jüdischen Orthodoxie Deutschlands*) and German-Jewish nationalist groups.

The Jewish veteran association, the *Reichsbund jüdischer Frontsoldaten* (RjF), was skeptical at first but eventually joined. Baeck, a former army chaplain in the Great War, was probably seen as a respected leader from the RjF perspective. He contributed to their journal *Der Schild* several times during the 1930s and wrote the lead article in 1934 for the organization's fifteenth anniversary. In an environment in which Jews were being

---

[21] Strauss, "Jewish Emigration from Germany"; Schleunes, *The Twisted Road to Auschwitz*, 186.

[22] Esriel Hildesheimer, *Jüdische Selbstverwaltung unter dem NS-Regime: Der Existenzkampf der Reichsvertretung und Reichsvereinigung der Juden in Deutschland* (Tübingen: Mohr Siebeck, 1994); Otto Dov Kulka, ed., *Deutsches Judentum unter dem Nationalsozialismus* (Tübingen: Mohr Siebeck, 1997); Salomon Adler-Rudel, *Jüdische Selbsthilfe unter dem Naziregime 1933–1939: Im Spiegel der Berichte der Reichsvertretung der Juden in Deutschland* (Tübingen: Mohr Siebeck, 1974).

[23] Baeck thought of leaving in early 1941 but decided against it. See Meyer, *Rabbi Leo Baeck*, 114.

Vulnerable Existence   79

legally and socially isolated – as early as 1932, fallen Jewish soldiers had been increasingly excluded from local and national memorials and memorial services – Baeck felt the need to defend the Jewish aspect of the RjF.[24] He insisted it was no ghettoization (*Ghettogebilde*) to have a Jewish veteran organization. While this term is striking, its usage in this context is in the sense of separation, in this case from the broader German experience of the war.[25] The war experience was shared among Jews and non-Jews, but it also had particular elements. City dwellers did not experience it the same way as those from rural areas, Catholics a bit differently than Protestants. It was for this reason, Baeck argued, that a Jewish veteran association was created.[26]

The RjF called the Jewish coming together of such various interest groups an inner-Jewish *Burgfrieden*, the same term used to describe the civic truce proclaimed by the Kaiser at the start of the Great War.[27] The imperial vocabulary from the days of the Wilhelmine Empire remained, but the civic truce was now not among various factions of German society, from which Jews had been increasingly pushed out, but an inner-Jewish affair. The alliance between the various factions was not always easy given the different agendas and personalities involved. Baeck ran into multiple conflicts with Heinrich Stahl of the Berlin Jewish community, who demanded to have more power in the decision making as the representative of the largest and wealthiest Jewish community. Even more vehement was the conflict with Gerog Kareski, an opportunistic revisionist Zionist who sought the favor of the Nazi regime and in 1937 unsuccessfully attempted to supplant Baeck. Despite the treacherous water, Baeck navigated the Reichsvertretung successfully through these inner tensions, among others thanks to the help and friendship of Otto Hirsch, the executive director of the Reichsvertretung. Hirsch was arrested by the Nazi authorities multiple times. In February 1941, he was sent to Mauthausen concentration camp, where he was murdered.

As the leader of German Jews, Baeck tried to come to terms with the new political constellation and its meaning. In an early interview, likely

---

[24] Penslar, "The German-Jewish Soldier," 440; Friedländer, *Nazi Germany and the Jews*, 292–93.

[25] On the development of the term ghetto, see Dan Michman, *The Emergence of Jewish Ghettos during the Holocaust*, trans. Lenn Schramm (Cambridge: Cambridge University Press, 2011); Daniel Schwartz, *Ghetto: The History of a Word* (Cambridge, MA: Harvard University Press, 2019).

[26] Leo Baeck, "15 Jahre RjF: Dem Frontbund zum Gedenktage seines Beginnes," *Der Schild* 18, no. 3 (February 2, 1934): 1.

[27] "Für Zusammenarbeit der jüdischen Organisationen! Bedeutungsvolle Resolution des Beirats der Reichsvertretung – Der innerjüdische Burgfrieden," *Der Schild* 13, no. 5 (February 16, 1934): 1.

80   The Jewish Imperial Imagination

before the 1933 April Boycott, apparently given to the French right-wing newspaper *L'Intransigeant* and taken up by the *Israelitisches Familienblatt*, Baeck described the "national German revolution" that was taking place as having two foci: the renewal of Germany and the fight against bolshevism.[28] Baeck pled for good working relations with the "new rulers in Germany" and affirmed that the renewal of Germany was "an ideal and longing" of German Jews.

In a letter addressed to Hitler from June 6, 1933, Baeck and Theodor Wolff from the C.V., as representatives of an early iteration of the Reichsvertretung, asked for an audience. Their request was denied.[29] The accompanying text to the request, which appeared in the Jewish press, began with the statement that the "German Jewish Question [*deutsche Judenfrage*] demands a clear word from German Jews." Although they were few – an earlier draft had "minority," a term likely deleted because legally it could be interpreted as suggesting different nationality – German Jews demanded respect and rejected the need to constantly refer to their millennia old German culture and connection to the land. Like Baeck's interview, the text stressed that German Jews had always shown themselves willing to be subordinated to any state-structure as long as their dignity and freedoms were kept.[30]

The national revolution was one side of the coin. The other was the rejection of bolshevism. In his statement for *L'Intransigeant*, Baeck attempted to counter the myth of Judeo-Bolshevism, which was an important pillar of the Nazi imagination of Jews.[31] According to Baeck, bolshevism was a godless movement that represented the most vehement and grim enemy of Judaism. Drawing on one of the harshest terms in the religious arsenal of Judaism, he stated that a "Jew who converts to

---

[28] Leo Baeck, "Das deutsche Judentum und die Erneuerung Deutschlands (1933)," *Werke* 6, 210. Like Michael Meyer (*Rabbi Leo Baeck*, 225n18), I was unable to locate in the original French newspaper any interview with Baeck between January 1933 and April 6, when Baeck is quoted by the *Israelitisches Familienblatt*. A possible explanation is that the interview was given but they decided against publishing it. On the discourse of "national revolution," see Mosse, *The Crisis of German Ideology*; Rose, *German Question/Jewish Question*.

[29] Kulka, ed., "Die Reichsvertretung der jüdischen Landesverbände an den Reichskanzler und die Reichsminister (June 6, 1933)," 48.

[30] Kulka, ed., "Erklärung der (alten) Reichsvertretung (June 9, 1933)," in *Deutsches Judentum unter Dem Nationalsozialismus* (Tübingen: Mohr Siebeck, 1997), 51–52. On petitions, see Wolf Gruner, "To Not 'Live as a Pariah': Jewish Petitions as Individual and Collective Protest in the Greater German Reich," in *Resisting Persecution: Jews and Their Petitions during the Holocaust*, eds. Thomas Pegelow Kaplan and Wolf Gruner (New York: Berghahn Books, 2020), 28–50.

[31] Paul Hanebrink, *A Specter Haunting Europe: The Myth of Judeo-Bolshevism* (Cambridge, MA: The Belknap, 2018); Yuri Slezkine, *The Jewish Century* (Princeton: Princeton University Press, 2006).

Vulnerable Existence

81

bolshevism is an apostate."[32] This was no mere apologetics or an attempt to acquiesce to a new ideology. Neither was it counterhistory. Rather, it reflected a point where Baeck's view of Judaism's role in the world and the contemporary imperial imagination were congruent.

Baeck was not alone in his rejection of bolshevism. A memorandum by the Free Association for the Interests of Orthodox Jews from October 1933 – likely a response to the founding of the Reichsvertretung – also opposed "Marxist materialism and Communist atheism," and stated that Orthodox Jews had fought against these threats long before the "National Revolution." The memorandum utilized the idea of a *Lebensraum*, an important tenet of the Nazi imperial imagination of the space needed for German expansion, by saying that Jews, too, "require some *Lebensraum* within the *Lebensraum* of the German people." The leading Orthodox rabbis undersigned – including Esra Munk, Jacob Rosenheim, and Isaac Breuer[33] – offered to send a public relations delegation abroad that would ask not to interfere in the relation between German Jews and their national government and explain the situation in Germany in a more favorable manner. In a striking passage that is hard to read without backshadowing, they added that they wanted to cooperate with the regime and did not believe that Nazism's aim was "to eradicate German Jewry from the German body politic." If that was the case, however, they asked that Jews should at least be honestly told about it so they would stop nourishing illusions.[34]

Despite their disagreements on other matters, Baeck and the Orthodox rabbis presented Marxism, communism, and bolshevism as a direct threat to Judaism. The Orthodox rabbis went further than Baeck, however, by implicitly denouncing Jewish scientists and journalists as "people whose

---

[32] Leo Baeck, "Das deutsche Judentum und die Erneuerung Deutschlands (1933)," 210; see also Hanebrink, *A Specter Haunting Europe*, 24.

[33] The Bundesarchiv copy has one of the signatories as "J. Breuer," which could be Joseph Breuer. Matthias Morgenstern, however, found a copy with handwritten comments that likely came from Isaac Breuer. Given the context of Orthodox leadership and the other signatories, this option is more likely. See Matthias Morgenstern, *From Frankfurt to Jerusalem: Isaac Breuer and the History of the Secession Dispute in Modern Jewish Orthodoxy* (Leiden; Brill, 2002), 283–84.

[34] Freie Vereinigung für die Interessen des orthodoxen Judentum, "Memorandum Sent from the Free Association for the Interests of Orthodox Judaism, Reich Alliance of Law Abiding Synagogue Communities in Halberstadt, and National Agudat Israel Organization in Germany to the Herr Reich Chancellor on Oct. 4, 1933," Bundesarchiv, Potsdam, R 43 II/602; Marc B. Shapiro, *Between the Yeshiva World and Modern Orthodoxy: The Life and Works of Rabbi Jehiel Jacob Weinberg, 1884–1966* (London: Littman Library, 1999), 226, 233; I was made aware of this text by Eliyahu Stern, "Anti-Semitism and Orthodoxy in the Age of Trump," *Tablet Magazine*, accessed March 15, 2019, www.tabletmag.com/jewish-arts-and-culture/281547/anti-semitism-orthodoxy-trump?fbclid=IwAR37lopQ1xyteNnDOeVVyAToEWKjtwCcd43Axi7SDSUgmQU4vxwKcOtMc6E.

82 The Jewish Imperial Imagination

intellectual outlook stamps them as twentieth-century Europeans, not Jews."[35] Orthodox Jewry, they wrote, did not look for economic supremacy and opposed baptism and intermarriage. The implication, of course, was that there were other Jews who aimed for these goals. Even if he defined Jewish bolshevists as apostates, Baeck did not go that far. As the head of the Reichsvertretung, he attempted to serve the largest possible constituency of Jews. Whereas the Orthodox rabbis undersigned on the memorandum saw only their community as proper Jews, Baeck remained true to his belief in large-tent Judaism and sought to bring assimilated Jews a stronger sense of their Judaism.

Baeck's work in the early years of the Reichsvertretung was an attempt to come to terms with the changing political landscape. Yet it would be wrong to interpret his work in this period as merely reactive. He also drew on his earlier understanding of Judaism and the Jewish existence as a minority in order to understand what can and should be done in these uncertain times. In the political sphere, this took the form of securing Jewish life through education, vocational training, and immigration. In his lectures and writings, this included rethinking the meaning of Jewish existence as a minority.

The Existence of the Jew

In the *Essence* (1905), Baeck argued that essence and existence were intertwined. Jewish existence was a precondition for Judaism to achieve its ethical mission actively, for example, by proselytizing. But even when missionizing was not an option, "also the existence can be a mission, *bare existence* is already a vivid sermon."[36] That is to say, Judaism served as a moral exemplar by being there and acting ethically. Thirty years later, "The Existence of the Jew," a public lecture in front of a Jewish audience from May 1935, developed this idea in a different vein by stressing the precarious position of existing as a minority.

The lecture began with an etymological exercise. The Hebrew word *saviv* (surrounding/round about), Baeck noted, was used in the Hebrew Bible to refer to the existence of the Jews as always surrounded. "Even in the centuries in which the independent state-life on Palestine's soil" took place, Jews lived "in the midst" of others.[37] It was this condition, said Baeck,

---

[35] Freie Vereinigung für die Intersse des orthodoxen Judentum, "Memorandum."
[36] Baeck, *Das Wesen des Judentums* (1905), 410 – emphasis in the original.
[37] Leo Baeck, "Die Existenz des Juden (1935)," *Werke* 6, 245–53; for an English translation see Leo Baeck, "Jewish Existence: A Lehrhaus Lecture of 30th May 1935," trans. Curtis Cassel, *European*

Vulnerable Existence 83

that led Jews to be perceived as *unheimlich*. *Unheimlich* can refer here to the fact that the Jews did not have a homeland and were not considered as part of an imagined bond between people and locality or *Heimat*.[38] *Unheimlich* also has psychoanalytical connotations derived from Freud's 1919 essay "The Uncanny" (*Das Unheimliche*), where it is described as a feeling of something strangely and disturbingly familiar.[39] As living amidst other people, Jews were under constant scrutiny and undesired visibility. Because the Jewish diaspora was worldwide, Jews appeared more powerful and numerous than they truly were.[40] Baeck's method here shifted slightly, from theology and the academic study of religion to sociological and psychological explanation of the origins of hatred of Jews.

To this spatial explanation, Baeck added a temporal explanation. Drawing on an imperial imagination of Jewish colonies spread outside the homeland of Palestine – the Jewish diaspora as having a civilizing mission – Baeck wrote in "The Jewish Person," an essay published in *Der Morgen* in 1935, that the Jew was a "colonial person."[41] That is to say, Jews colonized all over the world, but in order not to lose their particularity and get lost in a different surrounding, they needed their tradition. Time "for the Jews of the colonies" was unlike Chronos, Father Time who in Greek mythology devours his children like the present devouring the past in the ticking of the clock. Rather, Jewish temporality was loaded with meaning through the Jewish relation to God and tradition.[42]

Non-Jews, according to Baeck, recognized this feature of Jewish existence, and it gave rise to the legend of the Wandering Jew who refused to help Jesus carry the cross and was condemned to wander the world until Jesus's return. This legend was popular since the medieval period and often

---

    Judaism: A Journal for the New Europe 27, no. 1 (1994): 11–17; see also Leo Baeck, "Der jüdische Mensch (1935)," *Werke* 6, 234.

[38] Peter Blickle, *Heimat: A Critical Theory of the German Idea of Homeland* (Rochester, NY: Camden House, 2002); Alon Confino, *The Nation as a Local Metaphor: Württemberg, Imperial Germany, and National Memory, 1871–1918* (Chapel Hill: University of North Carolina Press, 1997).

[39] Sigmund Freud, "Das Unheimliche," *Imago: Zeitschrift für Anwendung der Psychoanalyse auf die Geisteswissenschaften* 5 (1919): 297–324.

[40] Baeck, "Die Existenz des Juden (1935)," 245.

[41] Baeck, "Die Existenz des Juden (1935)," 241–42.

[42] The different Jewish temporality is something that has been suggested by Franz Rosenzweig in the *Star of Redemption*. See Franz Rosenzweig, *The Star of Redemption*, trans. Barbara E. Galli (Madison: University of Wisconsin Press, 2005), 317–18. The language of chronos is a possible allusion to the work of Paul Tillich, who since the 1920s used the distinction between kairos, as a fullness of time, distinguishing it from the empty time of chronos. See Paul Tillich, "Kairos," in *The Protestant Era*, ed. James Luther Adams (Chicago: University of Chicago Press, 1948), 32–51; Daniel Weidner, "Prophetic Criticism and the Rhetoric of Temporality: Paul Tillich's Kairos Texts and Weimar Intellectual Politics," *Political Theology* 21, no. 1–2 (2020): 71–88.

84   The Jewish Imperial Imagination

served as an antisemitic trope, evident in the 1940 Nazi propaganda film
Der ewige Jude (The Eternal Jew).[43] Jews were hated, in Baeck's understanding, because they were in the midst of other people spatially, while
being outside the temporal order through their relation to God.

Alongside the spatial and temporal explanations of antisemitism, Baeck
implied that hatred of Jews was self-hate. The fact that Jews lived under
Islam and Christianity, both of which emerged from Judaism in Baeck's
account, led Christians and Muslims, but especially the former, to hate
their Jewish origins and project this hatred on the Jews. Antisemitism was
therefore nothing but self-loathing. This view was consistent with Baeck's
earlier argument that the Marcionite attempt to purify oneself of Jewish
elements was a Marcionite move that was not only an attack on the Jews,
but on Christianity itself.

This sublimated self-hate could also be experienced according to Baeck
by Jews with no grounding in Judaism. There was something that they
would rather get rid of but cannot.[44] Taken alongside Baeck's comments
about bolshevism and the activities of the Reichsvertretung, his claim
about the self-hatred of rootless Jews can be better understood. Some
might be "apostates" who had left the Jewish fold, but many were not
rootless by choice. They had been violently uprooted from German
culture, the only one they ever knew, without possessing Jewish knowledge
to ground them in their existence as Jews.

In "The Existence of the Jew," Baeck described this rootlessness as part of the
danger of being surrounded.[45] In a 1937 *Der Morgen* essay titled "Europe," he
analyzed the modernity of this phenomenon. Until the modern era, Jews and
Christians were separate, but with the emergence of a secular shared European
culture a new path seemingly opened. Only seemingly, because in the aftermath
of the French Revolution, Europe turned once more to Christianity. The
tragedy, Baeck argued, was that modern Jews tried to understand their
Judaism in light of European culture, instead of realizing that it was Europe
that should be interpreted in light of Judaism. The faith in and of Judaism,
Baeck wrote, would remain "even if Europe would cease to exist as a community of peoples [*Völkergemeinschaft*], as a spiritual, ethical unity."[46] The

---

[43] Galit Hasan-Rokem and Alan Dundes, eds., *The Wandering Jew: Essays in the Interpretation of a Christian Legend* (Bloomington: Indiana University Press, 1986); Richard Cohen, "The 'Wandering Jew' from Medieval Legend to Modern Metaphor," in *The Art of Being Jewish in Modern Times*, eds. Barbara Kirshenblatt-Gimblett and Jonathan Karp (Philadelphia: University of Pennsylvania Press, 2008), 147–75.

[44] Baeck, "Der jüdische Mensch (1935)," 242.   [45] Baeck, "Die Existenz des Juden (1935)," 246.

[46] Leo Baeck, "Europa (1937)," *Werke* 6, 280.

Vulnerable Existence

85

postimperial vision of peace after the Great War still existed for Baeck, but now he also recognized its potential dissolution, while claiming that Judaism stood above and outside any particular imperial order.

Given the deteriorating situation of German Jewry, the Reichsvertretung tried to help German Jews who could leave roots by assisting with emigration.[47] Booklets, produced by the Relief Organization of Jews in Germany, informed prospective German-Jewish migrants how to prepare for the tropical climate, learn the new language, and prepare for a new job.[48] Although many potential emigrants felt any destination would do, Palestine garnered the most attention. At times, this coincided with the position of some in the Nazi administration, who saw Zionism as an ideology was in line with the Nazi imperial imagination more than the position of assimilated Jews. With its insistence on Jewish otherness and fostering of emigration from Germany, Zionism became a potential unlikely bedfellow.[49]

Baeck visited Palestine with his wife Natalie in February 1935. A speech he gave on board the ship shows his understanding of settlement in the land. Although he did not explicitly mention the establishment of a state, he cited *Hatikva*, which at this point already served as the anthem of the Zionist movement. Using the categories he already developed in the *Essence*, he said that this land had never been "a place of power [*Macht*], but always a place of energy [*Kraft*], of thinking, of commandment, of hope."[50] Although the categories remained the same – not the violence involved in *Macht* but *Kraft* as a more spiritual ability was the Jewish way – their subject changed. Now the focus was on the land of Palestine and not on living in the diaspora. When Jews were not in the land, in Baeck's narrative, it was not part of history and did not reach greatness, as it had during the periods of Jewish sovereignty during the biblical period and the Second Temple period. Palestine was imagined as a Jewish *Kulturboden*, like Poland in the German imperial imagination, and Jews as having the right to settle it by virtue of its improvement. It is through the

---

[47] Adler-Rudel, *Jüdische Selbsthilfe unter dem Naziregime 1933–1939*, 72–109; Baeck insisted in a private conversation with Fritz Friedländer that "the young must go because they have no future in this land!" quoted in Leonard Baker, *Days of Sorrow and Pain*, 219.

[48] See, for example, Hilfsverein der Juden in Deutschland, ed., *Jüdische Auswanderung: Korrespondenzblatt über Auswanderungs- und Siedlungswesen* (Berlin: Schmoller & Gordon, 1937); and a special volume on South America: Hilfsverein der Juden in Deutschland, ed., *Jüdische Auswanderung nach Südamerika* (Berlin: Jüdischer Kulturbund, 1939).

[49] Francis Nicosia, *Zionism and Anti-Semitism in Nazi Germany* (Cambridge: Cambridge University Press, 2008).

[50] Leo Baeck, "Unsere Hoffnung (1935)," *Werke* 6, 472.

86 The Jewish Imperial Imagination

improvement of the land that Jews de facto guaranteed their claim to it, a point Baeck would return to in the postwar era.

Alongside emigration, the efforts of the Reichsvertretung during this period addressed the crisis of Jewish identity through educational and cultural activities to youth and adults alike.[51] The two types of rooting, the spiritual and physical, were connected in Baeck's view. In a celebration of the opening of a Jewish education center (*Lehrhaus*) in 1934, Baeck lectured on "History and the Present." He offered a striking comparison between Jews and Blacks. "Perhaps the worst crime that the white race has perpetrated against the Negroes," he said, "was tearing them from their homeland [*Heimat*] thereby suddenly separating them from their tradition." Jews in the nineteenth century, Baeck added, almost did the same to themselves, sacrificing their tradition for the price of assimilation.[52] Baeck worked within existing racial categories. In his telling, the Jews had agency, but it also meant that loss of tradition was their own doing. In connecting Jews and Blacks, Baeck alluded to the deteriorating legal status of Jews in Germany. The Nazi legislation meant to undo emancipation, a term whose origins traced to the ending of the slave trade in Britain and Catholic emancipation.[53]

The connection made between Blacks and Jews was in terms of spiritual danger as well as in legal precarity. Baeck was not alone in making this type of connection. That same year, in an essay titled "I Want to Be African," the Black musician, actor, and activist Paul Robeson compared the Black predicament to that of the Jew. Jews, "like a vast proportion of Negros, are a race without a nation; but, far from Palestine, they are indissolubly bound by their religious practice – which they recognize as such." Robeson called Blacks to similarly recognize the ties that bind them together, just as Jews recognized their "common origin, species, interest and attitudes."[54]

There is a spiritual and physical danger in existing as a minority, especially when rights are taken away and a homeland is not accessible.

---

[51] Adler-Rudel, *Jüdische Selbsthilfe unter dem Naziregime 1933–1939*, 19–46; Ernst Simon, *Aufbau im Untergang: Jüdische Erwachsenenbildung im mationalsozialistischen Deutschland als geistiger Widerstand* (Tübingen: Mohr, 1959); Rebecca Rovit, *The Jewish Kulturbund Theatre Company in Nazi Berlin* (Iowa City: University of Iowa Press, 2012).

[52] "Lehrhaus eröffnet. Ansprache der Leiter – Leo Baeck erhält der Eröffnungsvorlesung," 2.

[53] Jacob Katz, "The Term 'Jewish Emancipation': Its Origins and Historical Impact," in *Studies in Nineteenth-Century Jewish Intellectual History*, ed. Alexander Altmann (Cambridge, MA: Harvard University Press, 1964), 18–19; Sorkin, *Jewish Emancipation*, 210–12; Isabel Wilkerson, *Caste: The Origins of Our Discontents* (New York: Random House, 2020).

[54] Paul Robeson, "I Want to Be African," in *Paul Robeson Speaks: Writings, Speeches, and Interviews, a Centennial Celebration*, ed. Philip Foner (New York: Citadel Press, 1978), 90; George Bornstein, *The Colors of Zion: Blacks, Jews, and Irish from 1845 to 1945* (Cambridge, MA: Harvard University Press, 2011), esp. 73–74, 185–86.

Vulnerable Existence

To always be surrounded, Baeck said in "The Existence of the Jew," was to be in a "vulnerable situation" (*gefährdete Situation*). Jewish existence was "vulnerable existence" (*gefährdete Existenz*). For other people this was the exception; for Jews, according to Baeck, vulnerability was the norm.[55]

Baeck traced his use of the term "vulnerable existence" to Nietzsche and Kierkegaard. This is an interesting attribution for two reasons. First, while Nietzsche influenced many German-Jewish thinkers, he is not commonly cited by Baeck and his thought did not leave significant traces on Baeck's philosophy until this point. The same can be said of Kierkegaard.[56] Second, as far as I could tell, the term does not appear as such in either Nietzsche or Kierkegaard. This type of creative misreading of prominent thinkers is a pattern in "The Existence of the Jew."

The reference to Nietzsche and Kierkegaard was likely because Baeck was making an argument about Jewish existence, and he required existentialist language. In a postwar lecture at the Hebrew Union College, Baeck clarified this position by distinguishing two types of existentialism. There was the Lutheran, theological existentialism, which emerged "from man's deep anxiety" that it equated with existence. Judaism, which Baeck defined in the *Essence* as a religion of optimism, could not accept this position. The other type of existentialism was concerned with the "existential character of the individual" and "the responsibility of the individual resulting from his existence."[57] This position had a common ground with Judaism. It was the latter type of existentialism Baeck thought about when he said in 1935 that existential thinking "has special meaning for the understanding of the Jewish form of existence. Jewish thinking is just this thinking, in which the human is included with his concerns and concrete reality."[58]

Alongside Nietzsche and Kierkegaard, Baeck enlisted Martin Heidegger for his argument. Heidegger, who "intentionally or unintentionally, expressed a biblical thought," claimed that existence is not about "presence-at-hand [*Vorhandensein*], but a readiness-at-hand [*Zuhandensein*], something that is put in front of the human, so that he can form it, shape it, fashion it." According to Baeck, this readiness-at-hand was Jewish thinking, "which makes the commandment its own, which obeys the

---

[55] Baeck, "Die Existenz des Juden (1935)," 246.
[56] Baeck, "Romantic Religion," 212, 264; after the Holocaust, Baeck made somewhat more positive references, see Leo Baeck, "Israel und das deutsche Volk (1952)," *Werke* 5, 51; Leo Baeck, "The Interrelation of Judaism and Ethics (1949)," *Werke* 5, 136. On Nietzsche's influence on Jewish thought, see Jacob Golomb, ed., *Nietzsche and Jewish Culture* (New York: Routledge, 1997).
[57] Leo Baeck, "The Interrelation of Judaism and Philosophy (1949)," *Werke* 5, 130.
[58] Baeck, "Die Existenz des Juden (1935)," 249.

88 The Jewish Imperial Imagination

commandment."[59] What appears as a direct quote is not present in Heidegger, but a paraphrase of the distinction made in *Being and Time* between two modes of engaging objects in the world. Whereas "presence-at-hand" was considered by Heidegger detached and merely observing, "readiness-to-hand" was the way of being of equipment that was discovered through active engagement in the world.[60] Jewish disposition in the world was readiness-at-hand, a task to be fulfilled in this world. This understanding was in line with Baeck's emphasis on the commandment and his critique of Marcionite flight from this world.

Baeck, the official leader of the Jewish community in Nazi Germany, cited Heidegger approvingly in 1935.[61] It is unclear whether Baeck knew of Heidegger's support for the Nazi movement, but a hint that Baeck was aware of Heidegger's position was his comment that the expression of a biblical idea was "intentionally or unintentionally." This implies an insistence on the value of Heidegger's insight, perhaps despite the philosopher's Nazi allegiance. Baeck's decision to cite Heidegger shows an insistence on enlisting an existentialist tradition of Kierkegaard, Nietzsche, and Heidegger for his understanding of Jewish precarious existence.[62] Baeck could claim, in other words, that his understanding of Jewish vulnerability was in line not just with the Jewish tradition but also with one of the most prominent philosophical trends of the time.

Pointing Fingers

Jewish existence meant for Baeck coming to terms with vulnerability and gaining strength from looking beyond the current situation without

[59] Baeck, "Die Existenz des Juden (1935)," 250.
[60] Martin Heidegger, *Being and Time*, trans. John Macquarrie and Edward Robinson (New York: Harper, 2008), 98–99.
[61] On Heidegger's reception in Jewish thought, see Richard Wolin, *Heidegger's Children: Hannah Arendt, Karl Löwith, Hans Jonas, and Herbert Marcuse* (Princeton: Princeton University Press, 2001); Peter Gordon, *Rosenzweig and Heidegger: Between Judaism and German Philosophy* (Berkeley: University of California Press, 2003); Daniel Herskowitz, *Heidegger and His Jewish Reception* (Cambridge: Cambridge University Press, 2021); Elad Lapidot and Micha Brumlik, eds., *Heidegger and Jewish Thought: Difficult Others* (London: Rowman & Littlefield, 2018).
[62] This is the case even though some of these thinkers might not identify themselves with this label. In the entries of the *Historical Dictionary of Philosophy*, Nietzsche is not mentioned as part of this tradition, for he belongs more closely to *Lebensphilosophie*, see K. Hartman, "Existenzialismus," in *Historisches Wörterbuch der Philosophie*, eds. Joachim Ritter et al. (Basel: Schwabe, 1971), 850–52; K. Hartman, "Existenzphilosophie," in *Historisches Wörterbuch der Philosophie*, eds. Joachim Ritter et al. (Basel: Schwabe, 1971), 862–65; but compare Thomas R. Flynn, *Existentialism: A Very Short Introduction* (New York : Oxford University Press, 2006); Walter Kaufmann, ed., *Existentialism: From Dostoevsky to Sartre* (New York: Meridian Books, 1956).

Vulnerable Existence

wishing to flee this world. He found this orientation in the biblical stories of Abraham's leaving for Canaan and the Israelites' exodus out of Egypt. Abraham was leaving his ancestral home in response to God's call (Gen. 12:1). Similarly, the Israelites were slaves in Egypt who were ultimately rescued by God. These were two examples of leaving one's present home and following a higher call. Read in the context of Jewish emigration from Nazi Germany, these biblical stories could have been interpreted by Baeck's listeners as a justification for leaving their home in favor of a new beginning. Not only leaving one's home unites Abraham and the Exodus; this was a religious act whose telos was pointing toward God.

In making his claim about Jewish existence, Baeck turned to "the famous theologian Karl Barth" and his analysis of the crucifixion scene in Matthias Grünewald's Isenheim altarpiece. In particular, Baeck drew attention to the description of John the Baptist's gaze in this scene, and his almost supernaturally stretched arm, which pointed to something beyond that we cannot yet see. The reference to Barth and an altarpiece depicting the crucifixion in a text about Jewish existence in 1935 is a far from self-evident choice by Baeck. It therefore merits closer examination.

Barth's commentary on Paul's Epistle to the Romans (1st edition: 1919; 2nd edition: 1921) was nothing short of a theological earthquake, and his theology as a whole was an overthrow of liberal Protestantism that constituted, according to Gary Dorrien, "the major event of twentieth-century theology."[63] Barth emphasized God's radical otherness from the human and the world. God was the Wholly Other to whom human beings could have no access whatsoever through their own merit. As the Wholly Other, God could not be utilized for ethics, politics, or even religion as an institution. The knowledge of God came only through revelation, which is to say through Scripture. Historical knowledge, like any other field of knowledge, might be interesting, but according to Barth it had no bearing on the understanding of the message of the cross.[64] Barth had been chided in the 1920s, by Harnack and other liberal theologians, that his emphasis on God's otherness was Marcionite. While Barth was willing to recognize some parallels, he rejected the insinuation that his position was close to

---

[63] Gary Dorrien, *Kantian Reason and Hegelian Spirit: The Idealistic Logic of Modern Theology* (Malden, MA: Wiley-Blackwell, 2012), 454; Rudy Koshar, "Demythologizing the Secular: Karl Barth and the Politics of the Weimar Republic," in *The Weimar Moment: Liberalism, Political Theology, and Law*, eds. Leonard Kaplan and Rudy Koshar (Lanham, MD: Lexington Books, 2012), 313–36.

[64] Karl Barth, *The Epistle to the Romans*, trans. Edwyn Hoskyns (London: Oxford University Press, 1933).

90   The Jewish Imperial Imagination

that of the heretic, not the least because Barth insisted on the oneness of
God rather than a dualistic perspective. Baeck would have likely agreed
with Barth on this point, as he cited the theologian approvingly as expressing a Jewish position.[65]

Grünewald's Isenheim altarpiece was central for Barth. He returned to it
in several of his texts and had its reproduction on his writing desk.[66]
Barth's first main discussion of the image was in a 1920 lecture, "Biblical
Questions, Insights, and Vistas," which was published in a collection of his
essays in 1924. In this text, Barth noted how some of the people of Israel
and Judah were "a people to whom attention to a Wholly Other seems
never wholly to have lapsed."[67] It was in this context, alongside Abraham
and Moses – not coincidentally the two examples provided by Baeck – that
Barth addressed the image of John the Baptist as gazing beyond. Barth did
not call the movement of the hand "Jewish," but the context in which it
appeared in his text arguably supports Baeck's interpretation.

It was of particular importance for Baeck that John the Baptist's gaze
beyond the present would be described as Jewish and characteristic of what
he called "this extraordinary, this vulnerable existence."[68] Baeck's reading
of Barth, however, would only make sense if Baeck stopped halfway
through. Barth returned to Grünewald later in the same essay and argued
that recognizing God as the Wholly Other meant recognizing human
finitude. He then dramatically asked: "Shall we dare turn our eyes in the
direction of the pointing hand of Grünewald's John? We know whither it
points. It points to Christ. But to Christ the crucified, we must immediately add. That is your direction, says the hand."[69] What message did
Baeck send his Jewish listeners in 1935 using this image? The answer to
these questions depends on what Baeck found helpful in Barth, and what
associations were evoked by Grünewald's imagery.

Barth was part of the Confessing Church, an organization opposed to
the German Christians. In 1934, he was a principle author of the Barmen

---

[65] Martin Rumscheidt, *Revelation and Theology: An Analysis of the Barth-Harnack Correspondence of
1923* (Eugene, OR: Wipf & Stock, 2011), 37; George Hunsinger, "The Harnack/Barth
Correspondence: A Paraphrase with Commentary," in *Disruptive Grace: Studies in the Theology of
Karl Barth* (Grand Rapids: Eerdmans, 2000), 319–37; Karl Barth, *Der Römerbrief* (Zurich: TVZ,
2005), xxiv; Joseph Mangina, *Karl Barth: Theologian of Christian Witness* (Louisville: Westminster
John Knox Press, 2004), 15.

[66] Reiner Marquard, *Karl Barth und der Isenheimer Altar* (Stuttgart: Calwer Verlag, 1995).

[67] Karl Barth, "Biblical Questions, Insights, and Vistas," in *The Word of God and the Word of Man*,
trans. Amy Marga (Gloucester, MA: P. Smith, 1978), 264.

[68] Baeck, "Die Existenz des Juden (1935)," 248.

[69] Barth, "Biblical Questions, Insights, and Vistas," 278.

Vulnerable Existence 91

Declaration, which denounced German Christian teachings as a false doctrine that made the gospel subservient to the nation. Furthermore, Barth insisted over and against Harnack, and later also against Nazi theologians, on the indispensability of the Old Testament for any Christian witnessing. In short, Barth was about as much hope in and for Christian theology as Baeck could find in 1935.[70]

Barth was also a theological inspiration and provided Baeck with a theocentric vocabulary with which to think about Jewish existence.[71] Ernst Simon argued that Barth influenced Baeck's second edition of the *Essence*, in which the polarity between God's eternity and human finitude was stressed more than in the first edition.[72] It is only in the 1930s, however, that Barth's presence is sufficiently attested in Baeck's writings, for example, in the vocabulary Baeck used. In "The Jewish Person," Baeck defined the Jew as the one who is committed to the One God, as the "person of the theocentric, which he can neither evade nor elude; he is the person, before whom the demand stands always and everywhere."[73]

Existentialist and theocentric language appear mutually exclusive. The former focuses on the person, the latter on the perception of God. For Baeck, however, they were two sides of the same coin. Existentialism described human ethical action in the world as geared toward God; theocentrism offered the other side, namely, how the human is seen from God. Put differently, the former was about the finite's relation to the Infinite, the latter about the penetration of the Infinite into the finite. The theocentric

---

[70] Klaus Scholder, *The Churches and the Third Reich*, trans. John Brown (London: SCM Press, 1988), vol. 2, esp. 132–58; Doris Bergen notes (*Twisted Cross*, 21–22) that the Barmen Declaration failed to mention the persecution of the Jews. Furthermore, Barth's theology was limited in its ability to reflect on the conditions of contemporary Jews. See Katherine Sonderegger, *That Jesus Christ Was Born a Jew: Karl Barth's "Doctrine of Israel"* (University Park: Pennsylvania State University Press, 1992); Mark R. Lindsay, *Barth, Israel, and Jesus: Karl Barth's Theology of Israel* (London and New York: Routledge, 2016)..

[71] Baeck is hardly the only Jewish thinker to have been influenced by Barth. See Daniel Herskowitz, "An Impossible Possibility? Jewish Barthianism in Interwar Germany," *Modern Theology* 33, no. 3 (July 2017): 348–68; Randi Rashkover, *Revelation and Theopolitics: Barth, Rosenzweig, and the Politics of Praise* (New York: T&T Clark International, 2005); Samuel Moyn, *Origins of the Other: Emmanuel Levinas between Revelation and Ethics* (Ithaca: Cornell University Press, 2005); Mangina, *Karl Barth*, 78–85. For a contemporary Jewish engagement with Barth, see the work of David Novak, among others: David Novak, "Before Revelation: The Rabbis, Paul, and Karl Barth," in *Talking with Christians: Musings of a Jewish Theologian* (Grand Rapids: Eerdmans, 2005), 108–26; David Novak, "Karl Barth on Divine Command: A Jewish Response," in *Talking with Christians*, 127–45; David Novak, "How Jewish Was Karl Barth?," in *Karl Barth, the Jews, and Judaism*, ed. George Hunsinger (Grand Rapids: Eerdmans, 2018), 1–23.

[72] Ernst Simon, "Geheimnis und Gebot: Zum Leo Baecks 75 Geburtstag," *Aufbau* 14, no. 21 (May 21, 1948): 32.

[73] Baeck, "Der jüdische Mensch (1935)," 238.

92 The Jewish Imperial Imagination

was a term that allowed Baeck to reframe his argument about the paradoxes and polarities of human existence in light of Barth's thinking that stresses the commitment to Wholly Other precisely because of its complete otherness.[74]

Both the theocentric terminology and the creative misreading of Barth's comments on the Grünewald served the purpose of showing that despite the difficulty of existence in this world, Judaism had a more ultimate relation. The Jewish relation to God, based on the commandment, allowed Jews to exist in this world, knowing that there was more to it than the current vulnerability. This was a decision for God, and a decision for the world. "Jewish existence," explained Baeck, was never "existence for itself . . . The Jew lives before God, not in God . . . The Jew lives before God. Before God. And therefore he is ultimately risen above the surrounding" and "led away from danger."[75]

The question remains as to the use of Grünewald's striking image of the crucifixion in a text dealing with the existence of the Jew. Grünewald's work captivated the German imagination since the late nineteenth century, and particularly since the annexation of Alsace-Lorraine in the aftermath of the Franco-Prussian War. In the search for a shared German identity after the establishment of the Kaiserreich, art critics turned to the Gothic as the prime example of the German spirit. Grünewald, along with Albrecht Dürer, came to be perceived as the quintessential Gothic, and hence German, artist. Grünewald's magnificent altarpiece in question was originally commissioned by the Order of St. Anthony of Isenheim, but since 1852 it has been at the Musee d'Unterlinden in Colmar, Alsace.[76] Grünewald, in other words, was part of imagining the nation through its art.

Making a claim for the German character of the work was simultaneously an act of imperial imagination and a claim about Germany's territorial boundaries. In the immediate aftermath of the First World War, the altar – moved from Colmar by the Germans in 1917 for safekeeping and restoration – was presented in the Alte Pinakothek Museum in Munich. It was a sensational success, with many Germans making the pilgrimage to experience the altarpiece with their own eyes and bid it farewell, knowing that it was to be returned to France along with

---

[74] Leo Baeck, "Theologie und Geschichte (1932)," *Werke* 4, 46; Leo Baeck to Hans-Hasso von Veltheim-Ostrau, April 30, 1941, *Werke* 6, 612; on polarities as central to Baeck's thought, see Friedlander, *Leo Baeck*.

[75] Baeck, "Die Existenz des Juden (1935)," 252.

[76] Pantxika Béguerie-De Paepe and Magali Haas, *The Isenheim Altarpiece: The Masterpiece of the Musée Unterlinden*, trans. Chrisoula Petridis (Colmar: Musée Unterlinden, 2015), 50–51.

Alsace-Lorraine. The Great War and the experience of the soldiers on the front gave the twisted and tortured body of Grünewald's crucified Christ a new meaning. The altarpiece now became a symbol for German agony.[77] It was suffering Germans, and Germany, that were on the cross.

When invoking Grünewald, Baeck was therefore working within a German imperial imaginary during and in the aftermath of the Great War while making a claim about who suffered in contemporary Germany. Grünewald's altarpiece produced a double identification. First, through Barth, the theological language of pointing toward the beyond, the Wholly Other, turned into a Jewish language through the image of John the Baptist's gaze and his stretched hand. Second, the Baptist's hand points toward the suffering of the Crucified. Baeck did not mention the crucified Christ, but he did not have to. The image would have likely been well known to his listeners.[78]

In 1935, Baeck took the Jewish scholarly tradition of stressing Jesus's Jewishness a step further, extending it to the Crucified as a Jewish figure.[79] Suffering in the *Essence* was connected for Baeck to the Jewish task in the world. Both were a consequence of Jews striving toward the One God and a more ethical world. Jewish suffering was also a measurement for how far this ideal still was.[80] Now this suffering was encapsulated in the image of Grünewald. In having the crucified Christ as the absent presence in his discussion of Jewish existence, Baeck transformed the agony Germans saw in the painting to the suffering of Jewish vulnerable existence.

The Limits of Atonement

The number of violent acts against Jews reached new heights in the summer of 1935. In June and July, members of the SA and the Hitler Youth continuously attacked Jewish restaurants, coffee shops, and ice dealerships in Berlin, bullying customers, smashing windows, and beating the owners. The riots in "Berlin's fashionable Kurfürstendamm" were so shocking that they made the front page of the *New York Times* two days in

---

[77] Ann Stieglitz, "The Reproduction of Agony: Toward a Reception-History of Grünewald's Isenheim Altar after the First World War," *Oxford Art Journal* 12, no. 2 (1989): 87–103.

[78] For its presence in Jewish thought and literature, see, for example, Martin Buber, "The Altar," *Journal of Visual Culture* 4, no. 1 (2005): 116–22; Adam Stern, "Before the Altar: A Kafkan Study in Analytic Iconology," *Word & Image* 37, no. 4 (2021): 311–22.

[79] On Jewish adaptations of the crucifixion motif, see Neta Stahl, *Other and Brother: Jesus in the 20th-Century Jewish Literary Landscape* (New York: Oxford University Press, 2013); Amitai Mendelsohn, *Behold the Man: Jesus In Israeli Art* (Jerusalem: Magnes University Press, 2017).

[80] Leo Baeck, *Das Wesen des Judentums* (1905), 400, 415.

94 The Jewish Imperial Imagination

a row.[81] Violence was not limited to the big cities. In June, the synagogue of Wolfhagen was desecrated. In July, Jewish cattle traders were beaten in Wächtersbach. In August, in Greifswald, the Jewish businessman Georg R. was accused of race defilement, abducted from his house, and publicly humiliated.[82]

It is in this context that two pieces of legislation were passed in September 1935: The Law for the Protection of German Blood and Honor, and the Reich Citizenship Law. These laws – collectively known as the Nuremberg Laws – did not garner much attention among non-Jews. Yet they were not merely two more pieces of antisemitic legislation, adding to the numerous limitations enacted since 1933. Rather, the Nuremberg Laws were a crucial legal step in the disenfranchisement of German Jewry and signaled the reversal of the emancipation, which had been so central not only to the legal and political status of Jews in Germany but also to their own self-understanding.[83]

The organization Baeck headed, the Reich Representation of German Jews, had to rename itself. It was now called the Reich Representation of Jews in Germany, a subtle but significant change that served as a reminder that Jews could no longer call themselves Germans. Based on the Nuremberg Laws, Jews who converted were deemed Jewish. By one approximation, the number of those with one or two Jewish grandparents (thereby defined as *Mischlinge* or "mixed"), Jews married to Christians, and converted Jews was close to a million.[84]

---

[81] "Jews Are Beaten by Berlin Rioters; Cafes Are Raided," *New York Times*, July 16, 1935; "Reaction to Riot Alarms Germans; Baiting Continues," *New York Times*, July 17, 1935; Christoph Kreutzmüller, "Gewalt gegen Juden im Sommer 1935," in *Die Nürnberger Gesetze – 80 Jahre danach: Vorgeschichte, Entstehung, Auswirkungen*, eds. Magnus Brechtken et al. (Göttingen: Wallstein Verlag, 2017), 71–88.

[82] Data from Jüdisches Museum Berlin, "*Topography of Violence 1930–1938*," www.jmberlin.de/topographie-gewalt/#/en/vis, accessed July 5, 2022; Otto Dov Kulka and Eberhard Jäckel, eds., *The Jews in the Secret Nazi Reports on Popular Opinion in Germany, 1933–1945*, trans. William Templer (New Haven: Yale University Press, 2010); and Michael Wildt, *Hitler's Volksgemeinschaft and the Dynamics of Racial Exclusion: Violence against Jews in Provincial Germany, 1919–1939*, trans. Bernard Heise (New York: Berghahn Books, 2012).

[83] Bergen, *War and Genocide*, 74. On the influence of Jim Crow laws on Nazi legislation, see James Whitman, *Hitler's American Model: The United States and the Making of Nazi Race Law* (Princeton: Princeton University Press, 2017).

[84] Kaplan, *Between Dignity and Despair*, 78; Ursula Büttner, "The Persecution of Christian-Jewish Families in the Third Reich," *Leo Baeck Institute Year Book* 34, no. 1 (1989): 271. Jewish women in intermarriage were not recognized as part of the Jewish community. See Beate Meyer, "The Mixed Marriage: A Guarantee of Survival or a Reflection of German Society during the Nazi Regime," in *Probing the Depths of German Antisemitism: German Society and the Persecution of the Jews, 1933–1941*, ed. David Bankier (New York: Berghahn Books, 2000), 55.

Vulnerable Existence   95

Yom Kippur (Day of Atonement), the holiest day in the Jewish calendar, was less than a month after the Nuremberg Laws. The combination of the solemnity of the day along with the recent legal measures against the Jews in Germany led Baeck to compose a pastoral letter (*Hirtenbrief*) in which he called on Jews to stand strong and reject the accusations leveled against them. The theme of standing before God that concerned "Jewish Existence" was present throughout the text, which came to be known as Leo Baeck's Kol Nidre prayer. In fact, the expression "before God" appears five times in this short text.[85]

Baeck's pastoral letter began with a traditional understanding of Yom Kippur:

> In this hour, all Israel stands before its God, who is judging and forgiving. Before Him, we shall all examine our ways, examine, what we have done and what we have neglected, examine where we have gone and where we have remained distant. Wherever we have failed, we wish to confess openly: "we have sinned," and we shall pray with steadfast resolve to repent before God: "forgive us!"[86]

The asking for forgiveness for transgression is the core of Yom Kippur. Furthermore, the use of the "we" in Baeck's text was also in line with the use of the first-person plural throughout the liturgy, which is filled with prayers for repentance in which the community acknowledges its guilt before God, both for sins done knowingly, and for those that it fails to recognize.

Baeck's traditional opening did not prepare the listeners for the sentences that followed: "We stand before our God. With the same strength [*Kraft*] with which we have acknowledged our sins, the sins of the individual and those of the community, we speak with feeling of abhorrence that we see deep beneath our feet the lie directed against us and the slander of our faith and its witnesses."[87]

This was not the first time Baeck turned to liturgy to reject slander during the early years of the Nazi regime. Two months earlier, in a text for Shabbat Nahamu – in which the verse "comfort, oh comfort my people" (Is. 40:1) is read – Baeck wrote that Jews could find comfort in their religion, which can be posited against "all insults" and "all slights." "True honor," he consoled, "is that which each gives to himself" in the way one lives, "our honor is our honor before God; it alone will endure."[88]

---

[85] Meyer, *Rabbi Leo Baeck*, 107.
[86] Leo Baeck, "Ansprache zum Kol Nidre des Versöhnungstages 6. Oktober 1935," *Werke* 6, 312.
[87] Baeck, "Ansprache zum Kol Nidre (1935)," 312.
[88] Leo Baeck, "Tröstet, tröstet mein Volk (1935)," *Werke* 6, 312.

96 The Jewish Imperial Imagination

The rejection of the slander was twofold, aimed against the long anti-Jewish tradition associated with the Kol Nidre, and the specific Nazi imagination of the Jew. The Kol Nidre text, with its annulment of vows before God so that the person could repent, was utilized by Christians in disputations to claim that Jews are untrustworthy and do not respect their obligations. This type of interpretation remained part of the antisemitic repertoire, so that Jewish scholars had to reject it in standard Jewish works such as the early twentieth-century *Jewish Encyclopedia*.[89]

Furthermore, stressing the community's guilt under Nazi rule could lead to the thought that the Jews were suffering because they sinned. Baeck rejected such theodicy, suggesting a line be drawn. Outside claims about the Jews should not be mistaken as the result of their own guilt, not even for unintentional sins. In Yom Kippur, this was not just a bold political statement that rejected the degrading of the Jews. It was also a theological claim. Baeck transformed the moment of standing before God in repentance to a moment of protest and self-assertion in the name of God.

At a time in which they were being excluded and marginalized from German society, Baeck reminded his listeners of the centrality and indispensability of Judaism for morality. He used a series of rhetorical questions to proclaim the value of Jewish existence in and for the world: "Who proclaimed to the world the mystery [*Geheimnis*] of the Eternal, the one God? Who revealed to the world the sense for the pure conduct of life, for the purity of the family?" His answer: the prophetic spirit of the people of Israel. The slander and insults against Judaism "fall away when cast against these facts."[90]

Baeck's decision to emphasize the family in this context is significant. The Jewish family had been a central concern for rabbis and Jewish community leaders since the late nineteenth century. "The family," argues Paula Hyman, became "*the* issue on which concern for assimilation has focused within the Jewish community" with the result that Jewish women received a greater sphere of domestic responsibility while simultaneously being excluded from the public sphere. Women thereby became the primary culprit in the vexing issue of assimilation and intermarriage.[91]

---

[89] Joseph Jacobs et al., "Kol Nidre," in *Jewish Encyclopedia* (New York: Funk & Wagnalls, 1901–1906), 541–42.

[90] Baeck, "Kol Nidre," 312–13.

[91] Paula Hyman, "The Modern Jewish Family: Image and Reality," in *The Jewish Family: Metaphor and Memory*, ed. David Kraemer (New York: Oxford University Press, 1989), 179–93; Paula Hyman, *Gender and Assimilation in Modern Jewish History: The Roles and Representation of Women* (Seattle: University of Washington Press, 1995), esp. 50–92; Marion Kaplan, *The*

Vulnerable Existence

During the Weimar Republic this discourse gained a new sense of urgency. The rate of interfaith marriage in Germany during the Weimar Republic was high, and a source of concern for those in the Jewish community. In some places such as Hamburg it reached about 39 percent in 1930–1933. Rising divorce rates were also a source of concern.[92] In a volume about marriage edited by Keyserling and published in 1925, Baeck wrote of marriage as "mystery and commandment," the same terms he used in the eponymous essay to describe a relation to the divine. Marriage was in this sense a revelation, a relationship not only between two people but also with the divine. Baeck compared marriage to birth, and emphasized giving new life as part of the marriage. These suggest that for him divorce was like taking away life or committing suicide.[93]

The family for Baeck was based on heteronormative marriage as sanctioned by God. Men and women, he believed, were inherently different.[94] But he recognized changing gender attitudes, supporting, for example, the work of the Jewish Women's Federation (*Jüdischer Frauenbund*). He spoke there in 1929 and compared the emancipation of women to the emancipation of the Jews and said that women should have a greater role to play in communal affairs. That he chose to include this essay in his collection *Paths in Judaism* (1933) shows that this was not just catering to his audience.[95]

Baeck also intervened in rabbinical questions of gender such as the seating together of men and women in the Prinzregentenstrasse synagogue in Berlin. In his responsum in 1929, Baeck did not disallow mixed seating, but neither did he unequivocally approve, writing that it should be left for the individual congregation to decide.[96] Finally, Baeck also supported the first female rabbi, Regina Jonas, whom he congratulated upon her ordination in 1935. Jonas, like Baeck, would later be deported to Theresienstadt, where she would lecture, give sermons, and continue her pastoral work. She was murdered in Auschwitz in 1944.[97]

Making of the Jewish Middle Class: Women, Family, and Identity in Imperial Germany (New York: Oxford University Press, 1994); Benjamin Maria Baader, *Gender, Judaism, and Bourgeois Culture in Germany, 1800–1870* (Bloomington: Indiana University Press, 2006).

[92] Büttner, "The Persecution of Christian-Jewish Families in the Third Reich"; Sharon Gillerman, *Germans into Jews: Remaking the Jewish Social Body in the Weimar Republic* (Stanford: Stanford University Press, 2009), 58–66.

[93] Leo Baeck, "Die Ehe als Geheimnis und Gebot (1925)," *Werke* 6, 179–85.

[94] Baeck, "Die Ehe als Geheimnis und Gebot (1925)," 184.

[95] Leo Baeck, "Frauenbund (1929)," 226–31.

[96] Leo Baeck, "Das Zusammensitzen von Männern und Frauen in der Synagoge (1929)," *Werke* 6, 507–11.

[97] Elisa Klapheck, *Fräulein Rabbiner Jonas: The Story of the First Woman Rabbi*, trans. Toby Axelrod (Ann Arbor: University of Michigan Press, 2004); Stefanie Sinclair, "Regina Jonas: Forgetting and Remembering the First Female Rabbi," *Religion* 43, no. 4 (2013): 541–63.

98 The Jewish Imperial Imagination

The family for Baeck was a source of comfort and strength against the Nazi policies. The Nazis promulgated clear gender roles in which women – in continuation with a modern bourgeois ideology – were relegated primarily to the domestic sphere and to contributions limited to social help.[98] Relationships between Jewish and non-Jewish Germans occupied a special place in the Nazi imperial imagination as they posed a threat to the perceived purity of the *Volksgemeinschaft* and were considered a racial betrayal, a *Rassenschande*.[99] Marriages between Aryans and non-Aryans, primarily aimed at Jews but including Blacks and Roma and Sinti, were no longer possible after the Nuremberg Laws.

The regime did not go so far, however, as to annul existing marriages, likely for fear of social discontent. These couples, in which most commonly the husband was Jewish and the wife non-Jewish, numbered by some assessments around 35,000 in 1933.[100] Having a non-Jewish spouse offered some legal protection, but such marriages were not without their own tensions. The fact that men lost their jobs and status led in some cases to depressions and put even more stress on marriages. Decades later, Dennis Berend remembered how this affected his family, whose "morale was steadily broken ... One wrong word led to a quarrel ... The relationship between my parents was no longer as peaceful as it used to be. We were short of money and then finally we were short on food."[101] For some couples, these external tensions led to divorce, which held the promise of reintegration into the majority society for the non-Jewish spouse but could spell death for the Jewish partner.[102]

Whereas the Nazi imagination connected family, state, and race, Baeck envisioned the family as a counterweight to the power of the state. In a 1932 essay published in the *Jewish Welfare and Social Politics* journal under the title "State, Family, Individuality," he warned that "in our time, the

---

[98] For an overview of the Nazi policy toward the family, see Lisa Pine, *Nazi Family Policy, 1933–1945* (Oxford: Berg, 1997); Gisela Bock drew attention to the ways in which women were victims of Nazi body politics, see Gisela Bock, *Zwangssterilisation im Nationalsozialismus: Studien zur Rassenpolitik und Frauenpolitik* (Opladen: Westdeutscher Verlag, 1986). It would be wrong, however, to treat German women as lacking agency, see Claudia Koonz, *Mothers in the Fatherland: Women, the Family and Nazi Politics* (New York: St. Martin's Press, 1988); Lora Wildenthal, *German Women for Empire, 1884–1945* (Durham, NC: Duke University Press, 2001).

[99] Stefanie Schüler-Springorum, "Gender and the Politics of Anti-Semitism," *The American Historical Review* 123, no. 4 (2018): 1210–22.

[100] Büttner, "The Persecution of Christian-Jewish Families in the Third Reich."

[101] Quoted in Meyer, "The Mixed Marriage," 59.

[102] Meyer, "The Mixed Marriage"; Evan Bukey, *Jews and Intermarriage in Nazi Austria* (Cambridge: Cambridge University Press, 2010); Nathan Stoltzfus, *Resistance of the Heart: Intermarriage and the Rosenstrasse Protest in Nazi Germany* (New Brunswick, NJ: Rutgers University Press, 2001).

Vulnerable Existence 99

dominant violence of the state increases almost everywhere," adding that every form of government that aimed for absolute state power, from Plato's Republic to modern figurations, was a direct attack on the family. Only the "rooted energies [*Kräfte*] of independence and character" could withstand the state's power, and their source, the root of one's life, was the family.[103] Just as Judaism was the *Kraft* against the *Macht* of state power, the family could have a similar positive effect.

Baeck's pastoral letter in 1935 was meant to give Jews pride in their heritage, perhaps also to those who realized that after the Nuremberg Laws they were legally defined as Jews. But it was not just a celebration of Judaism, but also a recognition of the pain felt by members of the community. Near the end of the letter, Baeck brought together a verse from the Psalms with part of the Kaddish prayer: "'See, He does not sleep nor slumber, He, who guards Israel [Ps. 121:4]. He, who makes peace in His high places, He will make peace for us and all Israel.' [Kaddish]."[104] With few exceptions, interpreters of this Psalm claimed that the guardian of Israel was God, who neither sleeps nor slumbers. The divine providence remained with the people of Israel, a point Baeck himself made in an essay about the *Shekhinah*, the divine presence that accompanied the Jews into exile after the destruction of the Temple.[105]

By connecting this Psalm with the Kaddish prayer, Baeck was calling the people to stand before God in defiance against the atrocities of the world. The Kaddish is a doxology that begins with the words "Magnified and sanctified may His great name be," but its melancholic tone would not have been lost on Baeck's listeners. Although several forms and functions of the Kaddish are present in Jewish liturgy, since the twelfth and thirteenth century CE this prayer has been strongly associated with rites of mourning. Mourner's or Orphan's Kaddish (*kaddish yatom*) is recited at the grave, during the first year of mourning, and during the yearly commemoration (*Yahrzeit*) even among Jews who are otherwise not very observant.[106]

The juxtaposition of the Psalm with the Kaddish thus served as an encouragement – God was still with the people – and as a moment of reflection on the pain and losses experienced. It was with this association that Baeck ended the *Hirtenbrief*: "Mourning and pain fill us. Silently,

---

[103] Leo Baeck, "Staat, Familie, Individualität (1932)," *Werke* 3, 173–74.   [104] Baeck, "Kol Nidre."
[105] Leo Baeck, "Zwei Beispiele midraschischer Predigt (1925)," *Werke* 4, 178–79.
[106] Andreas Lehnardt, *Qaddish: Untersuchungen zur Entstehung und Rezeption eines rabbinischen Gebetes* (Tübingen: Mohr Siebeck, 2002), 277–305.

100 The Jewish Imperial Imagination

through moments of silence before our God, we want to express that, which fills our soul. More urgently than any words could, this silent devotion will speak."[107]

We do not know what effect Baeck's *Hirtenbrief* had or to what extent it was read in synagogues that day. It is highly unlikely that it was widespread. The Gestapo realized the subversive potential of Baeck's text and ordered that it "should not be read in any way, anywhere or at any time. Destroy it."[108] Baeck and his colleague Otto Hirsch were promptly arrested and released after several days. Even if Baeck's pastoral letter did not reach its intended audience, the *Hirtenbrief* reads as an attempt at protest and consolation without explaining away the suffering and loss experienced by Jews in Germany. At a dark moment for Jews in Germany, Baeck insisted that standing before God, gazing to the beyond like Grünewald's John the Baptist, was the only certainty available to Jews.

---

[107] Baeck, "Kol Nidre."
[108] In a surviving telegram to the Osnabruck community, but similar telegrams were sent to all congregations. See Kulka, *Deutsches Judentum unter dem Nationalsozialismus*, 246.

CHAPTER 4

Forced Labor

Reporting for the *New Yorker* on the Eichmann trial in Jerusalem in 1961, Hannah Arendt was highly critical of the role of the Jewish Councils. "To a Jew," she wrote, "this role of the Jewish leaders in the destruction of their own people is undoubtedly the darkest chapter of the whole dark history."[1] According to her highly contested thesis, the actions of the Jewish Councils helped the Nazis in the mass murder, regardless of the Councils' intentions. Arendt explicitly named Baeck, "scholarly, mild-mannered, highly educated," implying that his approach ended with the same results as the notorious policies of Chaim Rumkowski, head of the Jewish Council in Lodz, who ruled the ghetto as King Chaim I in an authoritarian style of leadership, printed currency with his own image, and was ruthless in facilitating the transports from the ghetto to the East.[2]

In the *New Yorker* and the first edition of *Eichmann in Jerusalem*, Arendt called Baeck, in a compound of English and German, the "Jewish Führer." Gershom Scholem wrote Arendt that the decision to use the German term reserved for Hitler had "horrific connotation." It was "most false and most insulting" to describe Baeck, "whom we both knew," using the term "Führer."[3] Without overtly acknowledging Scholem's point, Arendt omitted this phrase in subsequent editions while leaving the critique of Baeck intact. In her reply to Scholem, however, Arendt offered a more nuanced reflection, arguing one should distinguish between the actions of Jewish self-help organizations and the actions committed once the Second World

---

[1] Hannah Arendt, *Eichmann in Jerusalem: A Report on the Banality of Evil* (New York: Penguin, 2006), 117.

[2] Arendt, *Eichmann in Jerusalem*, 119; for a nuanced understanding of Rumkowski, see Michal Unger, *Reassessment of the Image of Mordechai Chaim Rumkowski* (Jerusalem: Yad Vashem, 2004).

[3] Hannah Arendt, "A Reporter at Large: Eichmann in Jerusalem—III," 42; Arendt, *Eichmann in Jerusalem*, 105; Meyer, *Rabbi Leo Baeck*, 247n14; Gershom Scholem, "Letter to Hannah Arendt," in *On Jews and Judaism in Crisis: Selected Essays*, ed. Werner Dannhauser, trans. John Mander (Philadelphia: Paul Dry, 2012), 302–3.

102 The Jewish Imperial Imagination

War began, or no later than the start of systematic annihilation in 1941. Earlier actions are understandable, "only later does it become highly problematic."[4]

Arendt's distinction between the two periods is important but insufficient. To understand Baeck in this period, one first needs to address the changing Nazi policies against the Jews, and the ways in which the Jewish sphere of action was being limited. This chapter therefore begins by describing the development of the Nazi genocidal policies and Baeck's actions in the dark years from 1938 until 1943. Even in this period, Baeck continued to be productive intellectually, and the center of my analysis is a 1200-page manuscript he co-wrote on the legal position of the Jews throughout history. The composition's background remains a matter of scholarly debate, but there are good reasons to maintain that it was written for Nazi authorities. The text, I contend, offers a rare glimpse into Baeck's engagement with Nazi imperial imagination under extreme conditions of intellectual forced labor.

Shifting Landscapes

The unification of Germany in 1871 under Prussian leadership left many Germans disappointed. A particular version of the German imperial imagination before and after unification envisioned a greater German state that included all Germans. First and foremost, such a view conceived Austria as part of a Greater German Empire (*Großdeutsches Reich*), but it also encompassed the eastern territories that were deemed German.[5]

The quest for a Greater German Empire reached new heights with the Anschluss, the annexation of Austria in March 1938, and the subsequent incorporation of the Czech Sudetenland in the Munich Agreement of September 1938. With the collapse of Austria on the night of March 11, pogroms erupted in Vienna, home to more than 90 percent of approximately 200,000 Austrian Jews. Jews were beaten and humiliated, their stores and houses plundered. The next day, members of the Austrian SA

---

[4] Hannah Arendt, "A Letter to Gershom Scholem," in *The Jewish Writings*, eds. Jerome Kohn and Ron H. Feldman (New York: Schocken Books, 2007), 468.

[5] For a contemporary usage of the term under Nazism, see Wilhelm Mommsen, "Bismarcks kleindeutscher Staat und das Großdeutsche Reich," *Historische Zeitschrift* 167, no. 1 (1943): 66–82; for postwar analyses: Mosse, *The Crisis of German Ideology*, 3; Stefan Manz, *Constructing a German Diaspora: The "Greater German Empire," 1871–1914* (New York: Routledge, 2014); Erin Hochman, *Imagining a Greater Germany: Republican Nationalism and the Idea of Anschluss* (Ithaca, NY: Cornell University Press, 2016); Mark Mazower, *Hitler's Empire: Nazi Rule in Occupied Europe* (New York: Allen Lane, 2008), 30.

Forced Labor

forced Jews to clean the streets of Vienna on their hands and knees. The profound shock, sense of betrayal, and helplessness led dozens of Austrian Jews to commit suicide by the end of the month.[6]

The change in Austria's status was swift. The country de facto ceased to exist, as expressed in its change of name. *Österreich*, which meant the Eastern Empire, was no longer. Now it became the *Ostmark*, "eastern border country."[7] In response to the Anschluss, the Reichsvertretung offered to send a delegation to Vienna with the purpose of incorporating the Austrian Jewish community under its wings. The reasoning for this idea was not provided, but there are three plausible and complementary explanations. First, this was an act of reaching out and helping the Jews in Austria, who could benefit from the experience and infrastructure established by Jews in Germany. A second explanation was practical. The Austrian Jewish community had not been dispossessed at this point and could provide much needed resources for the Reichsvertretung.

Finally, this suggestion reflected an imperial imagination in which Austrian Jews indeed belonged to Germany, just as many Germans believed Austria should be regarded as a legitimate part of a Greater German Reich. A parallel case helps understand this desire. The Saarland – a former German territory administered for fifteen years by the League of Nations following the Great War – was returned to Germany following a referendum in 1935. The Reichsvertretung greeted this development and offered the Jewish communities in the Saarland "a word of sincere bond . . . Shared is our fate once again, shared work, care, and task."[8] This idea of a shared bond and working together informed the reasons for the Reichsvertretung's request that the Jews in Austria be adjoined to it, even though, unlike the Saarland, they were never part of the Reich.

The Reichsvertretung adopted a position that would allow it to improve the situation of Jews in Germany and Austria by appealing, for practical or ideological reasons, to the imperial imagination of a Greater Reich. An

---

[6] Gerhard Botz, "The Dynamics of Persecution in Austria, 1938–1945," in *Austrians and Jews in the Twentieth Century: From Franz Joseph to Waldheim*, ed. Robert S. Wistrich (New York: St. Martin's Press, 1992), 200–2; Bruce Pauley, *From Prejudice to Persecution: A History of Austrian Anti-Semitism* (Chapel Hill: University of North Carolina Press, 1992), 279–86; Timothy Snyder, *Black Earth: The Holocaust as History and Warning* (New York: Tim Duggan Books, 2015), 77–85; Ilana Offenberger, *The Jews of Nazi Vienna, 1938–1945: Rescue and Destruction* (New York: Palgrave Macmillan, 2017), 31–38.

[7] Ruth Klüger, *Still Alive: A Holocaust Girlhood Remembered* (New York: The Feminist Press, 2001), 44–45; Victor Klemperer, *Language of the Third Reich*, trans. Martin Brady (London: Bloomsbury, 2013), 84.

[8] Leo Baeck, "Saar-Kundegebung der Reichsvertretung (1935)," *Werke* 6, 290.

SD-officer understood the Reichsvertretung's position in this light, writing that the Reichsvertretung's suggestion was meant "to complete the annexation also for their race-comrades in Austria."[9] The request was described as insolent, and "obviously to be refused."[10] The Nazi officer's fear was that "the accruing [to the RV] of, from our perspective not yet organized, Jews in Austria would lead to an obstruction of the emigration work in the Old Reich."[11] In Germany, the conflict between various government agencies led to a piecemeal process of Jewish emigration. The Nazis had different plans for Austria. Adolf Eichmann organized a centralized, streamlined process for the emigration of Austrian Jews. At its end, they were completely dispossessed and left the country. The policy proved so effective that by the end of October 1938 about 50,000 Jews emigrated from Austria.[12]

On November 9, 1938, non-Jewish Germans and Austrians attacked their Jewish neighbors. Committed Nazis and civilians alike, from members of the SA to people who never engaged in violence before, physically assaulted Jews, destroyed their property, and burnt synagogues. More than ninety Jews were murdered in the November Pogrom. The perpetrators vandalized some 7500 Jewish businesses and burnt down 267 synagogues. From big cities to small villages, violence was widespread. In the city of Breslau, the New Synagogue was burnt to the ground. The White Stork Synagogue was spared burning, but its Torah scrolls, the most sacred object in Judaism, were tossed out and burnt. Subsequently, six hundred Jewish men were arrested and sent to Buchenwald concentration camp. In the small village of Hoengen, the residents and local SA demolished the local synagogue with axes and sledgehammers. Eric Lucas remembered how "everybody tried to snatch some of the silver adorning the scrolls," while the scrolls themselves were "naked and open ... in the muddy autumn lane, children stepped on them and others tore pieces from the fine parchment on which the Law was written."[13] The violence was once again aimed not only against Jews but against Judaism, what Baeck understood as a Marcionite attempt to purify Christianity from its Jewish core.

---

[9] Kulka, ed., *Deutsches Judentum unter dem Nationalsozialismus*, 380.

[10] Kulka, ed., *Deutsches Judentum unter dem Nationalsozialismus*, 380–81.

[11] Kulka, ed., *Deutsches Judentum unter dem Nationalsozialismus*, 382.

[12] Hans Safrian, *Eichmann's Men*, trans. Ute Stargardt (Cambridge: Cambridge University Press, 2009), 14–45; Botz, "The Dynamics of Persecution in Austria, 1938–1945," 201; on the Jewish leadership's response, see Doron Rabinovici, *Eichmann's Jews: The Jewish Administration of Holocaust Vienna, 1938–1945*, trans. Nick Somers (Cambridge: Polity, 2014).

[13] Quoted in Martin Gilbert, *Kristallnacht: Prelude to Destruction* (New York: HarperCollins, 2006), 39–40.

Forced Labor

The shattered glass windows led to the Nazi euphemism Kristallnacht, the Night of Broken Glass.[14] The Nazi propaganda presented the riots as a spontaneous response to the assassination in Paris of the German diplomat Ernst vom Rath by Herschel Grynszpan, whose family was deported from Germany in October that year. In truth, the idea of a pogrom had been circulating among Nazi leadership for some time, and the violence was the product of an interplay between state propaganda and popular unrest. Jews were collectively blamed and held responsible and a fine of one billion Reichsmark was levied on the community. Thirty thousand Jewish men were arrested, many sent to concentration camps. In Regensburg, a city that could attest to nine hundred years of Jewish life by this point, Jewish men were led to Dachau concentration camp holding a sign. It read: The Exodus of the Jews.[15]

Fifteen years later, Baeck resorted to biblical imagery from the Book of Daniel to describe that night. "Far above the land of Germany," he said, "an invisible handwriting, adding word to word – three words which the Prophet had seen. The words: 'Mene, Mene, Tekel, Upharsin' which the Prophet had interpreted to mean: 'MENE, God has numbered the days of your kingdom and brought it to an end; TEKEL, You have been weighed in the balance and found wanting; PERES, your kingdom is divided and given to the Medes and Persians' (Dan. 5: 26–28)."[16] It is not clear to whom Baeck thought the writing on the wall was addressed. The most likely interpretation is that Baeck was referring here not to the Germans who would not listen to the Jewish prophecy, but to the Jews. Like Daniel in the court of Belshazzar, the Jews were able to interpret the writing on the wall. On the night the synagogues burnt, Baeck implied, Jews understood that their days in Germany were numbered.

The Reichsvertretung was transformed in the aftermath of Kristallnacht into the *Reichsvereinigung der Juden in Deutschland* (Reich Association of Jews in Germany), a Nazi controlled organization to which every racially defined Jew had to belong. The personnel of this organization remained the same as that of the Reichsvertretung, with Baeck at its helm. The Reichsvereinigung would later be tasked with helping in organizing the transports of Jews in Germany to the East. Baeck's decision to stay with his community despite multiple opportunities to emigrate doubtless

---

[14] The term Kristallnacht is attributed to Joseph Goebbels, but this cannot be ascertained. See Alan Steinweis, *Kristallnacht 1938* (Cambridge, MA: Belknap, 2009), 1–2.

[15] Gilbert, *Kristallnacht*, 35.

[16] Leo Baeck, "Excerpts from Baeck's Writings," *Leo Baeck Institute Year Book* 2, no. 1 (1957): 37.

contributed to the opinion that he was a martyr who offered spiritual and moral support to his flock at great personal risk. It is this image that turned him into the symbolic representative of Jews in Germany. Baeck was now, however, the face of a Jewish leadership that facilitated the transport of Jews to ghettos, concentration camps, and killing centers.

Women played an increasingly important role in the Reichsvereinigung, among others, because so many men were sent to concentration camps. A self-named "quartet" whose ties ran back to the Jewish Women Association during the Weimar Republic contributed to the work. Hildegard Böhme was a welfare officer for the Red Cross who until 1933 led a local chapter of the Jewish social welfare office. Cora Berliner was a scholar of social work and a leader of the department of emigration in the Reichsvereinigung. Paula Fürst, formerly a teacher in the Montessori method, became responsible for all the Jewish schools in Germany. Her romantic partner Hana Karminski headed the social welfare department of the Reichsvereinigung.[17] In a postwar speech reflecting on the April Boycott, Baeck praised the work and courage of German-Jewish women in this period, naming Karminiski as an example alongside Martha Hirsch, the wife of his friend Otto Hirsch.[18] None of them survived the Holocaust.

The Imperial Imagination of the Second World War

Richard Overy called the Second World War the "last imperial war." The German invasion of Poland on September 1, 1939, was in his view a struggle for territory and influence, deriving from envy and a desire to replace the remaining empires of Britain and France. It developed into a global affair once the Axis countries realized that their imperial ambitions would not be secured without invading the Soviet Union, in the case of Germany, and attacking the United States, in the case of Japan.[19]

Treating the Second World War as an imperial war touches on the question of historical continuities. Scholars debate whether there was a

---

[17] Gudrun Maierhof, *Selbstbehauptung im Chaos: Frauen in der jüdischen Selbsthilfe 1933–1943* (Frankfurt am Main: Campus Verlag, 2002).

[18] Leo Baeck, "Bewährung des deutschen Judentums (1953)," *Werke 6*, 396–97; Meyer, *Rabbi Leo Baeck*, 114.

[19] Richard Overy, *Blood and Ruins: The Great Imperial War, 1931–1945* (London: Penguin, 2021), 11–12; Gerhard Weinberg, *A World at Arms: A Global History of World War II* (Cambridge: Cambridge University Press, 2005); Reto Hofmann and Daniel Hedinger, "Axis Empires: Towards a Global History of Fascist Imperialism," *Journal of Global History* 12, no. 2 (2017): 161–65, and the articles in this special issue.

Forced Labor 107

historical line that led from German colonialism in Africa, especially the genocide of the Herero and Nama, to the Holocaust, for example, through certain concepts and military and cultural traditions. At stake are contested questions such as the Holocaust's uniqueness, the definition of genocide, and the memory of atrocities.[20] The continuity thesis is important in understanding the development of the German imperial imagination. Although it is hard to prove when it comes to German colonialism in Africa, the search for continuities holds more promise for the question of the German imperial imagination of central and eastern Europe.[21]

The East, as discussed in previous chapters, played a role in the German imperial imagination of the Kaiserreich, and as a result also among German-Jewish thinkers. In Baeck's imperial imagination, the East was ripe for colonization. His view of such settlements was agricultural and spiritual; it would be an opportunity for Jews to leave the artificiality of urban centers while spreading the monotheistic ethical message. As such it was an idea of self-improvement and missionizing, but Baeck stressed that it was to be done with *Kraft* and not *Macht*, that is to say without violence.

In Nazi Germany, the imperial imagination of the East turned into violent fantasies of total subjugation and annihilation. The Greater Germany the Nazis had in mind was connected to their view of the East – from Poland and in some visions all the way to the Ural region deep in Russia – as a German *Lebensraum*, or "living space," a term coined by the geographer Friedrich Ratzel in 1897. The East for the Nazis was a

---

[20] Steffen Klävers, *Decolonizing Auschwitz?: Komparativ-postkoloniale Ansätze in der Holocaustforschung* (Oldenbourg: De Gruyter, 2021).

[21] Supporters of the continuity thesis include Jürgen Zimmerer, *From Windhoek to Auschwitz: On the Relationship between Colonialism and the Holocaust* (London: Taylor & Francis, 2011); Benjamin Madley, "From Africa to Auschwitz: How German South West Africa Incubated Ideas and Methods Adopted and Developed by the Nazis in Eastern Europe," *European History Quarterly* 35, no. 3 (2005): 429–64; Shelley Baranowski, *Nazi Empire: German Colonialism and Imperialism from Bismarck to Hitler* (Cambridge: Cambridge University Press, 2011); Hull, *Absolute Destruction*; Mazower, *Hitler's Empire*; critiques in Birthe Kundrus, "Colonialism, Imperialism, National Socialism: How Imperial Was the Third Reich?," in *German Colonialism in a Global Age*, eds. Bradley Naranch and Geoff Eley (Durham, NC: Duke University Press, 2015), 330–46; Dan Michman, "The Jewish Dimension of the Holocaust in Dire Straits? Current Challenges of Interpretation and Scope," in *Jewish Histories of the Holocaust: New Transnational Approaches*, ed. Norman Goda (New York: Berghahn Books, 2014), 17–38; Robert Gerwarth and Stephan Malinowski, "Hannah Arendt's Ghosts: Reflections on the Disputable Path from Windhoek to Auschwitz," *Central European History* 42, no. 2 (2009): 279–300; Kuss, *German Colonial Wars and the Context of Military Violence*.

108   The Jewish Imperial Imagination

space to be tilled and colonized for the sake of the German *Volk*. To realize this *Lebensraum*, space had to be brutally colonized in the name of expansion and assertion of racial hierarchy.[22]

The imperial context of the Second World War highlights continuities of the German imperial imagination. Yet this argument does not sufficiently answer the question as to the special role of Jews in the Nazi imperial imagination.[23] When Hitler and Goebbels spoke about Jews as bolshevists and capitalists alike, this was not a simple contradiction. It points to the Nazi imagination in which Jews, as the ultimate enemy, were everywhere. The Holocaust was in this sense not another instance of colonial genocide. Rather, it was a genocide perpetuated throughout an entire empire that expanded its borders for the sake of mass murder, not for the sake of expansionism alone.[24]

With the Nazi occupation of western Poland, some two million Jews came under Nazi control. Although a systematic program of killing was not yet formulated, many were brutally murdered. Even more died in the ghettos, which concentrated and isolated Jews, as well as Sinti and Roma. Malnourishment and epidemics were the result. It is estimated that around 800,000 Jews were murdered in the ghettos of Eastern Europe.[25] Germany conquered much of Western Europe in 1940, most notably France. About three million more Jews would come under German rule with the attack on the Soviet Union in June 1941. The rapid advance of the German army in the Soviet Union was accompanied by mobile killing squads (*Einsatzgruppen*) whose task was to kill Jews alongside the progress of the army. It is in the context of this systematic annihilation by shooting that the establishment of the death camps and the decision for the Final Solution took place.[26]

---

[22] Pascal Grosse, "What Does German Colonialism Have to Do with National Socialism? A Conceptual Framework," in *Germany's Colonial Pasts*, eds. Eric Ames, Marcia Klotz, and Lora Wildenthal (Lincoln: University of Nebraska Press, 2005), 115–34; Woodruff Smith, *The Ideological Origins of Nazi Imperialism* (Oxford: Oxford University Press, 1986), 146, 218–24; Ben Kiernan, *Blood and Soil: A World History of Genocide and Extermination from Sparta to Darfur* (New Haven: Yale University Press, 2008), 31–33, 422–32.

[23] For this type of critique, see Roberta Pergher and Mark Rosman, "The Holocaust: An Imperial Genocide?" *Dapim: Studies on the Holocaust* 27 (2013): 42–49; Doris Bergen, "Imperialism and the Holocaust," *Dapim: Studies on the Holocaust* 27 (2013): 62–68; Michman, "The Jewish Dimension of the Holocaust in Dire Straits?."

[24] Pergher and Rosman, "The Holocaust: An Imperial Genocide?" 48; Gerhard Weinberg, "Some Myths of World War II," *The Journal of Military History* 75 (2011): 703. Jeffrey Herf, *The Jewish Enemy: Nazi Propaganda during World War II and the Holocaust* (Cambridge, MA: Belknap, 2006).

[25] Michman, *The Emergence of Jewish Ghettos during the Holocaust*, 61–89.

[26] Bergen, *War and Genocide*, 153–59.

Forced Labor 109

In Germany, there were no ghettos, but the conditions of the Jews continuously worsened, with a stream of legislation constantly curtailing their lives and narrowing the sphere in which they could move in public. Victor Klemperer, a professor of Romance languages at Dresden Technical University until his dismissal by the Nazis as racially Jewish, reflected in his diary about the "worst day for the Jews during those twelve years of hell." He concluded it was in September 1941, when they were ordered to wear a visible yellow Star of David inscribed with the word Jew. The yellow star was a humiliating act that marked Jews as a potential target for verbal and physical violence. Klemperer refused to let his non-Jewish wife walk with him on the street for fear that she would suffer because of his identification as a Jew.[27]

Klemperer also noted that there were a few people who, meaning well, made small gestures such as whispering to him words of disagreement with the regime.[28] Such small acts of kindness were meaningful for Baeck, who preferred to emphasize them. According to a story related by Eva Reichmann, Baeck told a Gestapo officer that he was not afraid to walk the streets of Berlin with the yellow badge. Some strangers, Baeck said, would make risky small gestures, smuggling a cigarette, a chocolate, or an apple to his pocket or quickly shaking his hand.[29] This story not only positions Baeck as someone who could answer a Gestapo officer with defiance. Its broader implication is that even amid totalitarianism, there was still hope that some people would exercise their agency against the regime. This point was crucial for Baeck when he came to think about the questions of guilt and responsibility in the aftermath of the Holocaust.

Jewish emigration from the Greater German Reich was severely limited with the outbreak of the war and completely prohibited in October 1941. Soon after, transports from Germany to ghettos, concentration camps, and killing centers began. By his own admission, Baeck knew the meaning of the transports, but he chose to remain silent, fearing that it would do no good and would only lead people to despair and suicide. There might be still some hope, he thought, for those in the East.[30] This difficult decision was not merely a political decision. Rather, it reflected the premium that Baeck's thought, from the *Essence* onward, placed on Judaism as a religion of optimism and hope.

---

[27] Klemperer, *Language of the Third Reich*, 171–72.
[28] Klemperer, *Language of the Third Reich*, 172.
[29] Reichmann, "A Symbol of German Jewry," 25.
[30] Eric Boehm, "A People Stands Before Its God: Leo Baeck," in *We Survived: Fourteen Histories of the Hidden and Hunted in Nazi Germany* (New Haven: Yale University Press, 1949), 288–90.

110   The Jewish Imperial Imagination

Also consistent with his earlier understanding was Baeck's condemnation of violent resistance to the Nazis. When the communist group around Herbert Baum set an anticommunist exhibition on fire in 1942, Baeck apparently said there was nothing the Jewish community could do for them and that it was "pure madness" from the beginning. His reasoning might have been pragmatic. He assumed there would be retaliation and indeed, the Nazi reaction was swift. Two hundred fifty Jews were executed and 250 more deported.[31] Baeck's rejection of violence and his aversion to bolshevism as apostasy likely also played a role in his reasoning. Pragmatic, justified fears were in line with Baeck's understanding of Judaism.

Baeck's decisions during this period were an attempt to come to terms with the Nazi antisemitic, violent, imperial imagination that viewed Jewish existence as a danger that needed to be addressed by increasingly radical means from legal restrictions to annihilation. In his actions, Baeck showed continuity and consistency with his earlier views of Judaism as a religion of optimism, spiritual energy, and the steadfastness of a minority facing adversity. One way to assess whether such a view could properly confront Nazi genocidal politics depends on whether one accepts Arendt's controversial judgment of the Jewish Councils.

Arendt's claim in her letter to Scholem about the difference between self-help and collaboration provides a helpful starting point. In this interpretation, Baeck's actions as the head of the Reichsvertretung were justified, whereas his action as the head of the Reichsvereinigung were not. There are several reasons, however, not to follow this neat distinction. First, it is historically inaccurate to lump together the Reichsvereinigung with the Jewish Councils established in occupied territories. For Jews in Germany there was no alternative course of action and no national partisan movement. The woods in the land of the perpetrators held no promise of resistance. Furthermore, the character of the population must be taken into account. At that point, many German Jews had already emigrated. Those who stayed behind were often those who could not leave; they were aged, ill, and in need of care. The idea that they would have been better off unorganized or that they could have rebelled is tenuous at best.[32]

[31] Arnold Paucker, "Resistance of German and Austrian Jews to the Nazi Regime 1933–1945," *The Leo Baeck Institute Year Book* 40, no. 1 (1995): 3–20; Avraham Barkai, "Im Schatten der Verfolgung und Vernichtung: Leo Baeck in den Jahren des NS-Regimes," in *Leo Baeck, 1873–1956: Aus dem Stamme von Rabbinern*, eds. Fritz Backhaus and Georg Heuberger (Frankfurt am Main: Jüdischer Verlag, 2001), 93.

[32] Barkai, *From Boycott to Annihilation*, 154; Beate Meyer, *A Fatal Balancing Act: The Dilemma of the Reich Association of Jews in Germany, 1939–1945*, trans. William Templer (New York: Berghahn Books, 2013), 122.

Forced Labor

Finally, there is an argument specific to Baeck's actions. In contrast to his active presence in the Reichsvertretung, starting in 1939, Paul Eppstein, a sociologist who was a member of the Reichsvereinigung and later the head of the Council of Elders in Theresienstadt, took over the everyday management. "There are hardly any traces in the files," writes the historian Beate Meyer, "of activity by the chair, Leo Baeck, during the time of the deportations," although there is evidence that he participated in the meetings, including those with Eichmann.[33]

Meyer describes the impossible dilemmas of the Reichsvereinigung as "a fatal balancing act." Working under these conditions was a tightrope walk to oblivion. This "fatal balancing act" is an apt metaphor not only for Baeck's activities as a leader, but also for his scholarly work in this period and the unpublished manuscript that was to be his lengthiest intellectual labor.

A Contested Manuscript

In a 1949 text published by Eric Boehm, Baeck first mentioned the existence of a manuscript he coauthored with Leopold Lucas, and Hilde Ottenheimer, describing how an official in the Ministry of the Interior suggested to him that a history of German Judaism's "contribution to European civilization" might support the "lenient group" among the Nazis. The secretaries for the project were Paula Glück and Johanna Nathan.[34] In a 1955 interview in London with Robert Weltsch and Hans Reichmann, Baeck further claimed to have stood in contact with the German conservative resistance. In this context, he said, a suggestion was made that "a book on the development of the position of the Jews in Europe should be written for the information of the public after liberation."[35] Baeck referred in this context to his contacts with some members of the conservative elite, most notably the former mayor of Leipzig, Carl Goerdeler, who was executed following the failed attempt of July 20, 1944, to assassinate Hitler.[36] A copy of the manuscript, titled *The*

---

[33] Meyer, *A Fatal Balancing Act*, 122; see also Barkai, "Im Schatten der Verfolgung und Vernichtung," 94–99.

[34] Boehm, "A People Stands Before Its God," 289. Another manuscript mentioned Peter Freund, about whom no information was found. See Fritz Backhaus and Martin Liepach, "Leo Baecks Manuskript über die Rechtsstellung der Juden in Europa: Neue Funde und Ungeklärte Fragen," *Zeitschrift für Geschichtswissenschaft* 50 (2002): 58.

[35] Hans Reichmann, "The Fate of a Manuscript," *The Leo Baeck Institute Year Book* 3, no. 1 (1958): 362.

[36] Peter Hoffmann suggests that traces of the *Legal Position* are present in Carl Goerdeler's memorandum "The Aim." See Peter Hoffmann, *Carl Goerdeler and the Jewish Question, 1933–1942* (Cambridge: Cambridge University Press, 2011), 113. This conjecture, however, is not based on any direct quotes or evidence from correspondence. "The Aim" also contains

112 The Jewish Imperial Imagination

Development of the Legal Position of Jews in Europe, Primarily in Germany from Antiquity to the Beginning of the Age of Enlightenment (hereafter *Legal Position*), was found behind a cupboard in his apartment after Baeck passed away. It is now housed at the Leo Baeck Institute in New York. Baeck assumed it was the only copy to have survived, but since then two more copies emerged, one in Frankfurt, another in the military archive in Prague.[37]

Less than a year after Baeck's death, Robert Weltsch asked two scholars to assess the first volume and the last one, which served as a summary of the entire project. The reviewers were Richard Koebner, a professor of history at the Hebrew University of Jerusalem and formerly a professor in Breslau until his dismissal by the Nazis, and Max Eschelbacher, Baeck's successor as a rabbi in Düsseldorf who emigrated to London after the November Pogrom and likely met Baeck there regularly after 1945. Both told Weltsch that the work was unsuitable for publication. Eschelbacher expressed genuine confusion. Some sentences, he insisted, simply could not have been written by Baeck and the text might have been reworked by a "foreign hand." Furthermore, the distinction between Jewish and non-Jewish authors in the text – the former were marked in the text with a J for *Jude* – was highly problematic. Finally, the treatment of the rise of Nazism in the manuscript suggested to Eschelbacher that it likely was not meant for the resistance.[38]

Documents revealed by Hermann Simon in 2001 shed light on the composition history.[39] Known as Aktennotizen K, these official memoranda from Berlin's Jewish community archives cover the timeframe from September 1941 to October 1942. They show that a "scientific work about

---

numerous antisemitic suggestions, such as the placement of Jews in Ghettos and the prohibition of mixed marriage. See Backhaus and Liepach, "Leo Baecks Manuskript über die Rechtsstellung der Juden in Europa," 68.

[37] Leo Baeck, Leopold Lucas, and Hilde Ottenheimer, "Die Entwicklung der Rechtsstellung und des Platzes der Juden in Europa, vornehmlich in Deutschland vom Altertum bis zum Beginn der Aufklärung" (Berlin, n.d., likely 1941–1942), Leo Baeck Collection, AR 66, folder 3/54, Leo Baeck Institute. Also Varia I (boxes 20–22), Prague Military Archive.

[38] Robert Weltsch, "Baecks Buch über die Rechtsstellung der Juden in Europa," April 25, 1957, Rabbi Leo Baeck Collection, LBIJER 104, series III, folder 12, Leo Baeck Institute Jerusalem. Max Eschelbacher, "Leo Baeck, Ueberblick über die Entwicklung der Rechtsstellung der Juden in Europa, vornehmlich in Deutschland. Die Entwicklung der Rechtsstellung und des Platzes der Juden in Europa, vohrnelmnlich in Deutechland, vom Altertum bis zum Beginn der Aufklärungszeit" (London, May 7, 1957), Rabbi Leo Baeck Collection, LBIJER 104, series III, folder 12, Leo Baeck Institute Jerusalem.

[39] Hermann Simon, "Bislang unbekannte Quellen zur Entstehungsgeschichte des Werkes die Entwicklung der Rechtsstellung der Juden Europa, vornehmlich in Deutschland," in *Leo Baeck, 1873–1956: Aus dem Stamme von Rabbinern*, ed. Fritz. Backhaus and Georg Heuberger (Frankfurt am Main: Jüdischer Verlag, 2001), 103–10.

Forced Labor

the history of the Jews in Europe" was discussed in the Reich Main Security Office (RSHA) headquarters in meetings between officers and the representatives of the Jews in Germany. The description matches the content of the *Legal Position*. Leo Baeck, the symbol of German Jewry, claimed to have produced a scholarly work for the resistance. Aktennotizen K tell a different story.

Baeck's biographer Michael Meyer concludes that "barring further new evidence, the issue cannot be finally resolved," although he describes the mitigating position by Arnold Paucker as plausible.[40] Paucker tried to reconcile Baeck's own statements with the evidence of Aktennotizen K and the structure of the manuscript. He surmises that the request for the manuscript first came from the resistance, and the Nazis took advantage of it upon learning of its existence.[41] I do not think this position brings us closer to solving the discrepancies. First, Baeck's story is not corroborated by external evidence, at least for the time being. Second, why would the resistance contact a Jew, let alone one that was monitored by the Nazis as the leader of German Jewry, to formulate such a document? Third, given the atmosphere in Germany at the time, the resistance could not have expected such a document to be needed or received with open arms by the public even in the days after the war. Finally, it is unlikely that the production of such a scholarly work would have been a priority for this group.

Aktennotizen K clarify the structure of the manuscript, which is otherwise unclear. The *Legal Position* is comprised of five volumes. The first three volumes cover the period from antiquity to the Enlightenment, the start of the modern period to the nineteenth century, and 1830–1930, respectively. The fourth volume is titled "Jews and Judaism in the Spiritual and Religious Movements of Antiquity." The fifth volume is a summary of the work. The fourth volume is thus out of sync with a chronological work, but this is explained by Aktennotizen K, which show that this volume was requested only after the completion of the first three volumes.[42]

It is more economical to assume that the document was ordered by the RSHA. This still leaves important questions open. To begin with, why would someone in the regime want this type of work? Fritz Backhaus and Martin Liepach offer an answer that connects the manuscript to the officer

---

[40] Meyer, *Rabbi Leo Baeck*, 140.
[41] Arnold Paucker, *Deutsche Juden im Widerstand 1933–1945: Tatsachen und Probleme* (Berlin: Gedenkstätte Deutscher Widerstand, 2003), 48.
[42] K63a in Centrum Judaicum Archive, 2 B1, 3.

114 The Jewish Imperial Imagination

demanding its production. The person in question was Sturmbannführer Regierungsrat Friedrich Suhr, who, among other roles in his career, was a member of Eichmann's IV B4 (Juden) department, as well as RSHA IIA3 (Justiziar). In the latter capacity, Suhr was responsible for legal aspects of the Jewish Question. It might explain his interest in the legal position of Jews in Germany. Such a work could have served as historical background for his work by framing Nazi policy in light of a broader historical narrative about the legal status of Jews in different countries.[43] That he could appropriate the work of leading Jewish scholars would be another incentive to pursue it.

Another question concerns the pace of production. If there was no work on the text before 1941, it means the authors produced a 1200-page manuscript in less than a year, which is remarkable by any standard. This does not necessarily imply, however, a work already in progress receiving retroactive approval. Baeck had thought about Jewish history for decades and had the assistance of two able co-authors in Leopold Lucas and Hilde Ottenheimer. Their contributions dramatically accelerated the work. Leopold Lucas was an expert on Judaism in the fourth century CE and a participant in the *Outline for the Complete Science of Judaism* and Germania Judaica project, two major enterprises to document and present the achievements of Jewish scholarship on all fields of Jewish history. Lucas was up to date, in other words, with the most recent Jewish contributions to Jewish history. Less is known about Hilde Ottenheimer, who likely worked in the Reichsvereinigung's social welfare department and authored an essay, published in 1941 in *Jewish Social Studies*, on Jewish demographics from 1900 to 1938.[44]

The three authors' specialties complement each other in crucial ways. In what follows, I read the work in light of Baeck's Jewish imperial imagination, but it is important to remember not only the extraordinary circumstances under which it was written, but also that it was a collaborative effort. I could not locate drafts or correspondences between the authors on the work, so it is hard to know who wrote what. Based on their specialties, it is possible that Lucas contributed to the sections on late antiquity and

---

[43] Backhaus and Liepach, "Leo Baecks Manuskript," 63, 66.

[44] Leopold Lucas, *Zur Geschichte der Juden im vierten Jahrhundert: Der Kampf zwischen Christentum und Judentum* (Hildesheim: G. Olms, 1985); Hilde Ottenheimer, "The Disappearance of Jewish Communities in Germany, 1900–1938," *Jewish Social Studies* 3, no. 2 (1941): 189–206; Albert Friedlander, "A Muted Protest in War-Time Berlin: Writing on the Legal Position of German Jewry throughout the Centuries: Leo Baeck, Leopold Lucas, Hilde Ottenheimer," *Leo Baeck Institute Year Book* 37 (1992): 372–74.

Forced Labor 115

the early medieval period and Ottenheimer to the section on modernity. There is also evidence that Lucas prepared part of the manuscript, transcribed by his wife, that covered the legal position of the Jews in the Balkan area. This section did not make it into the final version.[45]

The stakes for Baeck's image in discussions of the *Legal Position* are high. According to Arnold Paucker, if one rejects Baeck's narrative and accepts that the manuscript was ordered by the RSHA, one must accept that Baeck's statements were "pure inventions, really a pipe dream by him. And that contradicts everything we know about Baeck and his personality."[46] One final question to explore is why Baeck would describe the manuscript in a different fashion.

There are several possible explanations. First, Baeck's available comments are summaries of interviews, which means that conflations and other potential editorial mistakes cannot be ruled out. This is especially true in the case of Eric Boehm, who edited and paraphrased the text to present Baeck's words as a first-person account.[47] Even if mistakes had occurred, however, Baeck had time to fix them in other interviews or texts. In the case of the Boehm text, he had more than six years to do so. The fact that Baeck chose to keep this presentation implies he did not see a need for corrections in the text or in later statements.

Second, despite the image Baeck conveyed, by the time of the interviews in question he was more than seventy-five years old, had survived Theresienstadt Ghetto, and left Germany for London, a complete change of scene for the elderly rabbi. He was perhaps more fragile than either he or his interlocutors realized. That is to say, he might have misremembered the order of things or talked in a nonlinear manner that caused confusion. Similar problems arise regarding Baeck's account of Theresienstadt.

Finally, there is the possibility that Baeck himself was ambivalent about the manuscript. He was likely proud of the scholarly result, as evidenced by the fact that he took his copy with him to Theresienstadt. At the same time, he might have wanted to downplay or minimize the composition history. In this reading, Baeck wanted to present the manuscript, and himself, in a positive light.

In the Nazi empire, Jewish intellectuals and experts had a role in the process of dispossession as well as in the production of knowledge. The

---

[45] Leopold Lucas, "Rechtsstellung der Juden in Bulgarien, Griechenland, Rumanien, Serbien und der Turkei" (1942), 1D Ba 1, Nr. 36, Centrum Judaicum Archive.

[46] Paucker, *Deutsche Juden im Widerstand 1933–1945*, 48.

[47] Avraham Barkai, "Manhigut Be-Dimdumei Hidalun," in *Leo Baeck: Manhigut Ve-Hagut, 1933–1945*, ed. Avraham Barkai (Jeruslaem: Leo Baeck Institute, 2000), 69–70.

116   The Jewish Imperial Imagination

Legal Position is best theorized in this context as a product of intellectual forced labor.[48] In Prague, for example, Jewish scholars and curators such as Hana Volavková sorted and catalogized a collection of Judaica objects for a future Jewish Central Museum, an institution that was to present the extinct Jewish race after the end of the war. The collection grew hand-in-hand with the destruction of the Jewish communities of the Protectorate from around 1000 objects in 1941 to 200,000 by the end of the war.[49]

In Vilna, a group of Jewish experts known as the Paper Brigade was responsible for sorting and organizing the Nazi looting of the vast Jewish libraries and collections in Vilna, including the Strashun Library, the YIVO library, the An-ski Museum, and the treasures of the city's synagogues. The scholar and former co-director of YIVO Zelig Kalmanovitch was further tasked with leading a team of Jewish scholars that produced various scholarly works, including a bibliography and translation relating to the Karaite community, a historical overview of Lithuanian Jews from the Middle Ages, and a detailed account of the art and history of the Zarecha Jewish cemetery. The Nazi scholar Herbert Gotthard then reworked their research and gave it antisemitic tones in line with the Nazi imagination. Kalmanovitch noted the bitter irony of writing history at the time of destruction of the community. The Germans, he wrote in a diary entry from August 1942, "want to know the height of the mountain that they have leveled."[50]

Scholarly analysis of such case studies has focused on elements of resistance and agency. In Vilna, the Paper Brigade worked with smugglers and partisans to hide and rescue rare Jewish manuscripts that were otherwise likely to have been destroyed. In Prague, Volavková described the work of the museum's staff, of which she was the sole survivor, as courageous in that it tried to present Judaism in a respectful way under

---

[48] I thank Doris Bergen for pointing out this possibility. On the production of colonial knowledge as interplay between colonizer and colonized, see Siraj Ahmed, *Archaeology of Babel: The Colonial Foundation of the Humanities* (Stanford: Stanford University Press, 2018); Peter Gottschalk, *Religion, Science, and Empire: Classifying Hinduism and Islam in British India* (New York: Oxford University Press, 2013); David Chidester, *Empire of Religion: Imperialism and Comparative Religion* (Chicago: University of Chicago Press, 2013).

[49] Dirk Rupnow, "From Final Depository to Memorial: The History and Significance of the Jewish Museum in Prague," *European Judaism: A Journal for the New Europe* 37, no. 1 (2004): 142–59; Dirk Rupnow, *Täter, Gedächtnis, Opfer: Das "Jüdische Zentralmuseum" in Prag 1942–1945* (Wien: Picus, 2000).

[50] Quoted in David Fishman, *The Book Smugglers: Partisans, Poets, and the Race to Save Jewish Treasures from the Nazis* (Lebanon, NH: University Press of New England, 2017), 137.

Forced Labor

such adverse conditions.[51] She further argued after the war that the idea of collecting the items came from the Jewish community. A different account, notes Dirk Rupnow, attributed the genesis of this collecting to the SS.[52] As in the case of the *Legal Position*, the origins of the idea for the museum are contested, likely because there was a fear that this type of intellectual forced labor would be perceived as collaboration.

My argument that the *Legal Position* was not written *for* the resistance does not mean it is not a work *of* resistance. Treating it as intellectual forced labor highlights the conditions under which it was written and allows a move beyond the dichotomy of resistance or collaboration. Moments of subversion in the manuscript are rare, and at most take the form of omissions or refusal to engage, rather than outright counterhistory. That is explained through the precarious situation of its authors.

Thinking about the *Legal Position* as intellectual forced labor also means taking seriously the potential risk to the authors' well-being, as well as paying attention to the more technical aspects of the scholarly enterprise. Jews, for example, were no longer allowed to borrow books from the State Library, which meant Suhr had to approve loan requests. The authors received permission by Suhr, however, to continue to use the library of the *Lehranstalt für die Wissenschaft des Judentums*.[53] Baeck and his co-authors utilized various sources, including a remarkable array of Jewish authors. This is true not only with regard to primary sources, such as Josephus, Philo, or Glikl of Hamlen, but also anthologies and collections complied by contemporary Jewish authors such as Fritz (Yitzahk) Baer's first part of *Die Juden im christlichen Spanien* (1929) and a variety of secondary sources, most prominently the Jewish histories of Graetz and Dubnow.[54] All these authors were distinctly marked with the letter J.

The reliance on Jewish authors clearly irritated Suhr, who demanded that "primarily German authors" be consulted.[55] For both parties, German authors meant Aryan authors. Suhr's demand was only partly heeded. The section on "The Jews in Brandenburg-Prussia," for example, relied heavily on the first two volumes of the German-Jewish historian Selma Stern's *The*

---

[51] Hana Volavková, "The Jewish Museum of Prague," in *The Jews of Czechoslovkia: Historical Studies and Surveys*, ed. Avigdor Dagan, Gertrud Hirschler, and Lewis Weiner, vol. 3 (Philadelphia: Jewish Publication Society, 1984), 569, 576–77.

[52] Rupnow, *Täter, Gedächtnis, Opfer*, 62–69.

[53] K44, April 25, 1942; K46, May 21, 1942; K51, June 24, 1942. Simon, "Bislang Unbekannte Quellen," 105–6.

[54] See the bibliographies: Baeck et al., "Rechtsstellung," I.318–31, II.280–90, III.269–81.

[55] K50, June 20, 1942, in Simon, "Bislang unbekannte Quellen," 106.

118 The Jewish Imperial Imagination

Prussian State and the Jews. Stern managed to leave to the United States in 1941 on the last ship before emigration was stopped. There she was instrumental in the founding of the Leo Baeck Institute after the war.[56]

In his demand to incorporate German authors, Suhr had in mind articles from *Forschungen zur Judenfrage* (Research on the Jewish Question).[57] This journal was published by the Research Department on the Jewish Question at the Reich Institute for History of New Germany. The Institute's mission was to infuse the National Socialist perspective into historical research. Alongside historical explorations of antiquity, the journal also contained essays on Jews in German literature, philosophy, and culture, alongside studies of specific characters such as Benjamin Disraeli, Karl Marx, Baruch Spinoza, Kurt Tucholosky, and Walter Rathenau.[58] It was this type of scholarship Baeck and his co-authors had to engage as they wrote under persecution.

Colonies and Motherland

The *Legal Position* began with a programmatic statement: "Jewish settlements outside the motherland" could be dated at least to the sixth century BCE.[59] These settlements expanded dramatically at the time of Alexander the Great. Some Jews, according to the *Legal Position*, settled as soldiers, having received land after finishing their service. By presenting Jewish diaspora as emerging from the imperial army, the authors reject the antisemitic canard of the Jew as cowardly.[60] Whereas the text is straightforward, the footnotes offer an insight into the authors' engagement with Nazi scholarship.

Cited in support of the discussion of the Jewish settlements was an article from the *Forschungen zur Judenfrage*, titled "World Jewry in Antiquity." World Jewry (*Weltjudentum*) was itself an antisemitic trope that called to mind the presence of Jews everywhere. Victor Klemperer

---

[56] Irene Aue-Ben-David, *Deutsch-jüdische Geschichtsschreibung im 20. Jahrhundert: Zu Werk und Rezeption von Selma Stern* (Göttingen: Vandenhoeck & Ruprecht, 2017).

[57] See K52, July 2, 1942, in Simon, "Bislang unbekannte Quellen,"106; Baeck et al., "Die Rechtsstellung," III.18, 64.

[58] Reinhard Markner, "*Forschungen zur Judenfrage*: A Notorious Journal and Some of Its Contributors," *European Journal of Jewish Studies* 1, no. 2 (2007): 395–415; Dirk Rupnow, *Judenforschung im Dritten Reich: Wissenschaft zwischen Politik, Propaganda und Ideologie* (Baden-Baden: Nomos, 2011), 67–85.

[59] Baeck et al., "Die Rechtsstellung," I.2.

[60] After the Holocaust, Baeck kept this position, interpreting the etymology of *Iwri* (Hebrew) as related to "soldier." See Leo Baeck, "Epochen der jüdischen Geschichte (1956)," *Werke* 5, 242, 247.

Forced Labor

wrote in his diary in 1933 how *Weltjudentum* became an increasingly widespread word, marking the Jews in Germany as opponents to the Germans like their counterparts in France and England.[61]

"World Jewry in Antiquity" was written by Karl Georg Kuhn, who taught oriental languages and the history of Judaism in Tübingen and promoted the antisemitic study of the Jewish Question as an academic discipline. He distinguished in the article between Palestinian and diasporic Greco-Roman Jewry. The former had a "healthy national structure" whereas the latter was manifestly different and tended to assimilate into the culture without giving away their religion, a cause for resentment among the local populations. Only the diasporic Jews survived in Kuhn's telling and they came to pose the Jewish problem.[62]

The *Legal Position* did not elaborate Kuhn's position but by referencing it and insisting on the warrior-like nature of diaspora Jews, Baeck and his co-authors rejected Kuhn's distinction between diasporic and national Jews. In the *Legal Position*'s narrative, the Jewish soldiers established colonies throughout the ancient world. Despite the focus on soldiers, colonies stood in this context primarily for a designation of a group of people outside the homeland.

Another scholar cited in the manuscript in the context of Jewish settlements was Gerhard Kittel. In one of the earliest indictments of scholars during the Nazi era, published in 1946 in Yiddish, Max Weinreich, director of YIVO and a former student in Germany, singled Kittel as symbolizing "the beginning of the new anti-Jewish science."[63] Max Eschelbacher, for his part, was taken aback by the inclusion of Kittel in the manuscript, describing him in similar terms as expressing a Nazi way of writing the history of the Jews.[64]

Kittel, a professor of New Testament in the University of Tübingen, served as the chief editor of the important *Theological Dictionary of the New Testament* and was a frequent contributor to the *Forschungen*. More than most Christian scholars of his era, Kittel stressed the need to study rabbinic

---

[61] Klemperer, *Language of the Third Reich*, 30.

[62] Baeck et al., "Die Rechtsstellung," I.3n1; Karl Georg Kuhn, "Weltjudentum in der Antike," *Forschungen zur Judenfrage* 2 (1937): 9–29; on Kuhn, see Horst Junginger, *The Scientification of the Jewish Question in Nazi Germany* (Leiden: Brill, 2017), 159–88; Alan Steinweis, *Studying the Jew: Scholarly Antisemitism in Nazi Germany* (Cambridge, MA: Harvard University Press, 2006), 76–91; Susannah Heschel, "Jewish Studies in the Third Reich: A Brief Glance at Viktor Christian and Karl Schubert," *Review of Rabbinic Judaism* 13, no. 2 (2010): 247–49.

[63] Max Weinreich, *Hitler's Professors: The Part of Scholarship in Germany's Crimes against the Jewish People* (New Haven: Yale University Press, 2008), 40.

[64] Eschelbacher, "Leo Baeck, Ueberblick," 6.

120   The Jewish Imperial Imagination

sources to understand Christianity. In fact, until the rise of Nazism, he worked with Jewish scholars, and expressed views that would later stand in contrast with some Nazi ideas.[65]

This did not prevent Kittel from espousing antisemitic views. In 1933, shortly after the Nazis came to power, he published a speech he gave on the emergence of the Jewish Question. Kittel discussed several solutions for the Jewish Question: the murder of all Jews (senseless and impractical); the expulsion of Jews and the establishment of a Jewish state outside Europe (too pro-British and Zionism did not have the support needed among Jews); assimilation (impossible and had dire consequences for the races); and the treatment of Jews as a foreign minority with no equal rights. It was the fourth solution that he preferred and acted upon.[66]

Kittel believed Jews who converted to Christianity could still be Christians. They should not preach, however, in front of Germans. Mixing the two was an undesirable situation, just as "a Negro [*Neger*] in a white American congregation or a white in a Negro congregation." Jews who converted to Christianity, in other words, should establish their own churches, equivalent to the Black churches.[67] Kittel was aware that his position "must appear hostile" to Jews. He nonetheless sent a copy of his work to Martin Buber, whom he met three years earlier in a conference on the Jewish Question. Buber, of course, rejected Kittel's position and his pernicious claims about the influence of Jewish doctors, lawyers, and businessmen on German society.[68]

Kittel's articles cited in the *Legal Position* argued that Jewish colonies were an example of Jewish otherness, racially and sociologically.[69] Turning

---

[65] Awaiting his de-Nazification trial, Kittel's apologia after the war included references to his relation to Jewish scholars and his support for Jewish Christians. See Gerhard Kittel, *Gerhard Kittels Verteidigung: Die Rechtfertigungsschrift eines Tübinger Theologen und "Judentumsforschers" vom Dezember 1946*, eds. Matthias Morgenstern and Alon Segev (Wiesbaden: Berlin University Press, 2019); Matthias Morgenstern, "Erwägungen zur 'Verteidigung' Gerhard Kittels vom Dezember 1946," *Theologische Beiträge* 51 (2020): 260–71. See also Robert Ericksen, *Theologians Under Hitler: Gerhard Kittel, Paul Althaus, and Emanuel Hirsch* (New Haven: Yale University Press, 1985), 28–78; Gerdmar, *Roots of Theological Anti-Semitism*, 417–530.

[66] Gerhard Kittel, *Die Judenfrage* (Stuttgart: Kohlhammer, 1933), 13.

[67] Kittel, *Die Judenfrage*, 71.

[68] Martin Buber, *Briefwechsel aus sieben Jahrzehnten*, ed. Grete Schaeder (Heidelberg: Lambert Schneider, 1972), II.486–88; Junginger, *The Scientification of the Jewish Question in Nazi Germany*, 135–57.

[69] Baeck et al., I.9; Gerhard Kittel, "Die Entstehung des Judentums und die Entstehung der Judenfrage," *Forschungen zur Judenfrage* 1 (1937): 43–63; Gerhard Kittel, "Das Konnubium mit Nicht-Juden im antiken Judentum," *Forschungen zur Judenfrage* 2 (1937): 30–62. A 1941 article by Kittel is cited. See Baeck et al., I.4n5; Gerhard Kittel, "Die Ausbreitung des Judentums bis zum Beginn des Mittelalters," *Forschungen zur Judenfrage* 5 (1941): 290–310.

to the term colonies to describe Jews outside Palestine, he claimed that what distinguished the Jewish colonies, the diaspora, from other colonies, for example, those of the Egyptians, was their staunch refusal to assimilate. "The Jew," Kittel wrote, "remains what he is across peoples and centuries."[70] What he called the legalistic casuistry of World Jewry – the same antisemitic trope as Kuhn's – was for Kittel the consequence of an attempt to circumvent "the extermination of intermarriage" posed by Ezra and Nehemiah.[71] Whereas Ezra and Nehemiah tried to keep the race pure, the combination of intermarriage and Jewish proselytizing led according to Kittel to racial mixture. The ghettoizing of Jews in the medieval period brought an end to these interrelations, but after a thousand years of endogamy, when the Jews left the ghetto in the modern period, they were already a new, "second order," impure race.[72]

To a reader like Suhr, the references to Kittel and Kuhn served as an assurance that the *Legal Position* was in line with Nazi scholarship. Yet the references to this type of antisemitic scholarship was used to support a point Baeck had made already in the *Essence* about Judaism's appeal in antiquity. Converts to Judaism "were not a few," according to the *Legal Position*, and "the spiritual and social connections that were created this way are to be deemed not inessential."[73] Further consistent with Baeck's comments in the *Essence* was the claim that Hellenistic Judaism was able to combine the insights of Greek philosophy with the Bible while still maintaining its particularity, unlike many other cultures under Hellenism. In Baeck's imperial imagination, this powerful combination of Greek and Jewish – but unlike Paul, Hellenistic Judaism did maintain Jewish particularity – was, among other things, what made Jewish missionizing in antiquity attractive and effective.[74] Baeck cited scholars like Kittel and Kuhn for support on the fact that Jews were successful missionizers. What he left unsaid was their interpretation of this fact on racial terms, as well as his own interpretation of this conversion as propagation of ethical monotheism.

In the *Legal Position*, as a text concerned with rights, Jewish dispersion informed discussions of the Jewish right to autonomy. The Jewish colonies were described as legal entities that were recognized by the Romans as

---

[70] Kittel, "Die Entstehung des Judentums," 48.   [71] Kittel, "Das Konnubium," 41.
[72] Kittel, "Die Entstehung des Judentums," 48–50; Kittel, "Das Konnubium," 30, 45, 61. On the discourse about the "purity" of Jewry qua Semitic race, see John Efron, *Defenders of the Race: Jewish Doctors and Race Science in Fin-de-Siècle Europe* (New Haven: Yale University Press, 1994), 20–22.
[73] Baeck et al., "Die Rechtsstellung," I.10.   [74] Baeck et al., IV.121, 125–26.

"corporations" or "private associations," just like those of foreign merchants. Jewish communities had certain legal rights such as religious freedom and the voluntary jurisdiction over civil matters according to Jewish law.[75] In a 1940 unpublished lecture at the Lehranstalt in Berlin titled "The Development of the Talmud," Baeck emphasized the uniqueness of this arrangement. Jewish colonies were governed by Jewish, not Roman, law and without the support of police or state-apparatus.[76]

The question of Jewish autonomy resurfaced in the discussion of the early modern period in the *Legal Position*. When Jews started to resettle in Germany in the eighteenth century, this autonomy returned "as of old and everywhere," and was similar to that of foreigners living in Prussia.[77] The claim that Jewish communities enjoyed autonomy throughout the majority of their existence on German soil was of political relevance. The *Legal Position* argued for a historical precedence and a long tradition in favor of the right of autonomy and self-management of the Jewish community. Put differently, the dissolved Reichsvertretung as a self-governing Jewish organization was more in line with historical developments in Germany than the state-supervised and state-controlled Reichsvereinigung.

To talk about Jewish colonies was also to talk about a Jewish motherland. Kuhn and Kittel claimed that after the destruction of the Second Temple, Jerusalem lost its power as a political center, but instead of dissipating, it was transformed from an earthly political and religious center into a future-hope. It was in this condition of lacking a homeland (*Heimatlosigkeit*) that Jews lived in exile.[78] Jews, in other words, lived in colonies but without a homeland. They had no home to return to, but were also not assimilating, a situation that Kittel found illogical and disturbing.

The motherland in this context was Palestine. The *Legal Position* expressed the relation between motherland and colonies in antiquity by noting that the Jewish settlements "stood in relation to the homeland [*Heimatlande*] and were recognized by Roman officials" as Jewish colonies, for example, through the yearly Temple tax, the half shekel.[79] The colonies kept their legal autonomy but they often consulted with and appealed to authorities in the motherland, a further sign of the connection between the two.[80]

---

[75] Baeck et al., "Die Rechtsstellung," V.1–6.

[76] Leo Baeck, "Die Entwicklung des Talmud" (Lehranstalt für die Wissenschaft des Judentums, Berlin, June 5, 1940), 1D Ba 1, Nr. 36, Centrum Judaicum Archive, 8–9.

[77] Baeck et al., "Die Rechtsstellung," II.52.   [78] Kittel, "Die Entstehung des Judentums," 47–48.

[79] Baeck et al., "Die Rechtsstellung," V.2; Baeck, "Die Entwicklung des Talmud," 7.

[80] Baeck et al., "Die Rechtsstellung," I.15.

Over the years, Baeck saw more and more value in Jewish settlement in Palestine. In the mid-1920s, for example, in texts published both by Keren Hayesod, a fundraising organization for Jewish settlement in Palestine, and a journal of Liberal Judaism, he called for Liberal Judaism to play a more active role within the Zionist movement.[81] This was not an obvious position. Baeck's friend Claude Montefiore, president of the World Union of Progressive Judaism, saw Liberal Judaism and Zionism as incompatible and was concerned by Baeck's pro-Zionist tendencies. He ended a 1931 letter to Baeck with the plea that Baeck "[r]emain a staunch Liberal, and do not become too Zionistic or even too semi-Zionistic. We Liberals need you."[82]

Baeck praised Zionism in the *Legal Position* as the "idea and longing to establish a Jewish polity in the land of the fathers, in Palestine." This "idea and longing of a national rebirth" served as the "strongest, most lively energy [*Kraft*]" in the rejection of assimilation. Zionism was further described as a movement celebrating youth. It was an "inner revolution," which included willingness to sacrifice and often-heroic labor.[83] Like Baeck's missionizing Judaism, and in line with Baeck's comments in the 1930s, Zionism used *Kraft* and not *Macht*. Its justification was spiritual and creative, not violent and coercive. Suhr and other Nazi readership would have missed this point, central to Baeck's philosophy of Jewish minority. Yet the distinction shows that Baeck maintained some of his earlier views about Jews and their place in the world. He did so now in a much more implicit way given the context in which he was writing.

Jewish Difference

Nowhere is the predicament of writing as intellectual forced labor more evident than in the *Legal Position*'s treatment of Jewish difference. The penultimate section in volume three, concluding the historical presentation, is titled "Antisemitism." It described the rejection of Jews as a central motif of nineteenth-century politics in Europe and enumerated several factors for the perceptions of Jewish difference, including national, economic, social, religious, and implicitly racial reasons. Many of these

---

[81] Leo Baeck, "Das Palästinawerk (1926)," *Werke* 6, 464–67; Leo Baeck, "Stellung des religiös-liberalen Judentum zum Zionismus (1927)," *Werke* 6, 468–69.

[82] Claude Montefiore to Leo Baeck on February 20, 1931, DBa 1, Nr. 26, 63–64, Centrum Judaicum Archive.

[83] Baeck et al., "Die Rechtsstellung," III.266–67.

124   The Jewish Imperial Imagination

themes were present in earlier discussions, and here they were brought to the forefront in a short summary of the rise of modern antisemitism.

The rise of capitalism, the authors wrote, created financial difficulties for craftsmen and old nobility alike. Jews had "quickly acquired wealth, with an eye toward the fallen properties" and were "among the ranks of the capitalists, whom the oppressed and burdened knew to position themselves against."[84] Jews had, according to the *Legal Position*, "unusual, abnormal, and unhealthy" occupational patterns, which throughout the centuries "intentionally or unintentionally" concentrated on small commerce and money markets. This positioned some Jews to lead the fields of commerce and banking when these emerged.

Such comments could be read as replicating the antisemitic stereotypes of the Jew as worshipping mammon. The claim that Jews "almost appeared," "intentionally or unintentionally," to control fields such as banking might suggest a polemic, namely, that this was incorrect, and in any case involuntary.[85] This cannot be read merely as counterhistory, nor was it simply the result of the need to write for a Nazi audience. Rather, it shows once more a certain convergence, as this position was consistent with Baeck's political imagination before the *Legal Position*, expressed, for example, in his reserved attitude toward the metropolis during the Weimar Republic. At the same time, the tone might have been influenced by the context of writing for a Nazi audience.

A sociological argument was also used to explain Jewish political affiliations. The authors argued that politically, while most Jews remained liberal, "not few from the so-called intelligentsia" moved in the direction of socialism. This move was the result of their disenchantment with the liberal parties or personal tendencies, not something inherent to them or Judaism.[86] Here, too, one could locate a convergence between Baeck's rejection of bolshevism and the content of the *Legal Position*. Whereas in 1933 Baeck could still argue that a bolshevist Jew was an apostate, this type of argumentation no longer held when it was addressed to readers like Suhr in the early 1940s.

The forced character of Jewish vocational patterns was a recurring motif in the *Legal Position*. From its very first pages, the text mentions on multiple occasions that in antiquity Jews had the same professions as the

---

[84] Baeck et al., III.254.
[85] Baeck et al., III.255. A similar position was expressed in a Reichsvertretung memorandum from 1934. See Otto Dov Kulka, ed., "Denkschrift an die Reichsregierung zur gegenwärtigen Situation der Juden," in *Deutsches Judentum unter dem Nationalsozialismus*, 120.
[86] Baeck et al., III.145.

Forced Labor

majority of society for large swaths of their existence.[87] Jewish "almost monopoly" in the field of moneylending was a result of the Church's strict restrictions on their livelihood, which pushed Jews toward professions available to them such as commerce. It was not something Jews desired, but since laypeople and rulers needed loans, this task was imposed upon Jews.[88]

The economical limitations were tied to theological othering. The late medieval Church, the authors wrote, strove for homogeneity and determined the will to be different as heresy. Jews were seen as "the most prominent others, the exception. They stood from the outside, in a different religion, a different culture, and religion and culture were synonyms at the time."[89] This othering of Jews defined their legal status in the medieval period as negotiated between Church and king, the latter often being the guarantor of Jewish rights. After the Peace of Westphalia (1648), Christian minorities or foreign communities, say Protestants in France or Huguenots in Prussia, were also recognized as colonies, just as the Jewish community had been. Jews in this sense became not an exception but a model.[90] By turning to these examples, the authors of the *Legal Position* provided a historical precedent that showed the potential to tolerate difference in the European world.

Christianity as it developed throughout the centuries "thought itself to be" the single, true religion.[91] This "thought itself to be," like the "intentionally or unintentionally" could be read as a muted protest beneath the surface of the *Legal Position*. The Church was imagined as the cause of Jewish othering. If someone was to be blamed for Jewish vocational patterns, it was neither Jews nor the state. Rather, Christian perception led to marginalization of the Jews. This was the problem, not the relation between Jews and the imperial power.

In creating a historical image in which the Church – rather than the crown to which Jews most often belonged – was responsible for the condition of the Jews, the authors tried to avert arguments that there were grounds for discrimination of the Jews. Jews and Judaism in this historical imagination had no qualms with governments or regimes, and had enjoyed

---

[87] See, among others, Baeck et al., "Die Rechtsstellung," I.20–21, I.40–41, I.51, I.55–56, I.87–89.

[88] Baeck et al., I.176–77, V.26. On the association between Jews and usury, see Penslar, *Shylock's Children*, 17–18; Jerry Muller, *Capitalism and the Jews* (Princeton: Princeton University Press, 2010), 15–33; Julie Mell, *The Myth of the Medieval Jewish Moneylender*, vol. 1 (New York: Palgrave Macmillan, 2017).

[89] Baeck et al., "Die Rechtsstellung," II.176.   [90] Baeck et al., "Die Rechtsstellung," II.14–16.

[91] Baeck et al., "Die Rechtsstellung," III.254.

126 The Jewish Imperial Imagination

many communal and individual rights under the Roman Empire. This type of narrative tried to cater to the Third Reich's self-perception as the rightful heir of Rome.[92] Succeeding the Roman Empire, the *Legal Position* implied, also meant granting autonomy to the Jewish community.

The greatest unease when reading the *Legal Position* today comes from its discussion of the category of race, which appears in several key places in the work. It should be noted from the outset, however, that race played no significant role in Baeck's thought, unless it was used with clearly negative connotations, such as in his critique during the Weimar Republic of the infatuation with blood or the connection he made between Gnosticism and racism. Official announcements of the Reichsvertretung and Reichsvereinigung, his more scholarly work, and personal letters contain very little discussion of race otherwise.[93] But if the *Legal Position* is considered a document produced for the RSHA, the need to include race becomes evident. In the pages of *Forschungen zur Judenfrage*, for example, the category of race was prevailing, and Baeck and his co-authors might have felt forced to include at least brief references to the subject.

Race was not the main category of analysis in the *Legal Position*. Only at the end of the summary of the first volume, dedicated to Jews in antiquity and the Middle Ages, there is a comment about the "foreignness [*Fremdheit*]" of the Jews, which "presented itself also through the body-type ... Their Mediterranean-Near Eastern bodily constitution gave the impression of otherness [*Andersartigkeit*], which could come forth also in the spiritual and emotional sphere."[94] This was a use of a racialized language, but the text quickly clarified that differences were based not just on nature (*das Geborenen*) but also on nurture (*das Erworbene*), or natural and acquired traits. The vocational conditions of the Jews, along with hereditary characteristics, influenced physical formation. Race, however, did not account for the legal position of the Jews in the Middle Ages, which is attributed to the Church.

---

[92] Johann Chapoutot, *Greeks, Romans, Germans: How the Nazis Usurped Europe's Classical Past*, trans. Richard Nybakken (Berkeley: University of California Press, 2016), 229–84; Julia Hell, *The Conquest of Ruins: The Third Reich and the Fall of Rome* (Chicago: University of Chicago Press, 2018), 307–400.

[93] The Jewish race scientist Wilhlem Nußbaum used Baeck's name in 1933 to gain support for his Working Group for Jewish Hereditary Research and Care. It is likely that Nußbaum exaggerated Baeck's endorsement of the project. Baeck did write, however, a recommendation for Nußbaum in which he praised him as one of the foremost authorities on Jewish race research. See Veronika Lipphardt, *Biologie der Juden: Jüdische Wissenschaftler über »Rasse« und Vererbung 1900–1935* (Göttingen: Vandenhoeck & Ruprecht, 2008), 283–86, 296.

[94] Baeck et al., "Die Rechtsstellung," I.316–17.

A different approach to race is present in the second volume, which dealt with the period of the Enlightenment to the 1830s. The *Legal Position* defined this era as a struggle between Enlightenment and Romanticism. Baeck worked within a similar framework already in his critique of Prussia in the aftermath of the Great War. The former was characterized by an emphasis on natural law, universalistic tendencies, and mercantilism; the latter identified the law in the tradition, stressed the particularistic elements of the nation, and saw in the state an all-encompassing organic development of a people. This struggle between the two intellectual forces was described as giving way to a "new, even more comprehensive principle, fully exclusive and without compromise, that of race."[95] The text does not expand on this issue further. Yet what it achieved through this comment was to historicize the category, not treating it as a given and irrefutable fact of nature, but instead showing how race was a latecomer in the history of ideas.

The section in volume three titled "Antisemitism" contains the most detailed discussion of race. The rise of antisemitic parties in the nineteenth century was, according to this narrative, the result of various factors that coalesced different groups with varying interests through a shared "racial sensibility [*Rassenempfinden*]." "The development of a race-theory [*Rassen-Theorie*] and the formation of a racial teaching [*Rassenlehre*]" moved this sensibility from the unconscious into the conscious realm, as a demand on a people to act.[96] Race in this part of the text was a latent power already-in-existence. The rise of the Nazi party in the aftermath of the Great War was a rise of "*völkisch* consciousness in Germany" and the party's position against the Jews "was strengthened and sharpened by the [fact] that Jews in these fateful years had leading positions in the radical socialist and the communist parties. From this time the National Socialist German Worker's Party grew, which, primarily based on racial teaching, made the exclusion of the Jews a national task."[97]

What the authors managed to avoid in their discussion of Jews in antiquity was no longer possible when it came to the modern period. Jews were described in the "Antisemitism" section of the *Legal Position* as a foreign group in the middle of the nation and as free-spirited, frivolous, and temperamental. Some Jews, the text added, turned to think and write in the manner of the feuilleton, a popular modern form of journalism that was said by antisemites such as Heinrich von Treitschke to be inauthentic and superficial.[98] As Paul Reiter puts it, Treitschke's critique of the

---

[95] Baeck et al., "Die Rechtsstellung," II.268; Baeck, "Heimgegangene des Krieges (1919)," 287–88.
[96] Baeck et al., "Die Rechtsstellung," III.257.   [97] Baeck et al., "Die Rechtsstellung," III.260.
[98] Baeck et al., "Die Rechtsstellung," III.254–55.

128   The Jewish Imperial Imagination

feuilleton was similar to that of fast food: "Tasty, easy to obtain, and cheap, it proved hard to resist."[99] The feuilleton was thus a symbol of modern and unhealthy Jewish influence.

The critique of feuilletonist thinking in the *Legal Position* was a critique of the lack of Jewish substance. The choice of words was harsh, likely the result of the need to produce a manuscript for Nazi eyes. Yet in a sense the idea was consistent with Baeck's belief that Jews could always reach out for their spiritual resources. The promise of modernity, the authors wrote, led Judaism to lose itself and its ideas became alienating for many Jews. This left Judaism on unstable ground and many Jews became spiritually uprooted, converted to Christianity, or assimilated in the majority culture at the expense of their own tradition.[100]

The *Legal Position* argued that Judaism seemed doomed to disappear, but did not. The end of the historical presentation, a section at the end of volume three titled "Revival of Judaism," described how Judaism found itself again. The tide turned, for Jews as for other people. With the rise of historical cognition, "the past was discovered and thus the foundation of the present was gained . . . They began to reject assimilation, which wanted to grasp their inner-most being; the desire arose for the particular [*das Verlangen nach dem Eigenen*]," which in turn led to multiple renewal efforts in social and religious life.[101] Zionism, the *Legal Position* concluded, united all these renewals together, understanding itself as part of a historical continuity of Judaism and its aspiration for social duty, self-help, and national renewal of the Jewish people on its historical soil.

Based on ideas of struggle (*Kampf*) and task (*Aufgabe*) that had guided Baeck's understanding of Judaism's spiritual struggle as a minority among the people in the *Essence*, Zionism emerged in the *Legal Position* as Judaism's champion, leading the charge in the "historical struggle" for the whole of Judaism. The historical survey ended on a hopeful note: "every true great task is bound to remain above all in its certitude." With this, the authors both complied with presenting the otherness of the Jew in Nazi thought and at the same time asserted that Judaism had not ceased to exist due to the certainty in its calling.[102]

The *Legal Position* was a work of forced labor, written under extreme conditions of precarity. In it, a minority produced its own legal history for

---

[99] Paul Reitter, *The Anti-Journalist: Karl Kraus and Jewish Self-Fashioning in Fin-de-Siècle Europe* (Chicago: University of Chicago Press, 2008), 10.

[100] Baeck et al., "Die Rechtsstellung," III.263–64; Leo Baeck, "Europa (1937)," *Werke* 6, 276–80.

[101] Baeck et al., "Die Rechtsstellung," III.265–66.   [102] Baeck et al., "Die Rechtsstellung," III.268.

Forced Labor

the oppressing majority at a time of terror and genocide. This history had to contend with the Nazi imperial imagination, while at the same time managing to maintain Jewish dignity in a way that was consistent with Baeck's earlier ideas regarding the spiritual colonizing force of Judaism. Jewish otherness was not denied but instead described as a complex structure that was influenced from forces from the outside – economical and legal factors, theological biases, and racial assumptions – as well as springing out of a sense of mission to the world.

In the production of the manuscript, the authors might have been buying themselves more time. Soon after the completion of the work, Hilde Ottenheimer was likely murdered in Riga. Leopold Lucas died in Theresienstadt in 1943.[103] Baeck arrived in Theresienstadt in January 1943, not before he "purchased" a place there, a formality that served as a façade to the legality and normality of the process.[104]

---

[103] Albert Friedlander, "A Muted Protest in War-Time Berlin," 373.

[104] Fritz Backhaus, "'Ein Experiment des Willens zum Bösen': Überleben in Theresienstadt," in *Leo Baeck, 1873–1956: Aus dem Stamme von Rabbinern,* ed. Fritz Backhaus and Georg Heuberger (Frankfurt am Main: Jüdischer Verlag im Suhrkamp Verlag, 2001), 113.

CHAPTER 5

Seeking Hope

Theresienstadt (Terezín) – about sixty kilometers from Prague – had served as a ghetto since late 1941. During its existence, it was referred to by many names, including an "exhibition camp," "elders ghetto," and "Jewish settlement area." These euphemisms denote the ghetto's overlapping functions: transit and transport, a destination for privileged groups, propaganda, and – near the end of the war – a camp for holding Jews as exchange chips in negotiations.[1] Jews from Germany with military decoration, members of annulled mixed marriages, and Jewish functionaries were among those sent to Theresienstadt under the privileged designation. Baeck arrived in Theresienstadt under this category, and his stature and designation shaped his experience even prior to arrival. He was able to bring more luggage and had the significant privilege of travelling in a compartment by himself. This stands in stark contrast with the crowdedness of wagons experienced by others.[2]

Reconstructing Baeck's imperial imagination during this period is difficult due to the paucity of evidence. He rarely spoke of his time in Theresienstadt, but some information is available in letters and interviews. An important reflection is found in "Vision and Patience," written merely three months after liberation but published posthumously in 1967. Another source of information is Baeck's introduction to H. G. Adler's monumental study *Theresienstadt: The Face of a Coerced Community*.

---

[1] Anna Hájková, *The Last Ghetto: An Everyday History of Theresienstadt* (Oxford: Oxford University Press, 2020), 11. These multiple functions led some scholars to consider Theresienstadt as a transport camp. See Peter Klein, "Theresienstadt: Ghetto oder Konzentrationslager?" *Theresienstädter Studien und Dokumente*, no. 12 (2005): 111–23. Baeck himself referred to Theresienstadt as a camp, see Baeck's forward to Hans G. Adler, *Theresienstadt, 1941–1945: The Face of a Coerced Community*, trans. Belinda Cooper (Cambridge: Cambridge University Press, 2015); Virginia Irwin, "He Appreciates the Glories of Freedom," *St. Louis Dispatch*, February 23, 1948.

[2] Boehm, "A People Stands Before Its God," 290–91.

Seeking Hope 131

While Baeck gave many lectures and talks in the ghetto, only one full text is known to have survived. It is a lecture titled "Historiography" (*Geschichtsschreibung*), dated June 15, 1944. This text therefore serves as the backbone of the following analysis. More traces of Baeck's thinking in Theresienstadt are present in a notebook found in the Jewish Museum Berlin's archive. Titled *Judentumskunde*, it contains notes of lectures Baeck gave in Theresienstadt to a small circle of friends. Covering the period between November 1943 and August 1944, lecture titles in the notebook include "Prophetism," "Martyrdom," and "Humanity." The level of detail varies. At times, notes are sparse, and look like a summary. Other times, most notably in the lecture "Prophetism," notes are thorough and some of them might reflect verbatim Baeck's statements. The notebook was written by Kurt Crohn, who served as the head of the Jewish Orphanage in Pankow and knew Baeck from Berlin. Kurt and his wife Susanne, who later transcribed the notebooks, arrived in Theresienstadt along with their daughter Renate in 1943.[3] Kurt was murdered in Auschwitz in 1944. Susanne and Renate survived the war.

A final source for Baeck's thinking is a series of postwar lectures whose content overlap with Baeck's work in Theresienstadt. In May 1946, a year after liberation, Baeck gave three talks on the German channel of the BBC. The title, "The Meaning of History," is identical to a lecture Baeck gave in Theresienstadt.[4] It is significant that not only the title but also the content of the first lecture closely correlates to the surviving "Historiography" lecture. It is therefore reasonable to surmise that "The Meaning of History" provides further evidence of Baeck's thought about history in Theresienstadt. These lectures, despite potential changes after the war, serve a supporting role in understanding Baeck's thought in this period.[5]

There were important continuities in Baeck's imperial imagination in Theresienstadt. At a time when the Nazi empire attempted to kill all Jews and establish a new world order, Baeck turned to the prophets, whom he

---

[3] On Crohn, see Inge Lammel, "Alltagsleben im Waisenhaus," in *Verstörte Kindheiten: Das jüdische Waisenhaus in Pankow als Ort der Zuflucht, Geborgenheit und Vertreibung*, eds. Peter-Alexis Albrecht et al. (Berlin: Berliner Wissenschafts-Verlag, 2008), 135–39; Leo Baeck and Kurt Crohn, "Judentumskunde (n.d.)," 2018/151/1–2, Jewish Museum Berlin Archive. I thank Aubrey Pomerance, the head of archives at the Jewish Museum Berlin, for making this document available.

[4] Elena Makarova et al., eds., *University over the Abyss: The Story behind 520 Lecturers and 2,430 Lectures in KZ Theresienstadt 1942–1944* (Jerusalem: Verba, 2004), 434.

[5] The same can be said of Baeck's lecture "The Four Stages of Life," originally published in English in 1946, which might correspond to his Theresienstadt lecture "Epochs of Life." This, however, is harder to ascertain. See Leo Baeck, "The Four Stages of Life (1946)," *Werke* 6, 421–35.

The Jewish Imperial Imagination

long regarded as encapsulating the essence of Judaism. A new emphasis was reading the prophetic message as a way of narrating history. The prophets, Baeck argued, were correct in claiming that oppressive empires would collapse and be forgotten. Ethics would prevail and humanity rise again. Baeck held to this hope also after liberation, when he reflected on the conditions that gave rise to Nazism and the meaning of Jewish engagement with Germany after the Holocaust.

The Ever-Shrinking Space

Life in Theresienstadt, Baeck wrote a decade after liberation in his introduction to Adler's *Theresienstadt*, was characterized by three factors. First, "the realm of life was replaced by the realm of death."[6] Survival was a daily struggle. Malnourishment and poor sanitary conditions led to illnesses, most notably among the elderly. More than 140,000 people passed through Theresienstadt. About 34,000 died in Theresienstadt. The fear of being transported meant feelings of precarity were prevalent. More than 87,000 people were deported from Theresienstadt to killing centers in the East. Of them, only about 4000 survived.[7]

Second, there was the problem of overcrowding. The ghetto was an "ever-shrinking space," in which "all decency withered away" and selfishness and greed ruled.[8] Truda Sekaninová, a communist lawyer from Prague, described it as "abstract art" that "became a reality": "Each square centimeter was used … and so people lived in grocery stores, in former shops. In the old shopping windows were those ancient German women, and over them hung a sign saying 'fresh meat.'"[9] Read in light of Baeck's Jewish imperial imagination, the ghetto served as a dark negative. Earlier, Baeck thought about space as vast and inviting Jewish expansion. If Jewish missionizing across the world was concerned with the spread of ethics, then the limited and overcrowded space of the ghetto led to the opposite result.

The ever-shrinking space threatened the collapse of the moral order. The psychologist Emil Utitz, whom Baeck knew in Theresienstadt, claimed shortly after liberation that the best way to stave off this greediness

---

[6] Baeck's foreword to Adler, *Theresienstadt*, xi.

[7] Adler, *Theresienstadt*, 50; Anna Hájková, "Theresienstadt," in *Enzyklopädie jüdischer Geschichte und Kultur*, ed. Dan Diner, vol. 6 (Stuttgart: J.B. Metzler, 2014), 95.

[8] Baeck's forward to Adler, *Theresienstadt*, xi; see also Leo Baeck, "Vision und Geduld (1945)," *Werke* 6, 362–64.

[9] Quoted in Hájková, *The Last Ghetto*, 63.

Seeking Hope 133

and selfishness was through the establishment of better interpersonal relations.[10] Like Utitz, Baeck believed that community and morality were still possible under these conditions. In "Vision and Patience," he wrote that "the mass pressed from everywhere, from space and time. But in it, that was the profound experience, which everyone could make, the community was continuously alive."[11]

Community was essential for survival. The constitution of a community, however, was complicated by what Baeck identified as the third characteristic of Theresienstadt, namely its heterogeneity. The transports brought many different groups into the ever-shrinking space. Czech, Austrian, German, Dutch, and Danish Jews, "people, in other words, who for generations had been distinct from one another geographically, culturally, and linguistically" now came into contact. This in turn led to jealousy, a sense of group superiority, and the decay of "any sense of a collective identity."[12] National differences were accentuated under the harsh conditions of the ghetto.

In Theresienstadt, one's sense of identity was tied first and foremost with ethnicity and date of arrival at the ghetto. Along with these factors came access to certain advantages. Czech Jews, for example, were the social elite in Theresienstadt. They were often younger and arrived earlier, thereby occupying more desirable positions, such as the kitchens. Jews from Germany and Austria, by comparison, arrived relatively late in Theresienstadt and were often older. Old people in Theresienstadt often did not work, which meant they were allotted fewer food rations. Late arrivals also slept in the worst places, those left uninhabited for a reason, such as unheated attics with no sanitation.[13] Eighty-four percent of prisoners above the age of sixty who were not deported died in Theresienstadt.[14]

Theresienstadt was also religiously heterogeneous, as the Nazi racial criteria applied to Jews who practiced Christianity. Baeck extended spiritual care to some of them as well.[15] He lectured, for example, to a Catholic group and supported lay Catholics conducting marriage ceremonies in

---

[10] Emil Utitz, *Psychologie des Lebens im Konzentrationslager Theresienstadt* (Vienna: A. Sexl, 1948), 14; see also Adler, *Theresienstadt*, 560, 576.

[11] Baeck, "Vision und Geduld (1945)," 364.   [12] Baeck's foreword to Adler, *Theresienstadt*, xi.

[13] Hájková, *The Last Ghetto*, 62.   [14] Adler, *Theresienstadt*, 252–63; Hájková, *The Last Ghetto*, 77.

[15] Avraham Barkai, "Von Berlin nach Theresienstadt: Zur politischen Biographie von Leo Baeck 1933–1945," in *Hoffnung und Untergang: Studien zur deutsch-jüdischen Geschichte des 19. und 20. Jahrhunderts* (Hamburg: Christians, 1998), 143.

Theresienstadt.[16] When asked after the Holocaust why he, a Jew, did so, he "shook his head disapprovingly" and called it a "bad question." Noting the lack of Christian clergy, he added: "Jesus was a Jew of Jews. If talking with a Jewish clergyman, a rabbi, gave them any comfort so much the better, very much the better. You know that ours is the responsibility for all the peoples of the world."[17] The language Baeck used is by now familiar: the Jewishness of Jesus and the Jewish mission in the world. Earlier, the question of Jesus' Jewishness was used in a polemical fashion, to critique scholars who tried to separate Jesus from his Jewish origins. In Theresienstadt, the same argument was used to offer support for Christians.

The support for religious groups was consistent with Baeck's belief in the moral resolve that religion could provide. After the Holocaust, Baeck reflected on the importance of faith in Theresienstadt. "Without faith, without a religious philosophy to sustain us, we would have found it impossible to maintain our sanity," he said in a 1948 interview: "Perhaps, you don't appreciate an intangible such as faith until you have lived, almost without hope, in a concentration camp. But I can testify that the hours which my doomed congregation in the concentration camp at Theresienstadt spent in prayer and study were hours of contentment, the hours of freedom."[18]

Baeck received important benefits in comparison with other prisoners. He had a private two-bedroom apartment, with desk and chairs, a proper bed, and – as the poet Ilse Blumenthal-Weiss remembered – a functioning oven for heating during the cold winters.[19] Having a place of his own increased Baeck's chances of survival. Its importance was also as an antidote against the ever-shrinking space. Such an apartment in a crowded ghetto provided a certain shield from the experience of the ghetto and the domestic space allowed him privacy, as well as the ability to foster inter-human connections.

Baeck was also fortunate to receive packages from relatives and non-Jewish friends. In addition, Baeck had family ties in the ghetto. In the Boehm interview, Baeck mentioned that three of his sisters died in

---

[16] Adler, *Theresienstadt*, 541; Jana Leichsenring, "Die katholische Gemeinde in Theresienstadt und die Berliner Katholiken," *Theresienstädter Studien und Dokumente* 11 (2004), 183; Backhaus, "'Ein Experiment des Willens zum Bösen'," 119–21.

[17] Quoted in Makarova et al., *University over the Abyss*, 192.

[18] Irwin, "He Appreciates the Glories of Freedom."

[19] Ilse Blumenthal-Weiss, *Begegnungen mit Else Lasker-Schueler, Nelly Sachs, Leo Baeck, Martin Buber* (New York: Leo Baeck Institute, 1977), 22.

Seeking Hope 135

Theresienstadt before his arrival and a fourth shortly thereafter.[20] Anna Hájková, however, shows that only two sisters died by the time of Baeck's arrival at Theresienstadt. A third sister, Elisa, survived fourteen months after Baeck's arrival, a remarkable timespan by Theresienstadt standards. A fourth sister, Anna Fischerová, survived. Baeck also had connections with nieces and grandnieces who survived the war.[21]

Another important person in Baeck's life in the ghetto was Dora Czapski, his housekeeper from Berlin. Czapski, born 1882 in Breslau, continued to serve as Baeck's domestic helper in the ghetto. "Are housekeepers so important in the larger order of things?" asks Hájková rhetorically before replying: "They are central: Czapski made possible Baeck's entire political and spiritual activity at Theresienstadt, where everyday activities in the ghetto kept people exhausted and severely limited in their spare time."[22] It was also thanks to Czapski's resourcefulness that Baeck's manuscript of the *Legal Position* was hidden among his things and brought to Theresienstadt.[23] Czapski survived the war but there is no evidence she contacted Baeck, for example when applying for reparations.[24] While I focus in this chapter on Baeck's imperial imagination during this period, it is important to recognize that Baeck's intellectual and spiritual work would not have been possible without Czapski's labor.

The discrepancy in the description of the sisters, and the lack of recognition of Czapski, demand an explanation. Hájková sees in them a way for an informed functionary to highlight his own suffering.[25] The suggestion that Baeck offered a postwar gendered narrative in which he himself occupied the central place is compelling and explains why Czapski is mentioned in interviews but never by name, evidence of a narrative based on class and gender in which the "faithful maidservant" is relegated to a secondary role.[26] Yet if this is merely a constructed narrative, why mention the sisters at all but get the details mixed up? That Baeck repeated his narrative from the Boehm interview in a private letter suggests that this

---

[20] Postcards to Robert Baeck, April 18, 1944, and May 11, 1944, in Leo Baeck Institute Jerusalem, Rabbi Leo Baeck Collection, LBIJER 104, series II, folder 7. Leo Baeck letter to Robert Baeck, August 6, 1945, Rabbi Leo Baeck Collection, LBIJER 104, series II, folder 7, Correspondences, Leo Baeck Institute Jerusalem. Some of the original correspondence is in Beit Terezin, Givat Haim Ihud; Boehm, "A People Stands before Its God," 291.

[21] Hájková, *The Last Ghetto*, 51.

[22] Anna Hájková, "Israeli Historian Otto Dov Kulka's Auschwitz Account Tells the Story of a Czech Family That Never Existed," *Tablet Magazine*, October 30, 2014, www.tabletmag.com/jewish-arts-and-culture/books/186462/otto-dov-kulka.

[23] Reichmann, "The Fate of a Manuscript," 362. [24] Hájková, *The Last Ghetto*, 51.

[25] Hájková, *The Last Ghetto*, 54. [26] Reichmann, "The Fate of a Manuscript," 362.

was not a public story but a personal memory.[27] The discrepancies about Baeck's familial ties in the ghetto are hard to explain in this regard, and perhaps can be attributed to his lack of knowledge of all his family members' status at the time. Maybe there was also shame involved in not being able to help some of them despite his position.

Along with Baeck, the transports from Germany included senior members of the Reichsvereinigung, including Paul Eppstein, who soon replaced Jakob Edelstein at the head of the Council of Elders. Baeck was appointed the honorary head of the Council, but assumed official responsibilities, as the head of the Youth and Elderly Welfare Department, only in October 1944, the month the transports from Theresienstadt to Auschwitz ended. Baeck was in constant conflict with Paul Eppstein, Heinrich Stahl, and Benjamin Murmelstein, who became the last head of the Council after Eppstein's murder by the Nazis in September 1944. Their clash was substantial, on issues such as the proper food allocation for the elderly or the beautification of Theresienstadt before the Red Cross's visit in 1944. In the case of Eppstein and Stahl, it was also a conflict of personalities and tensions dating back to their shared work in Berlin.[28]

Baeck knew, by his own account, the fate awaiting those on the transports from Theresienstadt, but he chose to remain silent. He claimed to have been informed by a Czech escapee from Auschwitz by the name of Grünberg, who approached him in 1943. There are no details of such an escape, nor is there information about someone of that description in Theresienstadt. Rather, it is more likely that Baeck, along with two dozen other people, met Vítězslav Lederer, who escaped Auschwitz and came to Theresienstadt in April 1944. In this sense, Baeck was not bearing the secret alone. The difference in the descriptions can be explained once more in line with Hájková's argument as an attempt by Baeck to present himself in a more heroic and tragic manner. Another possible explanation is the problematic nature of Boehm's interview, which purported to be a first-person account but was a paraphrase of an interview.[29]

This contested decision, regardless of the exact details, was in line with Baeck's broader understanding of Judaism as providing hope and maintaining a steadfast position in front of God. In "Vision and Patience,"

---

[27] Leo Baeck's letter to unknown addressee, April 18, 1946, in *Werke* 6, 359.

[28] For varying assessments of these tense relations in light of the agency of the Council of Elders, see Adler, *Theresienstadt*, xix; Meyer, *Rabbi Leo Baeck*, 149, 154; Hájková, *The Last Ghetto*, 52–53; Wolfgang Benz, *The Holocaust: A German Historian Examines the Genocide*, trans. Jane Sydenham-Kwiet (New York: Columbia University Press, 1999), 110–14.

[29] Boehm, "A People Stands Before Its God," 292–93; Hájková, *The Last Ghetto*, 54.

Seeking Hope

Baeck emphasized the merit of Judaism as the combination of vision, or fantasy (*Phantasie*), and patience. Patience is a force of resistance that allows one to persist; vision is a type of imagination, one that can hope for a better future. Without vision, patience becomes enslaved to the present and goes about without hope. Vision without patience, on the other hand, is mere daydreaming out of touch with the present reality.[30] "Vision and Patience" was to an extent a justification after the fact. Telling people about their fate, Baeck would have argued, could lead either to an attempt to realize a fantasy of resistance that would be futile or to the giving away of all hope that would only foster further egoism and self-interest, immoral qualities that would make life in Theresienstadt more difficult. Although one could not control the external conditions – disease, hunger, and murder – Baeck implied one could preserve internally by combining vision and patience. This emphasis on hope was also a concern of his lectures and teaching in Theresienstadt.

Athens and Jerusalem

Among the people that arrived in Theresienstadt were renowned scholars and artists, among them the pianist Alice Herz-Sommer, the composer Rafael Schächter, the philologist Maximilian Adler, and the professor of medicine Hermann Strauss. Many cultural events happened in Theresienstadt, including theater productions in German, Czech, and Yiddish, operas to the accompaniment of a piano, readings from Goethe and Herzl, chamber music, and lectures on a variety of topics, including, to cite just few examples from one week: Nietzsche, Jewish mysticism, the chemistry of food, and the value of money. As Adler put it, "everything else was in short supply, but not the enterprising spirit."[31]

Although they generally took no interest in the content of the lectures or talks, the Nazis utilized the existence of a cultural apparatus for propaganda purposes. When the Red Cross came to inspect Theresienstadt, lectures, events, and music from the "coffee house" served to create the illusion of normality. For these reasons, Theresienstadt was also used as the site of a staged propaganda film, left unused, titled *Report from the Jewish Settlement Area* but more commonly known as "The Führer Gives the Jews

---

[30] Baeck, "Vision und Geduld (1945)," 361–62; and similarly in the postwar texts: Leo Baeck, "Rede von Ehren-Grosspräsident Rabbiner Dr. Leo Baeck (1955)," *Werke* 5, 470; Leo Baeck, "Why Jews in the World? A Reaffirmation of Faith in Israel's Destiny (1947)," *Werke* 5, 519.
[31] Adler, *Theresienstadt*, 526.

138   The Jewish Imperial Imagination

a City." It was another example of forced labor, as it was directed by Kurt Gerron, a Jewish inmate who was later murdered in Auschwitz. In one scene, Baeck, wearing a yellow Star of David, is shown attending a lecture by Utitz.[32]

The participation in the cultural life in the ghetto was not available to all. Many did not get tickets, were not interested or were simply too exhausted and had more pressing life-or-death priorities. For Baeck, however, these events were clearly meaningful. In "Vision and Patience," he reflected on how people "gathered in the cold and gloomy attic of a barrack, just under the roof. There they stood, pressed close to each other, to hear a talk about the Bible and the Talmud, about Plato, Aristotle ... or about days and problems of history, about poetry and art and music, about Palestine of old and today, about the commandments, the prophets and the messianic idea." In that time, "a community arose out of the mass and the narrowness grew wide. They were hours of freedom."[33]

The most productive organizer of cultural events was Philipp Manes, a former fur trader from Berlin. Until he was murdered in Auschwitz in the fall of 1944, Manes arranged more than 500 lectures, poetry competitions, and dramatic readings.[34] While in Berlin, Manes thought Baeck an uninspiring orator, but in Theresienstadt, Baeck "had changed completely; he was easy, fluent, and pleasant to listen to ... This was how we imagined a philosopher to be, at the evening of his life, having gathered the harvest of many decades and generously giving of his wisdom."[35] In fact, Baeck quickly became one of Manes' favorite lecturers and was invited to be the speaker at the 500th event, titled "Epochs of Life." The audience, wrote Manes in his diary, listened with "bated breath ... The appreciative applause did not want to end."[36]

Alongside these more formal events, Baeck took part in semi-formal discussion groups. Edith Kramer-Freund, a German-Jewish medicine student who arrived in Theresienstadt in 1943, remembered how each member of the group would choose a topic to talk about. Baeck then led the discussion before offering final comments, which "used to be the

---

[32] Kurt Gerron, *Theresienstadt: Ein Dokumentarfilm aus dem juedischen Siedlungsgebiet (Der Fuehrer schenkt den Juden eine Stadt)*, 1944, www.ushmm.org/online/film/display/detail.php?file_num= 2703; Wolfgang Benz, *Theresienstadt: Eine Geschichte von Täuschung und Vernichtung* (München: C. H. Beck, 2013), 186–98.

[33] Baeck, "Vision und Geduld (1945)," 364.

[34] On Manes, see Adler, *Theresienstadt, 1941–1945*, 532–33; editors' introduction to Philipp Manes, *As If It Were Life: A WW II Diary from the Theresienstadt Ghetto*, eds. Ben Barkow and Klaus Leist, trans. Janet Foster (New York: Palgrave Macmillan, 2009), esp. 1–6.

[35] Manes, *As If It Were Life*, 108, cf. 91.   [36] Manes, *As If It Were Life*, 201.

Seeking Hope 139

highlight of the evening. He was so well-versed in all areas of science, art, and politics that we were all quite enthusiastic about these evenings, which belonged to the few bright spots in T.[hereseinstadt]."[37]

Baeck's erudition allowed him to lecture on various topics. There were lectures on specific philosophers such as Plato, Spinoza (a lecture so popular Baeck apparently had to repeat it), Kant, and Hermann Cohen. Other lectures dealt with general themes in philosophy such as the problem of soul and body. There were also lectures on specifically Jewish themes, including the Talmud, Jewish holidays, and the worker according to Jewish teachings. Finally, there were lectures on historical themes, covering the gamut from the emergence of Christianity to the beginning of the nineteenth century.[38]

"Historiography," the only surviving lecture, belonged to this latter category and offered a reflection on the praxis of writing history. Baeck began by defining history as concerned with the "continuation of life" as "an existence that has become aware of itself." "The basic premise of all writing of history," argued Baeck, "is that there is sense and meaning behind all manifestations and that these are subject to laws."[39] Not all peoples, he added, reached a level of historical self-consciousness. A "so-called savage is a person without historical consciousness," for whom the succession of days does not indicate such a path. Implicitly, this meant that they were to an extent less human, because according to Baeck, animals were aware of their hereditary origins, but only humans possessed historical consciousness.[40]

In claiming certain people as without history, Baeck was reproducing an imperial imagination about those who were seen in racialized terms as uneducated natives. In its weak form, the argument implied that the savage would eventually progress by themselves. In a more demeaning understanding, people without history needed to be brought to the level of the civilized. This was a justification for colonization in the name of a civilizing mission. In its most harsh expression, this was an argument that the native or savage was beyond redeeming and would never be able to reach

---

[37] Edith Kramer-Freund, "As a Doctor in Theresienstadt" (n.d.), 7, LBIJMB MM 46 ME283c, LBI Berlin Collection.

[38] Leo Baeck, "Vorträge in Theresienstadt (n.d.)," *Werke* 6, 341–42; Makarova, Makarov, and Kuperman, *University over the Abyss*, 434–35.

[39] Leo Baeck, "Geschichtsschreibung (1944)," 344; Leo Baeck, "The Writing of History," *Synagogue Review* (November 1962), 51.

[40] Baeck, 343. Baeck reiterates this point in the postwar era. See Leo Baeck, "Epochen der jüdischen Geschichte (1956)," 227–29.

140 The Jewish Imperial Imagination

historical consciousness.[41] The European imperial imagination of the savage thus played a role in Baeck's historiography even as the lecture itself was meant to provide hope by showing that empires do not last.

The organizing framework of the lecture was an account of Greco-Roman historians and contrasting them with the prophets as historians. In this, Baeck alluded to Tertullian's classical question in the third century CE: "What does Athens have to do with Jerusalem?" It can be seen as a question about the compatibility of religion with philosophy or revelation and reason.[42] In the Enlightenment, Athens and Jerusalem turned into tropes. Judaism stood for revelation, or if treated critically, an irrational religion; Athens stood for reason and universality. As Miriam Leonard notes, the distinction was created neither in Athens nor in Jerusalem, but in Africa under the Roman Empire, that is to say in an imperial context.[43] Posed this way, the implication of the distinction between Athens and Jerusalem emerges. It is a question about the ability of Jews to be part of the body politic.[44]

Ancient Greece was an important pillar of how Germans imagined themselves. During the Enlightenment, ancient Greece represented the idea of *Bildung* or self-formation by cultivating oneself as a wholesome human being. Greek art, in particular sculptures, was central as a way for the rising educated middle-class to contemplate aesthetic sensibilities that stood in contrast to contemporary aristocratic Baroque taste. Reflecting on ancient Greece also shaped German educational politics. Following the efforts of Wilhelm von Humboldt, the completion of a classical school called *Gymnasium*, along with exams in Latin and Greek, became a requirement for admission to the university. The German spirit was thus seen as kindred with, and inheritor to, the Greek spirit of antiquity.[45]

During the Wilhelmine Empire, the focus on the material culture of ancient Greece and Hellenism became part of the German imperial imagination. Excavating Olympia, and even more so Pergamon, was seen not only as a scientific mission. It was part of empire-building. After the

---

[41] Zakiyyah Jackson, *Becoming Human: Matter and Meaning in an Antiblack World* (New York: New York University Press, 2020), 5.

[42] David Novak, *Athens and Jerusalem* (Toronto: University of Toronto Press, 2019).

[43] Miriam Leonard, *Socrates and the Jews* (Chicago: Chicago University Press, 2012), 3, 7–10.

[44] Martin Kavka, *Jewish Messianism and the History of Philosophy* (New York: Cambridge University Press, 2004), 2–5; Willi Goetschel, "Tangled Genealogies: Hellenism, Hebraism, and the Discourse of Modernity," *Arion* 21, no. 3 (2014): 114; Bernd Witte, *Moses und Homer: Griechen, Juden, Deutsche: Eine andere Geschichte der deutschen Kultur* (Berlin: De Gruyter, 2018).

[45] Suzanne Marchand, *Down from Olympus: Archaeology and Philhellenism in Germany, 1750–1970* (Princeton: Princeton University Press, 1996).

Seeking Hope 141

transportation of the Pergamon Altar to Berlin, a government official could boast that Germany's museums now possessed a "Greek work of art of dimensions that are equal (or nearly) to the great rows of Attic and Asia Minor sculptures of the British Museum."[46]

In the Nazi period, relation to classical ideas and architecture was more ambivalent. Education ideologues criticized what was seen as an impractical humanistic education and several leading party members wanted to shift the focus of archeology, and scholarship more broadly, to the Germanic roots of the nation. Hitler, on the other hand, was an admirer of Greek art. This fact was utilized time and again by archeologists of Hellenism and classicists in their defense of their fields of inquiry.[47]

Given the centrality of ancient Greece in the German imagination, it is no wonder that Baeck turned to the Athens and Jerusalem distinction long before Theresienstadt. His inaugural lecture at the *Lehranstalt* in Berlin was titled "Greek and Jewish Sermons," and he returned to the topic in "Perfection and Tension," a lecture that was given in Keyserling's School of Wisdom. In these texts, Baeck traced aspects of Greek philosophy as opposed at times to Jewish thought. Heraclitus, Pythagoras, and to an extent Plato offered in his reading exclusivist philosophies. They assumed that salvation was limited to a certain group of people with unique knowledge.[48] With this, they inspired Gnosticism, which for Baeck was an opponent of Judaism. In adopting this position, Baeck presented Judaism as universal rather than particular, inverting perceptions of Judaism and Hellenism at the time.

Baeck returned to the Greeks in the *Legal Position* (1941–1942). An entire volume of this work, titled "Jews and Judaism in the Spiritual and Religious Currents of Antiquity," traced the emergence of knowledge of Greeks and Jews on one another. In a text meant to justify the position of the Jewish minority within the legal order of Europe, Baeck began by arguing that Greeks held Jews in high regard, as a faraway people of philosophers akin to the people of India.[49] Implied in this claim in the context of the *Legal Position* was the idea that Germans should also take this insight into consideration when considering the current legal status of the Jews.

---

[46] Quoted in Marchand, *Down from Olympus*, 95.

[47] Marchand, *Down from Olympus*, 341–54; cf. Chapoutot, *Greeks, Romans, Germans*; Hell, *The Conquest of Ruins*, 307–445.

[48] Leo Baeck, "Greek and Jewish Preaching," in *The Pharisees and Other Essays* (New York: Schocken Books, 1966), 113; Leo Baeck, "Vollendung und Spannung (1923)," 29–44.

[49] Baeck et al., "Die Rechtsstellung,", IV.6.

142   The Jewish Imperial Imagination

In Theresienstadt, Baeck chose once more to stress the difference between Greek and Jewish cultures. The first historian he discussed was Herodotus, "the father of Greek history."[50] The main historical question for Herodotus was the fight between Greece and Persia, or more broadly between Europe and Asia. Baeck said that it was the British "great political artistry" that, in contrast with other empires, they did not try to unite Europe and Asia but instead left "each one within its own confines, each with its own characteristics."[51]

This was not the first time that Baeck praised England. In the aftermath of the First World War, Baeck explained that the victory of England and the United States in the Great War was based on their Calvinist – and therefore with strong Jewish roots – heritage as opposed to the Lutheran tradition of Prussia.[52] If at the time this could be seen as an inner-German critique, here the praise of England could be read as providing hope, from within the ghetto, for a new world order and the victory of England.

According to Baeck, all previous attempts at unification of East and West by the power of the sword – Alexander the Great, the Mongols, the Crusades, and Napoleon – had failed.[53] The British were the only empire to understand that the two could not be united. In support of this interpretation, Baeck cited a verse from Rudyard Kipling's "Ballad of East and West": "East is East, and West is West, and never the twain shall meet." The content of Kipling's tale, not described by Baeck, involved horse stealing and a power struggle at the outskirts of the British Empire between the chieftain Kamal and a British colonel's son. At its end, the mare chooses the British colonel's son freely, there is an exchange of gifts, and a blood brotherhood is formed between him and Kamal's son, who personally escorts him back to safety.[54]

Kipling's "Ballad" exemplifies an imperial imagination in which the noble savage comes to recognize the colonizer's rights of property as if by nature. Baeck followed this British imperial imagination and did not discuss the brutalities of British colonialism, preferring instead to highlight the positive side of those fighting Nazi Germany.[55] Baeck would maintain his positive view of the British Commonwealth after liberation and his move to London, where his daughter Ruth lived.

---

[50] Baeck, "Geschichtsschreibung (1944)," 346.   [51] Baeck, "Geschichtsschreibung (1944)," 346.

[52] Leo Baeck, "Heimgegangene des Krieges (1919)," 388.

[53] Baeck, "Geschichtsschreibung (1944)," 346.

[54] Rudyard Kipling, "The Ballad of East and West," in *The Collected Poems of Rudyard Kipling*, ed. R.T. Jones (Hertfordshire: Wordsworth Editions, 1998), 245.

[55] Cf. Caroline Elkins, *Legacy of Violence: A History of the British Empire* (New York: Knopf, 2022).

Seeking Hope

Alongside Herodotus, the political history of Thucydides served another key moment in European historiography. Together, Baeck told his audience in the ghetto, the two historians completed "what history writing was to become in Europe."[56] The third Greek historian Baeck discussed was Polybius, the second century BCE historian who wrote in Greek as a captive in Rome. "Liberated outwardly," Polybius, according to Baeck, "inwardly became a captive." His mode of writing history succumbed to the victorious powers and "personifies the problem of a man from a vanquished people who surrenders himself heart and soul to the conqueror ... The defeated had written a history for his ruler." In what was perhaps a self-reflexive moment for the author of the *Legal Position*, Baeck said Polybius might have "inwardly surrendered" but his readers get the impression that he was "concealing something" or "holding back his final views."[57] Baeck's discussion of Polybius highlights the dilemmas of writing history from the margins for the imperial oppressor, a predicament Baeck knew all too well.

Polybius is important for another reason. When Polybius described Scipio looking at the ruins of Carthage – according to Julia Hell the foundational scene of Western thinking about ruins – he made the general ponder the day in which the Roman Empire itself, now victorious, would be razed as well. Ruins reflect both the power of empire, but also its end, as ruins are what remain of empires that are recognized as such by the person or community looking at them.[58] The ruins of empires played a central role in Baeck's understanding as prophetic history, to which he turned after discussing several other historians, including Tacitus and Caesar. Despite the awakening of historical awareness alongside national consciousness in the nineteenth century, Baeck claimed the great historians of the nineteenth century – including Ranke, Mommsen, and Marx – followed the contours set by the ancient historians.[59]

---

[56] Baeck, "Geschichtsschreibung (1944)," 347; see also Leo Baeck, *This People Israel: The Meaning of Jewish Existence*, trans. Albert Friedlander (New York: Holt, 1964), 165–66.

[57] Baeck, "Geschichtsschreibung (1944)," 348–49. Instead of Polybius, Baeck could have chosen another famous example that he knew well, that of Josephus. In *This People*, Josephus is contrasted with Polybius. The former remained Jewish; the latter, Baeck suggests in this postwar work, gave up his identity. See Leo Baeck, *This People*, 252.

[58] Hell, *The Conquest of Ruins*, 45–51; Alain Schnapp, "Looking at Ruins, Then and Now," in Josef Koudelka, *Ruins* (New York: Aperture, 2020), 13–17; on fascination with ruins as sources of national history, see also Margaret Aston, "English Ruins and English History: The Dissolution and the Sense of the Past," *Journal of the Warburg and Courtauld Institutes* 36 (1973): 231–55.

[59] Baeck, "Geschichtsschreibung," 354–55.

144   The Jewish Imperial Imagination

The prophets offered for Baeck an alternative to Western historiography. The claim that the prophets were historians is counterintuitive, because a prophet can be thought of as future oriented, or at least a critic of the present, whereas the historian's gaze is toward the past. Yet history, argued Baeck, drawing on the romantic author Friedrich Schlegel, was at its core backward prophecy.[60] Just like Herodotus or Thucydides, the prophets tried to find the laws of history:

> They saw how structures of power [*Macht*] were erected, and how they collapse once again. And they asked themselves: Is this history? What the power erects, and through which it legitimizes itself in order then to be overthrown by another power, is this history? And they gave the answer: that is un-history, the opposite of history.[61]

Those who sought power for its own sake would eventually fall, according to Baeck, because "power can never last when it only wants to be power."[62] That led to the collapse of empires. To adopt a prophetic mode of history against empire was to see in the ruins of empires "the great hope" and the growth of justice in history.[63] Empires crumble; edifices of power are replaced by others.

Once more, as in his thought since the Wilhelmine Empire, *Kraft* as spiritual energy was contrasted with *Macht* as power and violence. Baeck made this point in connection to the fall of empires also in other texts from the era, as well as after the war. *This People: Jewish Existence* was published a decade after the end of the Second World War (1st vol. 1955, 2nd vol. posthumously in 1957) but Baeck worked on it in Nazi Berlin, sending a draft of the first volume to Hans-Hasso von Veltheim-Ostrau for safekeeping. There we find the following description of history: "where there is striving and struggling for justice, history builds. Without this justice, history only destroys, it heaps rubble [*Trümmer*] upon the earth."[64]

---

[60] Friedrich Schlegel, *Der Historiker als rückwärts gekehrter Prophet* (Leipzig: Reclam, 1991); Michael Brenner, *Prophets of the Past: Interpreters of Jewish History*, trans. Steven Rendall (Princeton: Princeton University Press, 2010).

[61] Baeck, "Geschichtsschreibung (1944)," 352; see also Leo Baeck, "Der Sinn der Geschichte (1946)," *Werke* 5, 25.

[62] Baeck, "Geschichtsschreibung (1944)," 353.

[63] Baeck, "Der Sinn der Geschichte (1946)," 26–27; Baeck and Crohn, "Judentumskunde - Transcribed," 28.

[64] Leo Baeck, "Dieses Volk (Veltheim-Ostrau) (1943)," 22, Leo Baeck Collection; AR 66; box 1, folder 10, Leo Baeck Institute. Julia Hell distinguishes between ruins, which contain traces of the empire and its downfall, and rubble (*Trümmer*), which signifies the erasure of the conquered. See Hell, *The Conquest of Ruins*, 22, 33.

Seeking Hope 145

Without justice, history is that of violence; with it, it is a constructive enterprise.

"The Meaning of History" lectures made a similar point using the motif of ruins. The edifices of bare power became ruins, Baeck said, because they were built on nothing but the attempt to exercise power over someone else. Such structures were never constructive and cannot persist. Baeck argued that historians such as Thucydides or Tacitus were historical pessimists because they saw in the downfall of empires and the sinking of their ruins something negative.[65] Baeck saw in pessimism a danger already in the *Essence* (1905), where he identified Buddhism as a religion of pessimism and Judaism as a religion of optimism.[66] By identifying Greek historiography as pessimist, Baeck placed pessimism, clearly a negative orientation in his thought, at the heart of the Western tradition.

In a postwar lecture series on "The Epochs of Jewish History," given in the last year of his life, Baeck extended the argument about the historical pessimism of the West from Greek historians through Tacitus to Gibbon and all the way to Oswald Spengler.[67] For them, the collapse of empires singled decline, as in Spengler's work *The Decline of the West* (1918–1922). In a 1929 essay titled "World History," Baeck criticized Spengler, writing that all books that espoused historical pessimism can have "decline" in their title, because they look only at the ruins and death and read them as world-history. But this was simply the history of individual peoples; it was not world-history because world-history was about finding unity and ethical progress.[68]

The rejection of Spengler was connected to a rejection of race theory, because for Baeck world-history was tied with relation to God, and not determined by racial struggles. The foundation of religion, in Baeck's view, was that each person is created in the image of God, hence there was no superior or inferior race. In Theresienstadt, he told the small circle that included Kurt Crohn that "in nationalism or in the myth of race [*Rassenmythos*], the human receives its value through the community, to which it belongs. In the Israelite religion the community receives its meaning through the people that belong to it."[69]

The prophets were talking about the downfall of empires built to last. Only names, and sometimes not even that, remained as their memory. Yet

---

[65] Baeck, "Der Sinn der Geschichte (1946)," 26–27.
[66] Baeck, *Das Wesen des Judentums* (1905), 406.
[67] Baeck, "Epochen der jüdischen Geschichte (1956)," 232.
[68] Leo Baeck, "Weltgeschichte (1929)," *Werke* 3, 151–52; Leo Baeck, "Neutralität (1929)," *Werke* 3, 167–72.
[69] Baeck and Crohn, "Judentumskunde - Transcribed," 7.

146   The Jewish Imperial Imagination

this is not pessimism but rather an optimistic vision. Against empire, justice in history would prevail. The allusion would not have been lost on the prisoners in Theresienstadt: Nazi power, Theresienstadt, would pass away, just as others before it failed. The One-Thousand-Years Reich proclaimed by Hitler was guaranteed to become sunken ruins.

Yosef Yerushalmi suggested the term "midrash of history" to describe a way of interpreting "the impact of ongoing historical events, and the ability to endure and overcome them, to see beyond them ... It is as though history became a text, capable of interpretation through a hermeneutic that flowed naturally and unselfconsciously out of the fundamental premises of Israelite faith."[70] As a teacher of homiletics and midrash for thirty years, Baeck looked at history through this perspective. In the *Essence*, his vision of the future was that of ethical progression in which each generation "receives its due from the preceding on, and in turn passes it on, fulfilled and enriched, to the one to follow."[71] "The wisdom of Judaism," he wrote, "is that it sees life as a task imposed upon man by God. Suffering is part of that task; every creative individual experiences it."[72] What was true of the individual was true of the community.

Jewish suffering was connected to the ethical task of converting the world, the spreading of ethical monotheism, and serving as a yardstick of morality. Even in the ghetto Baeck tied it to the idea of the Jewish mission as a minority under imperial rule. In the case of minorities such as the Jews, he argued, every individual was more meaningful. It was a quantitative argument. If there were fewer people, more was asked of each one. A majority did not need legal protection, or rather it had already secured protection by a recourse to power: "[E]very right is therefore a right, which is given to the few. Only there, where there are minorities, an ideal develops, and one fights for the idea." The meaning of the few for the many was that they exposed the meaning of the

---

[70] Yosef Hayim Yerushalmi, "Toward a History of Jewish Hope," in *The Faith of Fallen Jews: Yosef Hayim Yerushalmi and the Writing of Jewish History*, eds. David Myers and Alexander Kaye (Waltham, MA: Brandeis University Press, 2013), 313; Salo Baron used a similar term, "historical midrash," to refer to the ways in which the study of the past can help with the perplexities of the present. See David Myers, *The Stakes of History: On the Use and Abuse of Jewish History for Life* (New Haven: Yale University Press, 2018), 134–35n2.

[71] Leo Baeck, *Das Wesen Des Judentums* (1905), 276; in this he might have been influenced by Hermann Cohen, see Robert Gibbs, "Hermann Cohen's Messianism: The History of the Future," in *"Religion der Vernunft aus den Quellen ses Judentums": Tradition und Ursprungsdenken in Hermann Cohens Spätwerk*, eds. Helmut Holzhey et al. (New York: Georg Olms Verlag, 2000), 331–49.

[72] Leo Baeck, *Das Wesen des Judentums* (1926), 168.

Seeking Hope 147

individual, a fight for rights developed, and this fight was also a fight for an idea and ideal.[73]

Yet how can one see messianic hope amidst destruction? In the notes taken by Crohn, Baeck diverged from interpretations, including his own in the *Essence*, that focus on the meaning of the messiah as the Suffering Servant. Instead, he spoke of the messiah as "the one who comforts [*der Tröster*]."[74] Baeck likely had in mind the comment by R. Yuden son of Rabbi Aivu about the name of the messiah: "his name is Menachem," literally he who comforts or offers consolation (Y. Berakhot 2:4).[75] The duty under persecution, in other words, was not to despair but to offer comfort. Neither was the messiah in this reading a political leader freeing the people from the yoke of foreign rule. Instead, he was the one who offered a shoulder for their cries. This theological position was consistent with Baeck's actions as a political leader and public figure, most notably his decision not to share the news about the full meaning of the transports.

Baeck ended "Historiography" by telling his audience that they lived in new days. The question was whether these new times also required a new task for historical writing.[76] The prophetic mode of writing history recognized that only certain events – the encounter with God as ethics in the world – truly mattered. Other events, such as the conquests by empires, were un-history. The historian needed in the contemporary moment was one who should be a living conscience of his people while also recognizing the universal aspect of world history. In the aftermath of the Holocaust, Baeck would turn to this idea in thinking the Jewish relation to the German people.

After Catastrophe

After the liberation of Theresienstadt in May 1945, Baeck refused an offer to be one of the first to leave, citing the need to help other survivors in need. Only in July did he move to London. Based on comments spread throughout Baeck's postwar writing, a picture emerges as to what he saw as the underlying causes of the "years of horror" or the "terrible ordeal," as he

---

[73] Baeck and Crohn, "Judentumskunde - Transcribed," 28.
[74] Baeck and Crohn, "Judentumskunde - Transcribed," 10.
[75] Writing in Nazi Berlin, Baeck referred to the etiological meaning of Noah (Gen. 5:29) as the one who comforts, noting that this was later applied to "the redeeming person of the future." Baeck, "Dieses Volk (Veltheim-Ostrau) (1943)," 23, 64–65.
[76] Baeck, "Geschichtsschreibung (1944)," 355.

148 The Jewish Imperial Imagination

called it.[77] "This disaster," said Baeck in the World Union of Progressive Judaism in 1946, "has come over mankind because the moral enthusiasm, the moral passion, were lacking."[78] The same cause, he explained in "The Epochs of Jewish History," was also at the root of the downfall of Greek culture in antiquity. There was a connecting thread, in other words, leading from the Greek view of the world to the current political moment. It was the same type of critique he expressed against historical pessimism, which led in his view to lack of acting, or to acting immorally.[79]

This critique of passivity was something that Baeck identified during the Weimar Republic as a gnostic-Marcionite strand of Protestantism. It was embedded in Christianity and took over when it forgot its ethical roots in Judaism. In a lecture in Darmstadt in 1949, Baeck argued this had been the case with the rise of Nazism. The challenge "since the days of Marcion, against whom the Old Church had to fight," was to maintain the Hebrew Bible and its ethical essence in the Church. "The years of horror, which lie behind us," Baeck connected past and present, "had made this known to whomever did not know this yet, what remains of Christianity, when it wishes to get rid of the Jewish bible."[80] Baeck could not have been more explicit. The attempt to destroy Jews and Judaism was part of a deeper historical fight, that of Christianity against itself, against its own Jewish roots.

In a letter to Gershom Scholem in 1950, Baeck explained Nazism sanctified myth "as a personification of the German Torah." "I still remember," he wrote, "how at that time its canonization was taught in German schools and universities: he is 'the totality of faith and worldview forces of the people,' to a certain extent the *plērōma* from the Epistles to

---

[77] Leo Baeck, "Das Judentum auf alten und neuen Wege (1950)," *Werke* 5, 47; Leo Baeck, "The Task of Progressive Judaism in the Post-War World (1946)," *Werke* 5, 66; Eliezer Schweid argued that Baeck's position in the *Essence* and *This People*, and therefore in between them, does not change dramatically. Eliezer Schweid, "From *The Essence of Judaism* to *This People Israel*: Leo Baeck's Theological Confrontation with the Period of Nazism and the Holocaust," in *Wrestling until Day-Break: Searching for Meaning in the Thinking on the Holocaust* (Lanham: University Press of America, 1994), 3–84; cf. Feller, "What Hope Remains?," 364–68.

[78] Baeck, "The Task of Progressive Judaism in the Post-War World (1946)," 66.

[79] Baeck, "Epochen der jüdischen Geschichte (1956)," 237; see also Baeck, "Why Jews in the World? (1947)," 515.

[80] Baeck, "Das Judentum auf alten und neuen Wege (1950)," 47. Baeck offered here an early, neglected, intervention in what later would become a debate in postwar German philosophy about Gnosticism, modernity, and Nazism. See Willem Styfhals, *No Spiritual Investment in the World: Gnosticism and Postwar German Philosophy* (Ithaca, NY: Cornell University Press, 2019).

Seeking Hope 149

the Colossians and Ephesians."[81] The term *plērōma*, lit. fullness, reveals the connection Baeck continued to see between the apostle Paul, modern manifestations of gnosis, and the myth of the Führer. Eph. 3:19, along with Col. 2:9, has been associated with groups labeled gnostic, such as Valentinus and his disciples.[82] In this reading, the gnostic love that was in Christ in all its fullness was now expressed in the Führer. This mythological escape toward a redeeming figure was left morally unchecked due to the abandonment of the Hebrew Bible.

Baeck suggested that Germany developed a kind of modern myth or political religion that displaced God. The gnostic-Marcionite tendencies in Protestantism took over during the Nazi period and attempted to extinguish the Jewish kernel of Christianity. As in gnostic teachings, it led to the rise of new and fantastic myths that were unethical and detached from reality, primarily the primacy and unity of Volk and Führer. Already in the *Essence*, Baeck contrasted Judaism with myth, and in postwar texts such as his 1956 lectures about German-Jewish figures from Moses Mendelssohn to Franz Rosenzweig, he contrasted myth with "idea." The two stood as opposites. Myth catered to the human need; the idea made a demand. Myth, because it fulfilled one's need, could easily become overestimation and self-praise; the idea put the commandment to be fulfilled in front of the person.[83]

In the "Meaning of History," Baeck argued that the strength of a community was determined by its true members, that is to say, by those who remained honest to its ethical task. Individuality was exercised through the fulfillment of ethics in the world. It was politically dangerous, warned Baeck, when one's own self-definition and worth came from a belonging to a class or a people. In this case, "fanaticism, arrogance, and chauvinism lead their struggle against the spirit."[84]

Baeck saw the gnostic-Marcionite passivity also in the silence of the bystanders. Less than a year after liberation, a B'nai B'rith publication titled *National Jewish Monthly* published "A Message from Rabbi Leo

---

[81] Leo Baeck, "Baeck to Scholem, August 22, 1950," *Werke* 6, 650–51.

[82] Elaine Pagels, *The Gnostic Paul: Gnostic Exegesis of the Pauline Letters* (Philadelphia: Fortress Press, 1975), 122, 138–39; Gershom Scholem, *Major Trends in Jewish Mysticism* (New York: Schocken Books, 1995), 45, 73.

[83] Leo Baeck, "Von Moses Mendelssohn zu Franz Rosenzweig (1956)," 174; on Baeck's earlier rejection of myth, see Baeck, *Das Wesen des Judentums* (1905), 358–59; Baeck, *Das Wesen des Judentums* (1926) 68–69, 123–24. The rejection of myth in the first edition of the *Essence* is part of Baeck's understanding of Judaism as a religion of reason. In this, and in associating Christianity with myth, Baeck is once more indebted to Cohen. See Hermann Cohen, *Religion der Vernunft aus den Quellen des Judentums* (Wiesbaden: Fourier Verlag, 1988), 159–60, 166.

[84] Baeck, "Der Sinn der Geschichte (1946)," 34.

150 The Jewish Imperial Imagination

Baeck." Baeck, who was unanimously elected as the Great President of the German Lodges of B'nai B'rith in 1924, wrote that "the whole nation participated actively in the crime against the Jewish people, took pleasure in it and sought to derive benefit from it, or condoned it and would have applauded the criminals had they been victorious."[85] There were devout Nazis, as well as those industrialists and right-wing groups who enabled them in the first place. Yet there was a much broader group of the bystanders, who were faced with the demand of the hour and failed by choosing not to act. Baeck expressed a similar position that year in an interview to the German-Jewish émigré journal *Aufbau*. He differentiated between the nobility and working class on the one hand, and the middle-class on the other. It is the latter, and in particular spiritual leaders and university professors, who "did not raise a finger or dared a word of disapproval" thereby lending their support to the regime.[86]

The question of the bystanders occupied Baeck's thought. Reflecting in London in 1953 on the April 1, 1933, boycott of Jewish businesses, Baeck called it the day of "great cowardice" in which the churches, the universities, the chambers of commerce, the courts, and even president Hindenburg, whom Baeck eulogized in 1934, remained silent.[87] By emphasizing the silence of the bystanders, Baeck insisted that the responsibility for the rise and actions of National Socialism was shared by large swaths of society.

In response to reports claiming Baeck had "forgiven" Germans upon his first post-Holocaust visit to Germany in 1948, *Aufbau* invited him to make a clear statement on the subject. He was asked in Hamburg, Baeck explained, about collective guilt and replied that while this concept could be doubted, "there may be no doubt that there is collective responsibility [*Gesamtverantwortung*]."[88] He made a distinction between personal and collective forgiveness. Personally, Baeck was willing to forgive those who did him harm. But this encompassed only harm done to him directly and was an interpersonal matter. Unlike personal forgiveness, the German

---

[85] Leo Baeck, "Eine Botschaft von Leo Baeck (1946)," *Werke* 6, 372.

[86] Leo Baeck, "Ein Gespräch mit Leo Baeck im *Aufbau* (1945)," *Werke* 6, 371; see also Baeck, "Eine Botschaft von Leo Baeck (1946)," 373; Leo Baeck, "Die Idee bleibt (1946)," *Werke* 6, 389; Leo Baeck, "Bewährung des Deutschen Judentums (1953)," 394, 397; Leo Baeck, "Gedenken an zwei Tote (n.d.)," *Werke* 5, 16. On *Aufbau*, see Peter Schrag, *The World of Aufbau: Hitler's Refugees in America* (Madison: University of Wisconsin Press, 2019).

[87] Leo Baeck, "Zum Boykott Tag (1953)," *AJR Information* (April 1973), 3; Leo Baeck, "Ansprache auf der Trauergedenkfeier für Reichspräsident Hindenburg (1934)," *Werke* 6, 211–13.

[88] Leo Baeck, "Juden und Deutsche (1948)," *Werke* 6, 376–77. Discussions about German collective guilt started shortly after the war, when Karl Jaspers spoke about the "Guilt Question." See Karl Jaspers, *The Question of German Guilt*, trans. E.B. Ashton (New York: Fordham University Press, 2001), esp. 25–40.

Seeking Hope

people as a people could not be forgiven. This type of forgiveness, Baeck wrote, was outside human purview and "it would be arrogant ... when a person would want to pass judgement that is only God's."[89]

The collective responsibility, which cannot be doubted, required recognition of the need to make amends. In an essay titled "Israel and the German People," published in the German cultural magazine *Merkur* in 1952, Baeck wrote that new institutions or a new constitution, as important as they were, were not enough without a change of heart and taking concrete action in the world. The principle that should guide the new state was that it should always be ready to ask itself if its actions made the lives of those living in it – Baeck insists on a broad definition rather than one limited to the *Volk* or citizenship – and humanity as a whole better and more humane.[90]

Baeck addressed Germans, but this argument was consistent with his view of world history as exemplified by the prophets. For its deeds to have a lasting contribution and not be a mere exercise of politics and search for power, a people needed to extend beyond itself through moral acts. "A people dies," Baeck said while still in Theresienstadt, "when the spirit and its task die in it."[91] The Nazi belief that they were realizing the German spirit was distorted in this sense because it ignored the most crucial aspect of the prophetic understanding of history, namely that the task must be ethical.

This did not necessarily mean the end of the story. A people could die, but Baeck believed it could also be reborn. Just as the downfall of a people was related to its lack of morality, so was rebirth the result of taking an ethical task in the world anew.[92] Rebirth was a theoretical option, but in the immediate aftermath of the Holocaust, Baeck was highly skeptical that the German people was up to the task. In the *Aufbau* in 1945, Baeck said that while the older generation of Germans still showed decency during the difficult time, the youth, indoctrinated under Nazism, were corrupted beyond reeducation. The hope, he said, would perhaps come from the reeducation of children six years or younger.[93]

With discussions of reparations in the 1950s, Baeck became more hopeful. In the *Aufbau*, he wrote in 1951 that the answer to Bonn's proposal of reparations should be positive. Reparations, Baeck suggested, showed some taking of responsibility, a step that is not to be underestimated. In an interview upon his first visit to Berlin that year, he did not hesitate to critique

---

[89] Baeck, "Juden und Deutsche (1948)," 375–76.
[90] Leo Baeck, "Israel und das deutsche Volk (1952)," 56–59.
[91] Baeck, "Geschichtsschreibung (1944)," 356–57; Baeck, "Der Sinn der Geschichte (1946)," 33.
[92] Baeck, "Geschichtsschreibung (1944)," 357; Leo Baeck, "Tod und Wiedergeburt (1925)," *Werke* 3, 62.
[93] Baeck, "Ein Gespräch mit Leo Baeck im *Aufbau* (1945)," 371.

the German dragging of feet on this matter, saying it was possible to recognize the violation of law (*Vergewaltigung des Rechts*) that was characteristic of the Hitler-period in contemporary German attempts to inhibit reparations.[94] In the *Merkur*, a year later, he wrote reparations were a preliminary but insufficient step that might open once more a dialogue between Jews and Germans, each with its own task toward the shared goal of a better world.[95]

Baeck's visits to Germany after the war might have made him more hopeful about the possibility of some kind of meeting between Germans and Jews. He was not the only German-Jewish intellectual to re-visit Germany in the aftermath of the Holocaust. After initially rejecting speaking invitations, Martin Buber decided to come to Heidelberg in 1950. In 1951, Buber received the recently established Goethe Prize in Hamburg, and in 1953 he accepted the Peace Prize of the German Book Trade. Especially the acceptance of the former was hotly debated in Israel, where some saw it as an exoneration of Germany and the German people. For Buber, however, this meant a show of support of the Germans who tried to reclaim the humanistic tradition of Goethe.[96]

A central site for the meeting between Jewish and non-Jewish German-speaking intellectuals was the Eranos conference in Ascona, Switzerland. A leading figure of Eranos in this period was Carl Jung, whom Baeck likely met in the 1920s in Keyserling's School of Wisdom. Jung was a supporter of the Nazi movement in its early years, but Baeck nonetheless attended the conference in 1947, lecturing about "Individuum Ineffabile." In this lecture, he argued, shortly after the Holocaust and in line with his previous positions, that morality is based on a relation to a transcendent God and cannot be grounded in nature alone, thereby once more rejecting a racialized understanding of history.[97]

Gershom Scholem, the leading scholar of Jewish mysticism, received even more prominence in the German-speaking world through his repeated participation in the meetings in Ascona. Aniela Jaffé, Jung's last secretary, asked Scholem after Jung's death why he had accepted the invitation, having known of Jung's involvement with Nazism. Scholem

---

[94] Gerhard Löwenthal and Leo Baeck, "Die Zukunft der Juden in Deutschland," *Allgemeine Wochenzeitung der Juden in Deutschland. Beilage: Der Weg - Zeitschrift für Fragen des Judentums* 6, no. 35 (August 1951): 2.

[95] Leo Baeck, "Antwort an Bonn (1951)," *Werke* 6, 377–79; Baeck, "Israel und das deutsche Volk (1952)," 56.

[96] Paul Mendes-Flohr, *Martin Buber: A Life of Faith and Dissent* (New Haven: Yale University Press, 2019), 266–78.

[97] Leo Baeck, "Individuum Ineffabile," *Werke* 5, 72–108.

Seeking Hope 153

replied that he was initially hesitant but was pacified after Baeck told him in the summer of 1947 of a conversation with Jung in which the psychoanalyst admitted to having stumbled intellectually in his support of Nazism. According to Noam Zadoff, Scholem's account does not correspond to the archival evidence, which suggests that by the time of the supposed conversation Scholem had already accepted the invitation to attend. Rather, it was likely an attempt by Scholem to maintain an ambivalent position, while also relying on Baeck's moral authority.[98]

Although there might be renewed connections between Germans and Jews, Baeck famously argued in the *Aufbau* in December 1945 that an epoch has come to an end:

> the history of German Jewry had definitely ended. The clock cannot be turned back ... A return to Germany? I see no possibility whatsoever of that for the Jews. Between the German Jews and Germany of the 1933–1945 epoch stands too much. So much murder, looting, and plundering; so much blood and tears and graves cannot be erased anymore.[99]

There might be communities of Jews in Germany, and they should be assisted, but on the whole Baeck insisted this period in Jewish history had ended.[100] On the occasion of his first visit to Berlin, Baeck sounded different. Drawing once more on ruins and rubble, a metaphor but also a reflection on the bombed city, he said that "in the few years [that have passed] there is a rebuilding on the debris [*Trümmern*] of the Jewish community" in Germany. Future, Baeck suggested, was a big word and no one knew what it would bring, but among Jews in Germany there was a lot of energy and a "will to the future" so that today "there is true Jewish communal life in Germany."[101]

Baeck himself would not return to live in Germany or take an official leadership role among its Jewish communities. Neither did he see in West Germany, let alone in the communist East Germany, a center of Jewish existence. Baeck, the proud German Jew, an army chaplain in the Great War and the leader of the Jews in Germany, turned his gaze away from his homeland.

---

[98] Noam Zadoff, *Gershom Scholem: From Berlin to Jerusalem and Back*, trans. Jeffrey Green (Waltham, MA: Brandeis University Press, 2017), 163–64.

[99] Baeck, "Ein Gespräch mit Leo Baeck im *Aufbau* (1945)," 370.

[100] On the Jewish community in Germany in the aftermath of the war, see Andrea Sinn, "Despite the Holocaust: Rebuilding Jewish Life in Germany after 1945," *The Leo Baeck Institute Year Book* 64, no. 1 (2019): 143–58; Jay Geller, *Jews in Post-Holocaust Germany, 1945–1953* (Cambridge: Cambridge University Press, 2005).

[101] Löwenthal and Baeck, "Die Zukunft der Juden in Deutschland."

CHAPTER 6

Cold War Judaism

In late 1944, the Allied Forces were already making plans for after the war. Gathered in Dumbarton Oaks in Washington, DC, were representatives of the United States, the Soviet Union, Great Britain, and later also China. They were taking preliminary steps in establishing a new world organization intended to prevent another world war – the United Nations. One perceptive observer, W. E. B. Du Bois, noted the silence in Dumbarton Oaks about the question of colonialism. The problem of the suggested world organization, Du Bois wrote in *Color and Democracy: Colonies and Peace* (1945), was that it did not amount to true participation of the colonized people, primarily people of color, in governance. In addition to the colonized, he counted also "quasi-colonials" as practically excluded from this new organization. They could in turn be divided into "free nations which are not free" because they depended on imperial tutelage and capital, as well as minorities living among other nationalities.

In discussing the latter group, Du Bois connected the plight of Blacks in the United States to that of Jews in Germany. "The greatest tragedy of this war," he wrote, "has been the treatment of the Jewish minority in Germany. Nothing like this has happened before in modern civilization ... Considering the cultural accomplishments of this group of people, the gifts they have made to the civilization of the world, this is a calamity almost beyond comprehension."[1]

This was not the first time Du Bois reflected on German Jewry. A student in Berlin in the years 1892–1894, Du Bois admired the Kaiserreich and German culture. Some of his early writings show some of the common antisemitic tropes that were common at the time, for example, in his accusations that Jews controlled the stock market. Du Bois also contrasted the positive personal interactions he had, even in Nazi

---

[1] W. E. B. Du Bois, "Color and Democracy," in *The World and Africa and Color and Democracy*, ed. Henry Louis Gates (Oxford: Oxford University Press, 2014), 278, 285.

Germany, with the treatment of Blacks in the United States, using it as a way of critiquing racial discrimination at home. Visiting Germany in 1936, however, led him to write – only after leaving, likely for fear of repercussions – that "There has been no tragedy in modern times equal in its awful effects to the fight on the Jew in Germany. It is an attack on civilization comparable only to such horrors as the Spanish Inquisition and the African Slave trade."[2]

Leo Baeck, in Theresienstadt while Du Bois was contemplating the future United Nations, had himself compared Blacks and Jews during the Nazi period. He similarly shared an interest in the question of the postwar world order. Like Du Bois, Baeck's speeches and interviews after the war show that he did not hesitate to critique the United Nations. Unlike Du Bois, however, Baeck was primarily concerned with the place of religion, and with Jewish existence, in the postwar era. In Baeck's imperial imagination in the early Cold War era, the shortsightedness of the United Nations resulted from lack of religious conviction among its members. This emphasis on religion's role in the postwar world also determined Baeck's siding with the United States against the Soviet Union. Baeck drew, in other words, on his earlier imperial imagination while adjusting to the new global politics that emerged after the Holocaust.[3]

In "Why Jews in the World?," a 1947 essay for the American magazine *Commentary*, Baeck summarized a lot of what he had to say about the Jewish task throughout the years. Jews were in the world, he answered, "as witnesses – and here every witness becomes a herald, and every herald a pioneer. They are in the world as witnesses, heralds, and pioneers of the one God."[4] Jews were witnesses, he argued already in the *Essence*, to the level of morality in the world; they served as the yardstick for morality. In a lecture in the United States in 1949, he made a connection between this idea and the Holocaust, saying that "crimes against the Jews were nearly always the worst crimes against humanity."[5] At the same time, Jews also served as pioneers, as heralds of morality, wherever they were. They were

---

[2] Quoted in Kenneth Barkin, "W. E. B. Du Bois' Love Affair with Imperial Germany," *German Studies Review* 28, no. 2 (2005): 293; see also David Levering Lewis, *W. E. B. Du Bois: A Biography 1868–1963* (New York: Holt and Co., 2009).

[3] In the case of Baeck, this means accounting for a line of thinking that dated back to the Kaiserreich. On the impact of the Weimar period among a younger generation of leading Cold War intellectuals, see Udi Greenberg, *The Weimar Century: German Émigrés and the Ideological Foundations of the Cold War* (Princeton: Princeton University Press, 2015).

[4] Leo Baeck, "Why Jews in the World? (1947)," 518.

[5] Leo Baeck, "The Interrelation of Judaism and Ethics (1949)," 138; Baeck, "Das Judentum auf alten und neuen Wege (1950)," 39–40; Baeck, *This People*, 396.

156   The Jewish Imperial Imagination

not only passive witnesses but active agents. This idea of pioneering points to a broader interpretive network of Jewish imperial imagination in which Jews functioned once more as colonizers and missionaries.

These were the reasons, Baeck suggested, that Jews existed in the world. Yet the Holocaust changed Jewish demography, as well as the global balance of power. A pressing question was not only why Jews in the world, but where in the world. Abraham Shalom Yahuda, Baeck's former colleague from Berlin who was living in the United States, expressed disappointment with Baeck's decision to settle in England. "Your place is here first," he wrote Baeck in late 1945, "and Palestine next. A man like you is destined to rescue the last remnants of our people – and your voice shall be heard."[6]

Baeck's decision to settle in London after liberation was motivated by familial reasons. This was where his only daughter, Ruth, lived. On principle, however, Baeck agreed with Yahuda's assessment of the centrality of Palestine and the United States for Jewish life. At the Hebrew Union College in Cincinnati in 1953, Baeck spoke of a threefold sphere of Jewish life: "that of historic achievement, Europe; that of solid reality, America; that of faithful adventure, Israel." Although all three were "components of the Jewish people," the temporality in Baeck's comment implied different priorities.[7] Europe was part of Jewish past but had lost its relevance for contemporary Jewish life. It was a heritage but not a current focal point. The United States and Israel became the new foci of Jewish history.

The Ellipse of Jewish Existence

The imagination of a bifocal Jewish existence in Palestine and the United States was in line with Baeck's postwar ideas about Jewish history, as is evident in his last major work, *This People: Jewish Existence*. Despite the shared theme, the two volumes of *This People* diverge in style, a testimony to their composition-history. Baeck started the first volume under the Nazi regime but published it only in 1955. Although he had revised it in important ways, a comparison with a draft from Nazi Berlin shows the final work maintained much of the structure and style, tending toward a more theological orientation, and covering primarily biblical history until

---

[6] Shalom Yahuda to Leo Baeck, December 27, 1945, Ms. Var. Yah. 38 01 158, The National Library of Israel. For Baeck's appreciation of Yahuda, see Leo Baeck, "Epochen der jüdischen Geschichte (1956)," 249; on Yahuda's life and work, see Allyson Gonzalez, "Abraham S. Yahuda (1877–1951) and the Politics of Modern Jewish Scholarship," *Jewish Quarterly Review* 109, no. 3 (2019): 406–33.

[7] Leo Baeck, "Ein Meilstein in dem Leben eines Volkes (1953)," *Werke* 6, 550.

the entry to Canaan. Baeck's central concern in this volume was the covenant and the people who receive it. The second volume, written after the war in London and published posthumously in 1957, continued historically where the first ended. Yet in its structure and style it adhered much more closely to a chronological description of Jewish history the way Baeck understood it.

Baeck offered a fourfold division of Jewish history. Yet it was not the apocalyptic fourfold of the kind one finds in the Book of Daniel or Revelation. Descriptions of destruction are few and far between. The focus instead was on the development of Judaism within the context of the different empires. Each epoch in Jewish history lasted in Baeck's description about a millennium. First, there was the era of the prophets, which Baeck dated from the Exodus until Cyrus' edict and the return from exile. The first volume of *This People* primarily covers this era.

The second era was that of the teachers, characterized by the development of the Oral Torah, the Pharisees, and rabbis. Whereas the first era was characterized by the rejection of idolatry in favor of an inward gaze, the second included for the first time intellectual and spiritual engagement with other peoples in the context of the Persian and then the Greek culture. It was the epoch of paving the way. In this era, Jewish missionizing and colonizing were widespread and successful.

The third epoch roughly corresponds to the medieval period. It began with the violent oppression of the Jews by the Roman Empire. The Christianization of the Roman Empire and the rise of Islam led to the rise of empires of belief.[8] The question Jews faced was that of choice. A decision had to be made between the kingdom of God and being part of the empires through conversion. This period ended in the late fifteenth century with the expulsion of the Jews from Spain and Portugal.

The fourth epoch started where the last one ended and continues arguably until today. It is according to Baeck the millennium in which "the most important task ... became clinging to the one hope as against the many hopes that always appeared to be so close to fulfillment."[9] Hope was a central concern for Baeck in Theresienstadt, and he pronounced it the Jewish task in the postwar era. Despite the horror of the Holocaust, Baeck insisted on hope grounded in the commandment and mystery of the One God. He called it "the one hope" and posited it against what he saw as the modern false promises of universalism, nationalism, or communism, all of which demand that the Jews sacrifice their particular relation to God.

---

[8] Baeck, *This People*, 253.   [9] Baeck, *This People*, 291.

158 The Jewish Imperial Imagination

This outline of history shows how Jewish existence and thought were developed under the aegis of empires. Each epoch of Jewish history consists of a rebirth, which involved in this context an awakening of spiritual energy within the people. It described for Baeck the reformulation of the question or demand of a people, and the specific ethical task to which it is called. Rebirth was not limited to the Jews, yet it is characteristic of the Jewish people that they constantly experience this rebirth. Baeck made this point already in the *Essence*, writing that Judaism's "true history is a history of renaissance ... here history has always renewed."[10]

The periodization in *This People* was grounded by a twofold geographical constellation. In the sixth conference of the World Union for Progressive Judaism in London, Baeck offered a geometrical image for his historiography. Jewish existence was not a circle, but an ellipse, "a formation destined and determined by two focuses of strength, by two dynamic centers."[11] Baeck returned to this idea in a 1954 lecture in Düsseldorf commemorating the 750 anniversary of Maimonides' birth. In the medieval period, Baeck said, one encounters Maimonides and Rashi, representing Sepharad and Ashkenaz, respectively. The two had different approaches to the Jewish sources and their interpretation, but both are indispensable to Jewish learning.[12]

In *This People*, this idea of ellipse was carried throughout Jewish history. In biblical times, there were the northern and southern kingdoms. Following the destruction of the Second Temple and the failed Bar Kochba rebellion, "the motherland no longer could give strength as a visible, tangible center." The academies in Babylon managed to provide teachers and guidance serving the entire people.[13] Palestine and Babylon were the centers during the rabbinic period, with Babylon increasingly growing in prominence. Sepharad and Ashkenaz served as the two centers in medieval times. After the expulsion from Spain and Portugal, the foci became Western and Eastern Europe. Baeck's imagination of Jewish history was Eurocentric in this regard. He did not really account for the

---

[10] Leo Baeck, *Das Wesen des Judentums* (1905), 61. Baeck is likely inspired here by Nachman Krochmal, whom he called "one of the great pioneers" that "saw what others only later came to see" (Baeck, *This People*, 369, 391); see Schweid, "From *The Essence of Judaism* to *This People Israel*," 56–57; Meyer, *Rabbi Leo Baeck*, 201. Krochmal, however, attributed this ability to the Jewish people but not necessarily to all peoples. On the centrality of the idea of rebirth in modern Jewish thought, see Asher Biemann, *Inventing New Beginnings: On the Idea of Renaissance in Modern Judaism* (Stanford: Stanford University Press, 2009).

[11] Leo Baeck, "Die Mission des Judentums (1949)," *Werke* 6, 528.

[12] Leo Baeck, "Maimonides – Der Mann, sein Werk und seine Wirkung (1954)," *Werke* 5, 155–56.

[13] Baeck, *This People*, 254.

Jews of North Africa or the Ottoman Empire, which simply disappeared and were minimized in his grand narrative.

In his spatial understanding of Jewish existence as an ellipse, Baeck was likely influenced by Simon Dubnow (1860–1941), whose *World History of the Jewish People* Baeck knew. Dubnow offered a grand narrative of Jewish national and social history by distinguishing between the Oriental and Western periods in Jewish history, identifying within each of them two foci, for example, the Judean and Israelite kingdoms and the "epoch of the two hegemonies, Roman-Byzantine Palestine and Persian-Arab Babylonia."[14] Dubnow's history described a certain dynamism, and Baeck wrote similarly about a back-and-forth exchange between the poles. The prophets, for example, might have been residing in one kingdom but often preached to both. Similarly, the Talmud documents how rabbis and halachic decisions travelled between Palestine and Babylon.[15] Taken together, the two foci served as a guarantor for Jewish survival in the aftermath of disasters, be it the destruction of the Northern kingdom or the expulsion from Spain.

In modern times, Baeck argued, the two centers – Palestine or the state of Israel and the United States – needed each other, not only to survive but to thrive. Before he ever set foot in America, Baeck wondered in a 1911 article in *Liberales Judentum* if the United States would emerge as a center of Jewish life.[16] After returning from his first trip to the United States in 1925, Baeck remained unsure. In a speech in front of B'nai B'rith members, he said the United States and its Jews had civilization – they were technologically advanced and apt at solving problems – but they were lacking in culture (*Kultur*).[17] Baeck's understanding of culture as superior was grounded in his understanding of the term already in the Wilhelmine period, and in the postwar era Baeck used it to try and make sense of American Jewry. Culture, he cautioned, required many generations of development, and the United States was in his view simply too young and lacking history.

In making his argument about the recency of the United States, Baeck claimed its colonial origins were still present. "America is on the whole today still a colonial land (*Kolonialland*)," which meant it wished to be the

---

[14] Simon Dubnov, "Cedars of Lebanon: A New Conception of Jewish History," trans. Shlomo Katz, *Commentary Magazine*, March 1946, www.commentarymagazine.com/articles/simon-dubnow/cedars-of-lebanon-a-new-conception-of-jewish-history/; Baeck cited Dubnow in the *Legal Position*, see for example Baeck et al., "Die Rechtsstellung", I.14.

[15] Baeck, *This People*, 117, 225. [16] Leo Baeck, "Amerika (1911)," *Werke* 6, 533, 536.

[17] Leo Baeck, "Rede vor einer Bne Briss Loge (n.d., likely after 1925)," *Werke* 6, 540–41.

160 The Jewish Imperial Imagination

land of the new, without history.[18] This tendency was exacerbated according to Baeck by the fact that many immigrants reached the land relatively young, thereby coming without deep roots of their own. They were easily swept away by all that the country had to offer. The colonial land gave rise to what Baeck called the colonial person (*Kolonialmensch*), namely, someone whose historical memory was short, a newcomer who lacked depth. Whereas in 1935 Baeck would speak of Jews as a colonial people whose sense of tradition kept them from assimilating to the majority culture, in 1925 he identified in the colonial character of the United States the danger of assimilation, because Europeans who came to America sooner or later forgot their origins.[19]

After the Holocaust, Baeck revised his position and came to see in the United States a center of Jewish existence. He revisited a colonial image he used in order to encourage German Jews to emigrate in 1938 – Jews accompanying Columbus in the spirit of discovery – in a lecture he gave in Darmstadt in 1949. Jews followed Columbus, he told his listeners, because of the expulsion from Spain in 1492.[20] Through this reference to Columbus and the expulsion from Spain, Baeck made the connection between the destruction of European Jewry and the settlement in American explicit.

In an undated lecture, likely given in the years 1945–1948 in the United States, Baeck distinguished between the early Jewish settlement in South and North America and the immigration of Jews from Central and Eastern Europe to North America. The former "sprung from a medieval time and a medieval world." The passengers of the Mayflower, by contrast, did not take the old world with them. They were separated from the old soil by the ocean, and "the spirit has already divorced them from old times." The United States was thus a country "with more time for the future" in which the settlers "had the free, the unburdened and unchecked time."[21] What he had previously presented as a problem, Baeck saw as an opportunity in the postwar era. For all their differences, various American Jews recognized other Jews as Americans and were able to cooperate with them. It truly was a new kind of Judaism, he thought, American Judaism.[22]

---

[18] Baeck, "Rede vor einer Bne Briss Loge (n.d., likely after 1925)," 544.
[19] Leo Baeck, "Der jüdische Mensch," 241.
[20] Leo Baeck, "Die Ferne (1938)," 280–82; Leo Baeck, "Das Judentum auf alten und neuen Wege (1950)," 44.
[21] Leo Baeck, "America and the American Jews (n.d., likely 1945–1948)," Leo Baeck Collection; AR 66; Subgroup I, Series 2, Subseries A-b, 3.
[22] Baeck, "America and the American Jews (n.d., likely 1945–1948)," 22, 27.

Cold War Judaism

The newness of the United States meant Jews "lived in a land without precedent, really in a new land, the land of the new. They had to launch an American way of Jewish living and Jewish service . . . In their days, in great measure, *they had, so to speak, to be isolationist*, and perhaps at times also somewhat self-assertive. All this was their historical role."[23] Thinking of America as a so-called New World was imagining it on an imperial key as the settlement of an empty space devoid of people worthy of consideration such as the natives.

The language of isolationism reveals how Baeck imagined Jewish life in terms of international power structures. In the aftermath of the Second World War, in a lecture to American Jews, the term isolationism alluded to the United States' policy, primarily from the end of the Great War until its involvement in the Second World War, to remain uninvolved in the wars of Europe. This position was epitomized by Charles Lindbergh, the celebrated aviator and poster child of the America First movement, who in a speech in Des Moines on September 11, 1941, blamed the attempts to get the United States involved in the war on the Roosevelt administration, the British, and the Jews, utilizing antisemitic stereotypes of conspiracy and Jewish control of the media.[24] Baeck rejected isolationism as an international relations policy. Yet as the quote suggests, he thought American Jewry required a period of cocooning before it could take its place on the world stage and become a center of Jewish existence. The language Baeck used to describe American-Jewish isolationism constantly emphasized necessity, they "had to" develop this way to prepare for their historic task.

Baeck would visit the United States several times after 1945, routinely teaching at the Hebrew Union College in the 1950s. Most notable was Baeck's 1948 tour as a speaker in the American Jewish Cavalcade, a short-lived enterprise of the Union of American Hebrew Congregations – the umbrella organization of Reform Judaism in the United States – to strengthen Jewish life in the United States. Baeck's schedule included appearances in eleven cities throughout the entire country. He was received as a statesman without a state, dining with religious dignitaries

---

[23] Leo Baeck, "Ansprache zum Gründungstag des Hebrew Union College in Cincinnati (1953)," *Werke* 6, 553–54 – my emphasis.

[24] Charles Lindbergh, "Des Moines Speech – America First Committee," September 11, 1941, www .charleslindbergh.com/americanfirst/speech.asp; on Lindbergh's isolationism, see Lynne Olson, *Those Angry Days: Roosevelt, Lindbergh, and America's Fight over World War II, 1939–1941* (New York: Random House, 2014); Christopher McKnight Nichols, *Promise and Peril: America at the Dawn of a Global Age* (Cambridge, MA: Harvard University Press, 2011).

162 The Jewish Imperial Imagination

and mayors, receiving an honorary degree from Dropsie College, meeting President Truman at the White House, and opening a session of the House of Representatives with a short prayer, the first non-North American rabbi to receive such an honor.[25]

Baeck's visits to the United States were especially meaningful for German Jews who had settled there, a fact attested by the coverage he received in their leading journal *Aufbau*. But his presence was also meaningful for American Jewry more broadly. The image of Baeck, the Holocaust survivor and spiritual leader, was used, for example, in fundraising campaigns for postwar refugees under the title "Fill a Box for Baeck: Celebrate – 75th Birthday of Our Heroic Rabbi."[26]

Although meant primarily for American-Jewish audiences, the Cavalcade was also aimed at elevating the status of Judaism in the public sphere. Baeck's presence contributed to this goal. His lectures and statements were covered not only by Jewish newspapers but also in major news outlets such as *The New York Times* and *The Boston Globe*. Baeck was occasionally praised in hagiographical terms. The popular American rabbi Joshua Loth Liebman, author of the bestseller *Peace of Mind*, shared the stage with Baeck in Boston and Philadelphia and went to describe his aged colleague for *The Atlantic Monthly* and *Reader's Digest* as "a saint for our times" and "the most unforgettable character I've met."[27]

For his part, Baeck saw in the United States a crucial factor in the postwar global power constellations, and in Jewish life. Its importance for the latter was, to begin with, in terms of sheer numbers. Never before had so many Jews lived in the same country.[28] The United States provided a solid and stable place for Jews in the postwar era. It was a new country, but one in which progress in religious life could be made.

Conversely, Palestine served as the second pole of Jewish existence in the postwar era. It was the ancestral homeland, but also a place of the future, of "faithful adventure." The Promised Land, Baeck said in an

---

[25] Leo Baeck, "Gebet im Repräsentantenhaus am 12. Februar 1948," *Werke* 6, 549; on the Cavalcade, see "Scrapbook – American Jewish Cavalcade (n.d., likely 1948)," Leo Baeck Collection; AR 66; Subgroup I, Series 3; Michael Meyer, *Response to Modernity: A History of the Reform Movement in Judaism* (New York: Oxford University Press, 1988), 358.

[26] Hasia Diner, *We Remember with Reverence and Love: American Jews and the Myth of Silence after the Holocaust, 1945–1962* (New York: New York University Press, 2009), 192–95.

[27] Leo Baeck, "In diesen Tagen," *Aufbau* 14, no. 13 (March 26, 1948): 1; Leo Baeck and Richard Dyck, "Ohne Religion und Glaube – Keine Weltfrieden!," *Aufbau* 14, no. 2 (January 9, 1948): 1; Simon, "Geheimnis und Gebot"; "Dr. Baeck Visits Truman: He Thanks President for Our Aid to Jews in Europe," *The New York Times*, January 9, 1948; "Palestine Shift Scored Here by Dr. Leo Baeck," *The Boston Daily Globe*, March 31, 1948; Liebman, "A Saint for Our Times."

[28] Baeck, "Das Judentum auf alten und neuen Wege (1950)," 44–45.

Cold War Judaism

address to the World Union of Progressive Judaism in 1946, was also the Land of Promise, standing "in the centre of our hopes and of our cares."[29] Consistent with his earlier description of Zionism in the *Legal Position*, Baeck praised Zionism in 1949 as "a penetration of the millennia into the Jewish soul" and a "great renaissance, a rebirth" motivated by historical awareness and a newfound "national will." With Zionism, "a new epoch of Jewish life has begun," nothing short of the "unmediated great hope."[30] By describing Zionism as hope in the fourth millennium that is characterized by hope, Baeck emphasized its importance for Jewish life.

Palestine and the United States offered a future-orientation, but of different kinds. Palestine was saturated with Jewish history; the United States, by contrast was a colonial land, free, for better or worse, from history. American Jews had an advantage in that they did not have to constantly struggle with the past, but they were also under the risk of being swept away by the march of progress. Zionism was a rebirth, an actualization of the old idea and desire. It therefore did not have this problem but faced other challenges.

Baeck stressed in his postwar thought a geographical feature of Palestine, namely that it stood at the crossroads between Asia, Africa, and Europe.[31] In a series of weekly lectures on the epochs of Jewish history in 1956, Baeck explained this geography led to the potential influences of the Egyptian and Babylonian empires. He distinguished between the "struggle for the land" and the "struggle with the land." The former was the physical struggle against the Israelites' enemies, the ones who occupied the land. It was external and relatively short. The latter, by contrast, was an internal struggle against idolatry. It continued long after the land had been conquered and lasted until the exile.[32] This imperial imagination saw therefore a twofold Jewish struggle, one in which the spiritual element is more important, and harder to conquer, than the physical one.

The struggle for and with the land also shaped Baeck's view on the settlement in Palestine. The physical struggle was manifested in the relation to the Arab population. In a 1937 letter to Werner David Senator, a Zionist leader and supporter of a binational state, Baeck wrote that "the basis could be only that Jews and Arabs build a united front for

---

[29] Leo Baeck, "The Task of Progressive Judaism in the Post-War World (1946)," 67.
[30] Baeck, "Das Judentum auf alten und neuen Wege (1950)," 43.
[31] Baeck, *This People*, 119; Baeck, "The Task of Progressive Judaism in the Post-War World (1946)," 67; Leo Baeck, "Israel und das deutsche Volk (1952)," 60.
[32] Baeck, "Epochen der jüdischen Geschichte (1956)," 302; Baeck, *This People*, 121; Baeck, "Changes in Jewish Outlook (1947)," *Werke* 5, 499.

164 The Jewish Imperial Imagination

the renewed search and beginning of a united Palestine."[33] After the partition resolution of the United Nations in 1947, Baeck insisted in interviews and private letters on this binational idea, saying that partition was ultimately a step in the direction of "one state comprising one economic body with two administrations."[34]

A *New York Times* letter published on April 18, 1948, gives further indication of Baeck's position. It was co-signed by Baeck and Albert Einstein, but earlier drafts suggest the idea for the text and most of its composition likely emerged from Erich Fromm and Ernst Simon. Baeck and Einstein were chosen as the signatories because they were the most well-known figures to support the statement in its final version. The earlier drafts were harsh in tone, speaking of "the catastrophic events in Palestine," "the growing fanaticism of official Jewish statements," and the fact that the undersigned "view with alarm the growing cynicism in their own ranks which lightheartedly will dismiss any argument or any action that happens not to coincide with the Jewish interests as fullfledged proof of conscious, calculated hostility toward the Jewish people."[35]

In the published version, these ideas were tamed, but the overall critique remained. Baeck and Einstein decried the violence between Jews and Arabs and condemned, as Jews, "methods of terrorism and fanatical nationalism" on the Jewish side, just as if they were practiced by Arabs. They called on Jews in Palestine not to fall into "a mood of despair or false heroism which eventually results in suicidal measures. While such a mood is undoubtedly understandable as a reaction to the wanton destruction of six million Jewish lives in the past decade, it is nevertheless destructive morally as well as practically."[36] The Holocaust, in other words, did not justify violence in Palestine.

The *New York Times* letter cited approvingly members of Jewish groups supporting bi-nationalism (Brith Shalom and Ihud).[37] Alongside his other statements, it would therefore seem that Baeck imagined a Jewish-Arab federation or a binational state. Although this view was marginal in the political landscape of pre-state Palestine, Baeck's position is not surprising.

---

[33] Leo Baeck to David Senator on November 9, 1937, 476.
[34] Earl Barber, "Dr. Baeck Says Peace Possible in Holy Land," *The Miami Herald*, January 13, 1948; Leo Baeck to Hans Paeschke on November 4, 1949, *Werke* 6, 488.
[35] "For a Cooperation between Jews and Arabs (1990t-eng)," Erich Fromm Institute Tübingen. I thank Matheus Romanetto and Monique Scheer for drawing my attention to this source. See also Erich Fromm, "Für eine Kooperation zwischen Israelis und Palästinensern," in *Gesamtausgabe in Zwölf Bänden*, ed. Rainer Funk, vol. 11 (Munich: dtv, 1999), 523–27.
[36] Leo Baeck and Albert Einstein, "Kooperation in Palästina - Ein Appell (1948)," *Werke* 6, 481.
[37] Baeck and Einstein, "Kooperation in Palästina - Ein Appell (1948)," 481–82.

Cold War Judaism

Yfaat Weiss has shown that such ideas gained traction among Central European Jews, who in the 1920s saw the rise of ethnonationalism as a threat to the Jews. They preferred the multiethnic model they knew from places such as the Austro-Hungarian Empire to the nation-state and were afraid that a Jewish majority in Palestine would turn out to be no better than Polish, Romanian, or German nationalism, oppressing the minority in the same way Jews were discriminated in Europe.[38] Baeck, although working from within the German context, shared this concern, which was in line with his imperial imagination of Judaism as focused on spiritual energy (*Kraft*) and not state power (*Macht*). The state of Israel, he insisted, would rise or fall to the level of its morals and this entailed the relation to the Arab population.[39]

Despite whatever qualms he might have harbored about the conflict with the Arab population, Baeck firmly believed in the right of Jews to settle in the land. In "Judaism and Zionism: A Liberal View" (1947), a text published in London as part of a symposium on religious aspects of Zionism, Baeck justified a Jewish claim to the land on rational and ethical grounds:

> And reason says that mankind cannot afford – today even less than formerly – the wanton waste of unreclaimed regions of desert, swamp, and rocky desolation. Rather should these lands be entrusted to those pioneers who through labour and sacrifice can make them fertile. Ethics say that it is a commandment to give life to the soil. Judaism would add there is but one eternal owner of the soil, the one God ... and that the man who allows his portion of the soil to fall permanently into decay and ruins forfeits his right of possession. All moral right of possession is founded on this law and the right of colonisation and settlement issues therefrom.[40]

Drawing on the language of rights, Baeck wrote that "the recognition that every man has the right to live" meant first and foremost "the right to soil" that could support human existence.[41]

The claim to have a right to colonize was a common trope in the imperial justification of colonization of lands seen as less cultivated,

---

[38] Yfaat Weiss, "Central European Ethnonationalism and Zionist Binationalism," *Jewish Social Studies* 11, no. 1 (2004): 93–117; Zohar Maor, "Identity and Confusion: Another Look at the Whirlpool of Identities in Prague," *Zion* 71, no. 4 (2006): 457–72; Shumsky, *Beyond the Nation-State*; Adi Gordon, *Brith Shalom and Bi-National Zionism: The "Arab Question" as a Jewish Question* (Jerusalem: Carmel, 2008) (Hebrew).

[39] Baeck, *This People*, 132–33; Baeck, "Ansprache zum Gründungstag (1953)," 555; Baeck, "Das Judentum auf alten und neuen Wege (1950)," 45.

[40] Leo Baeck, "Judentum und Zionismus (1947)," 477.

[41] Baeck, "Judentum und Zionismus (1947)," 478.

166   The Jewish Imperial Imagination

whether culturally, agriculturally, or otherwise. It was part of the imperial imagination of the East that Baeck absorbed during the Wilhelmine Empire. For all his support of Arab-Jewish coexistence, Baeck thereby claimed the current inhabitants of the land had let it fall to disarray, thereby forfeiting their right to those who would make good use of the land, the Jewish pioneers.

The Jewish Tasks

In a 1948 interview as part of his visit to the United States, Baeck praised the settlement in Palestine, calling it "the most magnificent achievement" of any Jewish generation. "The Jews of Palestine," he said, "have become not only colonists of the soil but colonists of the spirit." Only the Pilgrims who came to America on the Mayflower, Baeck added, did something similar, not only settling the land but planting "a new spirit" in it.[42] Baeck thereby linked the two foci, also by pointing out on several occasions a congruence between Biblical and Jewish understanding of Law and the Pilgrims' infusion of broader life with religion. The roots of the American attempt to establish a kingdom of priests on earth were in this reading Jewish.[43]

To be a pioneer, a *chalutz*, in Palestine, Baeck said a month after the founding of the state of Israel, was to conquer the land "not by means of arms and guns, but to conquer it by labour, by sacrifice ... to redeem it from bareness, from unfertility."[44] This gendered language, in a speech in front of members of the Federation of British Progressive Women's Society, was building on Baeck's earlier imperial imagination and the distinction between *Kraft* and *Macht*. The former, improving the land supposedly without violence, gave Jews the right to settle. This kind of pioneering and colonial spirit, argued Baeck, was also constitutive of the United States, with its vast "free and wide space." The colonist, Baeck said in a speech in the United States, was "the man who means to have his home for good on a strange soil." This man must have individual strength

---

[42] Daniel Davis, "Baeck Comes to America," *Liberal Judaism* 15, no. 7, January 1948, 8; Baeck, "America and the American Jews (n.d., likely 1945–1948)," 8.

[43] Baeck, "Das Judentum auf alten und neuen Wege (1950)," 46; Baeck, "Epochen der jüdischen Geschichte (1956)," 237, 274. The Pilgrims also saw themselves as the Israelites reaching the Promised Land. See Ronald Hendel, "The Exodus in America," in *Found in Translation: Essays on Jewish Biblical Translation in Honor of Leonard J. Greenspoon*, eds. James Barker, Anthony Le Donne, and Joel Lohr (West Lafayette, IN: Purdue University Press, 2018), 156–61.

[44] Leo Baeck, "Religiöse Erziehung in Palästina (1948)," *Werke* 6, 482.

Cold War Judaism 167

of will in order to survive and thrive on the frontier, but it is not egoism because "on new soil, he cannot, not for long at least, be a recluse."[45] Colonist here is once more identified with a sense of changing the land and maintaining spiritual integrity, but not with occupation, exploitation, and subjugation.

The different geographies of Palestine and the United States determine for Baeck the challenges faced by Jews. In the United States, the vast spaces lead to tendencies of exaggeration and over-enthusiasm, but also, as Baeck suggested in 1925, to potential assimilation. In Palestine, one faces the opposite problem. Baeck cautioned in June 1948 that living in a narrow land, historically between empires, could lead to narrow-mindedness. Thinking of Palestine as the center of the world, Jews there risked adopting an insular mindset.[46] This isolationist mentality, Baeck further warned in an article in *Merkur* in 1952, could easily turn into a deification of the state and unbridled nationalism.[47]

This insular mentality also impacted the relation between the two centers. In an unpublished advisory opinion in 1951, Baeck contested the stronghold of the orthodoxy on religious affairs in Israel and the refusal of the chief rabbinate in Israel to recognize conversions to Judaism by liberal rabbis. This narrow-mindedness lamented Baeck to Senator in 1952, might create a schism between European and American Jews on the one hand, and Israeli Jews on the other, as the former would no longer be interested in Zionism because they would not feel welcomed.[48]

The two postwar centers of Jewish existence had different geographies, temporalities, and dangers facing them. They also had different goals. The state of Israel was a national center and as such was more concerned with Jewish particularity. The United States, by contrast, would serve "so to speak a centre of internationalism." Jewish existence circled around these two foci of the ellipse. The national center would remind American Jews of their particularity, thereby combating assimilation. The universal center would remind Israeli Jews of their ethical task for the sake of all of humanity. Only together, in "equipoise and equilibrium," as Baeck said

---

[45] Baeck, "America and the American Jews (n.d., likely 1945–1948)," 4–6; cf. Baeck, "Rede vor einer Bne Briss Loge (n.d., likely after 1925)," 546; Baeck, "Amerika (1911)," 536.

[46] Baeck, "Religiöse Erziehung in Palästina (1948)," 484.

[47] Baeck, "Israel und das deutsche Volk (1952)," 59; Baeck, "Die Mission des Judentums (1949)," 528.

[48] Leo Baeck, "Gutachten vom Oktober 1951," *Werke* 6, 488–90; Leo Baeck to David Werner Senator, December 12, 1952, in *Werke* 6, 491.

168 The Jewish Imperial Imagination

in the World Union of Progressive Judaism in 1949, would Jewish life flourish in the aftermath of the Holocaust.[49]

Religious education was a shared need of both centers, each separately and together.[50] For American Jews, Baeck suggested, religious education meant comprehending themselves and developing a unique culture that would be more than a mere civilization. This would anchor them in the history of both Judaism and the United States in a way that would mitigate the effects of the vastness of the land and the risk of assimilation. For Jews in Palestine, especially children born there who did not know anything else, religious education – meaning in Baeck's idiom more ethical and infused with relation to God but not a halakhic state limited to one denomination – would provide the antidote to the shortsightedness and narrowmindedness that were the result of the geography of the land and its geopolitical location. Without it, "there will be no future, no Jewish future in Palestine" but nationalism, chauvinism, and the violence they engender.[51]

The task of the Jewish settlers in Palestine, and later the state of Israel, was to serve as a national home for Jews. This task had a pragmatic aspect of providing shelter to those Jews displaced or persecuted. A Jewish national home ensured that "the survivors . . . at last be granted the right to their place and the place of their right."[52] Yet Baeck had higher hopes for the Jewish settlement than mere survival. Speaking on the religious aspects of Zionism in 1947, for example, he described the return of Jews to the land as a religious event and a fulfillment of the Jewish vocation in the world.[53] From an inner-Jewish perspective, Zionism had the potential to kindle a sense of Judaism in secular Jews otherwise removed from their heritage. This was one of the reasons why Baeck, unlike other German rabbis, had not opposed Zionism in its early days. In the postwar era he remarked that Hebrew, the language of the Bible, was once more being spoken in the Promised Land. For Baeck, this promoted a religious revival, because "Whoever has the Bible, to him religion will come today or tomorrow."[54] Through the language of the Bible, the younger generation

[49] Baeck, "Die Mission des Judentums (1949)," 528–29.
[50] Baeck, "The Task of Progressive Judaism in the Post-War World (1946)," 69; cf. Baeck, "Das Judentum auf alten und neuen Wege (1950)," 44–45.
[51] Baeck, "Religiöse Erziehung in Palästina (1948)," 484.
[52] Baeck, "America and the American Jews (n.d., likely 1945–1948)," 29.
[53] Baeck, "Judentum und Zionismus (1947)," Werke 6, 479.
[54] Baeck, "Das Judentum auf alten und neuen Wege (1950)," 44–46 (quote in 46); Baeck and Dyck, "Ohne Religion und Glaube – Keine Weltfrieden!"

Cold War Judaism 169

would become more religious, a phenomenon Baeck claimed to identify in 1950.

Baeck claimed a Jewish state with religious character would also serve a greater purpose for the nations of the world, in line with the messianic vision of Zion as a light unto to the nations.[55] In antiquity, he said in the 1947 speech about Zionism and Judaism, Jewish society was opposed to slavery or castes that were common in the pagan world. In medieval times, the Jewish community maintained its purity against the prevailing malaises of the time. After the Holocaust, in Palestine, "Jews have once again started to create an individual and novel social order on that old soil; a social order which is based on the respect of all for the individual human being, and on the respect of each for his fellow and for the community."[56] Now as then, Baeck suggested, Jews were leading the way morally.

Making the state more religious – in the sense of ethical monotheism – would accord it a place of pride among the nations. Other religiously oriented nations, in his view Great Britain and the United States, would be more inclined to support Israel that way. They would react positively, he told Shmuel Hugo Bergmann, to a Jewish state (*jüdischer Staat*), but would not know how to relate to "a secularized state of the Jews [*säkularisierten Judenstaat*]."[57] This vision was in line with his view of the Jew as a moral exemplar, but it also reflects an imperial imagination that was in line with his views of Great Britain and the United States after the Great War. A Jewish state would garner respect because in these countries Christianity often took the form of Calvinism, which in Baeck's understanding was deeply grounded in Judaism. The respect won by a Jewish state, in other words, would be a recognition of shared values.

The task of American Jewry according to Baeck was "probably the greatest and grandest that Jewish history outside Palestine ... has ever offered."[58] Like in Palestine, part of the task was pragmatic. As the largest and richest community, American Jews offered material support for Jews in need in general, and a much-needed help for the settlement in Palestine. To put it in terms we have already encountered, the Jewish colony should support the motherland, as had been done in ancient times.

Alongside the pragmatic role came a world-historical task. The creation of American-Jewish culture would bring Judaism respect. "We cannot ask

[55] Leo Baeck, "Leo Baeck in Palästina," *Aufbau* 13, no. 35 (August 29, 1947): 19.
[56] Baeck, "Judentum und Zionismus (1947)," 479.
[57] Schmuel Hugo Bergman, diary entry April 19, 1951, in *Tagebücher & Briefe*, ed. Miriam Sambursky (Frankfurt am Main: Jüdischer Verlag, 1985), II.85.
[58] Baeck, "America and the American Jews (n.d., likely 1945–1948)," 29–30.

170   The Jewish Imperial Imagination

for love," Baeck explained to students and teachers at the Hebrew Union College in Cincinnati in 1953, "but we can work for respect."[59] This respect would allow Jews to secure their place in the world. It would also be a respect for the teachings of Judaism, and hence for God. This respect would be gained, among other ways, when American Jews used their numbers in order to serve as the voice of conscience, decrying wrongs wherever they are found.[60]

In emphasizing the role of religion as commanding respect for American Jewry, Baeck drew upon a prevalent sense of the United States as a religious country with a shared Judeo-Christian tradition. The centrality of religion in one's life and in the public culture became a defining feature of what it meant to be an American. A day after Churchill's famous Iron Curtain speech in 1946, President Truman declared that for the civilized world to survive, the atomic bomb and military power alone would not be enough. What was required, he implored Americans, was a "moral and spiritual awakening."[61] This quickly got underway in the late 1940s, especially during Truman and Eisenhower's presidencies. Some of the more discernible consequences of this era are still with us today, for example, in the words "In God We Trust" that, circulating as early as the 1930s, were officially imprinted on all currency starting in the mid-1950s, when it was also enshrined as a national motto.

Unlike previous religious awakenings, this was not a grassroots movement, but a top-down effort of what Jonathan Herzog called "the spiritual-industrial complex," a cooperation of governmental and societal institutions, as well as business enterprises, in the promotion of Americanism as interwoven with religion and capitalism.[62] In line with this new vision for the United States, Truman warmly greeted the first American Jewish Cavalcade in late 1946. If there was to be progress toward "economic security and world peace, there will have to be a greater and greater acceptance of the basic tenets of religion," he said, singling out the "mutual

---

[59] Baeck, "Ansprache zum Gründungstag (1953)," 554.
[60] Baeck, "America and the American Jews (n.d., likely 1945–1948)," 29–30.
[61] Harry Truman, "Address in Columbus at a Conference of the Federal Council of Churches," March 6, 1946, www.trumanlibrary.gov/library/public-papers/52/address-columbus-conference-federal-council-churches.
[62] Jonathan Herzog, *The Spiritual-Industrial Complex: America's Religious Battle against Communism in the Early Cold War* (New York: Oxford University Press, 2011); Kevin Kruse, *One Nation Under God: How Corporate America Invented Christian America* (New York: Basic Books, 2015); Dianne Kirby, "The Cold War and American Religion," in *Oxford Research Encyclopedia of Religion* (Oxford: Oxford University Press, 2017), https://oxfordre.com/religion/view/10.1093/acrefore/9780199340378.001.0001/acrefore-9780199340378-e-398; James Wallace, "A Religious War?: The Cold War and Religion," *Journal of Cold War Studies* 15, no. 3 (2013): 162–80.

Cold War Judaism 171

Judaic Christian culture" as exemplified in the Ten Commandments and the Sermon on the Mount.

Mark Silk identifies two main meanings of the idea of a shared Judeo-Christian tradition in this period.[63] The first was theological. Reinhold Niebuhr, Paul Tillich, and other Christian theologians turned to the idea of a Judeo-Christian tradition in order to stress the dependence of Christianity, both historically and theologically, on Judaism. Baeck would approve of the attempts by Christian theologians to promote a return to the Hebrew Bible in a way that combated the danger of Marcionism.

The second meaning was sociopolitical. The United Stated described itself as a religious nation, unlike the Soviet Union. This, too, was in line with Baeck's imperial imagination. Baeck agreed with the rejection of Soviet communism, which he long saw as atheist and hence antithetical to Judaism. In his lectures on the epochs of Jewish history, Baeck maintained his objection to bolshevism, finding its origins in materialism, which he argued Judaism categorically rejected. Materialism understood the world as brutal and violent, which is why the political philosophy emerging from it – from Hobbes to Lenin, "the victorious leader and theorist of bolshevism" – always led to despotism and autocracy. Materialism, "the most dogmatic of all philosophies," refused to allow any metaphysical reality.[64] The rejection of dogma in Baeck's early polemic with Harnack in Imperial Germany was transformed here into an understanding of bolshevism qua dogma. Baeck's Judaism, grounded as it was in relation to a transcendent God, could only oppose this materialist view.

For Jews in the United States the idea of a shared Judeo-Christian heritage meant emphasizing their identity as a religious group, an American denomination akin to Protestants and Catholics. As Rachel Gordan shows, from the late 1940s and throughout the 1950s a middle-brow genre of Introduction to Judaism books developed whose aim was to provide accessible knowledge about Judaism for Jews and non-Jews alike.[65]

---

[63] Mark Silk, "Notes on the Judeo-Christian Tradition in America," *American Quarterly* 36, no. 1 (1984): 65–85; K. Healan Gaston, *Imagining Judeo-Christian America: Religion, Secularism, and the Redefinition of Democracy* (Chicago: University of Chicago Press, 2019).

[64] Baeck, "Epochen der jüdischen Geschichte (1956)," 339. Eliyahu Stern, by contrast, shows how central materialism was for the formation of some of the major Jewish ideologies, including Zionism and Reconstructionism. See Eliyahu Stern, *Jewish Materialism: The Intellectual Revolution of the 1870s* (New Haven: Yale University Press, 2018).

[65] Rachel Gordan, "'What the Jews Believe': A Liberal Rabbi Explains Judaism to the Readers of *Life* Magazine," in *New Perspectives in American Jewish History: A Documentary Tribute to Jonathan D. Sarna*, eds. Mark Raider and Gary Zola (Chicago: Chicago University Press, 2021), 273–80;

172 The Jewish Imperial Imagination

Baeck could be considered a popularizer of Judaism in this sense. *The Essence of Judaism* was first translated to English in 1936, but it was republished in the United States by Schocken Books in 1948, making it part of the Introduction to Judaism trend.

In a text likely addressed to an American-Jewish audience around 1948, Baeck said that alongside the colonial spirit, religious tolerance, and the spirit of Enlightenment, one of the foundations of America was the Great Awakening, which according to Baeck paved the way for profound social transformations such as abolitionism.[66] Baeck called for a contemporary Jewish revival, in line with the Great Awakening and the idea of the Cavalcade. His listeners needed to understand that they were "more pious, more religious, more Jewish than you yourselves know ... To awaken all this, is that great and urgent task, set for the sake of all Judaism, but no less for America's sake."[67] It was a call both for religious education as well as for a broader vision of American society as infused with religion.

In Baeck's imperial imagination, the post-Holocaust era was a time ripe for Jews to resume proselytizing and expanding. The 1949 conference of the World Union of Progressive Judaism was dedicated to "The Mission of Judaism: Its Present Day Application." Other religions, said Baeck in his contribution, did wonderful work in providing comfort and peace of mind to millions of people. They were, however, waning in influence. Buddhism failed to provide self-respect and self-esteem. Islam had been politicized, thereby losing its religious strength. Finally, the West, with Christianity at its core, committed "a serious crime against Africa" by introducing gunpowder, alcoholism, and maladies. Christianity further failed in remaining silent in the face of crimes and oppression, and compromised its religious purity by collaborating with earthly powers.[68] In a contribution to a volume titled *The Church and the Jewish People* (1954), Baeck returned to this theme and did not reject other religions' missionary duty, saying that "no community of faith has the right to take offence at the other's missionary work or purpose ... There can be no monopolies here."[69]

Baeck practiced what he preached. Some of his lectures in Germany after the Holocaust were in the Institutum Judaicum Delitzschianum,

---

Rachel Gordan, "The 1940s as the Decade of the Anti-Antisemitism Novel," *Religion and American Culture* 31, no. 1 (2021): 46.

[66] Baeck, "America and the American Jews (n.d., likely 1945–1948)," 9–11.
[67] Baeck, "America and the American Jews (n.d., likely 1945–1948)," 39.
[68] Baeck, "Die Mission des Judentums (1949)," 526–27.
[69] Baeck, "Some Questions to the Christian Church (1954)," *Werke* 5, 456.

Cold War Judaism 173

originally dedicated to missionizing the Jews. Karl Heinrich Rengstorf, the institution's head and founder of the German Evangelical Committee of the Service for Israel, was a proponent of Jewish-Christian dialogue after the Holocaust. His interest in Judaism, however, initially emerged when thinking about missionizing to Jews during the Weimar Republic. The Delitzschianum was no longer missionizing, and it is perhaps natural that earnest interest in Jewish-Christian dialogue would emerge from such a venue, which was closed by the Nazis.[70] Nonetheless, Baeck surely would have known its roots, but participated in the dialogue, perhaps because it was seen as standing in opposition to the Nazis or perhaps because he thought the conversation was now done with pure intentions.

After the Holocaust, with the weakness of the other religions' missionizing efforts and the new geopolitical context, the conditions merited in Baeck's opinion a return to active missionizing. Judaism, he said in 1949, could attract "educated people, high-minded people. Should we not begin anew? Should we not send out missionaries to Asia, to East Asia and to other places to the people there waiting for us? We are in need of expansion for our own sake."[71] Judaism's task as a world-historical religion meant that in order to spread ethical monotheism, one needed to gain converts. After the devastating murder of six million Jews, the need for expansion Baeck had in mind was likely also demographic.[72]

Missionizing required dedicated missionaries. Baeck singled out the Hebrew Union College in Cincinnati and the Theological Seminary of America (as the Jewish Theological Seminary was known) in New York. From there, these men – Baeck used a gendered language here, saying they must be "men, really men" – would go and it would be "a wonderful dissemination."[73] American Judaism was justified in concentrating its efforts inwardly in the period of inner-consolidation in the nineteenth century, but one of its burning tasks in the post-Holocaust world was to avoid isolationism, both internally between denominations, and between Jews and non-Jews. This was not only for the sake of Judaism, Baeck implied, but also for the entire world.

---

[70] Christian Wiese, "Institutum Judaicum," *Religion Past and Present*, 2011, https://referenceworks .brillonline.com/entries/religion-past-and-present/institutum-judaicum-SIM_10465.

[71] Baeck, "Die Mission des Judentums (1949)," 528.

[72] For that reason, Baeck was also lenient when it came to the re-admittance of Jews who had left Judaism into the community, see Leo Baeck, *Werke* 6, 399–405.

[73] Baeck, "Die Mission des Judentums (1949)," 528.

174   The Jewish Imperial Imagination

No World Peace without Religion

After the Holocaust, Baeck thought interfaith dialogue was not only possible, but also necessary. The central question was under what conditions it would take place: "will it be like a meeting of the Great Powers, invested with authority and vetoes, and a small country?" or between spiritual equals that were "neither diverted nor confused by any majority-complex on the one side or any minority-complex on the other?"[74] The mentioning of the Great Powers in this context alludes to the ways in which Baeck's thinking on religious matters was intertwined with the political discourse of the day.

Based on Baeck's earlier critique of Christianity, the majority-complex could be described as threefold. First, the Church's expansion in previous generations was "a kind of ecclesiastical imperialism and colonialism."[75] Too often, the Church turned to politics and the state consequently enlisted it for political aims. The use of violence and coercion, for example, by limiting access to certain professions, meant that some conversions to Christianity were dishonest or at least not fully pure. The Church, in short, needed to stop its reliance on violence and coercion. Second, overcoming the majority-complex entailed doing away with supersessionist claims in Christian theology. The Church should acknowledge and respect the legitimate existence of Jews in the world, not just as dejected witnesses, but as a living religion with a proud past, present, and future.

Finally, the Church should recognize just how important the Hebrew Bible was for its history and teachings. This was a point encapsulated in the title of Baeck's essay "Judaism in the Church" (1925) and Baeck's critique of Marcionite tendencies in Christianity. He did not spare the Church from this type of criticism after the Holocaust, linking Marcionism and Nazism.[76] In the postwar era, however, the harsh indictment of the Marcionite trends gave way to a slightly more positive tone. In several essays in the 1950s, Baeck commented that the fact that the emerging church adopted the Hebrew Bible as part of its canon, against the position of Marcion, was one of its great achievements.[77]

Like the Christian majority-complex, Judaism's minority-complex remained not fully elaborated by Baeck, but it is possible to unpack it

---

[74] Baeck, "Some Questions to the Christian Church (1954)," 454, 456.
[75] Baeck, "Some Questions to the Christian Church (1954)."
[76] Baeck, "Judaism in the Church."
[77] Baeck, "Judentum, Christentum und Islam (1956)," *Werke* 5, 484–85; Baeck, "Epochen der jüdischen Geschichte (1956)," 352; Baeck, "Some Questions to the Christian Church (1954)," 460; for the critique: Baeck, "Das Judentum auf alten und neuen Wege (1950)," 47.

Cold War Judaism

based on his thought as a whole. First, Judaism should insist on getting the respect it deserved. This would be the meaning of having Israel as a Jewish state, and of American Jews making their voice heard for just causes. Second, Judaism should recognize its own role within Christendom. The struggle against Marcionism was not Jewish. It was an inner-Christian struggle with their tradition. Yet a self-conscious and proud Judaism could serve as a valuable reminder for Christians of that part of their heritage.

Baeck returned in the postwar era to a point evident also in the *Essence* – Christianity had a world-historical task to fulfill, it was also part of the divine plan. Recognizing Judaism's place in this history could free Judaism from its minority-complex because such an understanding turned church history, indeed Western history, into Jewish history. *The Gospel as a Document of the History of the Jewish Faith*, which Baeck published in 1938, was an argument against the de-Judaizing attempts in Nazi Germany. In the postwar era, in search of dialogue, Baeck used the same logic, this time not as a protest but as an invitation to dialogue. Not only the Hebrew Bible, but also the New Testament was a shared source.[78]

Rethinking Judaism's relation to Christianity led Baeck to rethink his position regarding Paul. In "Romantic Religion" (1922), Baeck gave Paul the lion's share of criticism for the rise of Christianity as romantic religion. After the Holocaust, Baeck amended his perception in important ways that provide insight into his vision of a shared Judeo-Christian tradition. In a lecture delivered to the Society of Jewish Study in London, later published under the title "The Faith of Paul" (1952), Baeck wrote that "Paul was carried away ... far outside the Jewish boundaries" through the influence of Hellenistic culture. Paul turned the prophetic theocentric position into a Christocentric position, moving the focus from God to the messiah.[79]

Whereas during the Weimar Republic this claim was used to show the distance between Christianity and Judaism, Baeck now argued Paul's approach was an original and earnest attempt to deal with Jewish questions. The apostle's relation to Jewish law was no longer described as the foreign influence of gnostic lawlessness but as an attempt to come to terms with the question of epochal transition in rabbinic thought. Paul, having had the profound vision of the resurrected Christ, thought the epoch of Torah ended and the messianic epoch begun. This idea was now described as Jewish through and through. Even the mission to the gentiles, for which

---

[78] Baeck, "Das Judentum auf alten und neuen Wege (1950)," 47.
[79] Leo Baeck, "The Faith of Paul," in *Judaism and Christianity* (Philadelphia: Jewish Publication Society of America, 1960), 154, 146.

Paul is known, was rooted in ideas of Jewish missionizing. Paul turned to the gentiles after being rejected among the Jews, to whom he tried to preach first. Finally, Paul relied on the Hebrew Bible, "as a Jewish scholar."[80] Baeck read Paul as an exegete of the Hebrew Bible and the Jewish tradition, thereby implicitly rejecting his earlier idea about the connection between Paul and Marcion. The Jewish aspects of Paul's faith took center stage and the critique receded to the background.[81]

In Baeck's imperial imagination, the power of religion in the postwar era was not limited to Jewish missionizing or interfaith dialogue. Religion had a role to play in global politics. From a world formerly ruled by empires, two Great Powers emerged: the atheist Soviet Union and a religious United States. Framed this way, the choice for the latter was easy for Baeck. The postwar era, Baeck suggested, was a continuation of the United States' historical role in promoting morality and freedom. In the past, the United States had brought forth the idea of religious freedom and the concept of the rights of man in the Bill of Rights. Now, the American vision of freedom should be promoted through the United Nations. In a speech upon receiving an honorary degree from Dropsie College, Baeck described the United Nation as "a voluntary curtailment of the hitherto divine rights of the sovereign states to precipitate warfare and infringe on the basic human rights of their own citizens. This is an extension of the principle of reason out of which human rights and freedoms were born; upon its success rests the hope of the world."[82] In a post-Holocaust, postimperial world, states needed to give away some of their sovereignty to secure peace.

The phonograph, radio, telephone, and airplane were all invented or became readily available in Baeck's lifetime. It was a revolution in how people experienced space akin to how many think of the global village in the digital age today. These technological developments, Baeck believed, were making the world smaller. The shrinking of space in this regard could have a positive impact by bringing people together. But there were also

---

[80] Ibid., 166.

[81] While this was not the first reading of Paul in light of his Jewish background, it was relatively innovative for its time. See Samuel Sandmel, *Leo Baeck on Christianity* (New York: Leo Baeck Institute, 1975), 14–15. The New Perspective on Paul approach, which seeks to place him within the context of the Jewish background, would fully emerge only a decade later with the work of Krister Stendhal, who perhaps not incidentally knew Baeck's work, as he wrote an introduction to Leo Baeck, *The Pharisees and Other Essays* (New York: Schocken Books, 1966). See Krister Stendhal, "The Apostle Paul and the Introspective Conscience of the West," *Harvard Theological Review* 56, no. 3 (1963): 199–215.

[82] "Dr. Baeck given Honorary Degree," *Philadelphia Jewish Times*, March 12, 1948.

Cold War Judaism 177

dangers involved. Baeck described Theresienstadt as an ever-shrinking space that could lead to moral collapse.[83] In "The Meaning of History," shortly after liberation, Baeck said: "Now, every people has come nearer to another. At the same time, there is no place of refuge on earth, the people cannot avoid one another any longer."[84] Implied in this comment might be the idea that there were no longer "empty spaces" awaiting settlers, as if some territories were colonial spaces waiting to be conquered, through labor or otherwise. The entire world was populated and claimed.[85]

There was simply no alternative to learning to live together, even if one did not enjoy the idea of having neighbors. Isolationism, to return to Baeck's point about American Jews, was not an option. Baeck's imperial imagination was initially shaped by ideas of expansion and cultivation of land and people. After the Holocaust, he adopted an approach that saw the task as learning to live together. The United Nations was in this understanding the organization tasked with making sure coexistence in this populated, ever-shrinking world was possible.

Violent clashes in Palestine during the turbulent period following the U.N. declaration on the partition of Palestine in November 1947 caused the American position toward the establishment of the state of Israel to waver. Baeck described this as shortsighted and "an example of international immorality that is all too prevalent in a world with too little religious faith."[86] The way to combat such "international immorality" in Baeck's view was through promoting religion, which needed to be infused into the United Nations. "There can be no successful United Nations," argued Baeck, "until religions will have succeeded in elevating the souls of the peoples of the world. For even diplomacy, as practiced by the greatest of our statesmen, must be based upon faith. Faith and trust are the factors without which the United Nations cannot achieve success."[87]

Religion, Baeck argued, could foster peace in the age of the Cold War. In an interview on the occasion of his trip to the American Jewish Cavalcade, Baeck declared that "without religion and faith to inspire peace,

---

[83] Baeck's foreword to Adler, *Theresienstadt*, xi.

[84] Leo Baeck, "Der Sinn der Geschichte (1946)," 30; cf. Baeck, "Some Questions to the Christian Church (1954)," 451; Baeck, "Ansprache zum Gründungstag (1953)," 554; Baeck, *This People*, 311.

[85] The argument that Europe was suffering from overpopulation was a common one in the 1930s, see Mark Mazower, *No Enchanted Palace: The End of Empire and the Ideological Origins of the United Nations* (Princeton: Princeton University Press, 2013), 109.

[86] "U.S. Reversal on Palestine Fresh Symptom of World Immorality, Says London Rabbi," *The Boston Herald*, March 31, 1948.

[87] "U.S. Reversal on Palestine Fresh Symptom of World Immorality."

peace cannot be achieved," adding that religion was what kept him and other inmates of the concentration camp "spiritually healthy."[88] The United States was essential in this regard, as it could propagate religion and make sure the United Nations would be a religiously motivated organization. Without the full support of the United States, precisely because it was a religious nation, the United Nations would not endure. Like Atlas carrying the world, Baeck said, the fate of the world was on American shoulders.[89]

The twin ideas of propagating religion and the rejection of isolationism were therefore not limited to Baeck's vision of Judaism. They were part of the same postwar Jewish imperial vision in which Judaism and Jews played an exemplary role. President Truman spoke of the "mutual Judaic Christian culture" and gave the Ten Commandments and the Sermon on the Mount as examples. Baeck would have agreed with Truman's sentiment, because he too believed religion had the potential to bring about peace and moral progress. Baeck would have insisted, however, that even the Sermon on the Mount be considered Jewish. The order of things was clear. The Judeo-Christian tradition cannot exist without the Judaic part, for the Hebrew Bible, the New Testament, and Paul all belong to Judaism, part of its history within the Church.

As Baeck's writings from the Wilhelmine Empire onward show, Jews had a world-historical task. The postwar era was no different. This era in Jewish history was about hope, and for hope to thrive, religious ethics were needed in the aftermath of the destruction brought by the Second World War and the Holocaust. Jews should help American Atlas carry its burden. They could do so, Baeck suggested, by conducting themselves ethically based on the values of Judaism in both the centers of Jewish existence, by training Jewish missionaries that will go forth from the United States, and by offering a model society in Palestine. In this, they would not only gain respect but prove the value of religion in politics. At stake, according to Baeck, was not only Jewish existence but the fate of the world.

---

[88] Baeck and Dyck, "Ohne Religion und Glaube – Keine Weltfrieden!"
[89] *Philadelphia Jewish Exponent*, February 6, 1948; "Religion Is Termed Key to U.N. Success," *The New York Times*, February 1, 1948; "Jewish Leader Says Religion Vital to the U.N.," *The Baltimore News-Post*, February 14, 1948.

Epilogue
Remembering German Jewry, Forgetting Empire

Leo Baeck was a thinker attuned to changing constellations of power and domination. He lived through tumultuous times that saw the zenith and downfall of the Wilhelmine Empire, the Weimar Republic, the Third Reich, and the division of Germany. Colonialism, two world wars, the Holocaust, the establishment of the state of Israel, and the Cold War all left their mark on his thought. In response to those changes, Baeck developed various Jewish imperial imaginaries.

Moving beyond an abstract concept of a Jewish ethical mission to the nations, he claimed in *The Essence of Judaism* (1905) that Jews were, and should become, active missionaries. This idea of active missionizing was part and parcel of colonial discourse. Baeck kept this view in the *Legal Position*, the lengthy manuscript composed under Nazism, writing that Judaism appealed to the Hellenistic world and was successful in proselytizing. In the postwar era, Baeck hoped that American Jewry would train such missionaries. This task, he suggested, was more urgent than ever, given the destruction of world Jewry in the Holocaust.

Baeck's imperial imagination was not accompanied by a belief in the power and violence of imperial conquest. From the *Essence* onward , Baeck maintained a distinction between spiritual energy (*Kraft*) and violent power (*Macht*). The former, he suggested, was the Jewish way. Baeck maintained this position in Theresienstadt Ghetto, contrasting Greco-Roman and Western pessimist writing of history with prophetic hope. Empires built on violence, he said to inmates in the ghetto, would crumble and become nothing but ruins and rubble. Even in dark times, Baeck believed, it was possible to adopt prophetic hope and see the progress of justice in history.

Imperial imagination can be inconsistent and may contain multitudes and contradictions, such as rejecting violence while still endorsing a colonial mindset of expansion, hierarchy, and settlement. Baeck's was no exception in this regard. The position he saw for Judaism in the academic study of religion is a case in point. He worked with dichotomies that served to position Judaism as the highest – meaning most ethical – form of religion. In the *Essence*, he called Judaism a religion of optimism and contrasted it with Buddhism as a religion of pessimism. In making these classifications, Baeck participated in a prevalent colonial and orientalist discourse that shaped religious studies.

In "Romantic Religion," Baeck once again introduced a dichotomy building on classification of religions. Judaism was a classical religion versus Christianity, in particular Protestantism, which was a romantic religion. By positing this dichotomy, Baeck attempted to understand the theological roots of the society he was living in. Romantic religion, he argued, was in fact a dualistic, Marcionite flight from the world. As such, it had an unethical component that was only mitigated through the presence of Judaism within Christianity. Baeck would return to Marcion in the postwar era, when he tried to explain Nazism, as well as the challenges facing the contemporary church, along those lines.

Traces of imperial imagination are also evident in Baeck's work in Theresienstadt and postwar lectures, where he claimed savages have no history. He thereby marked them in contemporary understanding as potentially less than, or at least not yet, fully human. Finally, Baeck's ideas about Jewish *Kraft* and missionizing were similar to the notion of a civilizing mission and the right of a colonizer to the land in the name of its improvement. This was part of his justification of the Jewish settlement in Palestine.

The world upon Baeck's death in 1956 was radically different from the one into which he was born in 1873. What place do the imperial imaginations with which Baeck engaged have in the twenty-first century? What remains of Baeck's ideas? To show how Baeck is remembered today I turn to three institutions that bear his name: the Leo Baeck Temple in Los Angeles; the Leo Baeck Institute, with branches in New York, London, Jerusalem, and Berlin; and the Leo-Baeck-Haus in Berlin. They show how Baeck's memory is utilized in the public sphere as symbolizing the value of Jewish ethics, the creative power of German Jewry, and the continuity of the Jewish community in Germany in the aftermath of the Holocaust.

These are all facets of how Leo Baeck is remembered. As this book has shown, there is another Leo Baeck, the thinker engaging empire. Recognizing this aspect means the legacy of German Jewry and that of German colonialism need to be considered in tandem. By turning to recent debates in contemporary Germany, I show a similar dynamic at play in the politics of memory. Understanding Baeck as an imperial

Epilogue 181

thinker is therefore not only a question of the historiography of German-Jewish thought. It also points to the vexed contemporary relation between the memory of the Holocaust and that of German colonialism.

The Temple

The idea that the Jewish minority is the yardstick of morality and a bearer of ethics was a central tenet of Baeck's teachings. The term *tikkun olam*, mending or repairing the world, nowadays refers to similar ideas. Its usage as a catchall shorthand for Jewish social ethics began in the 1950s, but became more common in the 1970s and 1980s. Since then, *tikkun olam* has become such a buzzword among Jewish activists that some rabbis have urged greater restraint in its usage, arguing it is too removed from its original meaning in the second century *Aleinu* prayer and later in Lurianic kabbalah.[1]

Although Baeck's name is not often invoked in this context, the philosopher Emil Fackenheim, who was Baeck's student in Berlin in the 1930s, argued Baeck was interested in the notion of *tikkun olam*. In a sermon in Nazi Berlin on the *Aleinu*, Baeck preached, according to Fackenheim, "about the abomination of the false gods and everyone present knew what he had in mind," before ending "with the subject of *tikkun olam*," which in Baeck's interpretation was "preparing the world for the kingship of God."[2] Similar to the way in which he spoke of the Nazis as an empire bound to fall, here Nazism was the abomination of idolatry. *Tikkun olam*, in other words, may have been used by Baeck as a coded protest against the Nazi empire.

In emphasizing prophetic ethics, Baeck was part of the Reform and Liberal tradition in Judaism. This tradition was taken forward by Leonard

---

[1] Jill Jacobs, "The History of 'Tikkun Olam,'" *Zeek*, June 2007, http://www.zeek.net/706tohu/; Arnold Jacob Wolf, "Repairing Tikkun Olam," *Judaism* 50, no. 4 (2001): 479–82; Byron Sherwin, "The Assimilation of Judaism: Heschel and the 'Category Mistake,'" *Judaism*, no. 3–4 (2006): 40–51.

[2] Emil Fackenheim, *What Is Judaism?: An Interpretation for the Present Age* (New York: Summit Books, 1987), 198–99; Jonathan Krasner, "The Place of Tikkun Olam in American Jewish Life," *Jewish Political Studies Review* 25, no. 3/4 (2013): 67; Fackenheim himself would take up the term in his post-Holocaust philosophy, see Emil Fackenheim, *To Mend the World: Foundations of Post-Holocaust Jewish Thought* (Bloomington: Indiana University Press, 1994); Fackenheim's addresses in Baeck's memory are Emil Fackenheim, "After Auschwitz, Jerusalem: In Memory of My Teacher, Leo Baeck," *Judaism* 50, no. 1 (2001): 53–59; Emil Fackenheim, "In Memory of Leo Baeck, and Other Jewish Thinkers 'In Dark Times': Once More, 'After Auschwitz, Jerusalem,'" *Judaism* 51, no. 3 (2002): 282–92.

The Jewish Imperial Imagination

Beerman, the longtime rabbi of the Leo Baeck Temple in Los Angeles. Beerman and Baeck met at least once, in 1953 when Beerman was a young rabbi and Baeck visited the synagogue named in his honor. On several occasions, Beerman spoke with reverence of Baeck's life and religious thought, utilizing, for example, Baeck's idea of mystery and commandment as complementing one another.[3] As the rabbi of a synagogue bearing Baeck's name, Beerman serves as an example of the prophetic ethics that are part of Baeck's legacy.

Some of Beerman's views would have likely made the namesake of the Temple in Los Angeles uncomfortable. According to David Myers, Beerman espoused "lifelong agnosticism."[4] Baeck, on the other hand, insisted on prophetic hope and trust in God even in Theresienstadt and the aftermath of the Holocaust. The two also diverged in their assessment of communism. Baeck consistently rejected communism as atheist and hence antithetical to Judaism. Beerman, by contrast, saw in the "red scare" of the late 1940s and early 1950s a way to distract the public from real social problems in the United States.[5]

For all their differences, the two agreed on the need for interfaith dialogue and the role of Jewish ethics in the world. During the Wilhelmine period and even more so during the Weimar Republic and the early days of Nazism, Baeck was a sharp critic of Protestantism in Germany. He nonetheless sought to serve as a representative of Judaism for non-Jewish circles in order to correct misconception. It was only in the postwar era, however, that real theological rapprochement occurred. Baeck advocated for such interfaith dialogue and believed it held the key to a more ethical world.

Beerman, who came of age in the post-polemic era, tirelessly participated in interfaith efforts throughout his life. He developed, for example, decades-long collaborations with other religious leaders such as George Regas, the rector of All Saints Church in Pasadena, California. The two fulfilled Baeck's vision that religion had a role to play in the prevention of

---

[3] For Beerman's biography, see David Myers's introduction in David Myers, ed., *The Eternal Dissident: Rabbi Leonard I. Beerman and the Radical Imperative to Think and Act* (Oakland, CA: University of California Press, 2018), 12–50; reference to Baeck in Beerman, "My Troubles with God; God's Troubles with Me, February 9, 1979," in *The Eternal Dissident*, 129; Beerman, "Yom Kippur Eve, September 26, 1982," in *The Eternal Dissident*, 263.

[4] Myers's introduction to David Myers, ed., *The Eternal Dissident*, 19.

[5] Leonard Beerman, "Chapel Sermon, October 30, 1948," in *The Eternal Dissident*, 58; see also Beerman, "The Kindest Use of the Knife, October 16, 1953," in *The Eternal Dissident*, 136–44.

Epilogue 183

violence, helping, for example, to establish the Interfaith Center to Reverse the Arms Race.[6]

Both Baeck and Beerman followed the idea that the Jewish ethical task was grounded in prophetic ethics. Beerman spoke, for example, of the "Jewish mission among the nations" as that of "the doing of justice, the showing of mercy, and the pursuit of righteousness." He added that "the prophets of ancient Israel never died, for their spirit was resurrected not once, but a thousand times in the annals of the Jewish people."[7] These words came from a 1953 sermon reflecting on the legacy of the Reform leader Stephen Wise, but they were also in line with Baeck's teaching and could almost have been written by him.

Beerman, like Baeck, had strong emotional ties to the state of Israel but was not afraid to critique it when necessary. In a 1982 Yom Kippur sermon, a few months after Israel invaded Lebanon, Beerman cited Baeck's teaching that through Judaism, "the highest possible standard is imposed upon us." This ethical standard led Beerman to be "full of shame and horror and despair" of this war that "was doomed to be a moral and political failure."[8] The prophetic ethics remained valid when critiquing the actions of Jews, who were also held accountable.

Beerman was beloved by his congregation. He served as the rabbi of the Leo Baeck Temple between 1949 and 1986 and continued to give an annual Yom Kippur sermon until shortly before his death in 2014. Yet his views, especially when it came to the state of Israel, did not always sit comfortably with all community members. The former rabbi of the Leo Baeck Temple in Los Angeles thus represents only one way in which Baeck is remembered. Baeck's primary legacy is as the leader and symbol of German Jewry.

The Institute

The fact that Baeck was chosen to lead the Reichsvertretung in 1933 shows he was widely recognized as a leader representing many German Jews already during his lifetime. His fame only increased in the postwar era. For Baeck's eightieth birthday in 1953, a volume in his honor included, among

---

[6] Myers, *The Eternal Dissident*, 37–38; on Regas, see Jennifer Lu, "George Regas, Progressive Crusader and Longtime Rector of All Saints in Pasadena, Dies at 90," *Los Angeles Times*, January 6, 2021, www.latimes.com/california/story/2021-01-06/george-regas-social-justice-leader-episcopal-church-dead-at-90.

[7] Beerman, "Kindest Use of the Knife," 137–38.

[8] Beerman, "Yom Kippur Eve, September 26, 1982," in *The Eternal Dissident*, 263.

184 The Jewish Imperial Imagination

others, contributions by Nobel laureates Thomas Mann and Albert Einstein, the Jewish thinkers Abraham Joshua Heschel and Martin Buber, and the French Catholic thinker and proponent of human rights Jacques Maritain.[9] This tribute highlights his stature among intellectuals.

Baeck was also treated as a political dignitary. He met, as mentioned, President Truman at the White House and opened a session of the House of Representatives with a prayer. That he was on friendly terms with the first president of West Germany, Theodor Heuss, raised Baeck's stature further. Baeck first met Heuss through Otto Hirsch in the 1930s, and the two resumed contact after the Holocaust. When Baeck came to Germany to lecture on Maimonides in 1954, for example, Heuss made a point of attending.[10] A symbolic capital was being exchanged in those encounters with world leaders: Baeck situated himself as a leading figure after the war, while his interlocutors were benefitting from the moral authority Baeck conveyed.

Baeck was treated in the postwar era as the spiritual leader of German Jewry and its symbol. His lectures after the Holocaust helped cement this image. Shortly before his death, for example, he gave a series of four lectures in Münster, titled "From Moses Mendelssohn to Franz Rosenzweig." They were dedicated to the intellectual legacy of German Jewry that he himself came to embody. In the last lecture, Baeck celebrated German-Jewish contributions to intellectual life by noting that out of the four great "revolutions in the realm of spirit" in the modern era, three were initiated by German-Jewish intellectuals: Einstein, Freud, and Marx (the fourth being Darwin).[11]

The canonization of Baeck as a symbol of German Jewry reached its apex with an initiative by leading German-Jewish émigrés – including Hannah Arendt, Martin Buber, and Robert Weltsch – to establish an institution for the preservation of the legacy of German Jewry. They named it after Baeck, who was appointed its first president.[12] The locations of the three Leo Baeck Institutes (LBI) corresponded to Baeck's biography and thought. One is in London, where he lived after the war.

---

[9] *Essays Presented to Leo Baeck on the Occasion of His Eightieth Birthday* (London: East and West Library, 1954).

[10] Leo Baeck, "Maimonides – der Mann, sein Werk und seine Wirkung (1954)," 139–57. See also the letters in Baeck, *Werke* 6, 683–96.

[11] Leo Baeck, "Von Moses Mendelssohn zu Franz Rosenzweig (1956)," 195; see also Leo Baeck, "Das Überleben des Geistes (1953)," *Werke* 6, 486.

[12] Christhard Hoffmann, "The Founding of the Leo Baeck Institute, 1945–1955," in *Preserving the Legacy of German Jewry: History of the Leo Baeck Institute, 1955–2005*, ed. Christhard Hoffmann (Tübingen: Mohr Siebeck, 2005), 1–15.

Epilogue

The others are in Jerusalem and New York, two cities representing the two centers of Jewish existence in his postwar thought. In the early twenty-first century, a branch of the archives of LBI New York was established in the Jewish Museum Berlin, the city Baeck called home for decades. The public and scholarly activities emerging from LBI shape the way German-Jewish history is understood, and thereby how the name Leo Baeck is associated with this history.

An early major publication supported by the Leo Baeck Institute was Siegmund Kaznelson's *Jews in the German Cultural Sphere*. Kaznelson started this extensive bibliographic documentation of Jews in all spheres of German culture, from chess to politics and from art to economics, during the Weimar Republic. It was completed in 1934, but was banned by the Nazis. It was finally published in 1959, and Robert Weltsch, the first director of LBI London, wrote the foreword to this new edition. *Jews in the German Cultural Sphere* represents a common attitude among the founding generation of the LBI, namely the attempt to celebrate the Jewish contribution to culture.[13]

German-Jewish History in Modern Times (1996–1998), a four volume multi-author history, was the culmination of the LBI's attempt to produce a comprehensive history of Jews in Germany.[14] Critically reviewing this work, David Sorkin noted how categories shifted in the study of German Jewry: from earlier discussions of assimilation, the authors turned to acculturation and from contribution to culture to participation in culture.[15] Sorkin contended, however, that the work failed to offer a unified narrative. If there was coherency between the volumes and different authors, in his view it was found in what he called "the émigré synthesis." The work as a whole reflected in this reading the concerns of the first generation of LBI founders, including highlighting the contribution to culture, the question of liberalism and Zionism, and debates about

---

[13] Andreas Kilcher, "The Grandeur and Collapse of the German-Jewish Symbiosis: Hans Tramer and Jewish Literary Studies at the Leo Baeck Institute," in *Preserving the Legacy of German Jewry: History of the Leo Baeck Institute, 1955–2005*, ed. Christhard Hoffmann (Tübingen: Mohr Siebeck, 2005), 409–10. Kaznelson's anthology is not listed, however, as an official LBI publication. Cf. the list of publications in Christhard Hoffmann, ed., *Preserving the Legacy of German Jewry: History of the Leo Baeck Institute, 1955–2005*, 443–62.

[14] On earlier attempts, see Christian Wiese, "A Master Narrative? The *Gesamtgeschichte* of German Jewry in Historical Context," in *Preserving the Legacy of German Jewry: History of the Leo Baeck Institute, 1955–2005*, ed. Christhard Hoffmann (Tübingen: Mohr Siebeck, 2005), 317–31.

[15] On the centrality and contested nature of "assimilation" in such historiography, see Till van Rahden, "Treason, Fate or Blessing? Narratives of Assimilation in the Historiography of German-Speaking Jewry since the 1950s," in *Preserving the Legacy of German Jewry: History of the Leo Baeck Institute, 1955–2005*, ed. Christhard Hoffmann (Tübingen: Mohr Siebeck, 2005), 347–74.

186   The Jewish Imperial Imagination

German-Jewish dialogue or symbiosis. The issue with such an approach, he suggested, was that it focused on the elite, and the concepts were not applied systematically, thereby in fact replicating the concerns of the old terms with a more scholarly, objective language.[16] While some of Sorkin's critiques might be off the mark – one could argue the value of a multi-authored work is precisely in offering multiple perspectives and approaches, at times using different terminology – his review highlights the ways in which the historiography of Jews in Germany at the end of the twentieth century still worked with inherited categories while emphasizing the legacy of German-Jewish contributions to, or participation in, culture.[17]

Michael Meyer noted in the preface to this project that historiography was constantly evolving. *German-Jewish History in Modern Times*, in other words, was never intended to be a final statement.[18] One major historiographical development since then has been research on the German colonial legacy. How Jews participated in colonialism, or rejected it, was not a concern for authors of *German-Jewish History in Modern Times*, likely because it was also not a topic of concern for German historians at the time.[19] Yet as I have argued throughout this book, it is central for our understanding of Leo Baeck, and German-Jewish thought more broadly.

LBI shapes the memory of German Jewry not only through scholarship, but also by recognizing efforts of preservation of German-Jewish culture. The Leo Baeck Medal has been awarded by the LBI New York since 1978. It is its highest award, given to "people who have made extraordinary efforts to preserve the memory of German-speaking Jews." The medal is inscribed on its front with an image of Baeck and the words "Leader of German Jewry." The inscription on the back reads: "so that the memory of a great past may not perish." In recent years, the Leo Baeck Medal has been awarded to German politicians and state leaders. Presidents of Germany have received it, Frank-Walter Steinmeier in 2022 and Joachim Gauck in 2014. It was also awarded to the then chancellor

---

[16] David Sorkin, "The Émigré Synthesis: *German-Jewish History in Modern Times*," *Central European History* 34, no. 4 (2001): 532–33. See also Michael Steinberg, *Judaism Musical and Unmusical* (Chicago: Chicago University Press, 2007), 187–92.

[17] Christian Wiese, "A Master Narrative?," 343–45.

[18] Michael Meyer's preface to the series in Michael Meyer, ed., *German-Jewish History in Modern Times* (New York: Columbia University Press, 1996), 1:ix.

[19] Stefan Vogt, "Contextualizing German-Jewish History," in *Colonialism and the Jews in German History: From the Middle Ages to the Twentieth Century*, ed. Stefan Vogt (London: Bloomsbury, 2022), 7.

Epilogue

Angela Merkel in 2010 and former foreign minister Joschka Fischer in 2009.

Like Baeck's exchanges with world leaders in the postwar era, this award given by LBI functions in a twofold way. It conveys moral authority and legitimization for the recipient of the prize, while also supporting the mandate of the institution awarding the prize as the consolidator of the memory of German Jewry. Through this award, public events, and scholarship, LBI positions itself as a central site of memory of German Jewry. The name Leo Baeck stands for this memory.

The House

As the leader of German Jewry during the Holocaust, Baeck became a symbol also of the destruction of the community. After German reunification, the Central Council of Jews in Germany (*Zentralrat der Juden in Deutschland*) moved its offices in 1999 to the former site of the *Hochschule für die Wissenschaft des Judentums* in Berlin, where Baeck taught for three decades. They named the building the Leo-Baeck-Haus, thereby establishing a claim for historical continuity and moral authority.

The Leo Baeck prize has been awarded by the Zentralrat since 1957 to people who championed support for community and the future of Jewish life in Germany. Among recent recipients are politicians. In 2018, it was awarded to Norbert Lammert, former president of the Bundestag. Volker Beck of the Green Party received it in 2015, President Christian Wulff in 2011, and Angela Merkel in 2007.[20] As in the case of the Leo Baeck Medal, an exchange of recognition and social capital is working on both sides.

Representing around 100,000 people – likely about half the Jews in Germany and less than a quarter percent of the total population – the Zentralrat's voice is heard at a volume far stronger than its actual numbers. This is not surprising. The memory of the Holocaust is a pillar of German self-understanding in the postwar era and after reunification. Evidence of its importance is the vast memorial landscape that expands throughout Germany, including Jewish museums, the Memorial for the Murdered Jews of Europe near Brandenburg Gate in Berlin, restored synagogues, *Stolpersteine* – small golden plaques placed on the floor in front of houses that Jews were forced to leave, often to their death – and memorials in

---

[20] Zentralrat der Juden, "Preisträger Seit 1957," May 16, 2019, www.zentralratderjuden.de/der-zentralrat/auszeichnungen/leo-baeck-preis/preistraeger-seit-1957/.

188   The Jewish Imperial Imagination

train stations from which Jews were sent to ghettos, camps, and killing centers. It is because of this centrality that the official Jewish position in Germany receives careful attention.[21]

Baeck's name is present in this memorial constellation and in contemporary Jewish life in Germany. Baeck was a man of his time, and his time was that of empires. Highlighting this aspect of Baeck's thought means taking him not only as a symbol of German Jewry, but also of the entanglement of questions. It thereby brings forth the remembrance not only of the Holocaust but also of the German colonial legacy.

These issues are now being discussed in the German public sphere. In 2018, an official German government coalition document described the need for "working through colonialism" (*Aufarbeitung des Kolonialismus*) and "working through German colonial history" (*Aufarbeitung der deutschen Kolonialgeschichte*). Colonial history is now understood as an important aspect of public memory, discussed alongside Nazi atrocities, the East German dictatorship, and positive democratic moments.[22] The reckoning with colonial legacies of racism, xenophobia, and violence, however, is still sanctioned in German mainstream discourse, however, only insofar as the memory of the Holocaust takes precedence.[23] While such a position is clear in Germany, it is not limited to it. In the United States, a debate about the legitimacy of Holocaust comparisons was provoked by Congresswoman Alexandria Ocasio-Cortez's comments in 2019 that the conditions in U.S. Immigration and Customs Enforcement (ICE) migrant detention centers on the southern border were those of "camps," a word meant to evoke the concentration camps.[24]

---

[21] Dan Diner, "Negative Symbiose: Deutsche und Juden nach Auschwitz," *Babylon: Beiträge zur jüdischen Gegenwart* 1 (1988): 243–57; Y. Michal Bodemann, "The State in the Construction of Ethnicity and Ideological Labor: The Case of German Jewry," *Critical Sociology* 17, no. 3 (1990): 35–46; Aleida Assmann, *Shadows of Trauma: Memory and the Politics of Postwar Identity* (New York: Fordham University Press, 2016); Aleida Assmann, *Das neue Unbehagen an der Erinnerungskultur: Eine Intervention* (München: C. H. Beck, 2016); James Young, *At Memory's Edge: After-Images of the Holocaust in Contemporary Art and Architecture* (New Haven: Yale University Press, 2000); Irit Dekel, *Mediation at the Holocaust Memorial in Berlin* (New York: Palgrave Macmillan, 2013), 209–30.

[22] "Ein neuer Aufbruch für Europa. Eine neue Dynamik für Deutschland. Ein neuer Zusammenhalt für unser Land. Koalitionsvertrag zwischen CDU, CSU und SPD, 19. Legislaturperiode," 2018, 154, 167, www.bundesregierung.de/breg-de/themen/koalitionsvertrag-zwischen-cdu-csu-undspd-195906.

[23] For two different assessments of this trend, see Dan Diner, *Gegenläufige Gedächtnisse: Über Geltung und Wirkung des Holocaust* (Göttingen: Vandenhoeck & Ruprecht, 2007); Michael Rothberg, *Multidirectional Memory: Remembering the Holocaust in the Age of Decolonization* (Stanford: Stanford University Press, 2009).

[24] Michael Rothberg, "The Specters of Comparison," *Zeitgeister: International Perspectives from Culture and Society*, May 2020, www.goethe.de/prj/zei/gen/pos/21864662.html; Peter Gordon, "Why

Epilogue

The so-called Mbembe Affair highlights tensions in contemporary Germany's memorial politics, and the place of Jews and colonial subjects in them. Achille Mbembe, a leading postcolonial philosopher from Cameroon, was invited to give a keynote speech at the 2020 Ruhrtriennale festival in Bochum. Following critique by Lorenz Deutsch of the Free Democratic Party (FDP), Felix Klein, the Commissioner for Jewish Life in Germany and the Fight Against Antisemitism, chimed in and demanded the disinvitation of Mbembe. The argument he and others made was that Mbembe's work contained antisemitic stereotypes.

Josef Schuster, the president of the Zentralrat, went even further and demanded the firing of the festival's director Stefanie Carp for inviting Mbembe in the first place and defending him.[25] This was not the first time those deemed insufficiently pro-Israel were accused by the Zentralrat of antisemitism and anti-Jewish biases. Indeed, this seems to be a recurring theme emerging in several recent controversies. In 2019, for example, the director of the Jewish Museum Berlin, Peter Schäfer, a leading Jewish Studies scholars who came to the museum from Princeton University, resigned after a campaign against him and the museum. One of the leading critics was Schuster, who argued the museum was too critical of Israel and was therefore not worthy of the label Jewish.[26]

One can only surmise about Baeck's own position today regarding Israel, and whether he would approve of the positions taken by the people seated at the Leo-Baeck-Haus. His philosophy, shaped as it was by the imperial imaginations of the era, does not lend itself easily to contemporary discussions of the state of Israel or the German politics of memory. Given his views up to his death in 1956, however, it is very likely he would have supported the state of Israel. There was no question in Baeck's mind

---

Historical Analogy Matters," *The New York Review of Books*, January 7, 2020, www.nybooks.com/daily/2020/01/07/why-historical-analogy-matters/.

[25] Benjamin Weinthal, "German Jewish Head Opposes BDS Speaker, Anti-Israel Director," *The Jerusalem Post*, April 28, 2020, www.jpost.com/diaspora/antisemitism/german-jewish-head-opposes-bds-speaker-wants-anti-israel-director-fired-625858.

[26] Yaniv Feller, "Whose Museum Is It? Jewish Museums and Indigenous Theory," *Comparative Studies in Society and History* 63 (2021): 816–22; Itay Mashiach, "In Germany, a Witch Hunt Is Raging against Critics of Israel. Cultural Leaders Have Had Enough," *Haaretz.Com*, December 10, 2020, www.haaretz.com/israel-news/.premium.HIGHLIGHT.MAGAZINE-in-germany-a-witch-hunt-rages-against-israel-critics-many-have-had-enough-1.9362662; Sa'ed Atshan and Katharina Galor, *The Moral Triangle: Germans, Israelis, Palestinians* (Durham, NC: Duke University Press, 2020); Irit Dekel and Esra Özyürek, "What Do We Talk About When We Talk about Antisemitism in Germany?," *Journal of Genocide Research* 23, no. 3 (2021): 396–97.

190   The Jewish Imperial Imagination

that Jews had the right to settle in Palestine. True to his imperial imagination of establishing colonies and the task of Jews in the world, he believed that they improved the land, and this confirmed their right.

At the same time, Baeck was a proponent of prophetic ethics and the belief that Jews as a minority were the yardstick of morality and bearers of ethics. The Jewish state was and is not above this idea. Baeck believed that a Jewish state could not ignore the moral task at the heart of Judaism. Baeck made this point throughout his life with the emphasis on *Kraft* rather than *Macht*. He was not afraid to condemn Jewish violence in Palestine, for example, in the *New York Times* opinion column he co-signed with Albert Einstein in 1948.[27] An occupying state mistreating its minorities was hardly something for which Baeck would have offered his unequivocal support.

Accusations such as those made by the Zentralrat and Klein risk erasing such nuances. Following the Mbembe Affair and calls to have him removed from office, Klein refused to apologize but clarified his position in an interview to the newspaper *Die Zeit*. He posited a relationship between postcolonial studies and antisemitism and argued that "some of these theories very clearly stand in opposition to our culture of remembrance ... It could be that people in other countries aren't as sensitive to such issues, but something that is wrong from the German perspective doesn't become right just because it comes from elsewhere."[28] This clarification is illuminating in several ways.

First, Klein is representative of a broader perspective in German public and political discourse. In May 2019, the German Bundestag passed a resolution condemning the Boycott, Divestment, Sanction (BDS) movement as antisemitic and preventing federal funding to organizations that support it. In fact, Klein's claim that Mbembe was antisemitic was based primarily on Mbembe's support of BDS and a comparison he made between the state of Israel and Apartheid in South Africa. Comparing Israel to South Africa and supporting BDS implies in this understanding a denial of the state of Israel's right to exist, which constitutes antisemitism according to the current German definition.[29]

---

[27] Leo Baeck and Albert Einstein, "Kooperation in Palästina – Ein Appell (1948)," 480–82.

[28] Adam Soboczynski, "Felix Klein: 'I See No Need for an Apology,'" *Die Zeit*, May 20, 2020, sec. Kultur, www.zeit.de/kultur/2020-05/felix-klein-holocaust-achille-mbembe-protests-english; see also Philipp Dorestal, "Reassessing Mbembe: Postcolonial Critique and the Continuities of Extreme Violence," *Journal of Genocide Research* 23, no. 3 (July 3, 2021): 388–91.

[29] Aleida Assmann, "A Spectre Is Haunting Germany: The Mbembe Debate and the New Antisemitism," *Journal of Genocide Research* 23, no. 3 (2021): 403–6.

Epilogue

Second, the position taken by Klein was that while critiques of Israel were permissible, certain statements go too far and could not be allowed in the German public sphere, precisely because they stand in opposition to the German politics of memory. It is the memory of the Holocaust, in other words, that determines the relationship to the state of Israel and gives it primacy as representative of the Jews. This position is shared by Klein, a representative of the German government, and the Zentralrat.

Third, Klein's argument is nationally self-centered and does not recognize the transnational character of Holocaust memory. One of the features of the recent debate, as Michael Rothberg pointed out, was its global nature, with scholars from across the world – but primarily North America – intervening.[30] In this global controversy, the condemnation of Mbembe was far from universal, in Germany and outside it. He received support, for example, from intellectuals such as Aleida Assmann and Susan Neiman. They noted in a radio interview in Germany that Mbembe's voice deserves to be heard in the German public sphere, not least because, as a Cameroonian, his ancestors were subjected to German colonial rule.[31] German memory of the Holocaust is in this sense not limited to the confines of the German nation-state but transcends them and is open to multiple voices.

Finally, Klein argued that certain postcolonial theories espouse or support antisemitic views. This would make them illegitimate and beyond the pale of legitimate public discourse.[32] One can debate whether Mbembe's and other critics' positions extend all the way to a denial of Israel's right to exist or whether they are compelling critiques. But labeling Mbembe's views as antisemitic, or as drawing on antisemitic tropes, is a silencing mechanism that excludes this heir to German colonial violence from the public sphere.

The Mbembe Affair and current discourse about antisemitism in the German public sphere reveal how accusations of antisemitism, anti-

---

[30] Michael Rothberg, "Comparing Comparisons: From the 'Historikerstreit' to the Mbembe Affair," *Geschichte der Gegenwart*, September 23, 2020, https://geschichtedergegenwart.ch/comparing-comparisons-from-the-historikerstreit-to-the-mbembe-affair/.

[31] René Aguigah, "Die Welt reparieren, ohne zu relativieren: Aleida Assmann und Susan Neiman zur Causa Mbembe" (Deutschlandfunk Kultur, April 26, 2020); see also Aleida Assmann, "A Spectre Is Haunting Germany"; Susan Neiman and Anna-Esther Younes, "Antisemitism, Anti-Racism, and the Holocaust in Germany: A Discussion between Susan Neiman and Anna-Esther Younes," *Journal of Genocide Research* 23, no. 3 (July 3, 2021): 420–35.

[32] On Israel and postcolonial thought, see Bryan Cheyette, *Diasporas of the Mind: Jewish and Postcolonial Writing and the Nightmare of History* (New Haven: Yale University Press, 2013), 37–38.

The Jewish Imperial Imagination

Judaism, and anti-Israel biases serve to preclude engagement with post-colonial thought. This position is propagated by the Zentralrat from the Leo-Baeck-Haus. One effect of such discourse is that German-Jewish thinkers such as Leo Baeck are not discussed as participants in, and critics of, the German imperial imagination because of the insistence that the two spheres – German-Jewish thought and German colonialism – are completely separate.[33]

Almost 140 years after the Jewish and Colonial Questions were discussed in Germany, recent events such as the Mbembe Affair show the presence of the memory of empire is intertwined with the memory of the Holocaust. Nowadays, Leo Baeck is remembered primarily for the legacy of German Jewry, bravery in the face of Nazism, and prophetic ethics. Yet, as this book has shown, these convey only a partial view. The imperial imaginations Baeck developed draw attention to the themes of expansionism and missionizing, resistance and complicity, and the meaning of Jewish existence as a minority. Locating imperial imaginations in his work helps see the haunting of empire. Only with this imperial context can we fully understand Leo Baeck and the German-Jewish tradition.

[33] Stefan Vogt, "Contextualizing German-Jewish History," 2–4.

Bibliography

ARCHIVES

Beit Terezin, Givat Haim Ihud
Centrum Judaicum, Berlin
Erich Fromm Institute, Tübingen
Jewish Museum Berlin
Leo Baeck Institute Jerusalem
Leo Baeck Institute New York
National Library of Israel, Jerusalem
Prague Military Museum

SOURCES

Adler, Hans G. *Theresienstadt, 1941–1945: The Face of a Coerced Community.* Translated by Belinda Cooper. Cambridge: Cambridge University Press, 2015.

Adler-Rudel, Salomon. *Jüdische Selbsthilfe unter dem Naziregime 1933–1939: Im Spiegel der Berichte der Reichsvertretung der Juden in Deutschland.* Tübingen: Mohr Siebeck, 1974.

Aguigah, René. "Die Welt reparieren, ohne zu Relativieren: Aleida Assmann und Susan Neiman zur Causa Mbembe." *Deutschlandfunk Kultur,* April 26, 2020. www.deutschlandfunkkultur.de/aleida-assmann-und-susan-neiman-zur-causa-mbembe-die-welt-100.html.

Ahmed, Siraj. *Archaeology of Babel: The Colonial Foundation of the Humanities.* Stanford, CA: Stanford University Press, 2018.

Altmann, Alexander. *Leo Baeck and the Jewish Mystical Tradition.* New York: Leo Baeck Institute, 1973.

"Theology in Twentieth-Century German Jewry." *Leo Baeck Institute Year Book* 1 (1956): 193–216.

Anderson, Benedict. *Imagined Communities: Reflections on the Origin and Spread of Nationalism.* London: Verso, 2006.

Andreassen, Rikke. *Human Exhibitions: Race, Gender and Sexuality in Ethnic Displays.* New York: Routledge, 2015.

Bibliography

Angress, Werner. "The German Army's 'Judenzählung' of 1916: Genesis – Consequences – Significance." *The Leo Baeck Institute Year Book* 23, no. 1 (1978): 117–38.

Appelbaum, Peter. *Loyal Sons: Jews in the German Army in the Great War.* Portland, OR: Vallentine Mitchell, 2014.

Loyalty Betrayed: Jewish Chaplains in the German Army during the First World War. Portland, OR: Vallentine Mitchell, 2014.

Arendt, Hannah. *Eichmann in Jerusalem: A Report on the Banality of Evil.* New York: Penguin, 2006.

The Jewish Writings. Edited by Jerome Kohn and Ron Feldman. New York: Schocken Books, 2007.

The Origins of Totalitarianism. New York: Harcourt, 1973.

Armitage, David. "John Locke: Theorist of Empire?" In *Empire and Modern Political Thought,* edited by Sankar Muthu, 84–111. New York: Cambridge University Press, 2012.

Aschheim, Steven. *Brothers and Strangers: The East European Jew in German and German Jewish Consciousness, 1800–1923.* Madison: University of Wisconsin Press, 1982.

Assmann, Aleida. *Das neue Unbehagen an der Erinnerungskultur: Eine Intervention.* München: C. H. Beck, 2021.

Shadows of Trauma: Memory and the Politics of Postwar Identity. Translated by Sarah Clift. New York: Fordham University Press, 2016.

"A Spectre Is Haunting Germany: The Mbembe Debate and the New Antisemitism." *Journal of Genocide Research* 23, no. 3 (2021): 400–11.

Aston, Margaret. "English Ruins and English History: The Dissolution and the Sense of the Past." *Journal of the Warburg and Courtauld Institutes* 36 (1973): 231–55.

Atshan, Sa'ed, and Katharina Galor. *The Moral Triangle: Germans, Israelis, Palestinians.* Durham, NC: Duke University Press, 2020.

Aue-Ben-David, Irene. *Deutsch-jüdische Geschichtsschreibung im 20. Jahrhundert: Zu Werk und Rezeption von Selma Stern.* Göttingen: Vandenhoeck & Ruprecht, 2017.

Avraham, Doron. "Between Concern and Difference: German Jews and the Colonial 'Other' in South West Africa." *German History* 40, no. 1 (2022): 38–60.

Baader, Benjamin Maria. *Gender, Judaism, and Bourgeois Culture in Germany, 1800–1870.* Bloomington: Indiana University Press, 2006.

Bäck, Leo. "Harnack's Vorlesungen über das Wesen des Christentums." *Monatsschrift für Geschichte und Wissenschaft des Judentums* 45 (1901): 97–120.

Spinozas erste Einwirkung auf Deutschland. Berlin: Mayer & Müller, 1895.

Backhaus, Fritz. "'Ein Experiment des Willens zum Bösen': Überleben in Theresienstadt." In *Leo Baeck, 1873–1956: Aus dem Stamme von Rabbinern,* edited by Fritz Backhaus and Georg Heuberger, 111–28. Frankfurt am Main: Jüdischer Verlag, 2001.

Bibliography

Backhaus, Fritz, and Martin Liepach. "Leo Baecks Manuskript über die Rechtsstellung der Juden in Europa: Neue Funde und Ungeklärte Fragen." *Zeitschrift für Geschichtswissenschaft* 50 (2002): 55–71.

Baeck, Leo. "15 Jahre RjF: Dem Frontbund zum Gedenktage seines Beginnes." *Der Schild* 18, no. 3 (February 2, 1934): 1.

"In diesen Tagen." *Aufbau* 14, no. 13 (March 26, 1948): 1.

L'essence du judaïsme. Translated by Maurice-Ruben Hayoun. Paris: Presses Universitaires de France, 1993.

The Essence of Judaism. Translated by Victor Grubwieser and Leonard Pearl. New York: Schocken Books, 1961.

"Excerpts from Baeck's Writings." *Leo Baeck Institute Year Book* 2, no. 1 (1957): 35–47.

"Jewish Existence: A Lehrhaus Lecture of 30th May 1935." Translated by Curtis Cassel. *European Judaism: A Journal for the New Europe* 27, no. 1 (1994): 11–17.

Judaism and Christianity. Translated by Walter Kaufmann. Philadelphia: Jewish Publication Society of America, 1960.

"Die Kraft der Wenigen." *Der Schild* 14, no. 51 (December 20, 1935): 1.

Ma'hut Ha'yaha'dut. Translated by Lea Zgagi. Jerusalem: Bialik, 1967.

The Pharisees and Other Essays. New York: Schocken Books, 1966.

"Romantische Religion." In *Festschrift Zum 50jährigen Bestehen der Hochschule für die Wissenschaft des Judentums in Berlin*, 3–48. Berlin: Philo Verlag, 1922.

This People Israel: The Meaning of Jewish Existence. Translated by Albert Friedlander. New York: Holt, 1964.

Werke. Edited by Albert Friedlander, Berthold Klappert, Werner Licharz, and Michael Meyer. Gütersloh: Gütersloher Verlagshaus, 2006. 6 volumes.

"The Writing of History." *Synagogue Review*, November 1962, 51–59.

"Zum Boykott Tag." *AJR Information*, April 1973, 3.

Baeck, Leo, and Richard Dyck. "Ohne Religion und Glaube – keine Weltfrieden!" *Aufbau* 14, no. 2 (January 9, 1948): 1.

Baker, Leonard. *Days of Sorrow and Pain: Leo Baeck and the Berlin Jews*. New York: Macmillan, 1978.

Balibar, Étienne and Immanuel Wallerstein. *Race, Nation, Class: Ambiguous Identities*. London: Verso, 1991.

Bambach, Charles. *Heidegger, Dilthey, and the Crisis of Historicism*. Ithaca: Cornell University Press, 1995.

Baranowski, Shelley. *Nazi Empire: German Colonialism and Imperialism from Bismarck to Hitler*. Cambridge: Cambridge University Press, 2011.

Barber, Earl. "Dr. Baeck Says Peace Possible in Holy Land." *The Miami Herald*, January 13, 1948.

Barkai, Avraham. *From Boycott to Annihilation: The Economic Struggle of German Jews, 1933–1943*. Translated by William Templer. Waltham, MA: University Press of New England, 1989.

Hoffnung und Untergang: Studien zur deutsch-jüdischen Geschichte des 19. und 20. Jahrhunderts. Hamburg: Christians, 1998.

"Im Schatten der Verfolgung und Vernichtung: Leo Baeck in den Jahren des NS-Regimes." In *Leo Baeck, 1873–1956: Aus dem Stamme von Rabbinern*, edited by Fritz Backhaus and Georg Heuberger, 77–102. Frankfurt am Main: Jüdischer Verlag, 2001.

"Manhigut Be-Dimdumei Hidalun." In *Leo Baeck: Manhigut Ve-Hagut, 1933–1945*, edited by Avraham Barkai, 44–72. Jeruslaem: Leo Baeck Institute, 2000.

"Wehr Dich!": Der Centralverein deutscher Staatsbürger jüdischen Glaubens (C.V.) 1893–1938. Munich: C. H. Beck, 2002.

Barkin, Kenneth. "W. E. B. Du Bois' Love Affair with Imperial Germany." *German Studies Review* 28, no. 2 (2005): 285–302.

Bartal, Israel. *The Jews of Eastern Europe, 1772–1881*. Translated by Chaya Naor. Philadelphia: University of Pennsylvania Press, 2006.

Barth, Karl. *The Epistle to the Romans*. Translated by Edwyn Hoskyns. London: Oxford University Press, 1933.

Der Römerbrief. Zurich: TVZ, 2005.

The Word of God and the Word of Man. Translated by Amy Marga. Gloucester, MA: P. Smith, 1978.

Bauschulte, Manfred. *Religionsbahnhöfe der Weimarer Republik: Studien zur Religionsforschung 1918–1933*. Marburg: diagonal-Verlag, 2007.

Béguerie-De Paepe, Pantxika, and Magali Haas. *The Isenheim Altarpiece: The Masterpiece of the Musée Unterlinden*. Translated by Chrisoula Petridis. Colmar: Musée Unterlinden, 2015.

Beiser, Frederick. *Hermann Cohen: An Intellectual Biography*. Oxford: Oxford University Press, 2018.

Benor, Ehud. *Ethical Monotheism: A Philosophy of Judaism*. New York: Routledge, 2017.

Benz, Wolfgang. *The Holocaust: A German Historian Examines the Genocide*. Translated by Jane Sydenham-Kwiet. New York: Columbia University Press, 1999.

Theresienstadt: Eine Geschichte von Täuschung und Vernichtung. München: C. H. Beck, 2013.

Bergen, Doris. "Imperialism and the Holocaust." *Dapim: Studies on the Holocaust* 27 (2013): 62–68.

Twisted Cross: The German Christian Movement in the Third Reich. Chapel Hill: University of North Carolina Press, 1996.

War and Genocide: A Concise History of the Holocaust. Lanham: Rowman & Littlefield Publishers, 2016.

Bergmann, Schmuel Hugo. *Tagebücher & Briefe*. Edited by Miriam Sambursky. Frankfurt am Main: Jüdischer Verlag, 1985.

Berlin, Adele and Marc Zvi Brettler, eds. *The Jewish Study Bible*. New York: Oxford University Press, 2014.

Berman, Russell. *Enlightenment or Empire: Colonial Discourse in German Culture*. Lincoln: University of Nebraska Press, 1998.

Bhabha, Homi. *The Location of Culture*. London: Routledge, 2004.

Bibliography

197

Biale, David. *Gershom Scholem: Kabbalah and Counter-History*. Cambridge, MA: Harvard University Press, 1979.

Biemann, Asher. *Inventing New Beginnings: On the Idea of Renaissance in Modern Judaism*. Stanford, CA: Stanford University Press, 2009.

Bihl, Wolfdieter, ed. *Deutsche Quellen zur Geschichte des Ersten Weltkrieges*. Darmstadt: Wissenschaftliche Buchgesellschaft, 1991.

Bjork, James. *Neither German nor Pole: Catholicism and National Indifference in a Central European Borderland*. Ann Arbor: University of Michigan Press, 2009.

Blickle, Peter. *Heimat: A Critical Theory of the German Idea of Homeland*. Rochester: Camden House, 2002.

Blumenthal, Ilse Weiss. *Begegnungen mit Else Lasker-Schueler, Nelly Sachs, Leo Baeck, Martin Buber*. New York: Leo Baeck Instituts, 1977.

Bock, Gisela. *Zwangssterilisation im Nationalsozialismus: Studien zur Rassenpolitik und Frauenpolitik*. Opladen: Westdeutscher Verlag, 1986.

Bodemann, Y. Michal. "The State in the Construction of Ethnicity and Ideological Labor: The Case of German Jewry." *Critical Sociology* 17, no. 3 (1990): 35–46.

Boehm, Eric. *We Survived: Fourteen Histories of the Hidden and Hunted in Nazi Germany* New Haven: Yale University Press, 1949.

Bornstein, George. *The Colors of Zion: Blacks, Jews, and Irish from 1845 to 1945*. Cambridge, MA: Harvard University Press, 2011.

Bottici, Chiara. *Imaginal Politics: Images beyond Imagination and the Imaginary*. New York: Columbia University Press, 2014.

Botz, Gerhard. "The Dynamics of Persecution in Austria, 1938–1945." In *Austrians and Jews in the Twentieth Century: From Franz Joseph to Waldheim*, edited by Robert S. Wistrich, 199–219. New York: St. Martin's Press, 1992.

Bousset, Wilhelm. *Das Wesen der Religion, dargestellt an ihrer Geschichte*. Halle: Gebauer-Schwetschke, 1906.

Bowersox, Jeff. *Raising Germans in the Age of Empire: Youth and Colonial Culture, 1871–1914*. Oxford: Oxford University Press, 2013.

Boyarin, Jonathan. *The Unconverted Self: Jews, Indians, and the Identity of Christian Europe*. Chicago: Chicago University Press, 2009.

Braun, Christina von. *Versuch über den Schwindel: Religion, Schrift, Bild, Geschlecht*. Zurich and Munich: Pendo, 2001.

Brehl, Medardus. "'Das Drama spielte sich auf der dunklen Bühne des Sandfeldes ab': Die Vernichtung der Herero und Nama in der deutschen (populär-) Literatur." In *Völkermord in Deutsch-Südwestafrika: Der Kolonialkrieg (1904–1908) in Namibia und seine Folgen*, edited by Jürgen Zimmerer and Joachim Zeller, 86–96. Berlin: Ch. Links Verlag, 2016.

Brenner, Michael. *Prophets of the Past: Interpreters of Jewish History*. Translated by Steven Rendall. Princeton: Princeton University Press, 2010.

The Renaissance of Jewish Culture in Weimar Germany. New Haven: Yale University Press, 1996.

Bibliography

Breuer, Mordechai. *Modernity within Tradition: The Social History of Orthodox Jewry in Imperial Germany*. Translated by Elizabeth Petuchowski. New York: Columbia University Press, 1992.

Brocke, Bernhard von. "Wissenschaft und Militarismus: Der Aufruf der 93 'An die Kulturwelt!' und der Zusammenbruch der internationalen Gelehrtenrepublik im Ersten Weltkrieg." In *Wilamowitz nach 50 Jahren*, edited by William Calder, Hellmut Flashar, and Theodor Lindken, 649–716. Darmstadt: Wissenschaftliche Buchgesellschaft, 1985.

Brown, Wendy. *Regulating Aversion: Tolerance in the Age of Identity and Empire*. Princeton: Princeton University Press, 2006.

Brubaker, Rogers. *Citizenship and Nationhood in France and Germany*. Cambridge, MA: Harvard University Press, 2009.

"The Manichean Myth: Rethinking the Distinction between 'Civic' and 'Ethnic' Nationalism." In *Nation and National Identity: The European Experience in Perspective*, edited by Hanspeter Kriesi, Klaus Armington, Hannes Siegrist, and Andreas Wimmer, 55–71. West Lafayette: Purdue University Press, 2004.

Bruns, Claudia. "Antisemitism and Colonial Racisms: Genealogical Perspectives." In *Colonialism and the Jews in German History: From the Middle Ages to the Twentieth Century*, edited by Stefan Vogt, translated by Alissa Jones Nelson, 25–55. London: Bloomsbury, 2022.

Buber, Martin. "The Altar." *Journal of Visual Culture* 4, no. 1 (2005): 116–22.

Briefwechsel aus sieben Jahrzehnten. Edited by Grete Schaeder. Heidelberg: Lambert Schneider, 1972.

The Prophetic Faith. Translated by Carlyle Witton-Davies. New York: Harper, 1960.

Bukey, Evan. *Jews and Intermarriage in Nazi Austria*. Cambridge: Cambridge University Press, 2010.

Bülow, Bernhard von. "Bernhard von Bülow über Deutschlands 'Platz an der Sonne' (1897)." In *Deutsche Geschichte in Bilder und Dokumente*, edited by Roger Chickering, Steven Chase Gummer, and Seth Rotramel, vol. 5. Washington, DC: German Histroical Institute. Accessed June 29, 2020. http://germanhistorydocs.ghi-dc.org/sub_document.cfm?document_id=783.

"Bernhard von Bülows 'dynamische' Außenpolitik (1899)." In *Deutsche Geschichte in Bilder und Dokumente*, edited by Roger Chickering, Steven Chase Gummer, and Seth Rotramel, Vol. 5. Washington, DC: German Histroical Institute. Accessed June 29, 2020. http://germanhistorydocs.ghi-dc.org/docpage.cfm?docpage_id=2845.

Burton, Antoinette. "On the Inadequacy and the Indispensability of the Nation." In *After the Imperial Turn: Thinking with and through the Nation*, edited by Antoinette Burton, 1–23. Durham, NC: Duke University Press, 2003.

Büttner, Ursula. "The Persecution of Christian-Jewish Families in the Third Reich." *Leo Baeck Institute Year Book* 34, no. 1 (1989): 267–89.

Bibliography

Campos, Michelle. *Ottoman Brothers: Muslims, Christians, and Jews in Early Twentieth-Century Palestine.* Stanford, CA: Stanford University Press, 2011.

Case, Holly. *The Age of Questions, or, A First Attempt at an Aggregate History of the Eastern, Social, Woman, American, Jewish, Polish, Bullion, Tuberculosis, and Many Other Questions over the Nineteenth Century, and Beyond.* Princeton: Princeton University Press, 2018.

Casteel, Sarah Phillips. *Calypso Jews: Jewishness in the Caribbean Literary Imagination.* New York: Columbia University Press, 2016.

Castoriadis, Cornelius. *The Imaginary Institution of Society.* Translated by Kathleen Blamey. Cambridge: Polity, 1987.

Césaire, Aimé. *Discourse on Colonialism.* Translated by Joan Pinkham. New York: Monthly Review Press, 2000.

Chapoutot, Johann. *Greeks, Romans, Germans: How the Nazis Usurped Europe's Classical Past.* Translated by Richard Nybakken. Berkeley: University of California Press, 2016.

Chatterjee, Partha. *The Nation and Its Fragments: Colonial and Postcolonial Histories.* Princeton: Princeton University Press, 1993.

Nationalist Thought and the Colonial World: A Derivative Discourse. Minneapolis: University of Minnesota Press, 1993.

Cheyette, Bryan. *Diasporas of the Mind: Jewish and Postcolonial Writing and the Nightmare of History.* New Haven: Yale University Press, 2013.

Chickering, Roger. *Imperial Germany and the Great War, 1914–1918.* Cambridge: Cambridge University Press, 2014.

Chidester, David. *Empire of Religion: Imperialism and Comparative Religion.* Chicago: University of Chicago Press, 2013.

Ciarlo, David. *Advertising Empire: Race and Visual Culture in Imperial Germany.* Cambridge, MA: Harvard University Press, 2011.

Clark, Christopher. *The Politics of Conversion: Missionary Protestantism and the Jews in Prussia, 1728–1941.* Oxford: Clarendon Press, 1995.

Cohen, Hermann. *Jüdische Schriften,* edited by Bruno Strauss and Franz Rosenzweig. Berlin: C.A. Schwetschke, 1924. 2 volumes.

"The Polish Jew." In *The Jew, Essays from Martin Buber's Journal Der Jude, 1916–1928,* edited by Arthur A. Cohen, 52–60. Alabama: University of Alabama Press, 1980.

Religion der Vernunft aus den Quellen des Judentums. Wiesbaden: Fourier Verlag, 1988.

Cohen, Julia Phillips. *Becoming Ottomans: Sephardi Jews and Imperial Citizenship in the Modern Era.* Oxford: Oxford University Press, 2014.

Cohen, Richard. "'Jewish Contribution to Civilization' and Its Implications for Notions of Jewish Superiority in the Modern Period." In *The Jewish Contribution to Civilization: Reassessing an Idea,* edited by Jeremy Cohen and Richard Cohen, 11–23. Oxford: Littman Library of Jewish Civilization, 2008.

"The 'Wandering Jew' from Medieval Legend to Modern Metaphor." In *The Art of Being Jewish in Modern Times,* edited by Barbara Kirshenblatt-

Gimblett and Jonathan Karp, 147–75. Philadelphia: University of Pennsylvania Press, 2008.

Cohen-Skalli, Cedric. "Cohen's Jewish and Imperial Politics during World War I." In *Cohen im Netz*, edited by Hartwig Wiedebach and Heinrich Assel, 177–97. Tübingen: Mohr Siebeck, 2021.

Confino, Alon. *The Nation as a Local Metaphor: Württemberg, Imperial Germany, and National Memory, 1871–1918*. Chapel Hill: University of North Carolina Press, 1997.

A World without Jews: The Nazi Imagination from Persecution to Genocide. New Haven: Yale University Press, 2014.

Conklin, Alice. *A Mission to Civilize: The Republican Idea of Empire in France and West Africa, 1895–1930*. Stanford, CA: Stanford University Press, 1997.

Conrad, Sebastian. *German Colonialism: A Short History*. Cambridge: Cambridge University Press, 2012.

"Internal Colonialism in Germany: Culture Wars, Germanification of the Soil, and the Global Market Imaginary." In *German Colonialism in a Global Age*, edited by Geoff Eley and Bradley Naranch, 246–64. Durham, NC: Duke University Press, 2015.

Cooper, Julie. "In Pursuit of Political Imagination: Reflections on Diasporic Jewish History." *Theoretical Inquiries in Law* 21, no. 2 (2020): 255–84.

Darwin, John. *The Empire Project: The Rise and Fall of the British World-System, 1830–1970*. Cambridge: Cambridge University Press, 2011.

Davis, Christian. "Colonialism and the Anti-Semitic Movement in Imperial Germany." In *German Colonialism in a Global Age*, edited by Geoff Eley and Bradley Naranch, 228–45. Durham, NC: Duke University Press, 2015.

Colonialism, Antisemitism, and Germans of Jewish Descent in Imperial Germany. Ann Arbor: University of Michigan Press, 2012.

Davis, Daniel. "Baeck Comes to America." *Liberal Judaism* 15, no. 7, January 1948, 6–9, 44.

Dekel, Irit. *Mediation at the Holocaust Memorial in Berlin*. New York: Palgrave Macmillan, 2013.

Dekel, Irit, and Esra Özyürek. "What Do We Talk About When We Talk about Antisemitism in Germany?" *Journal of Genocide Research* 23, no. 3 (2021): 392–99.

Delitzsch, Friedrich. *Babel and Bible: Two Lectures*. Translated by Thomas McCormack and W. H. Carruth. Chicago: Open Court, 1903.

"Der Bettag am 5.August." *Allgemeine Zeitung des Judentums* 78, no. 33 (August 14, 1914): 385–88.

Derby, Lauren. *The Dictator's Seduction: Politics and the Popular Imagination in the Era of Trujillo*. Durham, NC: Duke University Press, 2009.

Derrida, Jacques. "Onto-Theology of National-Humanism (Prolegomena to a Hypothesis)." *Oxford Literary Review* 14, no. 1/2 (1992): 3–23.

Dickinson, Edward Ross. "The German Empire: An Empire?" *History Workshop Journal* 66, no. 1 (2008): 129–62.

Bibliography

Dietrich, Wendell. *Cohen and Troeltsch: Ethical Monotheistic Religion and Theory of Culture*. Atlanta: Scholars Press, 1986.

Dilthey, Wilhelm. *Das Wesen der Philosophie*. Hamburg: F. Meiner, 1984.

Diner, Dan. *Gegenläufige Gedächtnisse: Über Geltung und Wirkung des Holocaust*. Göttingen: Vandenhoeck & Ruprecht, 2007.

"Negative Symbiose: Deutsche und Juden nach Auschwitz." *Babylon: Beiträge zur jüdischen Gegenwart* 1 (1988): 243–57.

Diner, Hasia. *We Remember with Reverence and Love: American Jews and the Myth of Silence after the Holocaust, 1945–1962*. New York: New York University Press, 2009.

Dorestal, Philipp. "Reassessing Mbembe: Postcolonial Critique and the Continuities of Extreme Violence." *Journal of Genocide Research* 23, no. 3 (2021): 383–91.

Dorrien, Gary. *Kantian Reason and Hegelian Spirit: The Idealistic Logic of Modern Theology*. Malden, MA: Wiley-Blackwell, 2012.

"Dr. Baeck Given Honorary Degree." *Philadelphia Jewish Times*, March 12, 1948.

"Dr. Baeck Visits Truman: He Thanks President for Our Aid to Jews in Europe." *The New York Times*, January 9, 1948: 6.

Du Bois, W. E. B. *The World and Africa and Color and Democracy*. Edited by Henry Louis Gates. Oxford: Oxford University Press, 2014.

Dubnov, Simon. "Cedars of Lebanon: A New Conception of Jewish History." Translated by Shlomo Katz. *Commentary Magazine*, March 1946. www .commentarymagazine.com/articles/simon-dubnow/cedars-of-lebanon-a-new-conception-of-jewish-history/.

Dwork, Deborah. *Children with a Star: Jewish Youth in Nazi Europe*. New Haven: Yale University Press, 1991.

Efron, John. *Defenders of the Race: Jewish Doctors and Race Science in Fin-de-Siècle Europe*. New Haven: Yale University Press, 1994.

"Ein neuer Aufbruch für Europa. Eine neue Dynamik für Deutschland. Ein neuer Zusammenhalt für unser Land. Koalitionsvertrag zwischen CDU, CSU und SPD, 19. Legislaturperiode," 2018. www .bundesregierung.de/breg-de/themen/koalitionsvertrag-zwischen-cdu-csu-undspd-195906.

Eley, Geoff. *Reshaping the German Right: Radical Nationalism and Political Change after Bismarck*. Ann Arbor: University of Michigan Press, 1991.

Elkins, Caroline. *Legacy of Violence: A History of the British Empire*. New York: Knopf, 2022.

Ericksen, Robert. *Theologians under Hitler: Gerhard Kittel, Paul Althaus, and Emanuel Hirsch*. New Haven: Yale University Press, 1985.

Erlewine, Robert. *Judaism and the West: From Hermann Cohen to Joseph Soloveitchik*. Bloomington: Indiana University Press, 2016.

Monotheism and Tolerance: Recovering a Religion of Reason. Bloomington: Indiana University Press, 2010.

"Samuel Hirsch, Hegel, and the Legacy of Ethical Monotheism." *Harvard Theological Review* 113, no. 1 (2020): 89–110.

Bibliography

Essays Presented to Leo Baeck on the Occasion of His Eightieth Birthday. London: East and West Library, 1954.

Evers, Renate. "Die „Schocken-Bücherei" in den Nachlasssammlungen des Leo Baeck Institutes New York." *Medaon* 14 (2014). www.medaon.de/de/arti kel/die-schocken-buecherei-in-den-nachlasssammlungen-des-leo-baeck-insti tutes-new-york/.

Ezrahi, Yaron. *Imagined Democracies: Necessary Political Fictions.* Cambridge: Cambridge University Press, 2012.

Fabri, Friedrich. *Bedarf Deutschland der Colonien? Eine politisch-ökonomische Betrachtung.* 3rd ed. Gotha: Friedrich Andreas Perthes, 1879.

Fackenheim, Emil. "After Auschwitz, Jerusalem: In Memory of My Teacher, Leo Baeck." *Judaism* 50, no. 1 (2001): 53–59.

"In Memory of Leo Baeck, and Other Jewish Thinkers 'In Dark Times': Once More, 'After Auschwitz, Jerusalem.'" *Judaism* 51, no. 3 (2002): 282–92.

To Mend the World: Foundations of Post-Holocaust Jewish Thought. Bloomington: Indiana University Press, 1994.

What Is Judaism?: An Interpretation for the Present Age. New York: Summit Books, 1987.

Fanon, Frantz. *Black Skin, White Masks.* Translated by Richard Philcox. New York: Grove Press, 2008.

Feldman, David. "Jews and the British Empire c.1900." *History Workshop Journal* 63, no. 1 (2007): 70–89.

Feller, Yaniv. "From Aher to Marcion: Martin Buber's Understanding of Gnosis." *Jewish Studies Quarterly* 20, no. 4 (2013): 374–97.

"Romantic Politics in the Thought of Gustav Landauer and Leo Baeck." In *Skepsis and Antipolitics: The Alternative of Gustav Landauer,* edited by Cedric Cohen-Skalli and Libera Pisano, 273–96. Leiden: Brill, 2022.

"What Hope Remains? Leo Baeck as a Reader of Job." In *Hope,* edited by Ingolf Dalferth and Marlene Block, 353–68. Tübingen: Mohr Siebeck, 2016.

"Whose Museum Is It? Jewish Museums and Indigenous Theory." *Comparative Studies in Society and History* 63 (2021): 798–824.

Fischer, Jörg. "Zivilisation, Kultur." In *Grundgeschichtliche Begriffe,* edited by Reinhart Koselleck, Werner Conze, and Otto Brunner, 7:669–774. Stuttgart: Klett-Cotta, 1992.

Fishman, David. *The Book Smugglers: Partisans, Poets, and the Race to Save Jewish Treasures from the Nazis.* Lebanon, NH: University Press of New England, 2017.

Fitzpatrick, Matthew. *The Kaiser and the Colonies: Monarchy in the Age of Empire.* Oxford: Oxford University Press, 2022.

Liberal Imperialism in Germany: Expansionism and Nationalism, 1848–1884. New York: Berghahn Books, 2008.

Flynn, Thomas R. *Existentialism: A Very Short Introduction.* New York: Oxford University Press, 2006.

Fraiman, Sarah. "The Transformation of Jewish Consciousness in Nazi Germany as Reflected in the German Jewish Journal *Der Morgen,* 1925–1938." *Modern Judaism* 20, no. 1 (2000): 41–59.

Bibliography

Fredriksen, Paula. *Augustine and the Jews: A Christian Defense of Jews and Judaism.* Toronto: Doubleday, 2008.

Freud, Sigmund. "Das Unheimliche." *Imago: Zeitschrift für Anwendung der Psychoanalyse auf die Geisteswissenschaften* 5 (1919): 297–324.

Freytag, Gustav. *Soll und Haben.* Leipzig: S. Hirzel, 1866.

Friedlander, Albert. *Leo Baeck: Teacher of Theresienstadt.* London: Routledge and Kegan Paul, 1973.

———. "A Muted Protest in War-Time Berlin: Writing on the Legal Position of German Jewry throughout the Centuries: Leo Baeck, Leopold Lucas, Hilde Ottenheimer," *Leo Baeck Institute Year Book* 37, (1992): 363–380.

Friedländer, Moritz. *Geschichte der jüdischen Apologetik als Vorgeschichte des Christentums: Eine historisch-kritische Darstellung der Propaganda und Apologie im Alten Testament und in der hellenistischen Diaspora.* Amsterdam: Philo Press, 1973.

Friedländer, Saul. *Nazi Germany and the Jews: The Years of Persecution.* New York: Harper Collins, 1997.

Fromm, Erich. "Für eine Kooperation zwischen Israelis und Palästinensern." In *Gesamtausgabe in zwölf Bänden,* edited by Rainer Funk, 11:523–27. Munich: dtv, 1999.

Funkenstein, Amos. *Perceptions of Jewish History.* Los Angeles: University of California Press, 1993.

"'Für Zusammenarbeit der jüdischen Organisationen! Bedeutungsvolle Resolution des Beirats der Reichsvertretung - Der innerjüdische Burgfrieden.'" *Der Schild* 13, no. 5 (February 16, 1934): 1.

Galchinsky, Michael. "Africans, Indians, Arabs, and Scots: Jewish and Other Questions in the Age of Empire." *Jewish Culture and History* 6, no. 1 (2003): 46–60.

Gasman, Daniel. *The Scientific Origins of National Socialism.* New York: Routledge, 2017.

Gaston, K. Healan. *Imagining Judeo-Christian America: Religion, Secularism, and the Redefinition of Democracy.* Chicago: University of Chicago Press, 2019.

Gay, Peter. *Freud, Jews, and Other Germans: Master and Victims in Modernist Culture.* New York: Oxford University Press, 1978.

Geller, Jay. *Jews in Post-Holocaust Germany, 1945–1953.* Cambridge: Cambridge University Press, 2005.

Gerdmar, Anders. *Roots of Theological Anti-Semitism: German Biblical Interpretation and the Jews, from Herder and Semler to Kittel and Bultmann.* Leiden: Brill, 2009.

Gerron, Kurt. *Theresienstadt: Ein Dokumentarfilm aus dem juedischen Siedlungsgebiet (Der Fuehrer schenkt den Juden eine Stadt).* 1944. www .ushmm.org/online/film/display/detail.php?file_num=2703.

Gerwarth, Robert, and Stephan Malinowski. "Hannah Arendt's Ghosts: Reflections on the Disputable Path from Windhoek to Auschwitz." *Central European History* 42, no. 2 (2009): 279–300.

Bibliography

Gewald, Jan-Bart. *Herero Heroes: A Socio-Political History of the Herero of Namibia, 1890–1923*. Athens, OH: Ohio State University Press, 1999.

Gibbs, Robert. "Hermann Cohen's Messianism: The History of the Future." In *"Religion der Vernunft aus den Quellen ses Judentums": Tradition und Ursprungsdenken in Hermann Cohens Spätwerk*, edited by Helmut Holzhey, Gabriel Motzkin and Hartwig Wiedebach, 331–49. New York: Georg Olms Verlag.

"Lines, Circles, Points: Messianic Epistemology in Cohen, Rosenzweig, and Benjamin." In *Toward the Millennium: Messianic Expectations from the Bible to Waco*, edited by Peter Schäfer and Mark R. Cohen, 363–82. Leiden: Brill, 1998.

Gilbert, Martin. *Kristallnacht: Prelude to Destruction*. New York: HarperCollins, 2006.

Goetschel, Willi. *The Discipline of Philosophy and the Invention of Modern Jewish Thought*. New York: Fordham University Press, 2013.

"Tangled Genealogies: Hellenism, Hebraism, and the Discourse of Modernity." *Arion* 21, no. 3 (2014): 111–24.

Goetschel, Willi, and Ato Quayson. "Jewish Studies and Postcolonialism." *The Cambridge Journal of Postcolonial Literary Inquiry* 3, no. 1 (2016): 1–9.

Goldschmidt, Hermann. "Der junge Leo Baeck." *AJR Information* 28, no. 5 (May 1963): 2–3.

The Legacy of German Jewry. Edited by Willi Goetschel, translated by David Suchoff. New York: Fordham University Press, 2007.

Golomb, Jacob, ed. *Nietzsche and Jewish Culture*. New York: Routledge, 1997.

Gonzalez, Allyson. "Abraham S. Yahuda (1877–1951) and the Politics of Modern Jewish Scholarship." *Jewish Quarterly Review* 109, no. 3 (2019): 406–33.

Gordan, Rachel. "The 1940s as the Decade of the Anti-Antisemitism Novel." *Religion and American Culture* 31, no. 1 (2021): 33–81.

"'What the Jews Believe': A Liberal Rabbi Explains Judaism to the Readers of Life Magazine." In *New Perspectives in American Jewish History: A Documentary Tribute to Jonathan D. Sarna*, edited by Mark Raider and Gary Zola, 273–80. Chicago: Chicago University Press, 2021.

Gordon, Adi. *Brith Shalom and Bi-National Zionism: The "Arab Question" as a Jewish Question*. Jerusalem: Carmel, 2008.

Gordon, Peter. *Rosenzweig and Heidegger: Between Judaism and German Philosophy*. Berkeley: University of California Press, 2003.

"Why Historical Analogy Matters." *The New York Review of Books*, January 7, 2020.

Gottlieb, Michah. "Does Judaism Have Dogma? Moses Mendelssohn and a Pivotal Nineteenth-Century Debate." *Yearbook of the Maimonides Centre for Advanced Studies* 2 (2019): 219–42.

Gottschalk, Peter. *Religion, Science, and Empire: Classifying Hinduism and Islam in British India*. New York: Oxford University Press, 2013.

Grady, Tim. *A Deadly Legacy: German Jews and the Great War*. New Haven: Yale University Press, 2017.

Bibliography

Greenberg, Udi. *The Weimar Century: German Émigrés and the Ideological Foundations of the Cold War*. Princeton: Princeton University Press, 2015.

Grimmer-Solem, Erik. *Learning Empire: Globalization and the German Quest for World Status, 1875–1919*. Cambridge: Cambridge University Press, 2019.

Grosse, Pascal. "What Does German Colonialism Have to Do with National Socialism? A Conceptual Framework." In *Germany's Colonial Pasts*, edited by Eric Ames, Marcia Klotz, and Lora Wildenthal, 115–34. Lincoln: University of Nebraska Press, 2005.

Gruner, Wolf. "To Not 'Live as a Pariah': Jewish Petitions as Individual and Collective Protest in the Greater German Reich." In *Resisting Persecution: Jews and Their Petitions during the Holocaust*, edited by Thomas Pegelow Kaplan and Wolf Gruner, 28–50. New York: Berghahn Books, 2020.

Guettel, Jens-Uwe. *German Expansionism, Imperial Liberalism and the United States, 1776–1945*. Cambridge: Cambridge University Press, 2012.

Gusejnova, Dina. *European Elites and Ideas of Empire, 1917–1957*. Cambridge: Cambridge University Press, 2016.

Habermas, Rebekka. "'Do You Want to Help the Heathen Children?': Missionary Work in the German Colonies." In *German Colonialism: Fragments Past and Present*, edited by Sebastian Gottschalk, Heike Hartmann, Stefanie Müller, and Arnulf Scriba, 50–57. Berlin: Deutsches Historisches Museum, 2016.

Hacohen, Malachi. *Jacob & Esau: Jewish European History between Nation and Empire*. Cambridge: Cambridge University Press, 2019.

Haeckel, Ernst. *Natürliche Schöpfungsgeschichte*. Leipzig: A. Kröner, 1924.

Hájková, Anna. "Israeli Historian Otto Dov Kulka's Auschwitz Account Tells the Story of a Czech Family That Never Existed." *Tablet Magazine*, October 30, 2014. www.tabletmag.com/jewish-arts-and-culture/books/186462/otto-dov-kulka.

The Last Ghetto: An Everyday History of Theresienstadt. Oxford: Oxford University Press, 2020.

"Theresienstadt." In *Enzyklopädie jüdischer Geschichte und Kultur*, edited by Dan Diner, 6:94–98. Stuttgart: J.B. Metzler, 2014.

Hall, Catherine. *Civilising Subjects: Metropole and Colony in the English Imagination 1830–1867*. Chicago: University of Chicago Press, 2002.

Hanebrink, Paul. *A Specter Haunting Europe: The Myth of Judeo-Bolshevism*. Cambridge, MA: Belknap, 2018.

Hank, Sabine, Hermann Simon, and Uwe Hank, eds. *Feldrabbiner in den deutschen Streitkräften des Ersten Weltkrieges*. Berlin: Hentrich & Hentrich, 2013.

Harnack, Adolf von. *History of Dogma*. Translated by Neil Buchanan. New York: Dover Publications, 1961. 7 volumes.

Marcion, der moderne Gläubige des 2. Jahrhunderts, der erste Reformator: Die dorpater Preisschrift (1870). Edited by Friedemann Steck. Berlin: De Gruyter, 2003.

Marcion: Das Evangelium vom Fremden Gott. Leipzig: Hinrich, 1924.

Marcion: The Gospel of the Alien God. Translated by John Steely and Lyle Bierma. Durham, NC: Labyrinth Press, 1990.

The Mission and Expansion of Christianity in the First Three Centuries. Translated by James Moffatt. London: Williams and Norgate, 1908.

Das Wesen des Christentums: Sechzehn Vorlesungen vor Studierenden aller Facultäten im Wintersemester 1899/1900 an der Universität Berlin gehalten. Leipzig: J. C. Hinrichs, 1900.

What Is Christianity? Translated by Thomas Baily Saunders. London: Williams and Norgate, 1901.

Hartman, K. "Existenzialismus." In Historisches Wörterbuch der Philosophie, edited by Joachim Ritter, Karlfried Gründer, Gottfried Gabriel, and Rudolf Eisler, 850–52. Basel: Schwabe, 1971.

"Existenzphilosophie." In Historisches Wörterbuch der Philosophie, edited by Joachim Ritter, Karlfried Gründer, Gottfried Gabriel, and Rudolf Eisler, 862–65. Basel: Schwabe, 1971.

Hasan-Rokem, Galit, and Alan Dundes, eds. The Wandering Jew: Essays in the Interpretation of a Christian Legend. Bloomington: Indiana University Press, 1986.

Heidegger, Martin. Being and Time. Translated by John Macquarrie and Edward Robinson. New York: Harper, 2008.

Hell, Julia. The Conquest of Ruins: The Third Reich and the Fall of Rome. Chicago: University of Chicago Press, 2018.

Hendel, Ronald. "The Exodus in America." In Found in Translation: Essays on Jewish Biblical Translation in Honor of Leonard J. Greenspoon, edited by James Barker, Anthony Le Donne, and Joel Lohr, 155–78. West Lafayette, IN: Purdue University Press, 2018.

Herf, Jeffrey. The Jewish Enemy: Nazi Propaganda during World War II and the Holocaust. Cambridge, MA: Belknap, 2006.

Herskowitz, Daniel. Heidegger and His Jewish Reception. Cambridge: Cambridge University Press, 2021.

"An Impossible Possibility? Jewish Barthianism in Interwar Germany." Modern Theology 33, no. 3 (2017): 348–68.

Herzl, Theodor. "Das Bischari-Lager." Neue freie Presse, April 30, 1899.

Herzog, Jonathan. The Spiritual-Industrial Complex: America's Religious Battle against Communism in the Early Cold War. New York: Oxford University Press, 2011.

Heschel, Susannah. Abraham Geiger and the Jewish Jesus. Chicago: University of Chicago Press, 1998.

The Aryan Jesus: Christian Theologians and the Bible in Nazi Germany. Princeton: Princeton University Press, 2008.

"Ecstasy versus Ethics: The Impact of the First World War on German Biblical Scholarship on the Hebrew Prophets." In The First World War and the Mobilization of Biblical Scholarship, edited by Andrew Mein, Nathan MacDonald, and Matthew A. Collins, 187–206. London: T&T Clark, 2019.

Bibliography

"Jewish Studies as Counterhistory." In *Insider/Outsider: American Jews and Multiculturalism*, edited by David Biale, Michael Galchinsky, and Susannah Heschel, 101–35. Berkeley: University of California Press, 1998.

"Jewish Studies in the Third Reich: A Brief Glance at Viktor Christian and Karl Schubert." *Review of Rabbinic Judaism* 13, no. 2 (2010): 236–49.

"Revolt of the Colonized: Abraham Geiger's *Wissenschaft des Judentums* as a Challenge to Christian Hegemony in the Academy." *New German Critique* 77 (1999): 61–85.

"Theological Ghosts and Goblins: Martin Luther's Haunting of Liberal Judaism." In *Polyphonie der Theologie: Verantwortung und Widerstand in Kirche und Politik*, edited by Matthias Grebe, 325–44. Stuttgart: Kohlhammer Verlag, 2019.

Hess, Jonathan. *Germans, Jews and the Claims of Modernity*. New Haven: Yale University Press, 2002.

Heyden, Ulrich van der. "Christian Missionary Societies in the German Colonies, 1884/1885–1914/1915." In *German Colonialism: Race, the Holocaust, and Postwar Germany*, edited by Volker Langbehn and Mohammad Salama, 215–52. New York: Columbia University Press, 2011.

Hildesheimer, Esriel. *Jüdische Selbstverwaltung unter dem NS-Regime: Der Existenzkampf der Reichsvertretung und Reichsvereinigung der Juden in Deutschland*. Tübingen: Mohr Siebeck, 1994.

Hilfsverein der Juden in Deutschland, ed. *Jüdische Auswanderung: Korrespondenzblatt über Auswanderungs- und Siedlungswesen*. Berlin: Schmoller & Gordon, 1937.

Hilfsverein der Juden in Deutschland, *Jüdische Auswanderung nach Südamerika*. Berlin: Jüdischer Kulturbund, 1939.

Hochman, Erin. *Imagining a Greater Germany: Republican Nationalism and the Idea of Anschluss*. Ithaca, NY: Cornell University Press, 2016.

Hoffmann, Christhard. "The Founding of the Leo Baeck Institute, 1945–1955." In *Preserving the Legacy of German Jewry: History of the Leo Baeck Institute, 1955–2005*, edited by Christhard Hoffmann, 1–15. Tübingen: Mohr Siebeck, 2005.

Hoffmann, Peter. *Carl Goerdeler and the Jewish Question, 1933–1942*. Cambridge: Cambridge University Press, 2011.

Hofmann, Reto, and Daniel Hedinger. "Axis Empires: Towards a Global History of Fascist Imperialism." *Journal of Global History* 12, no. 2 (2017): 161–65.

Hollander, Dana. *Ethics Out of Law: Hermann Cohen and the "Neighbor."* Toronto: University of Toronto Press, 2021.

Exemplarity and Chosenness: Rosenzweig and Derrida on the Nation of Philosophy. Stanford, CA: Stanford University Press, 2008.

Holmes, Virginia. "Integrating Diversity, Reconciling Contradiction: The Jüdischer Friedensbund in Late Weimar Germany." *Leo Baeck Institute Year Book* 47 (2002): 175–94.

Homolka, Walter. *Jewish Identity in Modern Times: Leo Baeck and German Protestantism*. Providence: Berghahn Books, 1995.

Horne, John, and Alan Kramer. *German Atrocities 1914: A History of Denial.* New Haven: Yale University Press, 2009.

Hotam, Yotam. *Gnosis Moderni Ve-Tsiyonut: Mashber Ha-Tarbut, Filosofyat Ha-Ḥayim Ve-Hagut Le'umit Yehudit.* Jerusalem: Magnes University Press, 2007.

Hübner, Thomas. *Adolf von Harnacks Vorlesungen über das Wesen des Christentums unter besonderer Berücksichtigung der Methodenfragen als sachgemässer Zugang zu ihrer Christologie und Wirkungsgeschichte.* Frankfurt am Main: P. Lang, 1994.

Hull, Isabel. *Absolute Destruction: Military Culture and the Practices of War in Imperial Germany.* Ithaca, NY: Cornell University Press, 2013.

Hunsinger, George. *Disruptive Grace: Studies in the Theology of Karl Barth.* Grand Rapids: Eerdmans, 2000.

Hyman, Paula. *Gender and Assimilation in Modern Jewish History: The Roles and Representation of Women.* Seattle: University of Washington Press, 1995.

"The Modern Jewish Family: Image and Reality." In *The Jewish Family: Metaphor and Memory,* edited by David Kraemer, 179–93. New York: Oxford University Press, 1989.

Ilany, Ofri. "The Jews as Educators of Humanity: A Christian-Philosemitic Grand Narrative of Jewish Modernity?" In *The German-Jewish Experience: Contested Interpretations and Conflicting Perceptions,* edited by Steven Aschheim and Vivian Liska, 1–14. Berlin/Boston: De Gruyter, 2015.

Imber, Elizabeth. "Jewish Political Lives in the British Empire: Zionism, Nationalism, and Imperialism in Palestine, India, and South Africa, 1917–1939." Thesis, Johns Hopkins University, 2018.

Irwin, Virginia. "He Appreciates the Glories of Freedom." *St. Louis Dispatch,* February 23, 1948.

Jacobs, Jill. "The History of 'Tikkun Olam.'" *Zeek,* June 2007. www.zeek.net/706tohu/.

Jacobs, Joseph, Max Schloessinger, Cyrus Adler, and Francis Cohen. "Kol Nidre." In *Jewish Encyclopedia,* edited by Isidore Singer, 7: 539–46. New York: Funk & Wagnalls, 1901–1906.

Jackson, Zakiyyah. *Becoming Human: Matter and Meaning in an Antiblack World.* New York: New York University Press, 2020.

Janssen, Nittert. *Theologie fürs Volk: Der Einfluß der religionsgeschichtlichen Schule auf die Popularisierung der theologischen Forschung vor dem Ersten Weltkrieg.* Frankfurt am Main: Peter Lang, 1999, 124–81.

Jaspers, Karl. *The Question of German Guilt.* Translated by E.B. Ashton. New York: Fordham University Press, 2001.

Jay, Martin. *Songs of Experience: Modern American and European Variations on a Universal Theme.* Berkeley: University of California Press, 2005.

"Jewish Leader Says Religion Vital to the U.N." *The Baltimore News-Post.* February 14, 1948.

"Jews Are Beaten by Berlin Rioters; Cafes Are Raided." *The New York Times.* July 16, 1935.

Bibliography

Jonas, Hans. *The Gnostic Religion: The Message of the Alien God and the Beginnings of Christianity*. Boston: Beacon Press, 1963.

Joskowicz, Ari. *The Modernity of Others: Jewish Anti-Catholicism in Germany and France*. Stanford, CA: Stanford University Press, 2013.

Junginger, Horst. *The Scientification of the Jewish Question in Nazi Germany*. Leiden: Brill, 2017.

Kaplan, Marion. *Between Dignity and Despair: Jewish Life in Nazi Germany*. New York: Oxford University Press, 1999.

Dominican Haven: The Jewish Refugee Settlement in Sosua, 1940–1945. New York: Museum of Jewish Heritage, 2008.

The Making of the Jewish Middle Class: Women, Family, and Identity in Imperial Germany. New York: Oxford University Press, 1994.

Katz, Ethan, Lisa Moses Leff, and Maud Mandel, eds. *Colonialism and the Jews*. Bloomington: Indiana University Press, 2017.

Katz, Ethan, Lisa Moses Leff, and Maud Mandel, "Engaging Colonial History and Jewish History." In *Colonialism and the Jews*, edited by Ethan Katz, Lisa Moses Leff, and Maud Mandel, 1–25. Bloomington: Indiana University Press, 2017.

Katz, Jacob. *Out of the Ghetto: The Social Background of Jewish Emancipation, 1770–1870*. Translated by Henry Feingold. Syracuse: Syracuse University Press, 1998.

"The Term 'Jewish Emancipation': Its Origins and Historical Impact." In *Studies in Nineteenth-Century Jewish Intellectual History*, edited by Alexander Altmann, 1–25. Cambridge, MA: Harvard University Press, 1964.

Kauffman, Jesse. *Elusive Alliance: The German Occupation of Poland in World War I*. Cambridge, MA: Harvard University Press, 2015.

Kaufmann, Walter, ed. *Existentialism: From Dostoevsky to Sartre*. New York: Meridian Books, 1956.

Kaufmann, Yeḥezkel. *The Religion of Israel*, translated by Moshe Greenberg. New York: Schocken Books, 1972.

Kavka, Martin. *Jewish Messianism and the History of Philosophy*. New York: Cambridge University Press, 2004.

Keegan, John. *The First World War*. New York: Knopf, 1999.

Kiernan, Ben. *Blood and Soil: A World History of Genocide and Extermination from Sparta to Darfur*. New Haven: Yale University Press, 2008.

Kieval, Hillel. "Antisemitism and the City: A Beginner's Guide." *Studies in Contemporary Jewry* 15 (1999): 3–18.

Kilcher, Andreas. "The Grandeur and Collapse of the German-Jewish Symbiosis: Hans Tramer and Jewish Literary Studies at the Leo Baeck Institute." In *Preserving the Legacy of German Jewry: History of the Leo Baeck Institute, 1955–2005*, edited by Christhard Hoffmann, 409–33. Tübingen: Mohr Siebeck, 2005.

Kind, Amy. "Exploring Imagination." In *The Routledge Handbook of Philosophy of Imagination*, edited by Amy Kind, 1–12. Abingdon: Routledge, 2016.

Bibliography

King, Karen. *What Is Gnosticism?* Cambridge, MA: Harvard University Press, 2003.

Kinzig, Wolfram. *Harnack, Marcion und das Judentum: Nebst einer kommentierten Edition des Briefwechsels Adolf von Harnacks mit Houston Stewart Chamberlain.* Leipzig: Evangelische Verlagsanstalt, 2004.

Kipling, Rudyard. "The Ballad of East and West." In *The Collected Poems of Rudyard Kipling,* edited by R.T. Jones, 245–48. Hertfordshire: Wordsworth Editions, 1998.

Kirby, Dianne. "The Cold War and American Religion." In *Oxford Research Encyclopedia of Religion,* edited by John Burton. Oxford: Oxford University Press, 2017. https://oxfordre.com/religion/view/10.1093/acre fore/9780199340378.001.0001/acrefore-9780199340378-e-398.

Kittel, Gerhard. "Die Ausbreitung des Judentums bis zum Beginn des Mittelalters," *Forschungen zur Judenfrage* 5 (1941): 290–310

"Die Entstehung des Judentums und die Entstehung der Judenfrage." *Forschungen zur Judenfrage* 1 (1937): 43–63.

Die Judenfrage. Stuttgart: Kohlhammer, 1933.

"Das Konnubium mit nicht-Juden im antiken Judentum." *Forschungen zur Judenfrage* 2 (1937): 30–62

Klapheck, Elisa. *Fräulein Rabbiner Jonas: The Story of the First Woman Rabbi.* Translated by Toby Axelrod. Ann Arbor: University of Michigan Press, 2004.

Klassen, Pamela. "Fantasies of Sovereignty: Civic Secularism in Canada." *Critical Research on Religion* 3, no. 1 (2015): 41–56

Klävers, Steffen. *Decolonizing Auschwitz?: Komparativ-postkoloniale Ansätze in der Holocaustforschung.* Oldenbourg: De Gruyter, 2021.

Klein, Peter. "Theresienstadt: Ghetto oder Konzentrationslager?" *Theresienstädter Studien und Dokumente,* no. 12 (2005): 111–23.

Klemperer, Victor. *Language of the Third Reich.* Translated by Martin Brady. London: Bloomsbury, 2013.

Klinghardt, Matthias, Jason BeDuhn, and Judith Lieu, "Marcion's Gospel and the New Testament: Catalyst or Consequence? Roundtable Discussion," *New Testament Studies* 63, no. 2 (2017): 318–34

Klüger, Ruth. *Still Alive: A Holocaust Girlhood Remembered.* New York: The Feminist Press, 2001.

Koch, Angela. *DruckBilder: Stereotype und Geschlechtercodes in den antipolnischen Diskursen der "Gartenlaube."* Colonge: Böhlau Verlag, 2002.

Koebner, Richard, and Helmut Dan Schmidt. *Imperialism: The Story and Significance of a Political Word, 1840–1960.* Cambridge: Cambridge University Press, 1964.

Koonz, Claudia. *Mothers in the Fatherland: Women, the Family and Nazi Politics.* New York: St. Martin's Press, 1988.

The Nazi Conscience. Cambridge, MA: Belknap, 2003.

Kopp, Kristin. *Germany's Wild East: Constructing Poland as Colonial Space.* Ann Arbor: University of Michigan Press, 2017.

Bibliography

Koshar, Rudy. "Demythologizing the Secular: Karl Barth and the Politics of the Weimar Republic." In *The Weimar Moment: Liberalism, Political Theology, and Law*, edited by Leonard V. Kaplan and Rudy Koshar, 313–36. Lanham, MD: Lexington Books, 2012.

Krasner, Jonathan. "The Place of Tikkun Olam in American Jewish Life." *Jewish Political Studies Review* 25, no. 3/4 (2013): 59–98.

Kreutzmüller, Christoph. *Final Sale in Berlin: The Destruction of Jewish Commercial Activity, 1930–1945*. Translated by Jane Paulick and Jefferson Chase. New York: Berghahn Books, 2015.

"Gewalt gegen Juden im Sommer 1935." In *Die Nürnberger Gesetze – 80 Jahre danach: Vorgeschichte, Entstehung, Auswirkungen*, edited by Magnus Brechtken, Hans-Christian Jasch, Christoph Kreutzmüller, and Niels Weise, 71–88. Göttingen: Wallstein Verlag, 2017.

Krone, Kerstin von der. "Jüdische Wissenschaft und modernes Judentum: Eine Dogmendebatte." In *Die „Wissenschaft des Judentums": Eine Bestandsaufnahme*, edited by Andreas Kilcher and Thomas Meyer, 115–38. Paderborn: Wilhelm Fink Verlag, 2015.

Kruse, Kevin. *One Nation Under God: How Corporate America Invented Christian America*. New York: Basic Books, 2015.

Kucich, John. *Imperial Masochism: British Fiction, Fantasy, and Social Class*. Princeton: Princeton University Press, 2009.

Kuhn, Karl Georg. "Weltjudentum in der Antike." *Forschungen zur Judenfrage* 2 (1937): 9–29.

Kulka, Otto Dov, ed. *Deutsches Judentum unter dem Nationalsozialismus*. Tübingen: Mohr Siebeck, 1997.

Kulka, Otto Dov, and Eberhard Jäckel, eds. *The Jews in the Secret Nazi Reports on Popular Opinion in Germany, 1933–1945*. Translated by William Templer. New Haven: Yale University Press, 2010.

Kumar, Krishan. "Colony and Empire, Colonialism and Imperialism: A Meaningful Distinction?" *Comparative Studies in Society and History* 63, no. 2 (2021): 280–309.

Kundrus, Birthe. "Colonialism, Imperialism, National Socialism: How Imperial Was the Third Reich?" In *German Colonialism in a Global Age*, edited by Bradley Naranch and Geoff Eley, 330–46. Durham, NC: Duke University Press, 2015.

"Die Kolonien - 'Kinder des Gefühls und der Phantasie.'" In *Phantasiereiche: Zur Kulturgeschichte des deutschen Kolonialismus*, edited by Birthe Kundrus, 7–18. Frankfurt am Main: Campus Verlag, 2003.

Moderne Imperialisten: das Kaiserreich im Spiegel seiner Kolonien. Cologne and Weimar: Böhlau Verlag, 2003.

Kuss, Susanne. *German Colonial Wars and the Context of Military Violence*. Translated by Andrew Smith. Cambridge, MA: Harvard University Press, 2017.

Kutschera, U. "Struggle to Translate Darwin's View of Concurrency." *Nature* 458, no. 7241 (April 2009): 967.

Bibliography

Lagarde, Paul de. *Deutsche Schriften.* Göttingen: Dieterich, 1878.

Lammel, Inge. "Alltagsleben im Waisenhaus." In *Verstörte Kindheiten: Das jüdische Waisenhaus in Pankow als Ort der Zuflucht, Geborgenheit und Vertreibung*, edited by Peter-Alexis Albrecht, Leslie Brent, and Inge Lammel, 115–42. Berlin: Berliner Wissenschafts-Verlag, 2008.

Lapidot, Elad. *Jews Out of the Question: A Critique of Anti-Anti-Semitism.* Albany: SUNY Press, 2020.

Lapidot, Elad and Micha Brumlik, eds. *Heidegger and Jewish Thought: Difficult Others.* London: Rowman & Littlefield, 2018.

Lavsky, Hagit. *Before Catastrophe: The Distinctive Path of German Zionism.* Detroit: Wayne State University Press, 1996.

Lazier, Benjamin. *God Interrupted: Heresy and the European Imagination between the World Wars.* Princeton: Princeton University Press, 2008.

Lebovic, Nitzan. *The Philosophy of Life and Death: Ludwig Klages and the Rise of a Nazi Biopolitics.* New York: Palgrave Macmillan, 2013.

Leff, Lisa. *Sacred Bonds of Solidarity: The Rise of Jewish Internationalism in Nineteenth-Century France.* Stanford, CA: Stanford University Press, 2006.

Lehnardt, Andreas. *Qaddish: Untersuchungen zur Entstehung und Rezeption eines Rabbinischen Gebetes.* Tübingen: Mohr Siebeck, 2002.

"Lehrhaus eröffnet. Ansprache der Leiter - Leo Baeck erhält der Eröffnungsvorlesung." *Jüdische Allgemeine Zeitung* 14, no. 88 (November 7, 1934): 1–2.

Leichsenring, Jana. "Die katholische Gemeinde in Theresienstadt und die berliner Katholiken." *Theresienstädter Studien und Dokumente* 11 (2004): 178–222.

"Leo Baeck in Palästina." *Aufbau* 13, no. 35 (August 29, 1947): 19.

Leonard, Miriam. *Socrates and the Jews.* Chicago: Chicago University Press, 2012.

Leonhard, Jörn and Ulrike von Hirschhausen, eds., *Comparing Empires: Encounters and Transfers in the Long Nineteenth Century.* Göttingen: Vandenhoeck & Ruprecht, 2011.

Lerp, Dörte. "Beyond the Prairie: Adopting, Adapting and Transforming Settlement Policies within the German Empire." *Journal of Modern European History* 14, no. 2 (2016): 225–44.

Lewerenz, Susann. "Colonial Revisionism." In *Historical Companion to Postcolonial Literatures: Continental Europe and Its Empires*, edited by Prem Poddar, Rajeev Patke, and Lars Jensen, 224–25. Edinburgh: Edinburgh University Press, 2008.

Lewis, David Levering. *W. E. B. Du Bois: A Biography 1868–1963.* New York: Holt and Co., 2009.

Liebman, Joshua. "A Saint for Our Times: The Most Unforgettable Character I've Met." *Reader's Digest*, July 1948.

Lieu, Judith. *Marcion and the Making of a Heretic: God and Scripture in the Second Century.* New York: Cambridge University Press, 2015.

Lindbergh, Charles. "Des Moines Speech-America First Committee," September 11, 1941. www.charleslindbergh.com/americanfirst/speech.asp.

Linder, Ulrike. "Trans-Imperial Orientation and Knowledge Transfers." In *German Colonialism: Fragments Past and Present*, edited by Sebastian

Bibliography

Gottschalk, Heike Hartmann, Stefanie Müller, and Arnulf Scriba, 16–29. Berlin: Deutsches Historisches Museum, 2016.

Lindeskog, Gösta. *Die Jesusfrage im neuzeitlichen Judentum: Ein Beitrag zur Geschichte der Leben-Jesu-Forschung.* Darmstadt: Wissenschaftliche Buchgesellschaft, 1973.

Lindsay, Mark. *Barth, Israel, and Jesus: Karl Barth's Theology of Israel.* New York: Routledge, 2016.

Lipphardt, Veronika. *Biologie der Juden: Jüdische Wissenschaftler über »Rasse« und Vererbung 1900–1935.* Göttingen: Vandenhoeck & Ruprecht, 2008.

Liulevicius, Vejas Gabriel. *The German Myth of the East: 1800 to the Present.* Oxford: Oxford University Press, 2009.

War Land on the Eastern Front: Culture, National Identity, and German Occupation in World War I. Cambridge: Cambridge University Press, 2000.

Locke, John. *Two Treatises of Government and a Letter Concerning Toleration.* Edited by Ian Shapiro. New Haven: Yale University Press, 2003.

Loisy, Alfred. *The Gospel and the Church.* Translated by Christopher Home. New York: Scribner's Sons, 1912.

Lovejoy, Arthur. "On the Discrimination of Romanticisms." *PMLA* 39, no. 2 (1924): 229–53.

Löwenthal, Gerhard, and Leo Baeck. "Die Zukunft der Juden in Deutschland." *Allgemeine Wochenzeitung der Juden in Deutschland. Beilage: Der Weg - Zeitschrift für Fragen des Judentums* 6, no. 35 (August 1951): 1.

Lu, Jennifer. "George Regas, Progressive Crusader and Longtime Rector of All Saints in Pasadena, Dies at 90." *Los Angeles Times*, January 6, 2021. www .latimes.com/california/story/2021-01-06/george-regas-social-justice-leader-episcopal-church-dead-at-90.

Lucas, Leopold. *Zur Geschichte der Juden im vierten Jahrhundert: Der Kampf zwischen Christentum und Judentum.* Hildesheim: G. Olms, 1985

Lutz, Ralph Haswell, ed. *Fall of the German Empire, 1914–1918.* Stanford, CA: Stanford University Press, 1932.

Madley, Benjamin. "From Africa to Auschwitz: How German South West Africa Incubated Ideas and Methods Adopted and Developed by the Nazis in Eastern Europe." *European History Quarterly* 35, no. 3 (2005): 429–64.

Maierhof, Gudrun. *Selbstbehauptung im Chaos: Frauen in der jüdischen Selbsthilfe 1933–1943.* Frankfurt am Main: Campus Verlag, 2002.

Makarova, Elena, Sergeï Makarov, and Victor Kuperman, eds. *University over the Abyss: The Story behind 520 Lecturers and 2,430 Lectures in KZ Theresienstadt 1942–1944.* Jerusalem: Verba, 2004.

Mangina, Joseph. *Karl Barth: Theologian of Christian Witness.* Louisville: Westminster John Knox Press, 2004.

Manz, Stefan. *Constructing a German Diaspora: The "Greater German Empire," 1871–1914.* New York: Routledge, 2014.

Maor, Zohar. "Identity and Confusion: Another Look at the Whirlpool of Identities in Prague." *Zion* 71, no. 4 (2006): 457–72.

Bibliography

Marchand, Suzanne. *Down from Olympus: Archaeology and Philhellenism in Germany, 1750–1970*. Princeton: Princeton University Press, 1996.

    German Orientalism in the Age of Empire: Religion, Race, and Scholarship. New York: Cambridge University Press, 2009.

Marcuse, Ludwig. "Graf Klingeling und Leo Baeck." *Aufbau* 11, no. 50 (December 14, 1945): 3.

Margaliot, Abraham. "Emigration: Planung und Wirklichkeit." In *Die Juden im nationalsozialistischen Deutschland: The Jews in Nazi Germany, 1933–1943*, edited by Arnold Paucker, Sylvia Gilchrist, and Barbara Suchy, 303–16. Tübingen: Mohr, 1986.

Markner, Reinhard. "*Forschungen zur Judenfrage*: A Notorious Journal and Some of Its Contributors." *European Journal of Jewish Studies* 1, no. 2 (2007): 395–415.

Marks, Sally. "The Myths of Reparations." *Central European History* 11, no. 3 (1978): 231–55.

Marquard, Reiner. *Karl Barth und der Isenheimer Altar*. Stuttgart: Calwer Verlag, 1995.

Marshall, John W. "Misunderstanding the New Paul: Marcion's Transformation of the *Sonderzeit* Paul." *Journal of Early Christian Studies* 20, no. 1 (2012): 1–29.

Marx, Karl. "On the Jewish Question." In *The Marx-Engels Reader*, edited by Robert Tucker, 26–52. Princeton: Princeton University Press, 1978.

Mashiach, Itay. "In Germany, a Witch Hunt Is Raging against Critics of Israel. Cultural Leaders Have Had Enough." *Haaretz.Com*, December 10, 2020. www.haaretz.com/israel-news/.premium.HIGHLIGHT.MAGAZINE-in-germany-a-witch-hunt-rages-against-israel-critics-many-have-had-enough-1.9362662.

Masuzawa, Tomoko. *The Invention of World Religions, or, How European Universalism Was Preserved in the Language of Pluralism*. Chicago: University of Chicago Press, 2005

Mayer, Reinhold. *Christentum und Judentum in der Schau Leo Baecks*. Stuttgart: W. Kohlhammer, 1961.

Mayr, Ernst. *The Growth of Biological Thought: Diversity, Evolution, and Inheritance*. Cambridge, MA: Belknap, 1982.

Mazower, Mark. *Hitler's Empire: Nazi Rule in Occupied Europe*. New York: Allen Lane, 2008.

    No Enchanted Palace: The End of Empire and the Ideological Origins of the United Nations. Princeton: Princeton University Press, 2013.

McClintock, Anne. *Imperial Leather: Race, Gender, and Sexuality in the Colonial Contest*. New York: Routledge, 1995.

McGing, Brian. "Population and Proselytism: How Many Jews Were There in the Ancient World?" In *Jews in the Hellenistic and Roman Cities*, edited by John R. Bartlett and Sean V. Freyne, 88–106. Abingdon: Taylor & Francis, 2002.

Mehta, Uday Singh. *Liberalism and Empire: A Study in Nineteenth-Century British Liberal Thought*. Chicago: University of Chicago Press, 1999.

Bibliography

Mell, Julie. *The Myth of the Medieval Jewish Moneylender*. New York: Palgrave Macmillan, 2017.

Memmi, Albert. *The Colonizer and the Colonized*. Translated by Howard Greenfeld. Boston: Beacon Press, 1991.

Mendelsohn, Amitai. *Behold the Man: Jesus In Israeli Art*. Jerusalem: Magnes University Press, 2017.

Mendelssohn, Moses. *Jerusalem or On Religious Power and Judaism*. Translated by Allan Arkush. Hanover, MA: University Press of New England, 1983.

Mendes-Flohr, Paul. *Divided Passions: Jewish Intellectuals and the Experience of Modernity*. Detroit: Wayne State University Press, 1991.

Martin Buber: A Life of Faith and Dissent. New Haven: Yale University Press, 2019.

Meyer, Beate. "'Altersghetto', 'Vorzugslager' und Tätigkeitsfeld." *Theresienstädter Studien und Dokumente*, no. 12 (2005): 124–49.

A Fatal Balancing Act: The Dilemma of the Reich Association of Jews in Germany, 1939–1945. Translated by William Templer. New York: Berghahn Books, 2013.

"The Mixed Marriage: A Gurantee of Survival or a Reflection of German Society during the Nazi Regime." In *Probing the Depths of German Antisemitism: German Society and the Persecution of the Jews, 1933–1941*, edited by David Bankier, 54–77. New York: Berghahn Books, 2000.

Meyer, Michael. "Concerning D. R. Schwartz: 'History and Historiography — "A Kingdom of Priests" as Pharisaic Slogan.'" *Zion* 46, no. 1 (1981): 57–58.

Rabbi Leo Baeck: Living a Religious Imperative in Troubled Times. Philadelphia: University of Pennsylvania Press, 2020.

Response to Modernity: A History of the Reform Movement in Judaism. New York: Oxford University Press, 1988.

Meyer, Michael, ed. *German-Jewish History in Modern Times*. New York: Columbia University Press, 1996. 4 volumes.

Michman, Dan. *The Emergence of Jewish Ghettos during the Holocaust*. Translated by Lenn Schramm. Cambridge: Cambridge University Press, 2011.

"The Jewish Dimension of the Holocaust in Dire Straits? Current Challenges of Interpretation and Scope." In *Jewish Histories of the Holocaust: New Transnational Approaches*, edited by Norman Goda, 17–38. New York: Berghahn Books, 2014.

Mommsen, Wilhelm. "Bismarcks kleindeutscher Staat und das Großdeutsche Reich." *Historische Zeitschrift* 167, no. 1 (1943): 66–82.

Mommsen, Wolfgang. *Imperialismus: Seine geistigen, politischen und wirtschaftlichen Grundlagen*. Hamburg: Hoffmann und Campe, 1977.

Morefield, Jeanne. *Covenants without Swords: Idealist Liberalism and the Spirit of Empire*. Princeton: Princeton University Press, 2009.

Morgenstern, Matthias. "Erwägungen zur 'Verteidigung' Gerhard Kittels vom Dezember 1946," *Theologische Beiträge* 51 (2020): 260–71.

From Frankfurt to Jerusalem: Isaac Breuer and the History of the Secession Dispute in Modern Jewish Orthodoxy. Leiden: Brill, 2002.

Morrow, John. *The Great War: An Imperial History*. New York: Routledge, 2016.

Mosse, George. *The Crisis of German Ideology: Intellectual Origins of the Third Reich*. New York: Schocken Books, 1981.

Fallen Soldiers: Reshaping the Memory of the World Wars. Oxford: Oxford University Press, 1990.

Germans and Jews: The Right, the Left, and the Search for a "Third Force" in Pre-Nazi Germany. London: Orbach & Chambers, 1971.

Mosse, Werner. "From 'Schutzjuden' to 'Deutsche Staatsbürger Jüdischen Glaubens': The Long and Bumpy Road of Jewish Emancipation in Germany." In *Paths of Emancipation*, edited by Pierre Birnbaum and Ira Katznelson, 59–93. Princeton: Princeton University Press, 1995.

Moyn, Samuel. *Origins of the Other: Emmanuel Levinas between Revelation and Ethics*. Ithaca: Cornell University Press, 2005.

Mufti, Aamir. *Enlightenment in the Colony: The Jewish Question and the Crisis of Postcolonial Culture*. Princeton: Princeton University Press, 2007.

Muller, Jerry. *Capitalism and the Jews*. Princeton: Princeton University Press, 2010.

Muret, Eduard. *Geschichte der französischen Kolonie in Brandenburg-Preußen, unter besonderer Berücksichtigung der Berliner Gemeinde*. Berlin: Büxenstein, 1885.

Musch, Sebastian. *Jewish Encounters with Buddhism in German Culture: Between Moses and Buddha, 1890–1940*. New York: Palgrave Macmillan, 2019.

Myers, David, ed. *The Eternal Dissident: Rabbi Leonard I. Beerman and the Radical Imperative to Think and Act*. Oakland, CA: University of California Press, 2018.

Myers, David, *The Stakes of History: On the Use and Abuse of Jewish History for Life*. New Haven: Yale University Press, 2018.

Nahme, Paul E. *Hermann Cohen and the Crisis of Liberalism: The Enchantment of the Public Sphere*. Bloomington: Indiana University Press, 2019.

Neiman, Susan, and Anna-Esther Younes. "Antisemitism, Anti-Racism, and the Holocaust in Germany: A Discussion between Susan Neiman and Anna-Esther Younes." *Journal of Genocide Research* 23, no. 3 (2021): 420–35.

Nelson, Robert. "The Archive for Inner Colonization, the German East, and World War I." In *Germans, Poland, and Colonial Expansion to the East: 1850 through the Present*, edited by Robert Nelson, 65–93. New York: Palgrave Macmillan, 2009.

"A German on the Prairies: Max Sering and Settler Colonialism in Canada." *Settler Colonial Studies* 5, no. 1 (2015): 1–19.

Nichols, Christopher McKnight. *Promise and Peril: America at the Dawn of a Global Age*. Cambridge, MA: Harvard University Press, 2011.

Nicosia, Francis R. *Zionism and Anti-Semitism in Nazi Germany*. Cambridge: Cambridge University Press, 2008.

Nielsen, Philipp. *Between Heimat and Hatred: Jews and the Right in Germany, 1871–1935*. New York: Oxford University Press, 2019.

Novak, David. *Athens and Jerusalem*. Toronto: University of Toronto Press, 2019.

Bibliography

The Election of Israel: The Idea of the Chosen People. Cambridge: Cambridge University Press, 1995.

"How Jewish Was Karl Barth?" In *Karl Barth, the Jews, and Judaism,* edited by George Hunsinger, 1–23. Grand Rapids: Eerdmans, 2018.

Talking with Christians: Musings of a Jewish Theologian. Grand Rapids, Michigan: Eerdmans, 2005.

Offenberger, Ilana. *The Jews of Nazi Vienna, 1938–1945: Rescue and Destruction.* New York: Palgrave Macmillan, 2017.

Olson, Lynne. *Those Angry Days: Roosevelt, Lindbergh, and America's Fight Over World War II, 1939–1941.* New York: Random House, 2014.

Ottenheimer, Hilde. "The Disappearance of Jewish Communities in Germany, 1900–1938," *Jewish Social Studies* 3, no. 2 (1941): 189–206.

Overy, Richard. *Blood and Ruins: The Great Imperial War, 1931–1945.* London: Penguin, 2021.

Pagels, Elaine. *The Gnostic Paul: Gnostic Exegesis of the Pauline Letters.* Philadelphia: Fortress Press, 1975.

"Palestine Shift Scored Here by Dr. Leo Baeck." *Daily Boston Globe.* March 31, 1948: 1, 4.

Panter, Sarah. "Beyond Marginalization: The (German-)Jewish Soldiers' Agency in Times of War, 1914–1918." *The Leo Baeck Institute Year Book* 66 (2021): 25–39.

Jüdische Erfahrungen und Loyalitätskonflikte im Ersten Weltkrieg. Göttingen: Vandenhoeck & Ruprecht, 2014.

Paucker, Arnold. *Deutsche Juden im Widerstand 1933–1945: Tatsachen und Probleme.* Berlin: Gedenkstätte Deutscher Widerstand, 2003.

"Resistance of German and Austrian Jews to the Nazi Regime 1933–1945." *The Leo Baeck Institute Year Book* 40, no. 1 (1995): 3–20.

Pauley, Bruce. *From Prejudice to Persecution: A History of Austrian Anti-Semitism.* Chapel Hill: University of North Carolina Press, 1992.

Pearson, Lori. *Beyond Essence: Ernst Troeltsch as Historian and Theorist of Christianity.* Cambridge, MA: Harvard University Press, 2008.

Penslar, Derek. "The German-Jewish Soldier: From Participant to Victim." *German History* 29, no. 3 (2011): 423–44.

Jews and the Military: A History. Princeton: Princeton University Press, 2013.

Shylock's Children: Economics and Jewish Identity in Modern Europe. Berkeley: University of California Press, 2001.

Theodor Herzl: The Charismatic Leader. New Haven: Yale University Press, 2020.

Pergher, Roberta, and Mark Rosman. "The Holocaust – An Imperial Genocide?" *Dapim: Studies on the Holocaust* 27 (2013): 42–49.

Philipp Manes. *As If It Were Life: A WW II Diary from the Theresienstadt Ghetto.* Edited by Ben Barkow and Klaus Leist, translated by Janet Foster. New York: Palgrave Macmillan, 2009.

Pine, Lisa. *Nazi Family Policy, 1933–1945.* Oxford: Berg, 1997.

Bibliography

Pitts, Jennifer. "Political Theory of Empire and Imperialism: An Appendix." In *Empire and Modern Political Thought*, edited by Sankar Muthu, 351–88. Cambridge: Cambridge University Press, 2012.

A Turn to Empire: The Rise of Imperial Liberalism in Britain and France. Princeton: Princeton University Press, 2009.

Pollock, Benjamin. *Franz Rosenzweig's Conversions: World Denial and World Redemption.* Indianapolis: Indiana University Press, 2014.

"From Nation State to World Empire: Franz Rosenzweig's Redemptive Imperialism." *Jewish Studies Quarterly* 11, no. 4 (2004): 332–53.

Porter, Andrew. *European Imperialism, 1860–1914.* New York: Palgrave Macmillan, 1994.

Pratt, Mary Louise. *Imperial Eyes: Travel Writing and Transculturation.* New York: Routledge, 2008.

Prehn, Ulrich, ed. *"Überall Luthers Worte...": Martin Luther im Nationalsozialismus.* Berlin: Stiftung Topographie des Terrors, 2017.

Prell, Riv-Ellen, ed. "Empire in Jewish Studies." *AJS Perspectives*, Fall 2005, 7–19.

Pulzer, Peter. *Jews and the German State: The Political History of a Minority, 1848–1933.* Cambridge, MA: Blackwell, 2003.

Rabinovici, Doron. *Eichmann's Jews: The Jewish Administration of Holocaust Vienna, 1938–1945.* Translated by Nick Somers. Cambridge: Polity, 2014.

Rahden, Till van. "Germans of the Jewish Stamm: Visions of Community between Nationalism and Particularism, 1850–1933." In *German History from the Margins*, edited by Neil Gregor, Nils H. Roemer, and Mark Roseman, 27–48. Bloomington: Indiana University Press, 2006.

"Treason, Fate or Blessing? Narratives of Assimilation in the Historiography of German-Speaking Jewry since the 1950s." In *Preserving the Legacy of German Jewry: History of the Leo Baeck Institute, 1955–2005*, edited by Christhard Hoffmann, 347–74. Tübingen: Mohr Siebeck, 2005.

Rashkover, Randi. *Revelation and Theopolitics: Barth, Rosenzweig, and the Politics of Praise.* New York: T&T Clark International, 2005.

"Reaction to Riot Alarms Germans; Baiting Continues." *The New York Times.* July 17, 1935.

Rehlinghaus, Franziska. *Die Semantik des Schicksals: Zur Relevanz des Unverfügbaren zwischen Aufklärung und Erstem Weltkrieg.* Göttingen: Vandenhoeck & Ruprecht, 2015.

Reichmann, Eva. "A Symbol of German Jewry." *Leo Baeck Institute Year Book* 2, no. 1 (1957): 21–26.

Reichmann, Hans. "The Fate of a Manuscript." *The Leo Baeck Institute Year Book* 3, no. 1 (1958): 361–63.

Reitter, Paul. *The Anti-Journalist: Karl Kraus and Jewish Self-Fashioning in Fin-de-Siècle Europe.* Chicago: University of Chicago Press, 2008.

"Religion Is Termed Key to U.N. Success." *The New York Times.* February 1, 1948.

Reuveni, Gideon, and Edward Madigan. "The First World War and the Jews." In *The Jewish Experience of the First World War*, edited by Edward Madigan and Gideon Reuveni, 1–16. London: Palgrave Macmillan, 2019.

Bibliography

Robeson, Paul. *Paul Robeson Speaks: Writings, Speeches, and Interviews, a Centennial Celebration*, edited by Philip Foner. New York: Citadel Press, 1978.

Roemer, Nils. *Jewish Scholarship and Culture in Nineteenth-Century Germany between History and Faith*. Madison: University of Wisconsin Press, 2005.

Rogowski, Christian. "'Heraus mit unseren Kolonien!': Der Kolonialrevisionismus der Weimarer Republik und der 'Hamburger Kolonialwoche' von 1926." In *Phantasiereiche: Zur Kulturgeschichte des deutschen Kolonialismus*, edited by Birthe Kundrus, 243–62. Frankfurt am Main: Campus Verlag, 2003.

Rose, Jacqueline. *States of Fantasy*. Oxford: Clarendon Press, 1996.

Rose, Paul. *German Question/Jewish Question: Revolutionary Antisemitism in Germany from Kant to Wagner*. Princeton: Princeton University Press, 1990.

Rose, Sven-Erik. *Jewish Philosophical Politics in Germany, 1789–1848*. Waltham, MA: Brandeis University Press, 2014.

Rosenzweig, Franz. *Philosophical and Theological Writings*, edited and translated by Paul Franks and Michael Morgan. Indianapolis: Hackett, 2000.

Der Stern der Erlösung. Frankfurt am Main: Suhrkamp, 1988.

Rothberg, Michael. "Comparing Comparisons: From the 'Historikerstreit' to the Mbembe Affair." *Geschichte der Gegenwart*. September 23, 2020. https:// geschichtedergegenwart.ch/comparing-comparisons-from-the-historiker streit-to-the-mbembe-affair/.

Multidirectional Memory: Remembering the Holocaust in the Age of Decolonization. Stanford, CA: Stanford University Press, 2009.

"The Specters of Comparison." *Zeitgeister: International Perspectives from Culture and Society*, May 2020. www.goethe.de/prj/zei/en/pos/21864662 .html.

Rovit, Rebecca. *The Jewish Kulturbund Theatre Company in Nazi Berlin*. Iowa City: University of Iowa Press, 2012.

Rozenblit, Marsha, and Jonathan Karp, eds. *World War I and the Jews: Conflict and Transformation in Europe, the Middle East, and America*. New York: Berghahn Books, 2017.

Rubinstein, Ernest. *An Episode of Jewish Romanticism: Franz Rosenzweig's The Star of Redemption*. Albany: SUNY Press, 1999.

Rumscheidt, Martin. *Revelation and Theology: An Analysis of the Barth-Harnack Correspondence of 1923*. Eugene, OR: Wipf & Stock, 2011.

Rupnow, Dirk. "From Final Depository to Memorial: The History and Significance of the Jewish Museum in Prague." *European Judaism: A Journal for the New Europe* 37, no. 1 (2004): 142–59.

Judenforschung im Dritten Reich: Wissenschaft zwischen Politik, Propaganda und Ideologie. Baden-Baden: Nomos, 2011.

Täter, Gedächtnis, Opfer: Das "Jüdische Zentralmuseum" in Prag 1942–1945. Wien: Picus, 2000.

Rürup, Reinhard. "Jewish Emancipation and Bourgeois Society." *The Leo Baeck Institute Year Book* 14, no. 1 (1969): 67–91.

Bibliography

Ryland, Glen. "Translating Africa for Germans: The Rhenish Mission in Southwest Africa, 1829–1936." Thesis. University Of Notre Dame, 2013.

Safrian, Hans. *Eichmann's Men.* Translated by Ute Stargardt. Cambridge: Cambridge University Press, 2009.

Said, Edward. *Culture and Imperialism.* New York: Vintage, 1994.

Sandmel, Samuel. *Leo Baeck on Christinaity.* New York: Leo Baeck Institute, 1975.

Saperstein, Marc. *Jewish Preaching in Times of War, 1800–2001.* Oxford: Littman Library of Jewish Civilization, 2008.

Schilling, Britta. *Postcolonial Germany: Memories of Empire in a Decolonized Nation.* Oxford: Oxford University Press, 2014.

Schlegel, Friedrich. *Der Historiker als rückwärts gekehrter Prophet.* Leipzig: Reclam, 1991.

Schleiermacher, Friedrich. *Der christliche Glaube nach den Grundsätzen der evangelischen Kirche.* Halle: O. Hendel, 1897.

Schleunes, Karl. *The Twisted Road to Auschwitz: Nazi Policy toward German Jews, 1933–39.* Urbana: University of Illinois Press, 1990.

Schlör, Joachim. *Das Ich der Stadt: Debatten über Judentum und Urbanität, 1822–1938.* Göttingen: Vandenhoeck & Ruprecht, 2005.

Schmitt, Carl. *Political Romanticism.* Translated by Guy Oakes. Cambridge, Mass: MIT Press, 1986.

Schmokel, Wolfe. *Dream of Empire: German Colonialism, 1919–1945.* New Haven: Yale University Press, 1980.

Schnapp, Alain. "Looking at Ruins, Then and Now." In Josef Koudelka, *Ruins,* 13–17. New York: Aperture, 2020.

Scholder, Klaus. *The Churches and the Third Reich.* Translated by John Brown. London: SCM Press, 1988.

Scholem, Gershom. *Major Trends in Jewish Mysticism.* New York: Schocken Books, 1995.

    On Jews and Judaism in Crisis: Selected Essays. Edited by Werner Dannhauser, translated by John Mander. Philadelphia: Paul Dry, 2012.

Schorsch, Ismar. *Jewish Reactions to German Anti-Semitism, 1870–1914.* New York: Columbia University Press, 1972.

Schrag, Peter. *The World of Aufbau: Hitler's Refugees in America.* Madison: University of Wisconsin Press, 2019.

Schreier, Joshua. *Arabs of the Jewish Faith: The Civilizing Mission in Colonial Algeria.* New Brunswick, NJ: Rutgers University Press, 2010.

Schüler-Springorum, Stefanie. "Gender and the Politics of Anti-Semitism." *The American Historical Review* 123, no. 4 (2018): 1210–22.

Schwartz, Avshalom. "Political Imagination and Its Limits." *Synthese* 199, no. 1 (2021): 3325–43.

Schwartz, Daniel. *Ghetto: The History of a Word.* Cambridge, MA: Harvard University Press, 2019.

Schweid, Eliezer. *Wrestling until Day-Break: Searching for Meaning in the Thinking on the Holocaust.* Lanham: University Press of America, 1994.

Bibliography

Scott, David. *Refashioning Futures: Criticism after Postcoloniality*. Princeton: Princeton University Press, 1999.

Scott, Joan. "Fantasy Echo: History and the Construction of Identity." *Critical Inquiry* 27, no. 2 (2001): 284–304.

Segall, Jacob. *Die deutschen Juden als Soldaten im Kriege 1914–1918*. Berlin: Philo Verlag, 1921.

Shapiro, Marc B. *Between the Yeshiva World and Modern Orthodoxy: The Life and Works of Rabbi Jehiel Jacob Weinberg, 1884–1966*. London: Littman Library of Jewish Civilization, 1999.

Shavit, Yaacov, and Mordechai Eran. *The Hebrew Bible Reborn: From Holy Scripture to the Book of Books*. Translated by Chaya Naor. Berlin: De Gruyter, 2007.

Sherwin, Byron. "The Assimilation of Judaism: Heschel and the 'Category Mistake.'" *Judaism* 55, no. 3–4 (2006): 40–51.

Shumsky, Dmitry. *Beyond the Nation-State: The Zionist Political Imagination from Pinsker to Ben-Gurion*. New Haven: Yale University Press, 2018.

Sieg, Ulrich. "Empathie und Pflichterfüllung: Leo Baeck als Feldrabbiner im Ersten Weltkrieg." In *Leo Baeck, 1873–1956: Aus dem Stamme von Rabbinern*, edited by Fritz Backhaus and Georg Heuberger, 44–59. Frankfurt am Main: Jüdischer Verlag im Suhrkamp Verlag, 2001.

Jüdische Intellektuelle im Ersten Weltkrieg: Kriegserfahrungen, weltanschauliche Debatten und kulturelle Neuentwürfe. Berlin and Boston: De Gruyter, 2001.

Silk, Mark. "Notes on the Judeo-Christian Tradition in America." *American Quarterly* 36, no. 1 (1984): 65–85.

Simon, Ernst. *Aufbau im Untergang: Jüdische Erwachsenenbildung im nationalsozialistischen Deutschland als geistiger Widerstand*. Tübingen: Mohr, 1959.

"Geheimnis und Gebot: Zum Leo Baecks 75 Geburtstag." *Aufbau* 14, no. 21 (May 21, 1948): 31–33.

Simon, Hermann. "Bislang unbekannte Quellen zur Entstehungsgeschichte des Werkes *Die Entwicklung der Rechtsstellung der Juden Europa, vornehmlich in Deutschland*." In *Leo Baeck, 1873–1956: Aus dem Stamme von Rabbinern*, edited by Fritz. Backhaus and Georg Heuberger, 103–10. Frankfurt am Main: Jüdischer Verlag, 2001.

Simon, Oswald John. "Missionary Judaism." *Jewish Quarterly Review* 5 (July 1893): 664–79.

Simon, Oswald John, and Israel Zangwill. "The Mission of Judaism." *Jewish Quarterly Review* 9 (1897): 177–223.

Sinclair, Stefanie. "Regina Jonas: Forgetting and Remembering the First Female Rabbi." *Religion* 43, no. 4 (2013): 541–63.

Sinn, Andrea. "Despite the Holocaust: Rebuilding Jewish Life in Germany after 1945." *The Leo Baeck Institute Year Book* 64, no. 1 (2019): 143–58.

Slabodsky, Santiago. *Decolonial Judaism: Triumphal Failures of Barbaric Thinking*. New York: Palgrave Macmillan, 2015.

Slezkine, Yuri. *The Jewish Century*. Princeton: Princeton University Press, 2006.

Smith, Helmut Walser. *Germany: A Nation in Its Time*. New York: W.W Norton & Company, 2020.

Smith, Woodruff. *The Ideological Origins of Nazi Imperialism.* Oxford: Oxford University Press, 1986.

Snyder, Timothy. *Black Earth: The Holocaust as History and Warning.* New York: Tim Duggan Books, 2015.

Soboczynski, Adam. "Felix Klein: 'I See No Need for an Apology.'" *Die Zeit,* May 20, 2020, sec. Kultur. www.zeit.de/kultur/2020-05/felix-klein-holocaust-achille-mbembe-protests-english.

Sonderegger, Katherine. *That Jesus Christ Was Born a Jew: Karl Barth's "Doctrine of Israel."* University Park, PA: Pennsylvania State University Press, 1992.

Sorkin, David. "The Émigré Synthesis: German-Jewish History in Modern Times," *Central European History* 34, no. 4 (2001): 531–59

Jewish Emancipation: A History across Five Centuries. Princeton: Princeton University Press, 2019..

Spinner, Samuel. *Jewish Primitivism.* Stanford, CA: Stanford University Press, 2021.

Stahl, Neta. *Other and Brother: Jesus in the 20th-Century Jewish Literary Landscape.* New York: Oxford University Press, 2013.

Steigmann-Gall, Richard. *The Holy Reich: Nazi Conceptions of Christianity, 1919–1945.* Cambridge: Cambridge University Press, 2003.

Stein, Sarah Abrevaya. *Extraterritorial Dreams: European Citizenship, Sephardi Jews, and the Ottoman Twentieth Century.* Chicago: University of Chicago Press, 2016.

Steinberg, Michael. *Judaism Musical and Unmusical.* Chicago: Chicago University Press, 2007.

Steinmetz, George. *The Devil's Handwriting: Precoloniality and the German Colonial State in Qingdao, Samoa, and Southwest Africa.* Chicago: Chicago University Press, 2007.

"Empires and Colonialism." In *Oxford Bibliographies in Sociology, edited by Lynette Spillman.* Oxford: Oxford University Press, 2017. www .oxfordbibliographies.com/view/document/obo-9780199756384/obo-9780 199756384-0090.xml?q=Empires+an%E2%80%A6.

Steinweis, Alan. *Kristallnacht 1938.* Cambridge, MA: Belknap, 2009.

Studying the Jew: Scholarly Antisemitism in Nazi Germany. Cambridge, MA: Harvard University Press, 2006.

Stendhal, Krister. "The Apostle Paul and the Introspective Conscience of the West." *Harvard Theological Review* 56, no. 3 (1963): 199–215.

Stern, Adam. "Before the Altar: A Kafkan Study in Analytic Iconology." *Word & Image* 37, no. 4 (2021): 311–22.

Stern, Eliyahu. "Anti-Semitism and Orthodoxy in the Age of Trump." *Tablet Magazine.* Accessed March 15, 2019. www.tabletmag.com/jewish-arts-and-culture/281547/anti-semitism-orthodoxy-trump?fbclid=IwAR37lopQ1xyte NnDOeVVyAToEWKjtwCcd43Axi7SDSUgmQU4vxwKcOtMc6E.

Jewish Materialism: The Intellectual Revolution of the 1870s. New Haven: Yale University Press, 2018.

Stern, Selma. *Der preußische Staat und die Juden: Die Zeit des großen Kurfürsten und Friedrichs I.* Berlin: Schwetschke, 1925.

Bibliography

Stieglitz, Ann. "The Reproduction of Agony: Toward a Reception-History of Grünewald's Isenheim Altar after the First World War." *Oxford Art Journal* 12, no. 2 (1989): 87–103.

Stoler, Ann Laura, and Frederick Cooper. "Between Metropole and Colony: Rethinking a Research Agenda." In *Tensions of Empire: Colonial Cultures in a Bourgeois World*, edited by Frederick Cooper and Ann Laura Stoler, 1–56. Berkeley: University of California Press, 1997.

Stoltzfus, Nathan. *Resistance of the Heart: Intermarriage and the Rosenstrasse Protest in Nazi Germany*. New Brunswick, NJ: Rutgers University Press, 2001.

Stone, Dan. *Histories of the Holocaust*. Oxford: Oxford University Press, 2010.

Strauss, Herbert. "Jewish Emigration from Germany: Nazi Policies and Jewish Responses (I)." *The Leo Baeck Institute Year Book* 25, no. 1 (1980): 313–61.

Styfhals, Willem. *No Spiritual Investment in the World: Gnosticism and Postwar German Philosophy*. Ithaca, NY: Cornell University Press, 2019.

Sutcliffe, Adam. *What Are Jews For? History, Peoplehood, and Purpose*. Princeton: Princeton University Press, 2020.

Sweeny, Dennis. "Pan-German Conceptions of Colonial Empire." In *German Colonialism in a Global Age*, edited by Geoff Eley and Bradley Naranch, 265–82. Durham, NC: Duke University Press, 2015.

Sykes, Stephen. *The Identity of Christianity: Theologians and the Essence of Christianity from Schleiermacher to Barth*. Philadelphia: Fortress Press, 1984.

Tal, Uriel. "Al Bakashat 'Mahut Ha-Yahadut' Ba-Dorot Ha-Achronim U've-Yamenu." In *Mitos U-Tevunah Be-Yahadut Yamenu*, edited by Amos Funkenstein and Asa Kasher, 181–215. Tel-Aviv: Tel-Aviv University, 2011.

  "Theologische Debatte um das 'Wesen' des Judentums." In *Juden im wilhelminischen Deutschland, 1890–1914*, edited by Werner Mosse, 599–632. Tübingen: Mohr, 1976.

  Yahadut Ve-Natsrut Ba-'Raikh Ha-Sheni'. Jerusalem: Magnes University Press, 1969.

Taylor, Charles. *Modern Social Imaginaries*. Durham, NC: Duke University Press, 2004.

Ther, Philipp. "Beyond the Nation: The Relational Basis of a Comparative History of Germany and Europe." *Central European History* 36, no. 1 (2003): 45–73.

Tillich, Paul. *The Protestant Era*. Edited by James Luther Adams. Chicago: University of Chicago Press, 1948.

Jüdisches Museum Berlin. "Topography of Violence 1930–1938." Accessed July 5, 2022. www.jmberlin.de/topographie-gewalt/#/en/vis.

Toury, Jacob. "Emanzipation und Judenkolonien in der öffentlichen Meinung Deutschlands (1775–1819)." *Jahrbuch des Instituts für deutsche Geschichte* 11 (1982): 17–53.

  "'The Jewish Question': A Semantic Approach." *The Leo Baeck Institute Year Book* 11, no. 1 (1966): 85–106.

Trautner-Kromann, Hanne. *Shield and Sword: Jewish Polemics against Christianity and the Christians in France and Spain from 1100–1500*. Tübingen: Mohr Siebeck, 1993.

Bibliography

Troeltsch, Ernst. *The Absoluteness of Christianity and the History of Religions.* Translated by David Reid. Louisville: Westminster John Knox Press, 1971.

——. *Writings on Theology and Religion.* Edited by Robert Morgan and Michael Pye. Louisville: Westminster John Knox, 1977.

Truman, Harry. "Address in Columbus at a Conference of the Federal Council of Churches," March 6, 1946. www.trumanlibrary.gov/library/public-papers/52/address-columbus-conference-federal-council-churches.

Turits, Richard. *Foundations of Despotism: Peasants, the Trujillo Regime, and Modernity in Dominican History.* Stanford, CA: Stanford University Press, 2003.

Unger, Michal. *Reassessment of the Image of Mordechai Chaim Rumkowski.* Jerusalem: Yad Vashem, 2004.

"U.S. Reversal on Palestine Fresh Symptom Of World Immorality, Says London Rabbi." *The Boston Herald.* March 31, 1948.

Utitz, Emil. *Psychologie des Lebens im Konzentrationslager Theresienstadt.* Vienna: A. Sexl, 1948.

Valerio, Lenny. *Colonial Fantasies, Imperial Realities: Race Science and the Making of Polishness on the Fringes of the German Empire, 1840–1920.* Athens, OH: Ohio University Press, 2019.

Vatter, Miguel. *Living Law: Jewish Political Theology from Hermann Cohen to Hannah Arendt.* New York: Oxford University Press, 2021.

Vogt, Stefan, ed. *Colonialism and the Jews in German History: From the Middle Ages to the Twentieth Century.* London: Bloomsbury, 2022.

——. "Contextualizing German-Jewish History." In *Colonialism and the Jews in German History: From the Middle Ages to the Twentieth Century,* edited by Stefan Vogt, 1–21. London: Bloomsbury, 2022.

——. *Subalterne Positionierungen: Der deutsche Zionismus im Feld des Nationalismus in Deutschland, 1890–1933.* Göttingen: Wallstein, 2016.

Volavková, Hana. "The Jewish Museum of Prague." In *The Jews of Czechoslovkia: Historical Studies and Surveys,* edited by Avigdor Dagan, Gertrud Hirschler, and Lewis Weiner, 3:567–83. Philadelphia: Jewish Publication Society, 1984.

Volovici, Marc. *German as a Jewish Problem: The Language Politics of Jewish Nationalism.* Stanford, CA: Stanford University Press, 2020.

Walk, Joseph, ed. *Das Sonderrecht für die Juden im NS-Staat: Eine Sammlung der gesetzlichen Maßnahmen und Richtlinien.* Heidelberg: C. F. Müller Juristischer Verlag, 1981.

Wallace, James. "A Religious War?: The Cold War and Religion." *Journal of Cold War Studies* 15, no. 3 (2013): 162–80.

"Warns Prussian Poles." *The New York Times.* September 28, 1902.

Wehler, Hans-Ulrich. *The German Empire, 1871–1918.* Translated by Kim Traynor. New York: Berg Publishers, 1985.

Weidner, Daniel. "Prophetic Criticism and the Rhetoric of Temporality: Paul Tillich's Kairos Texts and Weimar Intellectual Politics." *Political Theology* 21, no. 1–2 (2020): 71–88.

Bibliography

Weinberg, Gerhard. *Germany, Hitler, and World War II: Essays in Modern German and World History*. Cambridge: Cambridge University Press, 1995.

"Some Myths of World War II." *The Journal of Military History* 75 (2011): 701–18.

A World at Arms: A Global History of World War II. Cambridge: Cambridge University Press, 2005.

Weinreich, Max. *Hitler's Professors: The Part of Scholarship in Germany's Crimes against the Jewish People*. New Haven: Yale University Press, 2008.

Weinryb, Sucher. *Der Kampf um die Berufsumschichtung: Ein Ausschnitt aus der Geschichte der Juden in Deutschland*. Berlin: Schocken, 1936.

Weinthal, Benjamin. "German Jewish Head Opposes BDS Speaker, Anti-Israel Director." *The Jerusalem Post*, April 28, 2020. www.jpost.com/diaspora/antisemitism/german-jewish-head-opposes-bds-speaker-wants-anti-israel-director-fired-625858.

Weiss, Yfaat. "Central European Ethnonationalism and Zionist Binationalism." *Jewish Social Studies* 11, no. 1 (2004): 93–117.

"'Wir Westjuden haben jüdisches Stammesbewußtsein, die Ostjuden jüdisches Volkesbewußtsein': Der deutsch-jüdische Blick auf das polnische Judentum in den Beiden ersten Jahrzehnten des 20. Jahrhunderts." *Archiv für Sozialgeschichte* 37 (1997): 157–78.

Wells, Allen. *Tropical Zion: General Trujillo, FDR, and the Jews of Sosúa*. Durham, NC: Duke University Press Books, 2009.

Whitman, James. *Hitler's American Model: The United States and the Making of Nazi Race Law*. Princeton: Princeton University Press, 2017.

Wiener, Theodore. "The Writings of Leo Baeck: A Bibliography." *Studies in Bibliography and Booklore* 1, no. 3 (1954): 108–44.

Wiens, Gavin. "A Mixed Bag of Loyalties: Jewish Soldiers, Ethnic Minorities, and State-Based Contingents in the German Army, 1914–1918." In *The Jewish Experience of the First World War*, edited by Edward Madigan and Gideon Reuveni, 137–58. London: Palgrave Macmillan, 2019.

Wiese, Christian. "'The Best Antidote to Anti-Semitism?' Wissenschaft des Judentums, Protestant Biblical Scholarship, and Anti-Semitism in Germany before 1933." In *Modern Judaism and Historical Consciousness: Identities, Encounters, Perspectives*, edited by Andreas Gotzmann and Christian Wiese, 145–92. Boston: Brill, 2007.

Challenging Colonial Discourse: Jewish Studies and Protestant Theology in Wilhelmine Germany, translated by Barbara Harshav. Boston: Brill, 2005.

"Counterhistory, the 'Religion of the Future' and the Emancipation of Jewish Studies: The Conflict between the Wissenschaft des Judentums and Liberal Protestantism 1900 to 1933." *Jewish Studies Quarterly* 7, no. 4 (2000): 367–98.

"Das Evangelium als 'Urkunde der jüdischen Glaubensgeschichte': Spuren der zeitgenössischen jüdischen geistigen Widerstand gegen die theologisch-völkische Religionswissenschaft des Eisenacher 'Entjudungsinstitut.'" In *Das Eisenacher 'Entjudungsinstitut': Kirche und Antisemitismus in der NS-*

Bibliography

Zeit, edited by Christopher Spehr and Harry Oelke, 119–54. Göttingen: Vandenhoeck & Ruprecht, 2021.

"Geheimnis und Gebot: Leo Baeck liberales Judentum zwischen Vernunftreligion und Mystik." In *Glaube und Vernunft in den Weltreligionen*, edited by Werner Zager, 99–132. Leipzig: Evangelische Verlagsanstalt, 2017.

"Institutum Judaicum." *Religion Past and Present*, 2011. https://referenceworks.brillonline.com/entries/religion-past-and-present/institutum-judaicum-SIM_10465.

"'Let His Memory Be Holy to Us!': Jewish Interpretations of Martin Luther from the Enlightenment to the Holocaust." *The Leo Baeck Institute Year Book* 54 (2009): 93–126.

"A Master Narrative? The *Gesamtgeschichte* of German Jewry in Historical Context." In *Preserving the Legacy of German Jewry: History of the Leo Baeck Institute, 1955–2005*, edited by Christhard Hoffmann, 315–48. Tübingen: Mohr Siebeck, 2005.

Wigard, Franz, editor. *Stenographischer Bericht über die Verhandlungen der deutschen constituirenden Nationalversammlung zu Frankfurt am Main*. Frankfurt am Main: J.D. Sauerländer, 1848.

Wildenthal, Lora. *German Women for Empire, 1884–1945*. Durham, NC: Duke University Press, 2001.

"Notes on a History of 'Imperial Turns' in Modern Germany." In *After the Imperial Turn: Thinking with and through the Nation*, edited by Antoinette Burton, 144–56. Durham, NC: Duke University Press, 2003.

Wildt, Michael. *Hitler's Volksgemeinschaft and the Dynamics of Racial Exclusion: Violence against Jews in Provincial Germany, 1919–1939*. Translated by Bernard Heise. New York: Berghahn Books, 2012.

Wilhelm, Kurt. "Leo Baeck and Jewish Mysticism." *Judaism* 11, no. 2 (1962): 123–30.

Wilkerson, Isabel. *Caste: The Origins of Our Discontents*. New York: Random House, 2020.

Williams, Michael. *Rethinking "Gnosticism": An Argument for Dismantling a Dubious Category*. Princeton: Princeton University Press, 1996.

Winter, Jay. *Remembering War: The Great War between Memory and History in the Twentieth Century*. New Haven: Yale University Press, 2006.

Wippermann, Wolfgang. *Die Deutschen und der Osten: Feindbild und Traumland*. Darmstadt: Primus, 2007.

Witte, Bernd. *Moses und Homer: Griechen, Juden, Deutsche: Eine andere Geschichte der Deutschen Kultur*. Berlin: De Gruyter, 2018.

Wolf, Arnold. "Repairing Tikkun Olam." *Judaism* 50, no. 4 (2001): 479–82.

Wolin, Richard. *Heidegger's Children: Hannah Arendt, Karl Löwith, Hans Jonas, and Herbert Marcuse*. Princeton: Princeton University Press, 2001.

Yerushalmi, Yosef Hayim. "Toward a History of Jewish Hope." In *The Faith of Fallen Jews: Yosef Hayim Yerushalmi and the Writing of Jewish History*, edited by David N. Myers and Alexander Kaye, 299–317. Waltham, MA: Brandeis University Press, 2013.

Bibliography

Young, James. *At Memory's Edge: After-Images of the Holocaust in Contemporary Art and Architecture*. New Haven: Yale University Press, 2000.

Zadoff, Noam. *Gershom Scholem: From Berlin to Jerusalem and Back*. Translated by Jeffrey Green. Waltham, MA: Brandeis University Press, 2017.

Zank, Michael. "Vom Innersten, Äußersten und Anderen: Annäherungen an Baeck, Harnack und die Frage nach dem Wesen." In *Religious Apologetics - Philosophical Argumentation*, edited by Yossef Schwartz and Volkhard Krech, 25–45. Tübingen: Mohr Siebeck, 2004.

Zantop, Susanne. *Colonial Fantasies: Conquest, Family, and Nation in Precolonial Germany, 1770–1870*. Durham, NC: Duke University Press, 1997.

Zentralrat der Juden. "Preisträger Seit 1957," May 16, 2019. www.zentralratderjuden.de/der-zentralrat/auszeichnungen/leo-baeck-preis/preis traeger-seit-1957/.

Zimmerer, Jurgen. *From Windhoek to Auschwitz: On the Relationship between Colonialism and the Holocaust*. London: Taylor & Francis, 2011.

Zirkle, Alexandra. "Re-Forming Professions: Salomon Herxheimer and Ludwig Philippson on the Past and Future of Jewish Farmers." In *Deutsch-jüdische Bibelwissenschaft: Historische, exegetische und theologische Perspektiven*, edited by Daniel Vorpahl, Sophia Kähler, and Shani Tzoref, 41–56. Berlin and Boston: De Gruyter, 2019.

Index

Note: The initials LB represent Leo Baeck.

Adler, Hans G., *Theresienstadt...*, 130, 130n1, 132, 137
Adler, Maximilian, 137
agency, and German Jews, 15–16, 86, 109, 116
Age of Questions, 8, 9, 9n24. *See also* Jewish Question
Alsace-Lorraine, 10, 59, 92–93
Ancient Greece. *See* Hellenism
Andersen, Friedrich, 66–67
Anderson, Benedict, 13
anti-Judaism, 49, 74–75, 76, 83, 84, 191–92.
    See also antisemitism
antisemitism
    Great Britain, 161
    Legal Position (Leo Baeck, Lucas, Ottenheimer), 118–19, 121, 123–24, 124n85, 127
    nation-state, 7, 9
    Nazis, 83–84, 118–19, 121, 127
    United States, 161
    Weimar Republic, 49, 60, 68
    Wilhelmine Empire, 9, 29, 30, 41, 49
    Zionists and, 41
    See also anti-Judaism
Arabs, 9, 163, 164, 165, 166, 177
Arendt, Hannah, 5, 9, 101–2, 110, 184
army chaplains, 3, 49, 51, 58, 78
Aschheim, Steven, 55
assimilation, 86, 96, 123, 128, 160, 167, 185
Assmann, Aleida, 191
atheism, and communism, 81, 171, 176, 182
Augustine (Saint), 46–47
Austria/Austrians, 102–4, 133

Bäck, Leo, 21. *See also* Baeck, Leo
Bäck, Samul, 36
Backhaus, Fritz, 113–14
Baeck, Elisa, 135

Baeck, Leo, and beliefs/interpretations, 19, 179.
    See also Baeck, Leo, and lectures/sermons/talks/writings; Baeck, Leo, and lectures/sermons/talks/writings during postwar era; Baeck, Leo, and lectures/sermons/talks/writings during Weimar Republic; Baeck, Leo, and lectures/sermons/talks/writings in Theresienstadt Ghetto; Baeck, Leo, and lectures/sermons/talks/writings in United States; *The Essence of Judaism* (Leo Baeck); First World War; leadership, and LB (1933–1935); leadership, and LB (1938–1943); *Legal Position* (Leo Baeck, Lucas, Ottenheimer); messianic era; Theresienstadt Ghetto
Baeck, Leo, and biographical information
    about, 2–3, 36, 180
    Bäck, Leo and name change, 21
    Baeck, Natalie as wife, 2, 85
    Berlak, Ruth as daughter, 2, 3, 142, 156
    doctorate dissertation, 2, 62
    eulogy, 5
    Germany and postwar era visits, 152, 153, 184
    Israel visits, 85
    legacy, 5, 180, 182, 183, 192
    life in London, England, 3, 112, 115, 142, 147, 150, 156
    rabbi as title, 2, 20–21, 40
    United States visits, 161–62, 184
    Wilhelmine Empire, 3, 17
    See also Baeck, Leo, and beliefs/interpretations; Baeck, Leo, and named buildings and institutions
Baeck, Leo, and honors
    essays in honor of eightieth birthday gift, 183–84
    honorary degree from Dropsie College, 161–62, 176

Index

229

Leo Baeck Medal (LBI New York), 186–87
Leo Baeck prize (Zentralrat), 187
See also Baeck, Leo, and named buildings and
  institutions
Baeck, Leo, and lectures/sermons/talks/writings
  about, 5
  "Christian Culture," 24
  Der Morgen essays, 1, 39, 73, 83, 84
  Der Schild essays, 54–55, 60, 78
  "The Development of the Talmud," 122
  "The Distance," 1, 2
  "The Drama of History," 51–52
  emancipation, 8
  "Europe," 84
  "The Existence of the Jew," 82–83, 84, 87
  existentialism, 87–88, 87n56, 88n62, 91
  First World War, 4, 49–50, 51–55, 57
  "The Foundation and Content of Life," 40
  The Gospel as a Document. . ., 76, 175
  "Greek and Jewish Sermons," 141
  Hellenism and Judaism, 121, 175, 179
  "History and the Present," 86
  Jewish mysticism, 5, 71–72, 72n92
  "The Jewish Person," 83, 91
  Jewish soldiers, 52–53, 119
  November Pogrom (1938), 105
  pastoral letter (*Hirtenbrief*), 95–96, 99–100,
    100n108
  peace, 52–53
  "Perfection and Tension," 141
  savages and historical consciousness, 11–12,
    32, 139–40, 180
  "State, Family, Individuality," 98–99
  Theresienstadt. . . (Adler) foreward, 130,
    130n1, 132
  world-history, 52, 145, 178
  "World History," 145
  See also Baeck, Leo; Baeck, Leo, and beliefs/
    interpretations; Baeck, Leo, and
    biographical information; Baeck, Leo, and
    lectures/sermons/talks/writings during
    Weimar Republic; Baeck, Leo, and lectures/
    sermons/talks/writings in United States;
    The Essence of Judaism (Leo Baeck); *Legal
    Position* (Leo Baeck, Lucas, Ottenheimer)
Baeck, Leo, and lectures/sermons/talks/writings
    during postwar era
  about, 147–48, 148n77
  bolshevism, 171
  bystanders' silence, 149–50
  Christianity without Judaism, 148–49,
    148n80
  The Church and the Jewish People
    (contributor), 172
  community, 149

culture, 159
emigrants and Jews, 160
epochs of Jewish history, 163, 171
"Epochs of Life" event, 131n5, 138
ethics, 149
existentialism, 87
"The Faith of Paul," 175–76
forgiveness by God, 150–51
"From Moses Mendelssohn to Franz
  Rosenzweig," 184
German children's reeducation, 151
guilt, 150–52, 150n88
historical context, 139n40, 152
hope, 132, 176
"Individuum Ineffabile," 152
isolationism and United States, 161
isolationism of Jews, 167
"Israel and the German People," 151
Israel, 85–86
Jewish community in postwar Germany,
  153
Jewish missionizing, 167–68, 172–73
"Judaism and Zionism. . .," 165, 169
letter to *New York Times* co-signed by LB and
  Einstein, 164, 190
materialism, 171, 171n64
"Meaning of History," 131, 131n5, 145, 149,
  177
Merkur essays, 151, 152, 167
"A Message from Rabbi Leo Baeck,"
  149–50
morality, 148, 155
morality and Jews/Judaism, 156
myth(s), 148–49, 149n83
Nazis, 148–49, 148n80
peace, 177–78
pessimism critique, 145, 148
religious education, 168, 172
reparations, 151–52
respect for Jews, 169 70
settlements and Jews, 160–61
space and Jews/Judaism, 156, 158–59
status of Jews/Judaism, 162, 169–70
"The Epochs of Jewish History," 145, 148,
  163, 171
This People: Jewish Existence, 61, 143n57, 144,
  144n64, 148n77, 156–58, 159
United Nations, 155
"Why Jews in the World?," 155
witnesses and Jews, 155
Baeck, Leo, and lectures/sermons/talks/writings
    during Weimar Republic
  "Classical and Romantic Religion," 67
  "Judaism in the Church," 68, 174
  marriage, 97

Index

Baeck, Leo, and lectures/sermons/talks/writings during Weimar Republic (cont.)
"Romantic Religion," 67, 68, 69, 69n82, 72, 73, 175, 180
See also Baeck, Leo, and lectures/sermons/talks/writings; Weimar Republic
Baeck, Leo, and lectures/sermons/talks/writings in Theresienstadt Ghetto
foreward to *Theresienstadt...* (Adler), 130, 130n1, 132
Hellenism and Judaism, 140, 142, 143, 143n57
"Historiography" (*Geschichtsschreibung*), 131, 139–41, 139n40, 142, 143, 147, 151
Jewish mysticism, 137
Judentumskunde (Leo Baeck and Crohn), 131, 144, 145, 146–47
justice, 144, 145, 146–47
lecture topics, 131n5, 138, 139
optimism, 145–46
oratorial skills, 138
prophets, 131–32, 140, 144, 147, 151
savages and historical consciousness, 139–40
"The Four Stages of Life," 131n5
"Vision and Patience," 130, 133, 136–37, 137n30, 138
Baeck, Leo, and lectures/sermons/talks/writings in United States
American Jewish Cavalcade, 161, 162, 172, 177–78
epochs of Jewish history, 163, 171
existentialism, 87
Hebrew Union College, 87, 156, 161, 169–70, 173
isolationism and United States, 161
Israel as homeland, 163–64
Jewish missionizing, 172, 173
letter to *New York Times* co-signed by LB and Einstein, 164, 190
morality and Jews/Judaism, 156
peace, 177–78
respect for Jews, 169–70
settlements and Jews, 160–61
status of Jews/Judaism, 162
witnesses and Jews, 155
See also Baeck, Leo, and lectures/sermons/talks/writings; Baeck, Leo, and lectures/sermons/talks/writings during postwar era; United States
Baeck, Leo, and named buildings and institutions
about, 5, 180
Leo-Baeck-Haus, 180, 187, 189, 192

Leo Baeck Institutes, 5, 112, 118, 180, 184–87, 185n13
Leo Baeck Temple, 180, 181–82, 183
See also Baeck, Leo, and biographical information; Baeck, Leo, and honors
Baeck, Natalie Hamburger, 2, 85
Baeck, Ruth, 2, 3, 142, 156
Baron, Salo, 146n70
Barth, Karl, 89–90, 91–92, 91nn70–71, 93
Baum, Herbert, 110
Beck, Volker, 187
Beerman, Leonard, 181–83
Berend, Dennis, 98
Bergen, Doris, 74, 91n70
Berlak, Ruth Baeck, 2, 3, 142, 156
Berliner, Cora, 106
Berman, Russell, 14n43
Beseler, Hans Hartwig von, 55
Bierschwale, Alfred, 75
Bjork, James, 37
Blacks, 8, 32, 86, 98, 120, 154–55
Blumenthal-Weiss, Ilse, 134
Bock, Gisela, 98n98
Bodenkulturverein (Association for the Advancement of Agriculture among the Jews of Germany), 39–40
Boehm, Eric, 111, 115, 130, 134–36
Böhme, Hildegard, 106
bolshevism, 75, 80–81, 82, 108, 110, 124, 171
Bousset, Wilhelm, 24, 25
Boycott, Divestment, Sanction (BDS), 190
Bronn, Heinrich Georg, 43–44
Brubaker, Rogers, 6
Buber, Martin, 4, 40, 56, 65, 120, 152, 183–84
Buddhism, 11, 24, 26, 145, 172, 180
Bülow, Bernhard von, 29, 44

Calvinism, 63, 69, 142, 169
Carp, Stefanie, 189
Case, Holly, 8
Castoriadis, Cornelius, 13
Catholics
First World War, 63n57
Germany, 8, 37, 50
Hebrew Bible and, 66
Jesus, 62
Luther/Lutheranism and, 62, 63
missionaries, 33
Poland, 36
Theresienstadt Ghetto and, 133–34
See also Christians/Christianity
Central Association of German Citizens of Jewish Faith (C.V., *Centralverein*), 41, 48–49, 78, 80
China, 10, 29, 44, 46, 154

Index

Christianity, and Jews/Judaism
Jewish Christians, 120, 128
Jewish foundation of Christianity, 25, 49, 63, 67, 68, 84
messianic era and, 46–47, 47n108
scholarship, 119–20
supersessionism/theological colonization, 15, 21–22, 23, 26
See also Christianity without Judaism; Christians/Christianity
Christianity without Judaism
about, 16, 148–49, 148n80
anti-Judaism, 49
Gnosticism, 69, 73, 141
Marcionism, 68, 84, 104, 148
Nazis and, 148–49, 148n80
Weimar Republic, 148, 148n80
See also Christianity, and Jews/Judaism
Christians/Christianity
Calvinism, 63, 69, 142, 169
conversions as forced, 34
diaspora, 35
equality/inequality and Jews, 125, 126
essence of Christianity, 17, 20, 21–23, 24, 43, 171
First World War and, 63, 63n57, 69, 142, 169
Hebrew Bible and, 62, 64, 66, 68, 75
historical context, 21–22
imperial power, 42n89, 43
interfaith dialogues, 174–76, 182–83
Jesus, 21, 22
Jesus as Jewish, 15, 22, 23, 134
Jewish Christians, 120, 120n65, 128, 133
Judeo-Christian tradition, 170–71, 175–76, 176n81, 178
missionaries, 33, 34, 35
morality, 21, 25, 28, 62–63, 70, 72
myth(s) and, 149, 149n83
national days of prayer, 49
othering of Jews, 14–15, 125
prophets, 25–26, 52
race and, 66–67
romantic religions and, 67–68, 70
Theresienstadt Ghetto, 133–34
völkisch movements, 66–67
Weimar Republic, 67–68, 69
See also Catholics; Christianity, and Jews/ Judaism; Christianity without Judaism; Pauline theology
Church. *See* Christians/Christianity
civilizing mission
Colonial Question, 38
imperialism, 4, 11, 32–33, 32n50, 139–40, 142
missionaries and, 4, 33–34

Poland, 38, 38n73
race and, 11, 32–33, 139
Weimar Republic, 59
Wilhelmine Empire and, 33–34, 38, 38n73
Zionists, 40–41
See also colonialism
classical religions, 68, 69, 70, 72, 73, 175, 180
Cohen, Hermann
ethics, 24n18, 27
existence/struggle for existence for Germans and Jews, 53
First World War, 4, 57, 58
justice, 146n71
LB on, 139
myth(s), 149n83
Cold War, 3, 155, 171, 177–78
Colonial Exhibition (1896), 31–32
colonialism
about, 11–12, 30–31, 139–40
First World War, 4, 11, 55
German Jews, 1, 2, 36, 39–40
imperialism versus, 12–13
Israel, 85–86, 165–67, 189–90
Jewish imperial imagination, 4, 83, 132
Jews/Judaism, 11–12, 14–15, 83, 107, 160
legacy of German colonialism, 180, 181, 188, 191, 192
morality and German colonialism, 32–33, 38, 45–46, 50, 51, 53
Poland, 36–37, 36n67, 37n69, 55, 59
Second World War, 106–7
United Nations, 154
United States, 159–60
Weimar Republic, 59–60
Wilhelmine Empire, 10, 29, 29n38, 31, 36–37, 36n67, 37n69, 44
See also civilizing mission
Colonial Question, 9, 9n24, 38
colonial violence, and Wilhelmine Empire, 31, 44–45, 44n98, 45n102, 46, 107
Columbus, Christopher, 1, 2, 160
commerce, and Jews/Judaism, 16, 124–25, 124n85
community
Jewish community in postwar Germany, 153, 187
national community (*Volksgemeinschaft*), 74, 98
Theresienstadt Ghetto, 133, 138, 145, 146, 149
concentration camps, 79, 104, 105, 108, 109, 131, 134, 177–78
conversion/s, 29, 34, 38–39, 42, 157, 167, 174.
See also Jewish missionizing
Crohn, Kurt, 131, 144, 145, 146–47

Index

Crohn, Renate, 131
Crohn, Susanne, 131
culture
  Legal Position (Leo Baeck, Lucas, Ottenheimer), 125, 128
  United States, 159, 170–71
  Weimar Republic, 61–62
  Wilhelmine Empire, 31–32, 159
  See also German culture
Czapski, Dora, 135
Czech Jews, 133, 136

de Lagarde, Paul, 9
Delitzsch, Friedrich, 24, 25
Derrida, Jacques, 28n37
Deutsch, Lorenz, 189
The Development of the Legal Position of Jews in Europe, . . . [*Legal Position*] (Leo Baeck). See *Legal Position* (Leo Baeck, Lucas, Ottenheimer)
diaspora
  Essence (Leo Baeck), 29, 35, 36, 38–39
  Jewish missionizing, 35, 38–39
  Legal Position (Leo Baeck, Lucas, Ottenheimer), 118, 119, 120–21
  settlements, 120–21
Dilthey, Wilhelm, 2, 62
Dorrien, Gary, 89
Dubnow, Simon, 117, 159, 159n14
Du Bois, W. E. B., 154–55

the East
  East European Jews, 55–57, 108
  German imperial imagination, 37–38, 55, 102, 107
  Jewish imperial imagination, 39, 55–57, 107
  Nazi imperialism, 74, 102, 103, 107–8
  See also Prussia
East European Jews, 55–57, 108
Edelstein, Jakob, 136
Eichmann, Adolf, 101, 104, 111, 114
Einstein, Albert, 164, 183–84, 190
emancipation, 6–7, 8, 39, 62, 86, 94, 97
emigration, and German Jews
  about and statistics, 77–78
  Evian Conference (1938), 1–2
  Great Britain, 3, 112
  Greater German Reich, 109
  Nazis, 74–75, 77–78, 85, 85n47, 89, 109, 112, 118
  Reichsvertretung, 78, 85, 85n47
  United States, 118, 160
  See also German Jews
empire/s
  about, 11, 11n32, 12–13, 180

culture and, 31–32
ethnic identity and, 10, 10n30
Germany and, 10–11, 11n32, 31–32
Greater German Empire, 102–4
Jews/Judaism and, 9–10, 15–16
  See also Roman Empire; Wilhelmine Empire (Kaiserreich)
energy (*Kraft*)/power (*Macht*)
  Essence (Leo Baeck), 42–43, 42n89, 47, 179
  Israel and, 85, 165, 166, 190
  leadership and LB (1933-1935), 85, 95, 99, 123
  leadership and LB (1938–1943), 107, 110
  Theresienstadt Ghetto, 144, 179
  Zionism, 123
Enlightenment, 28, 51, 62, 113, 127, 140, 172
Eppstein, Paul, 111, 136
equality/inequality, and Jews
  Christians, 125, 126
  Legal Position (Leo Baeck, Lucas, Ottenheimer), 120, 121–22, 126, 128, 141
  Roman Empire, 122, 125–26
  Wilhelmine Empire, 6, 7, 30, 39
Erlebnis (experience), 70, 70n86, 71, 72
Eschelbacher, Max, 112, 119
The Essence of Judaism (Leo Baeck)
  about, 20–21, 21n4, 27, 36, 148n77, 179
  diaspora, 29, 35, 36, 38–39
  dogma, 43, 43n90
  editions of, 20, 21, 29n38, 43, 91
  energy (*Kraft*)/power (*Macht*), 42–43, 42n89, 47, 179
  ethical monotheism, 35
  ethics, 23–24, 24n18, 26, 27, 46, 82, 146
  existence/struggle for existence, 43–44, 44n97, 52, 128
  Hellenism and Judaism, 121
  hope, 85, 109
  Jewish difference, 41
  Jewish missionizing, 27–29, 28n37, 29n38, 34–35, 38–39, 41
  Judeo-Christian tradition, 172
  justice, 146, 146n71
  messianic era, 26, 27, 35, 46, 147
  morality, 27
  myth, 149, 149n83
  optimism and Judaism, 26, 87, 109, 145, 180
  pessimism and Buddhism, 26, 145, 180
  prophets, 24, 27, 67
  rebirth, 158, 158n10
  Roman Empire, 34, 42
  status of Jews/Judaism, 26–28, 28n37, 41–42, 46, 47, 82
  translations, 20, 21, 172
  typology of religions, 26, 63, 68–69

Index

233

witnesses, 46, 155
world-history, 26, 27, 43, 46, 47
ethical monotheism
  about, 4, 40, 47, 146, 169
  The Essence of Judaism (Leo Baeck), 35
  Jewish missionizing, 28, 121, 173
ethics
  about, 16–17, 70, 72, 149
  First World War, 53, 57–58
  Harnack and, 23–24, 24n18, 66
  Luther/Lutheranism, 62–63
  prophets and, 25–26, 151, 183
  world-history, 27, 145
  See also ethical monotheism
ethics, and Jews/Judaism
  about, 35
  The Essence of Judaism (Leo Baeck), 23–24,
    24n18, 26, 27, 46, 82, 146
  Israel and, 183, 193
  tikkun olam, 181, 181n9
ethnic identity, 6, 7, 10, 10n30, 133
existence/struggle for existence, and Germans,
  53–55, 93
existence/struggle for existence, and Jews/
  Judaism
  Barth and, 89, 90
  Essence (Leo Baeck), 43–44, 44n97, 52, 128
  "The Existence of the Jew" (Leo Beck), 82–83
  existentialism, 88, 91
  German Jews and Nazis, 3, 74, 75, 77, 79,
    93–94, 109
  Israel, 163–64
  Legal Position (Leo Baeck, Lucas,
    Ottenheimer), 128
existentialism, 87–88, 87n56, 88n62, 91
Ezrahi, Yaron, 14

Fabri, Friedrich, 9n24, 33
Fackenheim, Emil, 181, 181n9
family, and Judaism, 96, 97, 98–99
fantasy/ies, 14, 14n43, 136–37
First World War
  about, 3, 17, 48, 49, 58
  Alsace-Lorraine, 59, 92–93
  army chaplain, 3, 49, 51, 58, 78
  Christians and, 63, 63n57, 69, 142
  colonialism, 4, 11, 55
  eastern front, 54–58
  East European Jews, 55–57
  ethics and, 53, 57–58
  France, 48, 54, 59, 63, 92–93
  German culture and, 50–51, 51n12, 52,
    53–55
  German imperial imagination, 57, 92, 93
  German Jews and, 48–49, 54, 60, 78–79

Great Britain, 48, 59, 63, 142
  Jewish imperial imagination, 4, 11, 52, 56–57
  Jewish missionizing, 4, 17
  Jewish soldiers, 52–53, 57–58
  Jews/Judaism, 55, 57–58
  Manifest of the Ninety-Three (1914), 53, 62
  othering of Jews, 55–56
  patriotism, 48–49, 55, 57–58
  remembrances after, 49–50
  Russia, 48, 49, 54, 59, 63n57
  sermons/talks/writings, 4, 51–55, 57
  Treaty of Versailles, 58, 59
  United States, 59, 142
  western front, 51–52, 54, 55
  Wilhelmine Empire and, 3, 29n38, 48, 59
  writings, 51–55, 57
Fischer, Joschka, 186–87
Fischerová, Anna, 135
France
  empire/s, 11, 59, 106
  First World War, 48, 54, 59, 63, 92–93
  nationalism, 6
  Second World War and, 106, 108, 119
Fredriksen, Paula, 47n108
Freud, Sigmund, 56, 83, 184
Freytag, Gustav, 38
Friedländer, Saul, 75
Fuchs, Eugen, 41
Funkenstein, Amos, 35
Fürst, Paula, 106

Gang-Salheimer, Lore, 77
Gauck, Joachim, 186
Geiger, Abraham, 15, 23, 28
gender, 46, 97, 98, 98n98, 106. *See also* women
German culture
  about, 53, 62, 84, 154
  First World War, 50–51, 51n12, 52, 55
  See also culture; Germany
German imperial imagination
  about, 14, 106–7, 108, 192
  the East and, 37–38, 102
  First World War, 55, 57, 92, 93
  Reichsvertretung, 103–4
  Wilhelmine Empire, 30–31, 32–33, 93, 107,
    140–41
  See also Germany
German imperialism, 2, 3–5, 9, 15, 29, 32, 74.
    See also German imperial imagination;
    Germany
German-Jewish History in Modern Times (LBI
    project), 185–86
German Jews
  about statistics, 1
  agency, 15–16, 86, 109, 116

Index

German Jews (cont.)
  colonialism, 1, 2, 36, 39–40
  expulsion of, 120
  First World War and, 48–49, 54, 60, 78–79
  minority position of, 12, 16, 17, 23, 49, 54, 154
  population statistics, 1n2
  remembrances after First World War, 49–50
  as soldiers, 52–53, 57–58, 119
  United States and, 118, 159, 160
  See also emigration, and German Jews; Jews/
    Judaism; Nazis, and German Jews; Nazis,
    and violence against German Jews;
    Reichsvereinigung (*Reichsvereinigung der
    Juden in Deutschland der Juden in
    Deutschland* or Reich Association of Jews in
    Germany)
Germany
  antisemitism, 41
  Catholics and, 8, 37, 50
  civilizing mission, 32–33, 32n50
  colonial fantasies, 14, 14n43
  colonialism, 44
  colonial violence, 44–45, 44n98, 45n102, 46
  empire/s and, 11n32
  First World War and, 48
  German Question, 7, 80
  German spirit, 53, 92, 140, 151
  Greater German Empire, 102
  Greater German Reich, 103, 109
  immigrants to United States, 37, 160
  imperialism, 2, 3–5, 9, 15, 74
  Jewish Question, 30
  Kaiser (emperor), 44, 45, 48, 49
  liberalism, 6, 7, 33
  rabbis, 40, 138
  race, 9, 30, 32–33, 41, 44
  rebellions overseas, 44–46, 44n98
  reparations, 135, 151–52
  See also German culture; German imperial
    imagination; Nazis; Prussia; Weimar
    Republic; Wilhelmine Empire (Kaiserreich)
Germany, and colonialism
  legacy, 180, 181, 188, 191, 192
  morality, 32–33, 38, 45–46, 50, 51, 53
  Second World War, 106–7
  See also Germany
Germany, and postwar era
  antisemitism, 189–91
  children's reeducation, 151
  Jewish community, 153, 187
  Jewish missionizing, 172–73

LB's visits, 152, 153, 184
  See also Germany; Holocaust
ghetto(s)
  as term of use, 79
  deaths, 106, 108, 138
  deportations/transport and, 1, 97, 105, 106, 109, 110, 111, 111n36
  Jewish leaders in, 101, 136
  survivors, 3, 115, 131, 132, 135, 147, 162
  See also Nazis, and violence against German
    Jews; Theresienstadt Ghetto
Glück, Paula, 111
Gnosticism
  Christianity and, 49, 69, 71
  Christianity without Judaism, 69, 73, 141
  gnosis, 64, 67, 69, 73, 149
  gnostic-Marcionism, 49, 65, 68, 69, 70, 148, 149
  Hebrew Bible and, 65
  Marcionism, 49, 64, 65, 67
  race and, 73, 126
  See also Marcionism
Goebbels, Joseph, 105n14, 108
Goerdeler, Carl, 111, 111n36
Goethe, Johann Wolfgang von, 51, 137, 152
Göring, Hermann, 75
Gotthard, Herbert, 116
Great Britain
  antisemitism, 161
  Calvinism, 63, 142, 169
  empire/s, 11, 59, 106, 142
  First World War, 48, 59, 63, 142
  Israel and, 169
  LB and life in London, 3, 112, 115, 142, 147, 150, 156
  Nazis and antisemitism, 119
  Second World War and, 106
  United Nations and, 154
Greater German Empire, 102–4
Greater German Reich, 103, 109
Great War. See First World War
Grimm, Hans, 59
Grünewald, Matthias, 89, 90, 92–93, 100n108
Grynszpan, Herschel, 105
guilt, 95, 96, 109, 134, 150–52, 150n88
Gusejnova, Dina, 61

Haeckel, Ernst, 44, 44n97, 50–51
Hájková, Anna, 135, 136
Halevi, Judah, 34
Hamburger, Natalie, 2, 85
Harnack, Adolf von
  Barth and, 89, 91
  Christianity, essence of, 17, 20, 21–23, 24, 43, 171

Index

235

critiques, 22–23
ethics, 23–24, 24n18, 66
German culture and, 50–51
Hebrew Bible, 65–66, 91
historical context, 21–22
Jesus, 22, 23, 24
Jewish missionizing, 35
Marcionism, 63, 64–67, 68
writings and lectures, 17, 20, 22, 43, 64n61, 65, 68n77
Hebrew Bible
about, 25–26
Christianity and, 62, 64, 66, 67, 68, 75
ethics and, 25
Gnosticism and, 65
Marcionism and, 64, 65–66, 171, 174
marriage/intermarriage, 121
originality/primacy of, 21, 23
prophets, 24, 25–26, 67
religious education, 168–69
Torah, 42, 52, 67, 75, 104, 148, 157, 175
Heidegger, Martin, 17, 73, 87, 88
Hell, Julia, 143, 144n64
Hellenism
Judaism, 121, 140, 142, 143, 143n57, 175, 179
morality, 148
Nazis, 141, 179
Wilhelmine Empire, 140–41
Herero Revolt (1904), 31, 44–45, 44n98, 45n102, 46, 106–7
Herzl, Theodor, 8, 31–32, 137
Herzog, Jonathan, 170
Herz-Sommer, Alice, 137
Heschel, Abraham Joshua, 183–84
Heschel, Susannah, 14–15, 23, 76
Heuss, Theodor, 184
Hirsch, Otto, 79, 100, 106, 184
Hirsch, Samson Raphael, 28
historiography
Jews/Judaism, 158, 180–81, 185, 186
the West, 142, 143, 144, 145
History of Religions School, 17, 21–22, 25, 26
Hitler, Adolf, 73, 74, 75, 80, 108, 111, 149
Holocaust
about, 108
bystanders' silence, 149–50
guilt and, 109, 134, 150–52, 150n88
historical context, 106–7
memory of, 107, 180–81, 187–88, 191, 192
morality and, 155
See also German Jews; ghetto(s); Nazis; Nazis, and violence against German Jews; Theresienstadt Ghetto

hope
Essence (Leo Baeck), 85, 109
Legal Position (Leo Baeck, Lucas, Ottenheimer), 122, 128
postwar era, 157, 178, 182
Theresienstadt Ghetto, 132, 136–37, 142, 157, 182
United Nations, 176
Zionists, 163
Hull, Isabel, 45n102
Hyman, Paula, 96

imaginary (social imagination), 13–14, 14n43, 136–37. See also German imperial imagination; Jewish imperial imagination
imperial imagination
about, 13
civilizing mission and, 32–33, 32n50, 139–40, 142
First World War, 17, 52, 56–57
Nazis, 15, 74, 98, 102, 103, 106–8
See also German imperial imagination; Jewish imperial imagination
imperialism, 11–13, 16–17, 30. See also German imperialism; imperial imagination; Jewish imperial imagination, and LB
intellectual forced labor, 102, 115–18. See also Legal Position (Leo Baeck, Lucas, Ottenheimer)
interfaith dialogues, 174–76, 182–83
Isenheim altarpiece (Grünewald), 89, 90, 92–93, 100n108
isolationism, and Jews, 161, 167, 173, 177, 178
Israel
Arabs, 9, 163, 164, 165, 166, 177
bi-nationalism, 164–65
colonialism, 85–86, 165–67, 189–90
critiques, 183, 189, 190–92
emigration of German Jews to, 85
energy (Kraft)/power (Macht) and, 85, 165, 166, 190
ethics, 183, 193
existence/struggle for existence and Jews/Judaism, 163–64
hope and, 85
isolationism, 167
Jewish missionizing, 40–41, 178
laws and Judaism, 35, 167
LB's visits to, 85
messianic era and, 46
nationalism, 10, 167
partition resolution (1947), 164, 177
religious education, 168–69
status of Jews/Judaism, 82
United States and, 169, 177

Index

Israel (cont.)
 violence and, 164, 177, 183, 190
 See also Zionists
Israel, and settlements
 about, 40–41, 122, 123
 space and settlements, 82–84, 156, 159,
  162–63

Jesus
 Catholics and, 62
 Christianity, 21, 22
 Harnack and, 22, 23, 24
 Jesus as Christ, 46–47, 90, 93, 149, 175
 Jesus as Jewish, 15, 22, 23, 76, 93, 134
 Nazis, 76, 149
Jewish Colonization Association, 39
Jewish imperial imagination
 about, 2, 3, 12, 16, 179–80
 coexistence, 166, 177
 Cold War, 155
 colonialism, 4, 83, 132
 the East and, 39, 55–57, 107
 First World War, 4, 11, 52, 56–57
 Jewish missionizing, 172, 176
 Legal Position (Leo Baeck, Lucas,
  Ottenheimer), 114, 121
 postwar era and, 178
 religions and, 171, 176
 Theresienstadt Ghetto, 130, 131–32, 135, 180
 Wilhelmine Empire, 107, 155n3, 166
Jewish imperial imagination, and LB
 about, 19, 179–80, 192
 Jewish missionizing, 172, 176
 Legal Position (Leo Baeck, Lucas,
  Ottenheimer), 121
 religion(s), 171, 176
 Theresienstadt Ghetto, 130, 131–32, 135, 180
 Wilhelmine Empire, 107, 155n3, 166
Jewish missionizing
 about, 4, 35
 diaspora and, 35, 38–39
 Essence (Leo Baeck), 27–29, 28n37, 29n38,
  34–35, 38–39
 ethical monotheism, 28, 121, 173
 historical context, 157
 Israel, 40–41, 178
 Jewish imperial imagination, 172, 176
 messianic era, 35, 47, 63
 postwar era, 29n38, 155–56, 157, 167–68,
  172–73
 settlements, 36, 38–40
 United States and, 173, 176, 179
 See also energy (*Kraft*)/power (*Macht*)
Jewish Question
 about, 7–8

emancipation and, 39, 62
Germany, 30
nation-state and, 7, 9, 30
Nazis, 80, 114, 118, 120
race, 9, 30
Jews/Judaism
 about, 24, 40, 156–57
 expulsion of, 2, 155, 157, 159, 160
 Jewish difference, 41, 123–24
 Judeo-Christian tradition, 170–72, 175–76,
  176n81, 178
 marriage/intermarriage, 96, 121
 morality and, 25, 28, 46, 70, 82, 96, 148, 156,
  169
 originality/primacy of, 21, 24, 25, 63
 respect, 80, 169–70, 174, 175, 178
 as witnesses, 46–47, 155–56, 174
 See also antisemitism; Christianity, and Jews/
  Judaism; Christianity without Judaism;
  emigration, and German Jews; energy
  (*Kraft*)/power (*Macht*); equality/inequality,
  and Jews; *The Essence of Judaism* (Leo
  Baeck); ethics, and Jews/Judaism; existence/
  struggle for existence, and Jews/Judaism;
  German Jews; Jewish missionizing;
  leadership, and LB (1933-1935); leadership,
  and LB (1938-1943); messianic era;
  othering, of Jews; settlements; status, and
  Jews/Judaism
Jonas, Regina, 97
Judaism. *See* Jews/Judaism
Judeo-Christian tradition, 170–72, 175–76,
 176n81, 178. *See also* Jews/Judaism
Jung, Carl, 152–53
justice, 144, 145, 146–47, 146n71

Kaiser (emperor), 10, 25, 44, 45, 48, 49, 59,
 79
Kaiserreich. *See* Wilhelmine Empire (Kaiserreich)
Kalmanovitch, Zelig, 116
Kant, Immanuel, 24n18, 51, 62, 139
Kareski, Gerog, 79
Karminski, Hana, 106
Kaznelson, Siegmund, 185, 185n13
Keyserling, Count Hermann von, 60–61, 61n49,
 97
Kierkegaard, Søren, 87, 87n56, 88
killing centers, 106, 109, 132, 136, 147
Kipling, Rudyard, 142
Kittel, Gerhard, 119–21, 120n64, 122
Klein, Felix, 189, 190–91
Klemperer, Victor, 109, 119
Koebner, Richard, 112
Koonz, Claudia, 74
Kopp, Kristin, 37

Index

Kraft (energy)/power (*Macht*). *See* energy (*Kraft*)/ power (*Macht*)

Kreutzmüller, Christoph, 77

Kristallnacht (November Pogrom [1938]), 1n2, 3, 78, 104, 105, 105n14

Kuhn, Karl Georg, 119, 121, 122

Kuss, Susanne, 45n102

Lammert, Norbert, 187

LBI (Leo Baeck Institute), 5, 112, 118, 180, 184, 185, 185n13

leadership, and LB (1933-1935)
  about, 3, 17, 73, 82, 100
  anti-Judaism and, 76, 83, 84
  antisemitism, 83–84
  Blacks and Jews comparison, 86
  bolshevism, 80–81, 82
  critiques, 101–2
  decision to stay versus emigrate, 78, 78n23, 105–6
  emigration of German Jews, 3, 85, 85n47
  energy (*Kraft*)/power (*Macht*), 85, 95, 99, 123
  family, 96, 97, 98–99
  Hitler and, 80
  morality and Jews/Judaism, 82, 96
  national revolution and, 79–80, 80n28
  nature/rural areas, 60, 124
  precarity and Jews, 82, 86, 88
  RjF, 54, 60, 78–79
  status of Jews/Judaism, 73, 82
  violence against Jews, 98–99
  women's role, 97
  See also Reichsvertretung (*Reichsvertretung der deutschen Juden* or Reich Representation of German Jews)

leadership, and LB (1938-1943)
  bolshevism, 110, 124
  critiques, 101–2, 110
  deportations/transport from Germany, 97, 105, 106, 111
  energy (*Kraft*)/power (*Macht*), 107, 110
  November Pogrom (1938), 104
  violence condemnation, 110
  See also leadership, and LB (1933-1935); *Legal Position* (Leo Baeck, Lucas, Ottenheimer)

Lederer, Vítězslav, 136

Legal Position (Leo Baeck, Lucas, Ottenheimer)
  about, 17–18, 102, 111–12, 111n36, 128–29
  antisemitism, 118–19, 121, 123–24, 124n85, 127
  assimilation, 123, 128
  authors and, 114–15, 116
  Boehm and, 111, 111n34, 115
  commerce, 124–25
  culture, 125, 128

diaspora, 118, 119, 120–21

Enlightenment, 113, 127

equality/inequality and Jews, 120, 121–22, 126, 128, 141

Hellenism, 141, 143, 179

historical context, 112, 113, 159n14

hope, 122, 128

intellectual forced labor, 102, 115–18

Jewish difference, 123–24

Jewish imperial imagination, 114, 121

memoranda and Aktennotizen K request, 111, 112–14, 115, 126

othering of Jews, 120, 125–26

race, 120, 121, 123, 126, 126n93, 127

rebirth, 123, 158

resistance, 111, 112, 113

RSHA and, 113, 114, 115, 126

settlements, 118–21, 122

sources, 117–18

Suhr and, 114, 117, 118, 121, 123, 124

Zionists, 123, 128, 163

Leo-Baeck-Haus, 180, 187, 189, 192

Leo Baeck Institute (LBI), 5, 112, 118, 180, 184–87, 185n13

Leo Baeck Medal (LBI New York), 186–87

Leo Baeck prize (Zentralrat), 187

Leo Baeck Temple, 180, 181–82, 183

Leonard, Miriam, 140

Lettow-Vorbeck, Paul von, 60

Liberal Judaism
  Beerman and, 181–82
  First World War, 48–49
  LB and, 42, 71, 123, 124, 165, 167, 181

Liebman, Joshua Loth, 162

Liepach, Martin, 113–14

Lindbergh, Charles, 161

Locke, John, 36n67

Loisy, Alfred, 22

Lucas, Leopold, 111, 114–15, 129. *See also Legal Position* (Leo Baeck, Lucas, Ottenheimer)

Lucas, Mrs. Leopold, 115

Ludendorff, Erich, 55

Luther, Martin, and Lutheranism
  ethics, 62–63
  existentialism, 87
  Nazis and, 75, 75n9
  Pauline theology, 65, 66, 69, 69n82, 71
  Prussia, 61–62, 142
  See also Protestants

Macht (power). *See* energy (*Kraft*)/power (*Macht*)

Makhshoves, Bal, 56

Manes, Philipp, 138

Manifest of the Ninety-Three (1914), 53, 62

Mann, Thomas, 183–84

Index

Marcionism
about, 63–64
Christianity without Judaism, 68, 84, 104,
148
critiques, 70, 88, 174
Gnosticism and, 49, 64, 65, 67
gnostic-Marcionism, 49, 65, 149
Harnack and, 63, 64–67, 68
Hebrew Bible and, 64, 65–66, 171, 174
Jews/Judaism and, 65, 84, 175
Marcionite-romantic religion, 16, 68, 180
Nazis and, 149, 174, 180
Protestants, 49, 65, 68, 69, 70, 76, 148
romantic religions, 68–69, 70, 71, 71n90,
175, 180
Weimar Republic, 16, 67, 68, 71
Maritain, Jacques, 183–84
marriage/intermarriage, 78, 94, 94n84, 96, 97,
98, 121, 130
Marx, Karl, and Marxism, 7, 81, 118, 143, 184
Mbembe, Achille, 189, 190, 191–92
Mendelssohn, Moses, 15, 149
Merkel, Angela, 186–87
messianic era
Jewish missionizing, 35, 47, 63
Jews/Judaism, 26, 27, 35, 46–47, 47n108, 63,
65
writings and LB, 26, 27, 35, 46, 147, 147n75
Meyer, Beate, 111
Meyer, Michael, 80n28, 113, 186
minority position, and Jews/Judaism
The Essence of Judaism (Leo Baeck), 21, 41–42,
46, 47, 128, 146, 175
German Jews, 12, 16, 17, 23, 49, 54, 154
leadership and LB, 82, 110
Legal Position (Leo Baeck, Lucas,
Ottenheimer), 123, 128–29, 141
morality, 181, 190
postwar era, 174–75
missionaries, 4, 33–34, 35. *See also* Jewish
missionizing
Mommsen, Theodor, 143
Montefiore, Claude, 123
morality
Christians, 21, 25, 28, 62–63, 70, 72
culture and, 31–32, 50, 51, 53
Jews/Judaism, 25, 28, 46, 70, 82, 96, 148,
156, 169
religions and, 24, 27
Theresienstadt Ghetto, 132–33, 134, 146
Mufti, Aamir, 9
Murmelstein, Benjamin, 136
Myers, David, 182
mysticism, 5, 71–72, 72n92, 137, 152
myth(s), 65, 73, 80, 148–49, 149n83

Nathan, Johanna, 111
national community (*Volksgemeinschaft*), 74, 98.
See also community
nation-state, 3, 6–7, 9, 30
nature/rural areas, 39, 60, 107, 124
Nazis
bolshevism, 75, 80, 108
Christianity without Judaism, 148–49,
148n80
German Christians (*Deutsche Christen*), 75,
90
Greater German Empire, 102
Greater German Reich, 102–3, 109
guilt, 150–52, 150n88
Hellenism and German spirit, 141, 151, 179
Hitler, 73, 74, 75, 80, 108, 111, 149
imperialism, 15, 74, 98, 102, 103, 106–8
Jesus and, 76, 149
Marcionism, 149, 174, 180
myth(s) and, 73, 80, 148–49
national community (*Volksgemeinschaft*), 74,
98
national revolution, 79–80, 80n28
Protestants, 75, 149, 182
Roman Empire and, 126
SA paramilitary, 93, 102–3, 104
space and, 74, 81, 83–84
völkisch movements, 127
women's role, 98, 98n98
Zionists and, 79, 85
See also Nazis, and laws; Nazis, and race;
Nazis, and violence against German Jews
Nazis, and German Jews
anti-Judaism, 74–75, 76
antisemitism, 83–84, 118–19, 121, 127
deportations/transports and, 1, 97, 105, 106,
109, 110, 111, 111n36
deported and refugee data, 1, 1n2
emigration, 74–75, 77–78, 85, 85n47, 89,
109, 112, 118
exclusion of, 75, 77, 127
existence/struggle for existence, 3, 74, 75, 77,
79, 93–94, 109
guilt and, 109, 134, 150–52, 150n88
Jewish Question, 80, 114, 118, 120
killing centers, 106, 109, 132, 136,
147
marriage/intermarriage, 78, 94, 94n84, 98,
130
memoranda/Aktennotizen K request, 111,
112–14, 115, 126
race, 74–75, 94, 98, 105, 109, 116
resistance, 110, 111, 112, 113, 116, 137
respect for Jews, 80
See also Nazis; Theresienstadt Ghetto

Index

Nazis, and laws
marriage/intermarriage, 78, 94, 94n84, 98, 130
Nuremberg Laws (1935), 54–55, 75, 78, 94, 98, 99
See also German Jews; Nazis
Nazis, and race
Aryan race, 74, 98, 117
Blacks and, 98, 154–55
the East, 107–8
German Jews, 74–75, 94, 98, 105, 109, 116
Legal Position (Leo Baeck, Lucas, Ottenheimer), 120, 121, 123, 126, 126n93, 127
Theresienstadt Ghetto, 133, 139, 145
See also Nazis; race
Nazis, and violence against German Jews
about and statistics, 98–99, 108, 110
Austrian Jews, 102–4
concentration camps, 79, 104, 105, 108, 109, 134, 177–78
desecration/destruction, 75, 94
East European Jews, 108
existence/struggle for existence, 3, 74, 75, 77, 79, 93–94, 109
expulsion, 120
November Pogrom (1938), 1n2, 3, 78, 104, 105, 105n14
patriotism of Jews, 55, 77
yellow Star of David, 109, 138
See also German Jews; ghetto(s); Holocaust; Nazis; Theresienstadt Ghetto
Negroes, 8, 32, 86, 98, 120, 154–55
Neiman, Susan, 191
Nietzsche, Friedrich, 87, 88, 137
non-whites, 32, 48
November Pogrom [1938] (Kristallnacht), 1n2, 3, 78, 104, 105, 105n14
Nußbaum, Wilhlem, 126n93

Ocasio-Cortez, Alexandria, 188
Old Testament. *See* Hebrew Bible
Oppenheimer, Franz, 56
optimism, 26, 87, 109, 110, 145–46, 180. *See also* pessimism
Orthodox Judaism, 48–49, 81–82, 167
othering, of Jews
Christians, 14–15, 125
First World War, 55–56
Legal Position (Leo Baeck, Lucas, Ottenheimer), 120, 125–26
Wilhelmine Empire, 9, 29, 30
Ottenheimer, Hilde, 111, 114–15, 129. See also *Legal Position* (Leo Baeck, Lucas, Ottenheimer)

Palestine. *See* Israel
Paper Brigade, 116
patriotism, 46, 48–49, 55, 58, 60, 77
Paucker, Arnold, 113, 115
Pauline theology
Erlebnis, 70, 71
Judeo-Christian tradition, 175–76, 176n81, 178
Luther/Lutheranism and, 65, 66, 69, 69n82, 71
Marcionism and, 65, 68
myth(s) and Nazis, 149
See also Christians/Christianity
peace, 52–53, 61, 84–85, 177–78
pessimism, 26, 145, 148, 180. *See also* optimism
Poland
colonialism, 36–37, 36n67, 37n69, 55, 59
Nazis, 106, 107, 108
Wilhelmine Empire, 36–37, 36n67, 37n69, 38, 38n73, 39
politics/political imagination, 13–14, 56, 61–63, 72, 124
postwar era
Cold War, 3, 155, 171, 177–78
hope, 157, 178, 182
interfaith dialogues, 174–76, 182–83
isolationism and Jews, 161, 167, 173, 177, 178
Jewish missionizing, 29n38, 155–56, 157, 167–68, 172–73
LB and life in London, England, 3, 112, 115, 142, 147, 150, 156
rebirth, 158, 158n10, 163
respect for Jews, 169–70, 174, 175, 178
settlements in United States, 160–61
space and Jews/Judaism, 158–59, 167
space and settlements, 177, 177n85
status of Jews/Judaism, 162, 169–70
Zentralrat, 5, 187–88, 189, 190, 191, 192
See also Baeck, Leo, and lectures/sermons/talks/writings during postwar era; United States
power (*Macht*). *See* energy (*Kraft*)/power (*Macht*)
precarity, and Jews, 82, 86, 88, 117, 128, 132
propaganda, and First World War, 50–51, 51n12, 55
prophets
Christian interpretation of, 25–26, 52
ethics and, 25–26, 151, 183
historical context, 132, 157
Judaism, 24, 25–26, 27, 67, 131–32
Theresienstadt Ghetto and lectures/sermons/talks/writings, 131–32, 140, 144, 147, 151
Protestants
about, 25–26, 33, 89

Index

Protestants (cont.)
German Christians (*Deutsche Christen*), 75, 90
gnostic-Marcionism, 49, 65, 68, 69, 70, 148
Hebrew Bible, 66, 67, 68, 75
Marcionism, 49, 76
Nazis, 75, 149, 182
supersessionism/theological colonization, 26
Weimar Republic, 49, 65, 148, 182
See also Luther, Martin, and Lutheranism
Prussia
colonialism, 36, 37, 37n69
East Prussia, 2, 11, 20–21, 36
German imperial imagination, 51, 102
Jewish population, 15, 122
Luther/Lutheranism, 61–62, 142
Weimar Republic, 61–62, 127

race
Blacks, 86
Christians, 66–67
civilizing mission, 11, 139
Germany, 9, 30, 32–33, 44
Gnosticism, 73, 126
Jewish Question, 9
Weimar Republic, 126, 126n93
Wilhelmine Empire, 41, 44
See also Nazis, and race
Rath, Ernst vom, 105
Ratzel, Friedrich, 107
rebellions overseas, and Wilhelmine Empire
(Kaiserreich), 44–46, 44n98
rebirth/renaissance, and Jews/Judaism, 123, 151, 158, 158n10, 163
Reform Judaism, 15, 62, 161, 181–82, 183
Regas, George, 182–83
Reich Main Security Office (RSHA), 113, 114, 115, 126
Reichmann, Eva, 5, 109
Reichmann, Hans, 111
Reich Representation of German Jews
(*Reichsvertretung der deutschen Juden* or
Reichsvertretung). *See* Reichsvereinigung
(*Reichsvereinigung der Juden in Deutschland
der Juden in Deutschland* or Reich
Association of Jews in Germany);
Reichsvertretung (*Reichsvertretung der
deutschen Juden* or Reich Representation of
German Jews)
Reichsbund ju ⟨discher Frontsoldaten (RjF), 54, 60, 78–79
Reichsvereinigung (*Reichsvereinigung der Juden in
Deutschland der Juden in Deutschland* or
Reich Association of Jews in Germany)
about, 105, 126
activities/lack of activities, 110, 111, 114, 122

deportations/transport from Germany, 105, 111
leadership and staff, 3, 105, 106, 110, 111, 114, 136
Reichsvertretung (*Reichsvertretung der deutschen
Juden* or Reich Representation of German
Jews)
about, 78, 86, 105, 122, 126
antisemitism, 124n85
Austrian Jews, 103–4
emigration of German Jews, 3, 85, 85n47
German imperial imagination, 103–4
leadership, 3, 78, 79, 80, 82, 110, 183
Orthodox Judaism and, 81–82
See also Reichsvereinigung (*Reichsvereinigung
der Juden in Deutschland der Juden in
Deutschland* or Reich Association of Jews in
Germany)
Reiter, Paul, 127–28
religion(s), 81, 155, 171, 176, 177–78, 182. See
also *specific religions*
Rengstorf, Karl Heinrich, 173
reparations, 135, 151–52
resistance, and German Jews, 110, 111, 112, 113, 116, 137
Robeson, Paul, 86
Roman Empire, 34, 35, 42, 122, 125–26, 140, 143, 157
romantic religions, 68–69, 70, 71, 71n90, 175, 180
Rosenzweig, Franz, 42n89, 68, 83n42, 149, 184
Rothberg, Michael, 191
RSHA (Reich Main Security Office), 113, 114, 115, 126
Rumkowski, Chaim, 101
Rupnow, Dirk, 117
Russia, 48, 49, 54, 59, 63n57, 107. *See also*
Soviet Union

savages, and historical consciousness, 11–12, 32, 139–40, 139n40, 180
Schächter, Rafael, 137
Schlegel, Friedrich, 67–68, 144
Schleiermacher, Friedrich, 71
Schnee, Heinrich, 59
Scholem, Gershom, 101, 152–53
Schuster, Josef, 189
Schweid, Eliezer, 148n77
Scott, David, 12
Second World War
colonialism, 106–7
Evian Conference (1938), 1–2
France, 106, 108, 119
German imperial imagination, 106–7
Great Britain, 106

Index

Poland, 106, 107, 108
Soviet Union, 106, 108, 154, 171, 176
United States, 106, 161
See also Holocaust; leadership, and LB (1938-1943); Nazis; Nazis, and German Jews; Nazis, and violence against German Jews; Reichsvereinigung (*Reichsvereinigung der Juden in Deutschland der Juden in Deutschland* or Reich Association of Jews in Germany)
Sekaninová, Truda, 132
Sering, Max, 38
settlements
Israel, 40–41, 122, 123
Jewish missionizing, 36, 38–40
Legal Position (Leo Baeck, Lucas, Ottenheimer), 118–21, 122
space(s), 82–84, 156, 159, 162–63, 177, 177n85
United States and, 160–61
Sienkiewicz, Henryk, 37
Silk, Mark, 170
Simon, Hermann, 112
social imagination (imaginary), 13–14, 14n43, 136–37. *See also* German imperial imagination; Jewish imperial imagination
Sorkin, David, 185–86
Soviet Union, 106, 108, 154, 155, 171, 176. *See also* Russia
space(s)
Jews/Judaism and, 82–84, 158–59, 167
Nazis, 74, 81, 83–84
settlements, 82–84, 156, 159, 162–63, 177, 177n85
Spain, and expulsion of Jews (1492), 2, 155, 157, 159, 160
Spengler, Oswald, 145
Spinner, Samuel, 56
Spinoza, Baruch, 62, 118, 139
Stahl, Heinrich, 79, 136
State of Israel. *See* Israel
status, and Jews/Judaism
about, 25, 26
The Essence of Judaism (Leo Baeck), 26–28, 28n37, 41–42, 46, 47, 82
leadership and LB (1933-1935), 73, 82
postwar era, 162, 169–70
Steinhardt, Martin, 49
Steinmeier, Frank-Walter, 186
Stendhal, Krister, 176n81
Stern, Eliyahu, 171n64
Stern, Selma, 117–18
Sternová, Elisa Baeck, 135
Strauss, Hermann, 137
Sudetenland, 103, 133, 136

Suhr, Friedrich, 114, 117, 118, 121, 123, 124
supersessionism (theological colonization), 11, 15, 17, 21–22, 23, 26
survivors, and ghetto(s), 3, 115, 131, 132, 135, 147, 162

Taylor, Charles, 13
temporality, and Jews/Judaism, 83–84, 83n41, 156, 167
Terezín. *See* Theresienstadt Ghetto
theological colonization (supersessionism), 11, 15, 17, 21–22, 23, 26
Theresienstadt Ghetto
about, 3, 18, 115, 130, 130n1, 147
Blacks and Jews comparison, 155
Christians, 133–34
comfort and, 136, 147
community, 133, 138, 145, 146
crowded/overcrowded spaces, 132, 134, 176–77
cultural events, 137–38
daily life described, 132–33, 134, 138–39
deaths, 97, 129, 131, 132, 133
energy (Kraft)/violent power (Macht), 144, 179
family ties, 134–36
hope, 132, 136–37, 142, 157, 182
Jewish imperial imagination, 130, 131–32, 135, 180
leadership conflicts, 111, 136
morality, 132–33, 134, 146
privileged groups, 129, 130, 134, 135
race, 133, 139, 145
resistance, 137
survival struggles, 132, 133, 134, 138
survivors, 3, 115, 131, 132, 135, 147, 162
transports to killing centers, 132, 136, 147
See also Baeck, Leo, and lectures/sermons/talks/writings in Theresienstadt Ghetto
Thun-Hohenstein, Count Paul, 60–61
tikkun olam, 181, 181n9
Tillich, Paul, 83n41, 171
Torah, 42, 52, 67, 75, 104, 148, 157. *See also* Hebrew Bible
Treaty of Versailles, 58, 59. *See also* First World War
Treitschke, Heinrich von, 127–28
Troeltsch, Ernst, 20, 22, 61
Trotha, Lothar von, 44–45
Truman, Harry S., 161–62, 170–71, 178, 184

Union of Progressive Judaism, 40
United Nations, 153, 154, 155, 164, 176, 177, 178
United States

242 *Index*

United States (cont.)
  American Jewish Cavalcade, 161, 162, 170, 172, 177–78
  assimilation, 160, 163, 167–68
  Blacks, 8, 120, 154–55
  Calvinism, 63, 142, 169
  Cold War, 155, 171
  colonialism, 159–60
  culture, 159, 170–71
  First World War, 59, 142
  German emigrants and, 37
  German Jews, 118, 159, 160
  Hebrew Union College, 87, 156, 161, 169–70, 173
  historical context, 86, 156, 160
  isolationism, 161, 173, 177, 178
  Israel, 168, 169, 177
  Jewish missionizing, 173, 176, 179
  Judeo-Christian tradition, 170–72, 175, 178
  LB's visits and activities, 161–62, 184
  religion and, 168, 170–71, 172, 178
  Second World War, 106, 161
  United Nations, 154, 178
  See also Baeck, Leo, and lectures/sermons/talks/writings in United States
Utitz, Emil, 132–33, 138

Veltheim-Ostrau, Hans-Hasso von, 60–61, 144
violence
  Israel and, 164, 177, 190
  against Jews/Judaism, 46, 98–99
  Wilhelmine Empire and colonial violence, 31, 44–45, 44n98, 45n102, 46, 107
  See also Nazis, and violence against German Jews
Volavková, Hana, 116–17
völkisch movements, 60, 66–67, 74, 127
Volksgemeinschaft (national community), 74, 98

Warburg, Otto, 40
Weimar Republic
  about, 3, 17, 49, 72
  antisemitism, 49, 60, 68
  Christianity without Judaism, 16, 68, 69, 148, 148n80
  Christians, 67–68, 69, 71
  classical religions, 67, 68, 70, 180
  colonialism, 59–60
  culture of memory, 61–62
  Erlebnis, 70, 70n86, 71, 72
  Gnosticism, 67, 69, 71
  gnostic-Marcionism, 49, 65, 148
  imperial intelligentsia, 60–61, 61n49
  Jewish foundation of Christianity, 49, 63, 67, 68

  Jewish mysticism, 5, 71–72, 72n92
  Marcionism, 16, 67, 68, 71
  Marcionite-romantic religion, 16, 68, 180
  nature/rural areas versus urban centers, 60, 124
  peace efforts, 61, 84–85
  political imagination, 61–63, 72
  Protestants, 49, 65, 148, 182
  race, 126, 126n93
  völkisch movements, 60, 66–67, 74, 127
  See also Baeck, Leo, and lectures/sermons/talks/writings during Weimar Republic
Weinreich, Max, 119
Weiss, Yfaat, 165
Wellhausen, Julius, 24
Weltsch, Robert, 111, 112, 184, 185
Wholly Other, 89–90, 91–92, 93
Wilhelm II (Kaiser), 25, 44, 45, 48, 49, 59, 79
Wilhelmine Empire (Kaiserreich)
  about, 10–11, 31–32
  Alsace-Lorraine, 10, 92–93
  antisemitism, 9, 30
  civilizing mission, 33–34, 38, 38n73
  colonialism, 10, 29, 29n38, 31, 36–37, 36n67, 37n69
  colonial violence, 31, 107
  culture, 31–32, 159
  the East and, 37–38, 107
  First World War and, 3, 29n38, 59
  Hellenism, 140–41
  imperialism, 9, 15, 29, 30–31, 32–33, 74, 93
  inner colonization and German Jews, 36, 39–40
  Jewish imperial imagination, 107, 155n3, 166
  Kaiser (emperor), 10, 25, 59, 79
  LB and biographical information, 3, 17
  othering of Jews, 9, 29, 30
  Poland and, 36–37, 36n67, 37n69, 38, 38n73, 39
  See also Germany
Wise, Stephen, 183
Wolff, Theodor, 80
women, 8, 94n84, 96, 97, 98, 98n98, 106. See also gender
world-history, 26, 27, 43, 46, 47, 52, 145, 178
World Union of Progressive Judaism, 148, 162–63, 167–68, 172
World War I. *See* First World War
World War II. *See* Second World War
Wulff, Christian, 187

Yahuda, Abraham Shalom, 156
Yerushalmi, Yosef, 146
Yuden son of Rabbi Aivu, 147

Index

Zadoff, Noam, 153
Zantop, Susanne, 14
Zentralrat (Central Council of Jews in Germany or *Zentralrat der Juden in Deutschland*), 5, 187–88, 189, 190, 191, 192
Zionists
  colonialism, 165–66
  First World War, 48–49

German Jews, 8, 41
  hope, 163
  isolationism and Jews, 167
  Jewish missionizing, 40–41, 178
  Legal Position (Leo Baeck, Lucas, Ottenheimer), 123, 128, 163
  Nazis and, 79, 85
  See also Israel